Beyond the Word of a Woman

Recovering the Bodies of the Syrophoenician Women

Alan H Cadwallader

ATF THEOLOGY

ATF Press
Adelaide

First published 2008
Second printing 2008
Third printing 2011

National Library of Australia Cataloguing-in-Publication entry

Author: Cadwallader, Alan.

Title: Beyond the word of a woman : recovering the bodies of the Syrophoenician women / Alan H. Cadwallader.

ISBN: 9781920691851 (pbk.)

Series: ATF Biblical series ; no. 1

Notes: Includes index.

Subjects: Jesus Christ--Teachings.
Jesus Christ--Political and social views
Bible. N.T. Mark--Criticism, interpretation, etc
Women in the Bible.
Children in the New Testament.

Dewey Number: 226.306

Published by ATF Press
An imprint of the Australasian Theological Forum Ltd
PO Box 504 Hindmarsh
SA 5007
ABN 90 116 359 963
www.atfpress.com

cover design
by Astrid Sengkey
based on
FW Farrar *The Life of Christ*
(London, Paris, New York: Cassell, Petter and Galpin, 1871), 368

Beyond the Word of a Woman

Alan H Cadwallader

For another woman

and her daughters

Table of Contents

Chapter Two
A Dog Returns to its Own Vomit
Ethological Constructions of Woman

Part Two
The Power of the Word and the Clash of Wisdom

Chapter Three
Dog in a Manger: The Ethological Words of Jesus

Chapter Four
The Scent of a Dog: The Ethological Words of Jesus in Context

Chapter Five
The Hair of the Dog that Bit You: The Ethological Word of a Woman

Part Three
Beyond the Word of a Woman to Somatic Restoration

Chapter Six
The Eloquence of a Barking Dog: Evaluating the Word of a Woman

Chapter Seven
The Power of The Dog: The Syrophoenician's Daughter

Conclusion
A Fondness for Bones
Reconsidering Mark's Syrophoenician Women

Acknowledgments

Time has haunted this book. The demands of full-time teaching and incessant claims of church insecurity have stretched energy and friendship. Moments of space for sitting with the Syrophoenician women had to be prised and prized. Nevertheless, graciousness adorns the years of labour and the labour of years, from many who through gentle enquiry and critical engagement helped me to shape the work.

Initially, Professor Dorothy Lee helped me to believe that I had ideas worth exploring. The Rev Dr Michael Trainor's large vision and constant demands that I state my ideas clearly, preserved my writing as much as possible from a state of thick pea-soup. Dr Vicky Balabanski's technical eye and political acumen saved me from many a jack-boot insensitivity. Any mistakes that remain are due either to my pig-headedness or myopic exhaustion.

The generosity and interest of people have been overwhelming. Cathy Laufer and Felicity Harley-McGowan, have read lesser and greater parts with unremitting attention to details of argument, style and format. Judy King has rummaged her fingers to the bone for the dogs of Pompeii. Paul Tuffin of Adelaide University's Classics Department, fostered my interest in Greek poetry and provided the occasional leash and redirection for my paths of enquiry. Scott Cowdell and the late John Roffey could not have been more encouraging, if at times cajoling of my chasing after a scent down some remote byway. Their red wine and Guinness almost always worked to draw me back to task.

A Flinders University Scholarship enabled me to expand contact with the rich and variegated resources in the northern hemisphere, and especially to have the opportunity of being exposed to concerted, supportive circles of learning. Arthur Holder of the Church Divinity School of the Pacific warmly welcomed me into the faculty colloquium, and Bill Countryman attentively heard me out as I was forging my ideas. Richard Rohrbaugh made space for me to attend the Portland meeting of the Context Group, an opportunity for supportive academic collegiality that is rare indeed. And Tom Olbricht gave me the chance of a lifetime to blend the brilliance of the exchanges in the meeting of the Rhetoric Group with the piazza evenings in Florence, where the group gathered in 1998. The staff and succession of researchers at St Deiniol's Library, Hawarden, deserve special mention for their promotion of a quite unique learning environment.

Delighted gratitude is felt for a man living up to his name, John Sweet, who deigned to show keen and engaged interest in the work of someone from a distant land. And to Hilary Regan of ATF Press, praise and thanks for his patience and belief amidst pressing schedules and the juggling of incessant demands.

There are others who probably have no appreciation of my debt to them. My students, who have had to indulge/endure constant reference to prostitutes, proverbs, poetry and dogs, have nevertheless asked those occasionally raw and guileless questions that pull flights of fancy back to the proper soil of earth.

But there are some who may be more conscious of my indebtedness. Librarians have a special call, I suspect, to chase, appease, support, and show a constant belief even when a writer has spiralled into a maelstrom of doubt. To the library staff at GTU and St Deiniol's who good-humouredly compensated for an Aussie accent and inexperience, I owe a great deal, but even more am I indebted to the librarians at the Adelaide Theological Library, Beth Prior, Rosemary Hocking, Val Canty and Wendy Davis who actually maintained an interest in my work in spite of my best efforts to tire them in the hunt for yet another reference.

No writing can be done without space, provision, and mountains of belief from those among whom I live and move and have my being. To Jess, Myf, Dan and Demelza, thanks; I look forward to hearing your side of the story. To Robyn, whose own research in medieval literature cross-pollinated my ideas so often over a coffee amongst the irises, gums and magpies, I owe . . . no, I don't owe. There are no debts, just determined, listening love and sheer shared gratitude at the chance to exchange help and belief, tease ideas together, embrace bodies, touch the earth, and hold the heritage of Tertullian, Augustine, Chrysostom and Jerome to account!

Abbreviations

The abbreviations for classical writers and their works and for inscriptions, papyri and ostraca are based on those used by HG Liddell, R Scott and HS Jones, *A Greek-English Lexicon* (Oxford: Clarendon Press, ninth edition (1940), with supplement, 1968), CT Lewis and C Short, *A Latin Dictionary* (Oxford: Clarendon Press, 1966), GW Lampe, *A Patristic Greek Lexicon* (Oxford: Clarendon Press, 1961), *Année Épigraphique*, *Journal of Biblical Literature* and JF Oates, RS Bagnall, WH Willis and KA Worp, *Checklist of Editions of Greek and Latin Papyri, Ostraca and Tablets* (Atlanta, GA: Scholars Press, fourth edition 1992). The following additional abbreviations are used:

ABD	Anchor Bible Dictionary
ABR	Australian Biblical Review
AE	Année épigraphique
AER	American Ecclesiastical Review
AHB	Ancient History Bulletin
AJA	American Journal of Archeology
AJAH	American Journal of Ancient History
AJP	American Journal of Philology
AncSoc	Ancient Society
AntCl	L'Antiquité classique
ANRW	Aufstieg und Niedergang der römischen Welt
AP	Palatine Anthology
AQ	Anthropology Quarterly
Archiv für lat Lexikogr	Archiv für lateinische Lexikographie und Grammatik
AW	Ancient World
b	Babylonian Talmud
BA	Biblical Archeologist
BAGD	W Bauer, WF Arndt, FW Gingrich

	and FW Danker (eds) *A Greek-English Lexicon of the New Testament* (Chicago and London: University of Chicago Press, second edition, 1979)
BDF	F Blass, A Debrunner and RW Funk *A Greek Grammar of the New Testament and Other Early Christian Literature* (Chicago and London: University of Chicago Press, ninth to tenth editions, 1961).
BGU	Berliner Griechische Urkunden
BibInt	Biblical Interpretation
BibRes	Biblical Research
BJRL	Bulletin of the John Rylands Library
BS	Beth She'arim Greek Inscriptions
BTB	Biblical Theology Bulletin
BZ	Biblische Zeitschrift
CA	Classical Antiquity
CBQ	Catholic Biblical Quarterly
CIG	Corpus Inscriptionum Graecarum
CIJ	Corpus Inscriptionum Judaicarum
CIL	Corpus Inscriptionum Latinarum
COP	Corpus des ordonnances des Ptolémées
CQ	Classical Quarterly
ET	Expository Times
Ethol	Ethology
ETL	*Ephemerides theologicae Lovanienses*
FemStuds	Feminist Studies
FGH	F Jacoby *Die Fragmente der griechischen Historiker* (Berlin)

GT	Gospel of Thomas
HSCP	Harvard Studies in Classical Philology
HTR	Harvard Theological Review
I Eph	Die Inschriften von Ephesos
ICUR	Inscriptiones Christianae Urbis, Romae
IEJ	Israel Exploration Journal
IF	Indogermansiche Forschungen
IG	Inscriptiones Graecae
IGNTP	International Greek New Testament Project
IGR	Inscriptiones Graecae ad Res Romanas pertinentes
ILS	Inscriptiones latinae selectae
Int	Interpretation
JAAR	Journal of the American Academy of Religion
JAOS	Journal of the American Oriental Society
JBL	Journal of Biblical Literature
JCS	Journal of Cuneiform Studies
JETS	Journal of Evangelical Theological Society
JECS	Journal of Early Christian Studies
JGBRS	Journal of Greek, Roman and Byzantine Studies
JFR	Journal of Folklore Research
JHS	Journal of Hellenic Studies
JQR	Jewish Quarterly Review
JRA	Journal of Roman Archeology
JRH	Journal of Religious History
JRS	Journal of Roman Studies

JSNT	Journal for the Study of the New Testament
JTB	Journal of Theoretical Behaviour
JTS	Journal of Theological Studies
LSJ	Liddell, Scott, Jones *Greek-English Lexicon*
LXX	Septuagint
m	Mishnah
NDIEC	New Documents Illustrating Early Christianity
NLH	New Literary History
NovT	Novum Testamentum
NTS	New Testament Studies
OGIS	Orientis Graeci Inscriptiones Selectae
OMich	Ostraca Michigan
Oud Stud	Oudtestamentische Studiën
PCG	Poetae Comici Graeci
PDM	Papyri Demoticae Magicae
PG	Patrologia Graeca
PGM	Papyri Graecae Magicae
PL	Patrologia Latina
P XV Congr	Papyrologica Bruxellensia du XVe Congrès
P Cair	Papyrus in the Musée du Caire
P Col Zen	The Columbia Zenon Papyri
P Duk	The Papyri at Duke University
P Ent	The Enteuxeis Papyri
P Fay	The Papyri of the Fayûm Towns
P Hamb	Griechische Papyrusurkunden der Hamburger Staats- und Universitätsbibliothek
P Hib	The Hibeh Papyri
P Lond	Greek Papyri in the British Museum (Kenyon)

P L Bat	Papyrologica Lugduno-Batava
P Lon Hay	Papyri of the London Hay Collection
P Oxy	The Oxyrhynchus Papyri
P Par	Greek Papyri in the Musée du Louvre
P Sakaon	The Archive of Aurelius Sakaon
P Strasb	Papyri of the University of Strasbourg
P Tebt	The Tebtunis Papyri
P Wisc	The Wisconsin Papyri
P Zen	The Zenon Papyri
PSI	Papiri della Società Italiana
PUG	Papiri dell'Università di Genova
QRB	Quarterly Review of Biology
RB	Revue biblique
RE	Pauly-Wissowa *Real-Encyclopädie der classischen Altertumswissenschaft*
RHPR	Revue d'Histoire et de Philosophie Religieuses
RSR	Religious Studies Review
RTL	*Revue théologique de Louvain*
SBLSP	Society of Biblical Literature Seminar Papers
SciExp	*Science et Ésprit*
SIG	Sylloge Inscriptionum Graecum
SO	Symbolae Osloenses
T	Testament
TAPA	Transactions of the American Philological Association
TDNT	Theological Dictionary of the New Testament
TGF	Tragicorum Graecorum Fragmenta

ThQ	*Theological Quarterly*
Tischendorf[8]	C Tischendorf Eighth Edition of the Greek New Testament
TLG	Thesaurus Linguae Graecae
TZ	Theologische Zeitschrift
UPZ	Urkunden der Ptolemäerzeit
VC	Vigiliae Christianae
VGT	Vocabulary of the Greek Testament
WUNT	Wissenschaftliche Untersuchungen zum Neuen Testament
ZNW	Zeitschrift für neutestamentaliche Wissenschaft
ZPE	Zeitschrift für Papyrologie und Epigraphik

Introduction
On Women, Word and Woofers

She has gained acclaim in Jewish and Gentile expressions of early Christianity. She names, under the guise of the 'Canaanitess', a Sunday in the liturgical year of the Orthodox Church. She was given twenty-seven sermons in one collection that ran through successive editions for over a hundred years.[1] She is a constant recipient of feminist re-conceptualisations of the early Jesus movement. She is the character in Mark's gospel (Mk 7:24–30) called 'the Syrophoenician woman'.

The prayer of humble access

The Syrophoenician woman has also provided inspiration for the most distinctive supplication of the foundational Anglican prayer-book. It is called 'The Prayer of Humble Access' and, 450 years after it was penned, many in the world-wide Anglican Communion still repeat it. The prayer comes at the critical transition from 'The Prayer of Thanksgiving' to 'The Prayer of Consecration' in 'The Order for the Administration of the Lord's Supper or Holy Communion':

> We do not presume to come to this thy Table, O merciful Lord, trusting in our own righteousness, but in thy manifold and great mercies. We are not worthy so much as to gather up the crumbs under thy Table. But thou art the same Lord, whose property is always to have mercy: Grant us therefore, gracious Lord, so to eat the flesh of thy dear Son Jesus Christ, and to drink his blood, that our sinful bodies may be made clean by his body, and our souls washed through his most precious blood, and that we may evermore dwell in him, and he in us. Amen.[2]

1. S Rutherford, *The Trial and Triumph of Faith* (The Free Church of Scotland, 1845).
2. This synaxis belongs to *The Book of Common Prayer* (1662), though from its origin in 1548, the prayer appears to have occupied different positions in the liturgy: see WE Scudamore, *Notitia Eucharistica* (London, Oxford & Cambridge: Rivingtons, 1872), 479.

The rubric of instruction for its use required the priest to say the prayer in the name of all, whilst kneeling, though community practice has swung the prayer into corporate repetition.

Several accents attach to the prayer: kneeling is the requisite posture to voice the petition, the body is sinful[3] (whereas the soul is without attribute) and no claims can be made upon God, even for crumbs under the table. Commentators on the prayer were quite clear that the allusion of the prayer was to the words of the Syrophoenician/ Canaanite woman.[4] One of the founders of the Oxford Movement, John Keble, held, 'We adopt her language in the deepest prayer of our Eucharistic Service.'[5] Hence, admission of wretchedness, expressed by a sinful body in a grovelling position, was set by intertextual relationship to a woman who was recalled as one under the table, a dog. The collapse of the man is portrayed as a descent into the feminine, or indeed, through the feminine to the bestial. The hallmark of unworthiness, of sin, and of dependency on a higher mercy, was the woman. In order to accentuate the destitution of the state, Jesus' own prior words to the woman are subtly restored: the denial of crumbs is accepted, even as it is blended with the woman's words confirming a position 'under the table'.

The perspective inculcated by the prayer was that redemption (ritually enacted by the movement through the Consecration Prayer to the reception of bread) consisted in moving up and away from being the animal—woman—indeed, from the bodily being of woman. God's mercy was pictured as securing an elevation from a bestial state. To receive bread was therefore to become a son not a daughter. Children and women were elided from express mention, seemingly collated with the animal recalled in the prayer's gospel reference, but never directly named—allusion being one of the most subtly powerful and self-protective forms of linguistic control.

---

3. 'Sinful body' may owe a connection to the dubious translation (found in early English translations through to the RSV) of Rom 6:6.
4. See, for example, E Daniel, *The Prayer Book: Its History, Language and Contents* (London: Wells Gardner, Darton & Co, fifteenth edition, nd), 322, A Barry, *The Teacher's Prayer Book* (London: Eyre & Spottiswoode, sixteenth edition, nd), 144a. The comparison to 'Prayers of Inclination' in ancient liturgies (for example, the Liturgy of St Basil) only reinforces the point—these ancient prayers lack any allusion to the story of the Syrophoenician woman.
5. See *Sermons for the Christian Year,* volume 4, sermon 14, quoted by MF Sadler, *The Gospel according to St Mark* (London: George Bell & Sons, 1892), 150.

The subtle liturgical socialisation was no novel development; it simply reiterated ancient constructions of woman, the body and the animal, and preserved male identity and control against the threat of womanly degeneracy. And with the self-indulgent and self-authenticating remarks that ascribe to the prayer a 'singular fervour and beauty ... in its confession of unworthiness and humility ...',[6] such attitudes were now deemed the acceptable worship of the christian god.

Toward a liberating reading of the Syrophoenician women's story

Accordingly, the story of the Syrophoenician woman must be the place where any potential for restoration and critique begins. But another and greater necessity accompanies a new reading of the story. The grave danger in the return to the story is that the use of the woman to delineate male salvation would continue. That is, whilst the prayer might use the image of the woman as the representation of the depths to which man can sink, a new reading must avoid constructing the woman as the means by which man can achieve salvation, via a revisioned posture towards God/Jesus. The paradigm would not have changed, merely the arrangement of the constituent elements. If the Syrophoenician's story has another reading which can withstand the 'Prayer of Humble Access', then it must be a reading that attends to the gender dynamics of the story rather than one that merely provides a woman's example (differently read) for the sake of a male in search of liberation. The missiological interpretation of the story that has accompanied western missionary expansion in the modern era—that the story represents the breaking into Gentile adherence of an originally Jewish-contained Jesus movement—is only partially redirected by an emphasis on women as 'determinative for the extension'.[7] Even more critically, the unabated emphasis on the words of the exchange between Jesus and the woman, which has shifted from privileging those of Jesus (in the nineteenth and early twentieth centuries) to those of the woman (in the last four decades) has done little to unsettle the logocentric presumptions that undergird both. In other words, missiological and logocentric interpretations leave the basic arena of male-controlled

6. Barry, 144a.
7. E Schüssler Fiorenza, *In Memory of Her: A Feminist Theological Reconstruction of Christian Origins* (New York: Crossroad, 1983), 138.

foundations largely unshaken.

An attempt must be made to attend to the gendered dynamics of the story. This will, of necessity, commence with the text itself, but will not be separated from the sociopolitical influences of its own time and the heightened awareness of gender issues in our own. Historical questions relating to the origins and authenticity of the story in Mark's gospel remain dormant throughout the body of the work, surfacing only as a postulate in the conclusion. At the same time, a consciousness of performance issues and the cultural materialism within which the text had its early life, provides an opportunity to move beyond a mere literary analysis of character. The resistance to the erasure of the woman from a story within which she figures so prominently is a small step towards according a subjectivity to the woman, at least at the level of performance and appropriation of the story, given that historical reconstruction may be too fragile a venture. Indeed, historical fixation may do a disservice to the groups that held, shaped and improvised the telling of the story of the Syrophoenician woman and sought to lead the story into the flesh of their own time.[8] Accordingly, both an essentialising of woman erected on the edifice of Markan literary dynamics and a thorough-going fictionalising that sacrifices somatic actualisation on the altar of the aesthetics of language are to be eschewed.

Moreover, the female adult and female child are not to be given a voice and a place as if by some beneficent male largesse. Rather, my hope, even as a male interpreter, is to recognise within and beyond the story 'her' self-authorised decision to occupy communication and space. It opens the possibility for this male writer to do likewise without demanding the presence or absence of the female (adult or child) in terms of gender dominance or dependence, utilisation or reification. The potential sought in a new reading is for women, children and men to cooperate in humanist transformation, or even to assert their own authorial subjectivity in resistance to any *demand* for cooperation that may lurk in such an aspiration.

The motivation for this writing is to purge the story of interpretations that require the expending of a woman and (female) child for male interests, whether of man's sin or redemption, of extolling/excusing a (male) saviour, or of maintaining a male privilege in identity constructs and rational discourse. This book is therefore about a woman and her

8. J Dewey, 'From Storytelling to Written Text: The Loss of Early Christian Women's Voices', in *BTB* 26 (1996): 71–78.

daughter's destabilisation of 'the powers of representation as powers of the Father',[9] of a male-constructed universe that has been naturalised by reference to the animal world.

The contemporary basis for the approach

Up until relatively recently, Mark's story has been overwhelmed by its dependent off-spring born(e) in a didactic, diasporan matrix (Mt 15:21–28).[10] The faith of a humble, gentile woman has characterised the reading of both pericopes. Such a (mis-) reading of Mark has a remarkable tenacity—Gerd Lüdemann, for example, has claimed that, although the woman's faith is not mentioned explicitly, 'as a phenomenon it is present in the story'.[11]

The retrieval of the blatant affirmation of the word of a woman (Mk 7:29) has brought considerable reassessment of the significance of the story. This 'word of a woman' has become prized in a socio-political climate of the recovery of distinctive and critical women's voices in contemporary church and society (especially in the West). However, even as this 'word of a woman' is still yielding a rich fecundity for the life of church and of those exploring other communal expressions of faith, I name three concerns (at least) for further reflection:

i) the problematisation of the accent upon word by the rehabilitation of corporeality as a positive, contributing presence.
ii) the significance of the application of animal epithets in an encounter *involving a woman*.
iii) the neglect of the daughter's role in/for the story.

The first concern arises from an awareness of the cost that may accompany a privileging of the woman's word. The corporeality, even carnality, of woman has been impaled with the long historical quill of demeaning de-, in- and pre-scription. The gaining of the word of a woman might simply become the final epitaph on/for her bodily subjectivity.

---

9. J Rancière, *The Flesh of Words: The Politics of Writing*, translated by C Mandell (Stanford, CA: Stanford University Press, 2004), 159.
10. Markan priority is assumed herein but does not affect the main arguments.
11. *Jesus After 2000 Years: What He Really Said and Did*, translated by J Bowden (London: SCM, 2000), 50.

Contemporary feminist theory, complemented by explorations in literary theory, have re-aligned attention from word to body.[12] The importance of the body has been reasserted not as a poor counterpoint to the primacy of the word, nor as a capitulation to ancient denigration of a woman's somatic 'troubling', but as a determinative subject in its own right. The challenge to the word, to the hegemony of this 'logocentricity', does not seek the establishment of a rival for the throne of the word. It looks for a new way of understanding both word and body and the relationship(s) exchanged between them, removed from a competitive striving for supremacy. Body in this understanding is not an ink-injected project of the word, but a gendered, materialist actor and performer engaging both world and word.

The second concern arises from a more rigorous assessment of the sociopolitical and sociocultural background for the story of the Syrophoenician woman, one that acknowledges an influence stretching from the ancient world into the present. The animal world that is called upon in the key metaphor of the story (the dog) bears manifold disruptive attributes. The most fundamental description of the animal was and remains that it is irrational. Rationality stands as the singular mark of distinction of the human from the animal. Here scientific axiom and cultural distinctive are glued by the appeal to nature. By extrapolation, the animal was also the mark of anarchic potential and unmastered bodily instincts. Antiquity's stock dualisms extended the characterisation to woman. The upholding of the word of the Syrophoenician woman in the Markan story is compelled to confront the anomaly of Jesus' description of the woman and her daughter as dogs. The primary spur to exploration here is the question: how can one who is collated with the dumb beasts yet be declared to have uttered *logos*, the mark of rationality?

The third concern confronts the centuries of neglect of the child in the story. For all that the miracle story hinges on the disturbance to the life of the child, little attention has been given to the Syrophoenician daughter's significance for the story, nor to the relationship and exchange with her mother. Even when the expansive power of the

12. See the work of the Australian writers: Elizabeth Grosz, *space, time and perversion: The Politics of Bodies* (London: Allen & Unwin, 1995), especially chapter 2, and Sara Ahmed, *Differences That Matter: Feminist Theory and Postmodernism* (Cambridge: Cambridge University Press, 1998), especially chapter 3.

word of the woman is appreciated, the absence of any accompanying revaluation of the child may result in a denial of the very achievement of the woman's word, namely, the release of the daughter. The child remains as bound and marginalised as in the opening of the story.

There is no intention in exploring these concerns to resuscitate a biological determinism for the life of women, nor to reify their positions as mothers or dependent daughters. The history of interpretation of the story of the Syrophoenician women testifies too plainly to a backlash against the power of the word of a woman and to a reinstatement of boundaries upon and around a woman's body.[13] Moving beyond the word of a woman must not be a retrogression. The careful analysis that follows therefore seeks to meet with these questions raised of the word of a woman in the hope that attention to issues of corporeality, rationality and generational succession will yield not only a strengthening of the woman's connection with the word she speaks, but also an alternative to the absorption of her word into an unchallenged logocentric framework. It will require constant reminder of the gendered dynamics replete in the story.

The structure of the argument

The argument presented here unfolds in three sections. The first two chapters seek to establish the *prima facie* case for a new investigation of the story, one which takes seriously the tension between logocentric accent and bestial metonymy such that a new methodology is required so as to guide the analysis.

The metaphor of the dog that dominates the contest of proverbs[14] in the Markan dialogue of Jesus and the Syrophoenician woman will be explored in the context of the larger schema of the scientific assessment and rhetorical deployment of animals in the ancient world. More particularly, the commitment to the gendered dynamics of the story will require an investigation of the use and purpose of 'dog' as a term of abuse by men against women, rather than replay the standard

13. Nineteenth century commentators turned the Syrophoenician story into a repudiation of women's agitation for access to universities and electoral franchise. See my 'Dog-throttling: Nineteenth Century dogmatic/cultural constructions of the Syrophoenician Woman', in V Balabanski and AH Cadwallader (editors), *Hermeneutics and the Authority of Scripture* (Adelaide: ATF Press), forthcoming.

14. It will become clear in chapter 3 that of the three contenders for the form of Jesus' saying in Mark, that is chreia, *tobspruch* and proverb, that the last is the foundation for his first response.

interpretation that alleges a common Jewish label for Gentiles, even as it subtly removes women from consideration.

The recognition of the problems raised by the complexities of the conjunction of women, dogs and reason in the ancient world generates the need for an adequate methodology. The modern discipline of ethology provides a useful beginning because of its accent upon the conclusions for human behaviour that can be derived from the animal world. It also bears the marks of ancient forebears that similarly constructed conclusions about human beings from animals, most especially a fundamental accent on the unequal dimorphic division between male and female. Feminist critiques of ethology enable a specific accountability for the limitations and socio-biological interests of the discipline.[15]

The second section applies to the Markan text four insights distilled from a feminist-critical appraisal of ethology. These are:

i) the conjunction of scientific/philosophical axioms with cultural values reinforced through long-standing literary expression,
ii) the moral implications which attach to the inferior partner categorised in any hierarchical exchange,
iii) the territorial boundaries which afford spatial protection for dominant and submissive entities, and
iv) the socio-political conclusions which assert a foundation in the natural order.

In chapters three to five, the saying of Jesus and the reply of the woman in particular will be screened through the grid of these emphases. This grid aids the recognition of the power within the whole story of a mutually reinforcing connection between ethological investigation and ancient literary characterisation. Further, the critical application of a feminist challenged ethology awakens an awareness of literary and popular values operating in the ancient world, of the literary techniques and interests of the text, and of a reliance upon both the performance of the story (the 'performance act') and the reception of the story (the 'performance event').

15. I have briefly explored the potential of ethology, critically handled, for the analysis of this gospel story in 'When a Woman is a Dog: Ancient and Modern Ethology meet the Syrophoenician Women', in *BCT* 1.4 (2005): 1–35.

The third section diverts attention from the exchange of words towards the relationship between the two Syrophoenician women in the story. The problems of the dominance of a logocentric approach to the Syrophoenician's story will be named most clearly in chapter six, especially as it threatens both the achievement of the woman affirmed in the story and any attempt to recover the importance of the role of the daughter. In chapter seven, the final verse of the pericope receives concerted attention, not least because it constructs a situation that is *not* centred upon Jesus and his benchmark of approval (v 29), but on the encounter between two women, an encounter that displaces an exchange of words in favour of somatic performance.

Problematising the word of this work and its writer

There are significant dangers in this overall discourse, precisely because the prime avenue of communication is linguistic. A number of factors preclude the inclusion of reproductions of material artefacts even though they would provide at least a symbolic gesture of interrupting a written scholarly enterprise.[16] However, it is hoped that the re-evaluation of the body and the bodies of two women in a story from late antiquity will confront the colonialist tendency of writing as an inherited cultural disposition and activity of (at least) Western male history.[17]

By educational opportunities, canonical and manufacturing control over transmission of literature, and myriad reinforcements in the scientific-political nexus, privilege in writing has been granted to men.[18] In the ancient Mediterranean world, this privilege was one expression of the supremacy of *logos*, of word as both reason and literary words. Speech, at least as defined as credible, public and

---

16. The demand for a materialist approach to biblical studies haunts the literary approach. Stephen Moore has produced a succession of essays reflecting this concern: 'Illuminating the Gospels without the benefit of colour: a plea for concrete criticism', in *JAAR* 60 (1992): 257–279, *God's Gym: Divine Male Bodies of the Bible* (New York/London: Routledge, 1996), *God's Beauty Parlor: and Other Queer Spaces In and Around the Bibl*e (Stanford, CA: Stanford University Press, 2001), 90–172.
17. See B Ashcroft, G Griffiths and H Tiffin, *The Empire Writes Back: Theory and Practice in Post-Colonial Literatures* (London/New York: Routledge, 1989), 1–12.
18. S Johnson, 'Theorizing Language and Masculinity: A Feminist Perspective', in S Johnson and UH Meinhof (editors), *Language and Masculinity* (Oxford: Blackwell, 1997), 16.

authorised, was the other key aspect. In a sense, both are combined in the story in Mark's Gospel—speech, and the writing thereof, appear to be privileged, although I will argue that both are problematised.

These recognitions demand a (self-)reflection beyond the admission of my own socio-political location. Such disclosure can never deliver a complete guarantee of the direction of theoretical argumentation nor adequate evidence for any allegation or excuse.[19] However, the methodological and analytical insights that unfold in argument cannot (dare not) be monolithic. Any self-protective metastructure would defy the very suggestions that are presented herein. The refraction of political potential in the arguments inextricably touches upon my own gender expression and the wanted and unwanted historical inheritance highlighted by the feminist-critical insights I employ.[20]

The dependence on feminist critiques of contemporary ethology is a means of compelling a critical analysis of ancient modes of (re) presentation of women and patterns of being. Satisfaction with mere description of the ancient evidence participates in the same mystifying of socio-political structures that ancient writers frequently manipulated through their writing of prescription through innocuous description. Even without that regulatory intent, contemporary scholarship becomes complicit in the inscription, when it questions neither the extant sources nor the community/history of interpretation.

Eva Stehle and Amy Day have argued, 'Sexual representations engage any viewer according to his or her social identity and place in the sex-gender system and elicit readings that are at least in part based on bodily identification . . .'[21] For some men, albeit trained in feminist discourse and even aligned with its political programmes, this compromises participation, even when it may be acknowledged that it is an imperative.[22] Paul Smith lamented:

19. Note the comments of Kwok Pui-lan: ' . . . should a person's race and gender be decisive in discussing the myths of origin?' ('Response to the Semeia volume on Postcolonial Criticism', in *Semeia* 75 (1996): 216).
20. Compare Joseph Boone, 'Of Me(n) and Feminism: Who(se) is the Sex that Writes?', in L Kaufmann (editor), *Gender & Theory* (Oxford: Basil Blackwell, 1989), 158–180.
21. E Stehle and A Day, 'Women Looking at Women: Women's Ritual and Temple Sculpture', in NB Kampen (editor), *Sexuality in Ancient Art* (Cambridge: Cambridge University Press, 1996), 101.
22. AJ Frantzen, 'When Women Aren't Enough', in *Speculum* 68 (1993): 445.

> There is always the probability of being incriminated, the continual likelihood of appearing provocative, offensive, and troublesome to the very people who have taught me to ask the questions, even at the very moment when I begin to grapple with the only theoretical language available. These feelings, these fears, are in a large part the result of having to engage with a discourse whose laws I can never quite obey.[23]

As expressed, this might stray into the familiar male cry for (maternal) sympathy and/or yet again, provide evidence of the legacy of logocentricity where one constantly (though unsuccessfully) strives to rise above the complex entanglements in the very materiality it seeks to explicate and order.[24] The desire to be 'outside' is, in this sense, nothing other than nostalgia for the symbolic public position which ancient (free) man was granted and expected to occupy, with woman constrained to the 'inside'.

Analysis of the patriarchal, hierarchical structure of the ancient Mediterranean world and contemporary philosophical discussion of masculine and feminine identities demonstrate that a range of subjectivities is available.[25] Men can themselves be oppressed by patriarchy and its legitimating, constricting ideologies—this is the reason for Elisabeth Schüssler Fiorenza's preference for the term 'kyriarchy'.[26] There is no universal 'female or male voice' nor a reflexive implication that relations between the sexes predetermine theoretical discourse and political stances. This is part of my own rejection of socio-biology. Adopting ways of thinking and commitment

---

23. P Smith, 'Men in Feminism: Men and Feminist Theory', in A Jardine and P Smith (editors), *Men in Feminism* (New York: Methuen, 1987), 38; compare P Rabinow, 'Representations are Social Facts: Modernity and Post-Modernity in Anthropology', in J Clifford and GE Marcus (editors), *Writing Culture: The Poetics and Politics of Ethnography* (Berkeley and Los Angeles: University of California Press, 1986), 257–259.
24. EF Keller, *Reflections on Gender and Science* (New York and London: Yale University Press, 1985), 22.
25. RW Connell, *Gender and Power* (Sydney: Allen & Unwin, 1987), 110, Johnson, 'Theorizing Language', 19–21.
26. E Schüssler Fiorenza *But She Said: Feminist Practices of Biblical Interpretation* (Boston: Beacon Press, 1992), 114–120.

can be both personally transformative and socially reconstructive.[27] At the same time, there can be no fantasy about or attempt at an invulnerability of argument or person.

Finally, the arguments presented prepare the way for transformational thinking and acting with respect to the animal world. Whilst this falls outside my purpose here, there is more than a human and feminist liberation to be gained from the critique of ethological and sociobiological determinism in both its ancient and modern forms. This liberation does not assert a triumphalist human uniqueness apart from creation (particularly the animal world). Rather it invites complementary, respectful engagements that allow, indeed celebrate, commonalities and differences without re-imposing hierarchies of relationship.[28]

27. E Schüssler Fiorenza, *Discipleship of Equals* (London: SCM, 1993), 369; *cf* AS Kahn and WP Gaeddert, 'From Theories of Equity to Theories of Justice: The Liberating Consequences of Studying Women', in VE O'Leary, RK Unger and BS Wallston (editors), *Women, Gender and Social Psychology* (Hillsdale, NJ: Lawrence Erlbaum Associates, 1985), 129–145.
28. See N Habel (editor), *Readings from the Perspective of the Earth* (Sheffield: Sheffield Academic Press, 2000), 38–53.

Part One

The Primacy of the Word: And its Ethological Reinforcement

1

Cave Canem, Have Canis When a Woman is a Dog

Logos and the dog: the contradiction

The intertwining of logocentricity and socio-political dimensions in the exegetical commentary of the last two centuries is nothing new. The accent on word betrays an uncanny resonance with ancient concerns and constructions of human affairs. The classical training and inheritance of the nineteenth century shows through even when coloured by christological commitments. One fundamental issue related to the importance of *logos* in the ancient world was however sidelined—the conjunction of *logos* with an element in the story that is diametrically opposed to it, namely, the dog. The woman and her daughter are polarised against Jesus by his collation of them with an irrational animal. This chapter launches the exploration of the tensions involved in the conjunction of women, animals and reason in the ancient world. The purpose is to delineate these key elements and something of their inter-relationship to establish a *prima facie* case that must guide the search for a methodology.

Both woman and child are caught into a naturalist fallacy by being aligned with the animal. The bestial realm attracts male interest and desire for control even as it threatens both. They are thereby made to require 'zoning' by reason,[1] the faculty that characterises gods and men. This highlights the problem of the story's connection of reason and the dog. A lengthy study of the various evaluations of the dog exposes both its pariah and companion characteristics in ancient cultures and the susceptibility of humans to the enormous range of metaphors built upon the dog in literary characterisation. Women in particular are found to have an almost metonymic connection with dogs in ancient literature, but the rhetoric of characterisation is hidden or assumes an unchallenged foundation. This chapter therefore builds the case for a critical ethological reading of the story of the Syrophoenician woman, a method that will be outlined in the following chapter.

1. MJ Bennett, *Belted Heroes and Bounded Women* (Lanham: Rowman & Littlefield, 1997), 136–142.

Naming key elements: women, animals and reason

The fundamental problem in the contemporary study of the story remains the exchange between Jesus and the Syrophoenician woman. Jesus' words set the encounter in the division between man and beast. A missiological interpretation (in manifold permutations) adds a further pairing, Jew and Gentile, to the basic division between (hu) man and animal. Any attention to gender dynamics in the story merely compounds the dualistic counterpoint of Jew-male-human over Gentile-female-dog.

Twentieth century preoccupation with a missiological interpretation has obscured the larger question of the use of animal 'metaphors', even when ranged against other pejorative references to dogs in the New Testament (Mt 7:6, Phil 3:2, Rev 22:15). Studies of the use of animal metaphors in verbal abuse are absent;[2] certainly, analysis of the story of the Syrophoenician woman rarely moves beyond a stock equation of Gentiles and dogs.[3]

Bestial-laced abuse is relatively frequent in the New Testament, emanating from the lips of Jesus and Paul amongst others: snake (Mt 23:33), viper (Mt 3:7 || Lk 3:7, Mt 12:34, 23:33), fox (Lk 13:32) pig (Mt 7:6), wolf (Mt 7:15, Acts 20:29).[4] The frequency of such metaphors in Jesus' discourse suggests that the use of 'dog' for the woman and her daughter in the Syrophoenician's story is not unusual. Even if none of the instances be authentic to the historical Jesus (unlikely), the evangelists apparently were open to making/recognising such

---

2. Robert Grant briefly mentions the metaphorical application of 'wolf' and 'fox': *Early Christians and Animals* (London and New York: Routledge, 1999), 14.
3. Bruce Malina is one of the few to have noted the connection made between animals and human character but this is not explored at any length nor does he include dogs in his survey—the most prolific term of abuse in the ancient world: 'Is there a Circum-Mediterranean Person? Looking for Stereotypes', in *BTB* 22 (1992): 74. The study is more advanced in classical disciplines: see S Lilja, *Dogs in Ancient Greek Poetry* (Helsinki: Societas Scientarum Fennica, 1976), especially 21–25.
4. Sometimes the referents are less obvious: for example, Lk 10:19, Jn 10:12. This may be an example of 'insider language' where the audience knows (or thinks it can identify) the intended recipients. A detailed study of such language use in the New Testament must await another opportunity. Michael Goulder has noted however that *logia* with pairs of animal images are confined to Matthew-Luke: *Luke, A New Paradigm* (Sheffield: JSOT Press, 1989), volume 2, 463.

a speech pattern for Jesus. Bestial characterisation of enemies was familiar in the period.[5]

Hence, for all the importance of the recovery of emphasis on the word of the woman in recent interpretation, what remains unrecognised is *the dissonance between the description of a woman as a dog and the affirmation that she has spoken logos*. Jude's collation of instinct-driven humans with irrational (ἄλογα) animals (Jude 10; *cf* 2 Pet 2:12)[6] is merely a canonical instance of an almost universally held ancient understanding.[7] Animals are the antithesis of *logos*. They often provided the typologies of various vices,[8] moral depravity being especially represented in the various examples of lack of restraint (for example, Tit 1.12).[9] Lack of restraint was a clear manifestation of the absence of reason.

5. Dogs, boars and foxes figure prominently in such portraits: see P Tiller, *A Commentary on the Animal Apocalypse of 1Enoch* (Atlanta, GA: Scholars Press, 1993), 32–36.
6. Richard Bauckham considers the clause to parallel 'defile the flesh' in v 8, suggestive of sexual indulgence: *Word Bible Commentary: Jude, 2 Peter* (Waco, TX: Word, 1983), 63. The connection of the animal world with sexual license is noteworthy—an aspect explored in chapter 3.
7. Xen *Cyro* 2.3.9, *Rhet ad Her* 2.19.29, Varr *L L* 6.56, Sen *Ira* 1.3.3–8, Phil Jud *Opif* 73, Jos *C Ap* 2.213, *Ant* 10. 262, Wis 11:15, 4 Macc 14:14, 19, Ps-Phoc 188, Just M *Apol* 1.43.8. The word ἄλογα could be used as a substantive meaning 'brutes': Plat *Prot* 321b, Democritus fr 164, Xen *Hiero* 7.3, *TZeb* 5.1, Phil Jud *Opif* 148, *Virt* 133. Philo extrapolates from animal irrationality to the justification of (hu)man's dominion over creation, as reason ruling over that which does not possess reason: P Borgen, 'Man's Sovereignty over Animals and Nature', in T Fornberg and D Hellholm (editors), *Texts and Contexts: Biblical Texts in Their Textual and Situational Contexts* (Oslo: Scandinavian University Press, 1995), 371–379. Elsewhere, the same principle undergirds Philo's understanding of relations between men and women: *Mig Abr* 7–8, *Opif* 151,165.
8. Jeffrey Rusten, 'Introduction' to Loeb edition of *Theophrastus* (edited by J Rusten, IC Cunningham, AD Knox) (Harvard: Harvard University Press, 1993), 17; for an example, see Timaios of Locri *Mund Anim* 86; *cf* 1 En 85–90.
9. See WW Fortenbaugh, 'Aristotle: Animals, Emotion and Moral Virtue', in *Arethusa* 4 (1971): 137–165. Human lawlessness was equated with animal behaviour: Xen *Anab* 5.7.32, Sen *Ep* 60.4; *cf* the Christian appropriation of these associations: Iren *C Haer* 5.8.2–3, Epiph *Pan* 4.5.2.

Occasionally, debates surface as to whether any intelligence was to be found in animals,[10] but it is clear that the measure of intelligence was the human and the well-ordered one at that. John Winkler dismisses the proponents as projectors 'of a patriarchal image onto the screen of the animal world'.[11] The supremacy of human beings was assured; it resided in the (or 'his') mind[12] and in the ability to communicate what was therein.[13] Speech was the expression and exposition of *logos*.

Rationality made a (hu)man (hu)man, and declared 'man alone of animals' the imitation of deity, welcoming everything marked by 'mind and reason'[14] and demonstrating the divinised hierarchy by animal sacrifices.[15] Euripides captured the widespread sentiment:

---

10. *Eg* Plut *Mor* (*Sol Anim*), Porph *Abst* 3.3, 188.17–189.4. Diogenes Laertius (*Vit* 5.49) avers that Theophrastus wrote a work *On the Wisdom and Character of Animals*, no longer extant. Quintilian (*Inst* 2.16.16) allows some intelligence to animals but their inability to speak warranted the usual designation. Compare Plat *Leg* 196e. See generally the (slightly polemical) treatment by Richard Sorabji, *Animal Minds and Human Morals: The Origins of the Western Debate* (Ithaca, NY: Cornell University Press, 1993), J Heath, 'Disentangling the Beast: Humans and Other Animals in Aeschylus' *Oresteia*', in *JHS* 119 (1999): 17–47, and CR Matthews, 'Articulate Animals: A Multivalent Motif in the Apocryphal Acts of the Apostles', in F Bovon, AG Brock and CR Matthews (editors), *The Apocryphal Acts of the Apostles* (Cambridge, MT: Harvard University Press, 1999), 213–222.
11. JJ Winkler, *The Constraints of Desire: The Anthropology of Sex and Gender in Ancient Greece* (New York: Routledge, 1990), 23 (responding to Phil Jud *Anim.*). This explains Christopher Matthews' puzzle that the extolling of reason in animals could yet be matched with the extreme brutality and blood sports of the Romans ('Articulate Animals' 219n46)—animal reason was merely a fictional postulate not to obstruct (hu)man rational dominance. In fact, the debates over reasoning animals were only jousts, gladiatorial games made the more interesting because of the difficult terms of the contest. Dominance was the industry to which reason was harnessed as the rationale: see S Brown, 'Death as Decoration: Scenes from the Arena on Roman Domestic Mosaics', in A Richlin (editor), *Pornography and Representation in Greece and Rome* (New York and Oxford: Oxford University Press, 1992), 180–211.
12. Eur *Aeol* fr 27, Dem *Decl 60* (*Epitaphius*) 30.
13. Xen *Mem* 4.3.11–12, Cic *De Or* 8.32, Lucret *Nat Rer* 5.1041–1061, Quint *Inst* 2.16.15. A talking dog, 'a dumb animal which received a human voice', is taken as a miracle (*Acts of Peter* 9, 11–12); *cf* a seven month old child who miraculously received a manly voice (15); *cf* also *Acts of Philip* 8.
14. Plut *Mor (Conv)* 673e.
15. J-P. Vernant, 'At Man's Table: Hesiod's Foundation Myth of Sacrifice', in M Detienne and J-P Vernant (editors), *The Cuisine of Sacrifice*

Man's strength is small and yet
In the turns of his subtle mind
He masters the monstrous brood
Of the sea and the beasts
Of the air and the earth.[16]

Gender-specificity was regarded as *essential* to the argument in the ancient world.[17]

Similarities might sometimes be drawn with animals—such as in the common need for nourishment, the procreation and nurture of the young,[18] the sexual divide. But such comparisons also reinforced distinctions. There was a general consistency in philosophical arguments that there were essential characteristics that delineated particular animals and separated them from different species and from human beings.[19] Just as it was in the nature of a lion to have a truculent temper, for a fox to have craftiness, or a deer to have timidity, so it was in the nature of a (hu)man to be rational.[20] Philo was just this blunt, notably collating reason and speech: 'For as neighing is peculiar to a

---

translated by P Wissing (Chicago: University of Chicago Press, 1986), 28–29, 37–38. Jews and Christians rejected the anthropomorphism of divine representation, but readily agreed with the relative hierarchy of relations between God, man, woman and animals. Moreover, Jewish efforts to define themselves rigorously against Egyptian practices, despised the collation of god(s) with animals (Phil Jud *Dec* 76–80); they were not alone: see Grant, *Christians and Animals*, 7–8.

16. *Aeol* fr 27. This understanding occurs in different genres and disciplines in esteemed and mediocre writers alike; hence compare the preamble for Euryphamus' *Concerning Human Life* where the accent on the divine connection is even more blatant.
17. S Stowers, 'Greeks Who Sacrifice and Those Who Do Not', in LM White and OL Yarbrough (editors), *The Social World of the First Christians: Essays in Honor of Wayne A Meeks* (Minneapolis: Fortress Press, 1995), 325–329.
18. Interestingly, Anna's lament about her barrenness in *The Protoevangelium of James* humiliates her *below* bird and beast, precisely because of her inability to procreate (3.2).
19. Lucret *Nat Rer* 1.159–173, Gal *MM* 2.7.3–5, a passage strikingly parallel to 1 Cor 15:39.
20. Lucret *Nat Rer* 3.741–753; *cf* 5:1036–1042. Compare also Quintilian 'It is natural for a man to reason, as for birds to fly, for horses to gallop and for wild beasts to be savage. So special is the brain to us in activity and ingenuity that the origin of the mind is believed to be heaven.' (*Inst* 1.1.1, my translation); *cf* Sen *Ep* 76.8–10.

horse, and barking to a dog, and lowing to a cow, and roaring to a lion, so is speech and reason itself to man.'[21]

For human beings to behave irrationally was either to cross boundaries between species, with its resultant satyric chaos,[22] or, more mildly, to betray inborn temperaments which should be controlled, if unable to be eliminated completely.[23] Thus the import of calling someone a cynic (that is, 'dog-like') is οὐκ ἀνθρωπίζεις, 'you are not human'.[24] Conversely, Philo of Alexandria cherished the hope that the taming of the wild beasts within a person would result in animals becoming tame and gentle.[25]

Woman as animal

When the human was a woman however, the collation of woman and animals could become, in some assessments, virtually tautologous.[26] One of the most common equations of the natural realm and the human in the ancient world was that relating to gender. Sherry Ortner's famous question, 'Is female to male as nature is to culture?',[27] meets with a decided 'yes' in the ancient world.[28] The Middle Platonic

21. Phil Jud *Somn* 1.108. This is the endowment of God; *cf* Xen *Mem* 4.3.11–12, Quint *Inst* 2.16.16–17.
22. Hor *Ars Poet,* 12-13.
23. Lucret *Nat Rer* 3.319–322.
24. Luc *Dem* 21.
25. Phil Jud *Praem* 88. The animals would be 'awe-struck into respectful fear of him as, by nature, their ruler and master' (89). Compare *Sib Or* 3.788–795, 2 Bar 73.6. The harmony of humans and animals is a hope shared by other traditions as well; see, for example Verg *Ecl* 4.18–25, Tibullus 1.2.40–52, *Tabula Ceres* 22.2, Mk 1:13, 11:2.
26. Phocylides held that there were four tribes of women (φῦλα γυναικεί-ων)—all of which were named as animals: the dog, the bee, the pig, the horse: *apud* Stob *Flor* 73.60,61.
27. SB Ortner, 'Is Female to Male as Nature is to Culture?', in MZ Rosaldo and L Lamphere (editors), *Women, Culture and Society* (Stanford, CA: Stanford University Press, 1974), 67–87. See also SJ Hekman, *Gender and Knowledge: Elements of a Postmodern Feminism* (Oxford: Polity Press, 1990), 111–135 who points to Frederick Nietzsche's same formulation of the question with a genealogical exploration that spanned from ancient to modern times.
28. Ortner's universalising of the nature-culture dichotomy has been criticised: see C MacCormack and M Strethern (editors), *Nature, Culture, and Gender* (Cambridge: Cambridge University Press, 1980). The Mediterranean world of antiquity however almost completely justifies her critical observations, even though it was not the basis for her anthropological conclusions. See also Schüssler Fiorenza, *In*

pseudepigraphal writing *Timaios of Locri*, probably to be dated just prior to the gospel writings, applied the scalpel thus: 'There being two, these are the foundations: on the one hand, the idea is expressed as (of the) male and of the father; on the other hand, matter is (of the) female and of the mother.'[29] Woman is the sign of the material, the natural, over against the intellect and its chief instrument, language.[30] And given that animals often were the emblems of shame, women were similarly collated: 'No animal more shameless.'[31]

This is not simply a derivation from female physiology. Rather, the links between woman and the natural world were both frequent and literary.[32] The uncontrolled license associated with harlots[33] drew manifold connections with animals[34] and provided constant demonstration of the 'natural' proclivities of women.[35] Little wonder

---

Memory, 89, *Discipleship of Equals* 302. The resilience of the woman-nature collation into the present time is found in manifold examples: see SL Hacker, 'The Culture of Engineering: Woman, Workplace and Machine' in J Rothschild (editor), *Women, Technology, and Innovation* (Oxford: Pergamon Press, 1982), 345–346.

29. §5. Text from TH Tobin, *Timaios of Locri, On the Nature of the World and the Soul* (Chico, CA: Scholars Press, 1985), 32 (my translation.) Tobin's translation unfortunately blurs the lines of division between λόγον . . . ἄρρενός τε καὶ πατρός and ὕλα θήλεός τε καὶ ματέρος by drawing λόγον ἔχει across the asseverative construction, whereas a copula is to be understood in the second clause. Note also that εἶδος is frequently equivalent to ἰδέα in Platonic philosophy (for example, Plat *Phd* 103e, *Rep* 597a), and appears to be so in this writing: compare §§2, 7, and Tobin's own introduction (16).
30. See EV Spelman, 'Woman as Body: Ancient and Contemporary Views', in *Fem St* 8 (1982): 109–131.
31. Alexis fr 302; *cf* Eubolos fr 117.8–15.
32. Plato insisted that earth does not imitate woman, but woman earth (*Men* 238a) a citation reiterated by Plut *Mor* 638a.
33. Lilja, *Dogs,* 88.
34. See Athen *Deip* 583a where there is a sophisticated and literary allusion to a proverb. There is no formal designation of a proverb but it must be known by the audience for the satire or humour in the distortion to work..
35. See the speech of Cato the Elder attributed to him by Livy *Hist* 34.2.11–3.2. Addressing the issue of whether to repeal the Oppian Law limiting women's right to property (195 BCE), he declaimed, 'Give rein to their unbridled natures and these unmastered creatures, and hope that they will put limits on their own freedom! They want freedom, nay licence (if we are to speak the truth) in all things . . .' The mythological debate about who enjoyed sex more, men or women, merely provided the ideological metaphysics for such ready ascriptions. According to

that women were credited the ability to morphe into animals.[36] However, regardless of sexual constraint, nature also dictated that no woman has the power to rule.[37] By contrast, collation with an animal for a (free) man was likely a charge castigating a descent into a state beneath him.[38] The connections of man-woman-animal were played out in Lucian's satire *The Dream of the Cock*, where Pythagoras descends to the level of the beast via a woman, the courtesan Aspasia.[39] Descent to the animal was also possible via a 'foreigner' who according to Isocrates was closer to the beasts than Greeks or, especially, Athenians (15.293). Of course, if the person was both a woman and a foreigner, the proximities were reinforced.

Care must be taken in the collation. Only certain animals were conducive to a denigrating turn of phrase. Other animals (such as the ever-productive bee)[40] might become a comparison of praise for human beings. And some animals were inherently ambiguous, much more subject to context (including gender).[41]

Teiresias, who had been both man and woman, the ratio of enjoyment was 1:9. Such knowledge however was viewed as dangerous, linked as it was with the troubled and troubling life of woman: see Luc *Gall* 19.

36. Such as Empousa, Hecate, and Mestra.
37. Menand *Sent* 157.
38. Note Plato's language of 'descent' *Rep* 586a, particularly associated with such banquets and festivities where men become 'cattle'. Dio Chr (*Or* 3.50) uses the effeminate dimensions of the legendary Syrian king, Sardanapallus, to describe the shame of a man's decline to the position of a woman. Strikingly, the classic spatial signifiers of enclosure in a house—where Sardanapallus lay—are taken as indicating domestication, required of women but not of men. These connections are as common in paraliterary texts: effeminate men are connected with women in *P Hib* 54: 'woman' is used terminologically to degrade a man in *CPJ* 1.19.20.
39. *Gall* 19 (with an additional excursion through the 'not human Cynic' Crates). The movement to the bestial via a woman was precisely that envisaged by Plato for the man concerned about his body (*Tim* 42b-c, 76e, 91a). Compare the correlation of courtesans and beasts in the descent into vice and the passions in *The Tabula of Ceres* 5, 22–24, Athen *Deip* 558d.
40. The bee is the only animal Semonides, in his iambic attack on women, offered in 'praise' of a woman (fr *Mul* 83–93; *cf* Xen *Oecon* 7.32, 38).
41. Note the warnings against inappropriate alignments in Hor *Ars Poet* 1, Ps-Arist *Phys* 805a. Unlikely connections become serviceable for comic relief—a Maltese terrier named Tauros (*Pal Anth* 7.211; Gow and Page V); *cf* the ferocious gladiatorial bear named *Innocentia*: Amm Marcel 29.3.9.

Nature provided, alternately, a warning (to man) and a confirmation (of woman). Menelaus' abuse of the Trojans in the *Iliad* captures this. By calling them κακαὶ κύνες he is not merely deprecating them as animals but also, through the feminine qualifier, compounding insult upon insult.[42] The connection between women and animals was reinforced religiously as well—prohibitions excluding 'women, dogs and flies' or barring from the sacred area a man who had contacted a woman, dog or donkey indicated the common juxtaposition.[43]

Logos as the control for woman

The upshot of the collation of the woman with the dog is that she cannot speak *logos*. Rather, as the frequent application of the saying 'a barking dog' to women demonstrated,[44] shouting (κράζειν)[45] characterised women; unlike speech, shouting was an 'irrational impulse'.[46] Accordingly, woman must be governed *by logos*, just as surely as a dog must be restrained by a chain.[47] Without such restraint,

42. *Il* 13.623, following the preferred reading of Lilja, *Dogs* 21n30. See also Margaret Graver, 'Dog-Helen and Homeric Insult', in *CA* 14 (1995): 50. The use of words for woman or the feminine gender combined with an animal was a particularly damning expression; see S Lilja, *Terms of Abuse in Roman Comedy* (Helsinki: Academia Scientiarum Fennicae, 1965), 68, EJ Vodoklys, *Blame-Expression in the Epic Tradition* (New York and London: Garland Publishing, 1992), 20, citing *Il* 1.158–159.
43. Susan S Cole, 'Women, Dogs and Flies', *The Ancient World* 26 (1995): 182–183 citing Phylarchos fr 81 F 33 and F Sokolowski, *Lois sacrées de l'Asie mineure* (Paris: E de Boccard, 1955), 91 (sanctuary at Lindos). That these two instances range from the third century BCE to the third century CE indicates how stable such correlations were in the ancient world.
44. *Eg* Menand fr 546.4f. See W Headlam and AD Knox (editors) *Herodas: The Mimes and Fragments* (Cambridge: Cambridge University Press, 1922), 286.
45. Κράζειν was an onomatopoeic word derived from the rasping cry of a crow. The assonantial proximity to the dog-noise ἀράζειν, to snarl, meant that the two words were often interchanged, as in the alternate readings to Phil Jud *Somn* 2.267. In Matthew 15:22, a large number of manuscripts chose to accentuate the canine baying of the woman by the reading ἐκραύγασεν (for example C G K W F) a word also used to evoke the caw of crows (Arr *Epict* 3.1.37).
46. Phil Jud *Ebr* 98.
47. Plut *Vit* 754a (where the imagery of breeding and the collar are applied to a woman); *cf* Arr *Cyn* 11.1. Alternatively, and especially in a Jewish context, the dog is to be driven off, separated, guarded against (for example b*Shab* 155b)—much as the disciples in Matthew's version of

woman's true nature would wreak havoc.[48] The stable dominance of this attitude is shown in the axiomatic precept 'nothing more like a dog than a woman' which runs from the authoritative Poet to his episcopal commentator, Eustathius, nearly two millennia later.[49]

Aristotle's bipartite psychology (the division between logical and alogical sides of the soul) saw a woman's deliberative faculty as intrinsically weak, constantly overridden by the emotional, alogical side. She was constitutionally *and politically* in need of an imposed temperance.[50] Similarly, the first century, Hellenised Jew, Philo, constructed the parallel of the mind and the house as belonging to the man, with the sensual woman requiring the bridle that the walls provided.[51]

The medical sphere 'naturalised' the testimony. The 'wandering womb' became a gynaecological confirmation of the lack of restraint women shared with the animals.[52] 'The womb,' said Aretaeus, 'is like an animal within an animal.'[53] Dogs were prone to wander prolifically,[54] an indication to Democritus that the dog had more than one womb—a

---

the story recommend to Jesus about the dog yapping/clamouring at their heels.

48. MR Lefkowitz, *Women in Greek Myth* (Baltimore: Johns Hopkins University Press, 1986), 114.

49. Hom *Od* 11.427, *GA* App 61, Cl Al *Strom* 6.2.5 (adding ῥίγιον 'colder/more miserable'), Eust *Comm Od* 1.425.45.

50. *Pol* 1.5.3–5 (1259b–1260a). Slave, woman and child manifested the alogical in humanity; man expressed the logical: see WW Fortenbaugh, 'Aristotle on Slaves and Women', in J Barnes, M Schofield, and R Sorabji (editors), *Articles on Aristotle 2: Ethics and Politics* (London: Duckworth, 1977), 137–139, G Clark, *Women in Late Antiquity: Pagan and Christian Lifestyles* (Oxford: Clarendon Press, 1993), 121.

51. Phil Jud *Opif* 165, *Spec* 3.169–70. See generally, JR Wegner, 'Philo's Portrayal of Women—Hebraic or Hellenic?', in A-J Levine (editor), *'Women Like This' New Perspectives on Jewish Women in the Greco-Roman World* (Atlanta, GA: Scholars Press, 1991), 41–66, D Sly, 'The Plight of Women: Philo's Blind Spot?', in WE Hellemann (editor), *Hellenization Revisited: Shaping a Christian Response within the Greco-Roman World* (Lanham: University Press of America, 1994), 173–187.

52. Medical speculation frequently drew comparisons between humans and animals. See L Dean-Jones, 'The Cultural Construct of the Female Body', in SB Pomeroy (editor), *Women's History and Ancient History* (Chapel Hill/London: University of North Carolina Press, 1991), 125, 127.

53. Aret 287. His opinion was not isolated: see G Roccatagliata, *A History of Ancient Psychiatry* (New York: Greenwood Press, 1986), 205.

54. Ael *NA* 9.54. This was especially a trait of the female: Grat 161–164.

conclusion confirmed, so it was reasoned, by its large litters.[55] Aelian provides a striking overlap, suggesting that dogs (and women) were fit for household management, *provided* they were properly trained.[56] This adds a sinister edge to the familiar philosophical topos on the training of a wife for household affairs.[57]

Child as animal

Similarly, 'Children were regarded as physically weak, morally incompetent, mentally incapable.'[58] They were non-speakers: νήπιοι, *in-fantes*.[59] Plato and Aristotle both made direct equations of children and animals in their comments.[60] For Plato, that part of the soul called τὸ λογίστικον was not present in animals or children (παιδία).[61] His misopaedy was so pronounced that he held the child to be the hardest to manage of all the beasts.[62] For Aristotle, no one feels shame before small children or animals, since no shame is felt before those whose opinion is held in contempt.[63] Seneca reflects the same sentiments closer in time to christian writings.[64] And the same description of the child as ἄφρων and ἀλογίστος is found in near-contemporary Jewish writings.[65]

Generally, such a distinction was gender related—the program for the male child was self-control, that for the female child, protective

55. Ael *NA* 12.16.
56. Ael *NA* 6.10(i).
57. Xen *Oecon* 6.17–10.13; *cf* Plut *Mor* 138a–146a.
58. M Golden, *Children and Childhood in Classical Athens* (Baltimore/London: Johns Hopkins University Press, 1990), 5. Extraordinary children (boys) were those who defied the norm—indicated by their ability to match adults already versed in wisdom: Lk 2:46–47, Jos *Vit* 1.1–2, Diog Laert *Vit* 10.14.
59. T Wiedemann, *Adults and Children in the Roman Empire* (London/New York: Routledge, 1989), 20–21.
60. Plato's groupings were often children, women, slaves, animals; see *Clit* 409d-e, (*cf Epin* 355c), *Leg* 710a, *Theaet* 177b, *Gorg* 470c; *cf* Arist *GA* 728a, *HA* 588a, *Rhet* 1.11 (1371a), 2.6 (1384b). Interestingly, children were used in theatre to play dogs and puppies: see Lilja, *Dogs,* 74.
61. *Rep* 441a-b; *cf Tim* 44a-c, *Prot* 321b, Arist *HA* 588f. However Plato, in playful mode, was prepared to regard the dog at times highly—'as a most philosophic animal' *Rep* 376a.
62. *Leg* 808d.
63. Arist *Rhet* 2.6 (1384b).
64. Sen *Ep* 124.9.
65. Wis 12:24–25. The use of these terms for idolators underscores the demeaning assessment.

parameters.[66] These were the two sides of the development of reason for the child.[67] The child was largely unformed and therefore required a pedagogy that either enabled the *logos* to achieve its ascendancy over the material of the subject[68] or provided the *logos* as a close hedging control around that materiality. Hence, writers were adamant that parental responsibility must be extremely cautious about the formative influences on a child.[69]

The rule of reason

This government by *logos* was achieved, *inter alia*, through the key expression of reason, namely speech and its forms. Thus the multitude of problematic aspects of the dog was encapsulated in narrative sayings, such as proverbs and fables. Sayings in such forms evoked a sense of natural universality that only their lost origins could confer.[70]

Nature, manifest in microcosm in the dog, functioned in two ways. Firstly, it pointed to the universals governing the cosmos and especially human affairs. Secondly, it was also the borderland of that cosmos that constantly menaced its order with the chaos of the beyond.[71] The appearance of contradiction is resolved in the control that *logos* (reason) imposed upon it.

Reason provided more than understanding of the universals governing the world. It was a *participation* in the divine organization of primal matter,[72] a synergy that enabled one to preserve, conserve and capitalise its universals. For Stoics especially, 'the verbal logos corresponded with the logos of the physical world'.[73] In this sense, animals having their own distinctive nature helped to prove by analogy

66. Thus, for example, Xen *Mem* 1.5.2.
67. See H Cancik-Lindemaier, 'Seneca's Collection of Epistles: A Medium of Philosophical Communication', in AY Collins (editor), *Ancient and Modern Perspectives on the Bible and Culture* (Atlanta, GA: Scholars Press, 1998), 89–90.
68. Sen *Ep* 41.8.
69. *Eg* Quint *Inst* 1.1.4–5 (citing Chrysippus).
70. Philosophical and scientific debates frequently cite proverbs and fables (as well as poets and playwrights) as 'proofs' of propositions; see, for example, Plut *Mor* 968f.
71. Winkler, *Constraints of Desire*, 20–23.
72. This is exactly the defence of careful organization of armies and meals in Plutarch's *Moralia* (*Table Talk*) 615f–616a where Plato's account of the 'great god' (τὸν μέγαν θεόν) ordering chaos in the *Timaeus* (30a) provides the seal upon the argument.
73. ML Colish, *The Stoic Tradition From Antiquity to the Early Middle Ages* (Leiden: EJ Brill, 1990), volume 1, 57, FE Peters, *The Harvest of*

and by contradistinction the discrete nature of a human being.[74] Thus, the imposition of *logos* revealed nature's ontology and its teleology. This was the important function of classification—knowledge meant power and revealed power.

Aristotle, for example, deemed the domestication of animals as enabling an increase in their productivity,[75] which itself confirmed the value and power of *logos* in harnessing what otherwise might deteriorate into anarchy. Animals were 'servants'.[76] In fact, a dog was often called a slave—both were collared, the mark of appropriate subjection by *logos*.[77]

The threat and attraction of the wild

A standard argument of ancient commentators on husbandry and the natural world was that all domesticated animals had a corresponding wild form.[78] These two poles become mutually reinforcing, providing symbolic foci for the many dichotomies that enabled the cosmic and societal world to be upheld and negotiated. In the Greco-Roman world especially, there was no animal that more pointedly demonstrated this than the dog, whose various domestic breeds were set over against the wolf, the fox and even the scavenging pariah roaming the streets and city-walls.[79] At their most occultic, dogs characterised the snatching

---

Hellenism: A History of the Near East from Alexander the Great to the Triumph of Christianity (London: George Allen & Unwin, 1970), 142.

74. See for example, Galen *MM* 2.7.3–10. The supposed conflict between Philo's emphasis on the idea and Aristotle's preference for nature is resolved in this expanse of *logos*, each merely accenting one arm above the other; *cf* K von Fritz and E Kapp, 'The Development of Aristotle's Political Philosophy and the Concept of Nature', in Barnes, *Articles on Aristotle 2,* 116–117.
75. R Sallares, *The Ecology of the Ancient Greek World* (Ithaca, NY: Cornell University Press, 1991), 396. Similar notions are found in Quint *Inst* 8.3.75, 9.4.3–5), Lucret *Nat Rer* 1.208–214; *cf* Jas 3:7.
76. Aesch *Prom* fr 194.
77. Eur *Med* 54, Ael *NA* 6.10. According to a source used by Justin the second-century (CE) historian, slaves were only capable of spite, never of wisdom: Justin 18.3.14.
78. Arist *PA* 643b, *HA* 488a, Pl *HN* 8.213–214; *cf* Porph *Abst* 1.14.
79. Jewish classifications of animals followed a different formal patterning: see S Stern, *Jewish Identity in Early Rabbinic Writings* (Leiden: EJ Brill, 1994), 33–42; at a more popular level, see RH Isaacs, *Animals in Jewish Thought and Tradition* (Northvale, NJ: Aronson, 2000). The implications of this element of the intercultural conflict between Jew and Greek for the analysis of the exchange about dogs between Jesus and the Syrophoenician woman are explored in chapters 4 and 5.

demons (for example, Keres),[80] or the dreaded night-terrors of Hecate.[81] Sometimes the polar connection was recalled humorously—as with a prize pedigree house ornament named Λύκαινα ('Wolverine').[82]

The hound provided the bridge, played out in political and symbolic fashion, between the two poles, being the key member of the hunt. Hunting was the enterprise that expressed in rawest exposure the superiority of the *logos* over untamed nature.[83] It entered militaristic augmentation in war[84]—enemies frequently being portrayed in bestial terms,[85] warriors as almost rabid.[86] It was, as Robin Fox observed, an 'all-male activity'.[87] Barbarian women engaged in hunting escape his notice, but, in Greco-Roman understanding, this simply confirmed the bestial proximity of barbarians.[88]

The borderlands of the hunt, barbarian practices, and the female generally, fostered a fascination and a rationale. Hunting enabled the immense force of the wild to be touched in controlled circumstances,

80. *GA* 7.439. Dogs frequently invited a portentous interpretation: see Ter *Phorm* 705–710.
81. Athen *Deip* 149c. Compare the hound demon in Philostr *Vit Apol* 4.10. On the occult sympathies of animals, see F Klingender, *Animals in Art and Thought to the End of the Middle Ages* (edited by E Antal and J Harthan) (London: RKP, 1971), 91–92.
82. *Vit Aes* 45.
83. Brown, 'Death as Decoration', 197–198. Katherine Dunbabin describes the hunt as 'an allegory of man's fight against strong and hostile forces.' (*The Mosaics of Roman North Africa: Studies in Iconography and Patronage* (Oxford: Clarendon Press, 1978), 63.)
84. MH Jameson, 'Sacrifice before Battle', in VD Hanson (editor), *Hoplites: The Classical Greek Battle Experience* (London and NY: Routledge, 1991), 209–211. The earliest reference to dogs in war appears to be an epigram attributed to Pisander of Rhodes (*GA* 7.304, Ael *NA* 7.38).
85. For example, Ap Rh *Arg* 2.2, 4.421, Aesch *Eum* 131–138, Hom *Il* 8.299.
86. See B Lincoln, 'Homeric *lússa*: Wolfish Rage', in *IF* 80–81 (1975–1976): 98–105.
87. R Fox, 'Ancient Hunting: From Homer to Polybios', in G Shipley and J Salmon (editors), *Human Landscapes in Classical Antiquity: Environment and Culture* (London and New York: Routledge, 1996), 128; *cf* Dunbabin, 60–62. Fox omits the metaphorical use of the hunt which was regularly applied to the activity of adulterous women, courtesans and prostitutes: Xen *Mem* 3.11.11.
88. Hdt *Hist* 4.115–116. Dio Chrysostom's customary phrase 'Greeks and barbarians, men and women' clearly indicates the duality that aligned barbarians with women (and thence to animals): see, for example, *Or* 1.14.

appropriately re-animating society.[89] Training for the hunt expressed the control that enabled the transition to a hunting hound: bread was to replace meat as recommended food for the dogs—a sign, like the collar,[90] of appropriate control.[91]

The fragility of the dog's behaviour in this liminal exercise[92] was captured in comments about hounds whose native fierceness became so unlocked that quarry and husbanded animals were both rabidly devoured,[93] compared with those hounds who remained under the invisible leash of their master.[94] Or again, there was the comparison between those hounds that remained focussed on the task at hand and those that wandered off on undirected meanders.[95] The dog epitomises the ambiguity and necessity of control by *logos*.

From an anthropological viewpoint, according to Edmund Leach, '. . . it is the ambiguous categories that attract the maximum interest and the most intense feelings of taboo'.[96] Such ambiguities charge the story of the Syrophoenician woman, all the more because of the clash of the natural (dogs) and the rational (word) that occurs between Jesus' two sayings. Moreover, a suspicion arises that the affirmation of the *logos* ('this word': Mk 7:29) implies a re-establishment of proper

---

89. Xen *Cynegetics,* Grattius *The Hunt* and Pollux *Onomasticon* offer lengthy treatments of the value and joys of the hunt; see also Plut *Mor* 959e.
90. Tibullus 2.4.32-36, Ov *AA* 1.6, Suet *Rhet* 3; *cf* the door-servant in Acts 12.13 fulfilling a canine role as guardian of the threshold.
91. Dio Chr *Or* 7.16. Compare the overview of dog feeding provided by DB Hull, *Hounds and Hunting in Ancient Greece* (Chicago: University of Chicago Press, 1964), 46–48.
92. Fox suggests that hunting was a transgression of earthly reality and its boundaries and uses this to explain how a female god (Artemis) could be the patron of this male preserve (127). It may also explain the frequency of hunting (and battle) scenes on sarcophagi—another indication of a liminal zone: see M Grant, *Art in the Roman Empire* (London and New York: Routledge, 1995), 25.
93. Dio Chr *Or* 1.28, Damocharis 206.1; *cf* Lucret *Nat Rer* 5.1308–1337 on the general principle as applied to many species trained for battle but whose training deserted them in the fury of engagement.
94. The Argives reportedly had an annual feast, the Κυνοφόντις, during which dogs were killed in atoning memory for the death of Linus (the son of Apollo), who had been dismembered in a canine attack: Athen *Deip* 99e, *P Oxy* 2263 Fr 1.ii.5.
95. Dio Chr *Or* 20.15–16.
96. 'Anthropological Aspects of Language: Animal Categories and Verbal Abuse', in EH Lenneberg (editor), *New Directions in the Study of Language* (Cambridge, MA: MIT Press, 1964), 39.

control and order. Certainly, *logos* was exactly the requirement for the control of the dog.

The signification of the dog— an introduction

Cave canem

The importance of the control by *logos* is visually represented in the entrance hall mosaic at Casa del Porta Tragico, Pompeii. The chained, snarling dog enjoyed considerable popularity among Roman cultured classes; its '*Cave Canem*' design and inscription wandered through Pompeii, Herculaneum and beyond,[97] though firmly tethered to the homes of the wealthy.[98]

Whilst the pretentious provinciality of domiciliary adornment brought ridicule from such hardened city-dwellers as Petronius,[99] the key significations of the mosaic are echoed in a popular Aesopian fable of the ordered dog and the wild wolf:

> A dog who was very plump met with a wolf who began to question him: where was he fed that he had become such a big dog and so well lined with fat? 'A rich master feeds me,' said the dog. 'But your neck' asked the wolf 'how come the bare spot on it?' 'The flesh has been rubbed by the iron collar which my keeper forged and put upon me.' The wolf laughed at him mockingly and said: 'Away with that kind of luxury! It's not for me at the cost of having my neck frayed with an iron collar.'[100]

97. It was repeated sometimes without inscription; for example, at Casa di Paquius Proculus, an entrance mosaic displays a chained dog lying at a half-open door (Pompeii I.7.1). *Cave canem* was apparently the title of a satire by the Roman poet-playwright Varro (A Otto, *Die Sprichwörter und Sprichwörtlichen Redensarten* (Leipzig: BJ Teubner, 1890), 69); see also *CIL* 10.877, *AE* 1978: 0444, 1989: 0470.
98. M de Vos, 'Pavimenti e mosaici', in F Zevi (editor), *Pompei 79. Raccolta di studi per il decimonono centenario dell'eruzione vesuviana* (Naples: 1979, 1984 repr,) considers that the rarity of mosaics (2.5% of total floor space) indicates that mosaics demonstrated the luxury of the élite (cited from A Wallace-Hadrill, *Houses and Society in Pompeii and Herculaneum* (Princeton, NJ: Princeton University Press, 1994), 228n24).
99. See *Sat* 15.29; *cf* Pl *HN* 36.184, Hom *Od* 17.400–402.
100. Loeb edition (edited by Perry) §100. A later Latin fabulist, Avianus, replaced the wolf with a lion and embellished the dog's lavish fare by

Fable collections, such as that by Babrius, a hellenised Italian living in Syria in the first century CE, drew on epigrams, apophthegms, anecdotes and even proverbs that distilled a narrative of animals.[101] These forms were part of the staple oral/aural instruction of the young[102] and ensured that the values distilled in the mosaics and literature of society's elite, were inculcated into a wider audience—a subtle assertion of *logos*.

The centre-point of 'Aesop's' dog-and-wolf story is the chain, evoking the familiar philosophical topos of 'who is the truly free person'.[103] However, there was an added point to the chain in relation to an animal, namely, that there was something threatening and dangerous here. Such a threat needed to be contained for the safety of the house-dwellers—hence the chain. But the threat remained, albeit hedged about, becoming a warning to thieves[104] or other undesirables.[105] Of course, the chain inevitably leads into the house indicating that the occupant was the one who controlled this dangerous animal.[106] The master was the one who handled the *logoi*, the words *Cave Canem*, carved in close connection with the fierce animal.[107]

The inscription asserted not only the owner's power over the bestial, but the power of word to master, control and direct that which, of itself, was unchecked and chaotic. The words redeemed the natural to the service of civilised culture. So Vergil sees such a dog's role as warning off visitor or intruder.[108] Strikingly, Theophrastus portrays the

having it share the master's food at table (37).

101. The connection between proverbs and fables was noted: see Quint *Inst* 5.11.20–21.

102. Quint *Inst* 1.1.36, 1.9.1, Plut *Mor* 673f, Sen *Ep* 88.20.

103. See, for example, Dio Chr *Or* 4, 15, Epict *Disc* 4.1, Phil Jud *Prob* The emphasis throughout is upon self-control.

104. TH Feder *Great Treasures of Pompeii and Herculaneum* (New York: Abbeville Press, 1978), 30. It is clear from the cast of a dog taken from the ash-inundated remains of Pompeii that the chain was an actual not merely a symbolic reality: see JMC Toynbee, *Animals in Roman Life and Art* (London: Thames & Hudson, 1973), 108, 120.

105. Pers *Sat* 1.107, Tibullus 2.4.32, Theocr *Id* 15.43, Aristoph *Thesmo* 423.

106. Aristoph *Lys* 1215–1217, *cf* Hom *Od* 14.22–35.

107. AM Bowie reads dogs as 'regularly markers of margins': *Aristophanes: Myth, Ritual and Comedy* (Cambridge: Cambridge University Press, 1993), 89.

108. *Hylax in limine latrat*—Verg *Ecl* 8.107; *cf* Juv *Sat* 6.413, Tibullus 1.6.32, Plaut *Most* 162–170.

boor as one who fails to recognise hierarchical ordering over nature, confusing himself with the role of the trained guardian.[109]

The wolf remains in the dog as anarchic potential;[110] so the dog requires a constant reminder of its position—hence the well-worn patch on the neck. The mark, much like the tattoo-branding of slaves,[111] prevented the descent into the contemptible garbage-collectors which roamed the city walls and streets, poxed and pilloried, themselves refuse of the earth.[112] The pointed double-reference in this regard was when dogs were placed as guards on women's apartments within a house.[113]

The striking picture of the menacing dog was not, however, Cerberus[114] or Anubis[115] or other mythological being. Rather the point at which the menace was most pronounced in the ancient world was in connection with a woman—Hecuba.[116]

---

109. Theophr *Char* 4.12. Theophrastus may also be suggesting that the boor insults his visitor by adopting the dog's role of accusing another of a threat to property and household—acceptable in a dog but not in the master.

110. See other Aesopic fables of the wolf and the dog—Babr §128, Phaedr §3.7, suppl §134; *cf* §407, the much-recalled death of Euripides—torn to death by wolf-hounds as recalled in the proverb προμέρου κύνες; *cf P Oxy* 2263 Fr 1.ii.5, and the death of Acteon, and Apollo's son, Linus which drew a proverb warning against keeping those who would later injure the carer (Isocr *Demo* 29, Varr *RR* 2.9.8–9). Otto Keller suggested that λύσσα, rabies, used to describe a dog's enraged erratic behaviour as much as the disease, is etymologically related to λύκος wolf: *Thiere des classichen Altertums in culturgeschichtlicher Beziehung* (Innsbruck: Verlag der Wagner'schen Universitäts-Buchhandlung, 1887), 168. Magic similarly equated them: see CA Faraone, *Talismans and Trojan Horses: Guardian Statues in Ancient Greek Myth and Ritual* (Oxford: Oxford University Press, 1992), 45–46.

111. See CP Jones, '*Stigma*: Tattooing and Branding in Greco-Roman Antiquity', in *JRS* 77 (1987): 139–155.

112. Aristophanes plays on this dual notion of the dog in *The Wasps*, one being an οἰκούρος, a 'stay-at-home' (970), the other never staying in the same place (969): see Bowie, 89.

113. Aristoph *Thesmo* 414-418, Eratosthenes 5.242.8.

114. The ultimate guardian of the threshold (for example, Verg *Aen* 6.400–404, Mart *Epig* 5.34).

115. Juvenal, in line with his conservative defence of Roman particularity, sees Anubis as an example of Egyptian atrocities (*Sat* 15.8).

116. This is based largely on a critical assessment: see also AP Burnett, 'Hekabe the Dog', *Arethusa* 27 (1994): 151–164. From Homer's treatment of Clytemnestra (*Od* 24.200-202) and Helen (*Il* 6.354–355, *Od* 4.145–146) to that of Clodia by Cicero (*Cael* 13.30–29.69), rhetorical

Beware the woman

Dio Chrysostom described Hecuba:

> the poets say of Hecuba, that as a climax to all her terrible misfortunes, the Furies made her like to a hound with flashing eyes; and when she poured her brazen cry from hoary jaws,
> Ida gave ear and sea-girt Tenedos
> And all the wind-swept crags of Thrace.[117]

Euripides explained her metamorphosis as the result of her grief/rage-driven fury over the death of her children.[118] An alternate suggestion was that her vicious vituperation of her enemy Polymestor was the cause.[119] Juvenal pinpointed the transformation to her kinship with the 'savage barking of a dog'.[120] Because the woman had transgressed what was proper, and had adopted what was natural for another creature in instinct and noise, she became that creature.[121]

The evasiveness in this common androcentric rendering is that Hecuba's own slander is treated as unacceptable whereas others' pejorative portrayal of her as a savage dog was a literary commonplace. Such invective extended to the woman's racial connections—Hecuba was a Phrygian, a race that Greeks considered wild, uncultured and cowardly.[122]

The late first-century (CE) philosopher and historian, Plutarch, compounds the horror at Hecuban instinct and noise by a further characterisation of the dog—gluttony. His Hecuba whines, 'I wish I might eat up his liver, Biting it 'tween my teeth.'[123] That this is a citation from Homer[124] only adds to the authority and atemporality of the characterisation, reinforced by the continued popularity of

---

defamation turned these women into infamous exemplars of womanly degradation.

117. *Or* 33.59; *cf* 11.154.
118. Eur *Hec* 237, 511, 1252-53; *cf* Ov *Meta* 13.569f.
119. Cic *Tusc* 3.26, Plaut *Men* 718.
120. *Sat* 10. 271–272.
121. The Greek rendition of *cave canem* turned the dog into a bitch: εὐλαβοῦ τὴν κύνα.
122. Theophr *Char* 28.2, Aristoph *Ach* 141–171, Eur *Hec* 1064–1066, Tert *Anim* 20 (279a).
123. *Mor* 170c.
124. Hom *Il* 24.212.

Euripides' plays into and beyond the first century CE.[125] Her final resting-place on sea-cliffs, the 'bitch's tomb', was named Cynossema, supposedly a constant warning to sailors,[126] paralleling the destructive sexual allure of the Sirens.

Thus, Hecuba became the bearer of a combination of characteristics of the (wild) dog: irrationality, noisiness, gluttony and dangerous promiscuity. Such 'shamelessness' inspired a range of Greek words anchored to the dog: κύνεος, κυνοθαρσής, κυνόφρων, κυνῶπις, κύντερος, κύντατος.[127] These characterisations 'naturally' attached to Hecuba, Cassandra, Helen and so on because of their gender: 'no creature as shameless as women.'[128]

Cave canem without the chain

This disgust at the dog is more undifferentiated and uncompromising in Jewish tradition. Such a response was not confined to racial antipathies, but reflected long-held traditions about dogs themselves. Hence, 'dog' as a term of abuse was not racially specific (for example, 1 Rgn 17:43,[129] 2 Sam 16:9[130]). The basic attitude to dogs was to see them as scavengers, mangy parasites on the landscape, especially in towns (*cf* Lk 16:31). Dogs were often associated with a blighted end, butchers of rebellious individuals in the prophetic curse of God (1 Kgs 14:11, 16:4, 21:23; 2 Kgs 9:10,36; *cf* Ps 22:16, Prov 26:11, Jer 15:3, Eccl 9:4) or with a sad and terrible demise at the hands of unjust powers (1 Kgs 21:19).

Other Jewish writers, writing in the Hellenistic diaspora, acknowledge some of the attainments of dogs—as trained hunters, sheep herders, watch-dogs, and as endowed with a remarkable sense of smell.[131] Indeed, there is evidence in the Zenon papyri that at least some Jews, despite the literary indictments, were prepared to curry

125. Epict *Disc* 5.22, Juv *Sat* 9.324; *cf* Ps-Mart *Epig* 20, Athen *Deip* 557e, Luc *HC* 1.
126. Ascepl Sam fr 1, Eur *Hec* 1273.
127. *Cf* Lilja, *Dogs*, 22.
128. Aristoph *Lys* 368–369 (*cf* Semon *Mul* fr, Archil fr 161, Phocyl fr 2, Soph *El* 622).
129. David's reply ('worse than a dog') to Goliath's questioning taunt is found only in the LXX.
130. In Josephus, it is David not Abishai who calls Shimei 'a dead dog': see *Ant* 7.209.
131. Jos *Ant* 4.206, Phil Jud *Abr* 266, *Dec* 114, *Post C* 161.

favour with their Hellenistic superiors through gifts, *inter alia*, of dogs.[132]

Nevertheless, the stock view is negative.[133] Dogs are predators in and around cities, often providing the fitting end for opponents. Indeed, Josephus repeats many of the scriptural stories noted above in a way that indicates that such a horror end was well-known in contemporary experience.[134] Dogs are consigned flesh that has been torn (which cannot be eaten by pious Jews). They are expendable in human endeavours to obtain toxic plants; the plant's acquisition is worth far more than the death of the dog.[135]

Thus, any recognition of the hunting qualities of dogs must baulk at the unacceptability of the game so obtained. Philo, in particular, reckoned the goal of the hunting dog (the tearing of flesh) one of the distinguishing marks between Jewish and Greek culture and law.[136] The knowledge that some nations deified dogs and other animals merely corroborated the impressions of the degeneracy of the idolaters amongst whom Jews were situated.[137] He delivers his dominant understanding of dogs when he uses them as an analogy for the untempered senses:

> Let not our appetites, then, be whetted and incited towards anything that is dear to the flesh. The

---

132. *CPJ* 1.5 Toubias to Apollonios, regarding a gift to Philadelphos Ptolemaic king of Egypt, 12 May 257 BCE. This would indicate that although the literary indications are generally uniform, practice reflected a broader range of responses to the dog.
133. W Houghton expresses an assessment repeating nineteenth century judgements, and repeated throughout the twentieth century: 'The Scripture references to the dog are numerous and in all cases show the aversion in which it was held by the Hebrews. It was regraded as a half-wild, greedy creature, running about at will, without a master and eating human corpses.' See his 'Zoology of the Bible', in WE Barnes (editor), *A Companion to Biblical Studies* (Cambridge: The University Press, 1916), 448; *cf* E Firmiage, 'Zoology', in *ABD* 6.1143.
134. Jos *BJ* 3.192, 6.367, *Ant* 8.271, 289, 361, 9.124; *cf* 15.289–290.
135. Ps-Phocyl 147–148, Jos *BJ* 7.178–185.
136. *Spec* 4.119–121. Philo makes Nimrod a mighty hunter 'against the Lord', an archetypal sinner embroiled in a detestable profession: *QG* 166. Plutarch's extolling of the hunting dog in the military terminology of victory, clearly demonstrates the difference in cultural values: *Mor* 971a.
137. Phil Jud *Leg* 139. The Egyptians of course were particularly targeted (*Dec* 76–80).

> undisciplined pleasures are often as dogs; they fawn on us, then turn against us and their bite is fatal.[138]

Dogs become ready images for actions that are to be criticised—thus Josephus polemicises against the Jewish leadership in the Jewish War comparing them to 'dogs … who continue to maul the very carcass of the people'.[139] 'Dog' in connection with any human being was abusive or derisive.[140]

The only woman included in these references is Jezebel. Even so, women were generally regarded as more inferior beings in creation.[141] They were more akin and susceptible to both animal and demonic realms.[142] Thus a woman might be collated with a swine (Prov 11:22) or a night-demon (Isa 34:14).[143]

A religious colouring was applied to the attitude—distancing from dogs was one mark of distinction from the surrounding practices of other nations (Deut 23:18). Josephus and the Mishnah take the deuteronomic injunction literally: money derived from dog-mating or the dog itself, 'whether hound of the chase or guardian of the flocks', could not be used to purchase sacrifices for the Temple.[144] Dogs had no place in God's temple.[145] In Pseudo-Philo's *Biblical Antiquities* the dog itself is repudiated as an acceptable sacrifice (39.11). More recent archaeological discoveries have sponsored this more literal interpretation[146] rather than taking the injunction euphemistically as

---

138. *Gig* 35.
139. *BJ* 5.526; *cf* 6.196.
140. Jos *Ant* 12.210–214, Phil Jud *Prob* 90, *Vit Con* 40. In *Dec* 115, Philo describes the dog as 'the most audacious of brutes' (τοῦ θηρίων θρασυτάτου). It was not a compliment.
141. See A Brenner, *The Intercourse of Knowledge: On Gendering Desire and 'Sexuality' in the Hebrew Bible* (Leiden: Brill, 1997), 132f.
142. See LJ Archer, *Her Price is Beyond Rubies: The Jewish Woman in Graeco-Roman Palestine* (Sheffield: JSOT Press, 1990), 306.
143. Lilith; *cf* b*Shab* 151b.
144. *Ant* 4.206, m*Tem* 6.3.
145. Other deities, most notably that of Asclepius, regularly employed dogs for healing: see Toynbee, *Animals,* 122–124.
146. LE Stager, 'Why Were Hundreds of Dogs Buried at Ashkelon?', *BAR* 17 (1991): 26–42. The debate is far from over however: see P Wapnish and B Hesse, 'Pampered Pooches or Plain Pariahs? The Ashkelon Dog Burials', in *BA* 56 (1993): 55–80. Dogs are occasionally represented in later synagogue zodiac mosaics (that is, from the fifth century CE) and in astral symbolism on funerary caskets: see E Goodenough, *Jewish Symbols in the Greco-Roman Period* (edited by J Neusner), (Princeton, NJ: Princeton University Press, 1988), 116–121. There are also late (that

'male prostitute'.[147]

Modern commentary has tended to identify a parallelism with 'prostitute' in the first part of Deuteronomy 23:18,[148] so that 'dog' is drawn to 'whore'.[149] The distinction between daughters and sons of Israel in the previous verse is taken to make the dog gender specific (=male prostitute). Alternately, verse 18 may utilise a synthetic parallelism, with dogs and prostitutes viewed as synonymous.

Certainly, the term כלב translated as 'prostitute' (LXX: πόρνη) taps into the levitical distinctions of clean and unclean. The 'dog' belongs to the latter category, banned from kitchen and house,[150] along with the woman stereotyped according to sexual economy.

The proximity of dog and prostitute is unequivocal in the miscellany on women in Sirach 26:19-27.[151] Here the Greco-Roman

---

is, sixth century CE) 'chase' friezes, rare in Jewish art: see R Hachlili, *Ancient Jewish Art and Archeology in the Land of Israel* (Leiden and New York: EJ Brill, 1988), 339. I am grateful to Dr Felicity Harley-McGowen for bringing these to my attention.

147. A Van den Branden, 'Notes phoeniciennes', in *Bulletin de Musée de Beyrouth* 13 (1956): 92–95; DW Thomas, '*Kelebh*, "Dog": Its Origin and some Usages of it in the Old Testament', in *VT* 10 (1960): 417, 425–426.

148. For example, SR Driver, *Deuteronomy* (ICC) (Edinburgh: T&T Clark, 1895), 265, JA Thompson, *Deuteronomy* (London: IVP, 1974), 242, PC Craigie, *The Book of Deuteronomy* (Grand Rapids: Eerdmans, 1976), 302.

149. W Houston, 'What was the Meaning of Classifying Animals as Clean and Unclean?', in A Linzey and D Yamamoto (editors), *Animals on the Agenda* (London: SCM Press, 1998), 22.

150. The only favourable view of dogs is in Tobit (5:16, 11:4) where the animal is portrayed as a companion for journeying; it is found only *outside* dwellings. The novella genre of this writing however may have imported greater Hellenistic influence: J Craghan, *Esther, Judith, Tobit, Jonah, Ruth* (Wilmington, DE: Michael Glazier, 1982), 130–135. Houghton credits 'Magian influence': 'Zoology', 448.

151. Alexander Di Lella considers the miscellany to be a series of expansions on 25:13–26:18, extant only in some Greek manuscripts and a Syriac text, but presumed to have been a Hebrew composition originally: PW Skehan and A Di Lella, *The Wisdom of Ben Sira* (ABC), (New York: Doubleday, 1987), 346. Substantial textual qualifications need to be made (59–60). Warren Trenchard, on structural grounds, does not accept the genuineness of the verses: *Ben Sira's View of Women: A Literary Analysis* (Chico, CA: Scholars Press, 1982), 12. Nevertheless, he opts for a Hebrew *Vorlage* to the section, dated to the first century BCE.

conjunction of dog with shame[152] reverberates onto a woman who acts disgracefully:

> γυνὴ ἀδιατρέπτος ὡς κύων λογισθήσεται,
> ἡ δὲ ἔχουσα αἰσχύνην τὸν κυρίον φοβηθήσεται (v 25)

Various negative characterisations of women are dispensed throughout this passage: γυνὴ μισθία, γυνὴ ἀσεβῆς, γυνὴ ἀσχήμων, γυνὴ ἀδιατρέπτος, γυνὴ μεγαλόφωνος καὶ γλωσσώδης. Probably, a composite has been compiled of the woman to avoid.[153] Nevertheless, the animal epithet is reserved for the γυνὴ ἀδιατρέπτος,[154] and is directly set off against the Lord, who supports the honour of the father/husband. The woman who thus acts 'without shame', is vilified in religious tones—shame-*bearing* is construed as a pious action for a woman.[155] The dog here is seen not merely as unclean but as shame*less*.

The specific content of this can be surmised from other refrains of the evil woman—her habitual characteristic is sexual promiscuity.[156] The absence of reference to a man/husband (ἀνήρ) may imply that γυνή is to be understood simply as 'woman', the additional descriptors reflecting the consequence of a failure to provide the necessary protective boundaries for a daughter having identical untameable inclinations:[157]

---

152. The author expressly mentions travels abroad (Sir 34:9–13). There are many indications that Ben Sira was thoroughly embedded in Hellenistic values, including the importance of honour and shame (see, especially 41:14–42:8). See generally, Collins, *Jewish Wisdom,* 23–41.
153. Skehan and Di Lella, 352; *cf* also CV Camp, 'Understanding a Patriarchy: Women in Second Century Jerusalem Through the Eyes of Ben Sira', in Levine, *Women Like This*, 20–21 (here commenting on Sirach 9:1–9; Camp does not deal with the miscellany).
154. Contempt is apparent in the designation of the prostitute (γυνὴ μισθία).
155. A vivid recounting of the shame/honour dimensions of male-female relations amongst Jews is found in *CPJ* 1.19: Dositheos and Herakleia, both Jews accused each other of abuse, demanding compensation in the former case and exoneration in the latter.
156. JT Sanders, *Ben Sira and Demotic Wisdom* (Chico, CA: Scholars Press, 1983), 87; PW van der Horst, 'Conflicting Images of Women in Ancient Judaism', in his *Hellenism—Judaism—Christianity: Essays on Their Interaction* (Kampen: Kok Pharos, 1994), 74–75.
157. *Cf* Sir 42:11–14, which culminates in a stock *Tobspruch* comparing the wickedness of a man favourably even to the goodness of a woman,

ἐπὶ θυγατρὶ ἀδιατρέπτῳ στερέωσον φυλακήν,
ἵνα μὴ εὑροῦσα ἄνεσιν ἑαυτῇ χρήσηται· (Sir 26:10a)

Thus a woman and a daughter betray the same breach of acceptable female propriety. The word ἀδιατρέπτος is extremely rare, found only in Sirach in the LXX and sparsely elsewhere.[158] The word may have a positive sense, denoting an extreme steadfastness.[159] Of a woman however, such resistance to male control and reason was culpable in the extreme, threatening the very order of creation.[160] By implication, dog becomes the apt censure for such behaviour, curs who scrounge society's refuse.

Whatever the accolades for dogs amongst non-Jews, in Jewish culture the dog was a blight on the landscape. In metaphorical application, it connoted abuse, uncleanness of habit and eating, distance from the house and certainly the Lord's house,[161] shamelessness, persistence, judgement. The dog was equated with the foxes and wild beasts, not contrasted from them (En 89:42, 43, 46). There is nothing in Jewish literature or other non-literary remains that indicates general acceptance or domestication of the dog.[162]

Jewish agreement with the Greco-Roman world was simply at the level of the danger of the dog; it cannot be mollified by reference to a more positive appreciation, even of 'puppies'. Moreover, it is not enough simply to recite the equation of gentile and dog. The metaphor had a much richer range of application, from personal enemy to any woman betraying independence from a man.[163] For the Jew, *cave*

---

since she is the shame-bearer!

158. Suet *Cal* 29. Suetonius' reference cites Caligula's proud boast in Greek. But Suetonius' own explanatory intrusion, 'shameless' [*inverecundiam*], suggests that he reads the word differently from the emperor's intent.

159. *Cf* Cl Al *Ped* 3.2.8, Eus *HE* 8.6.3, *Comm Is* 1.32.82.

160. Archer, *Price Beyond Rubies*, 212.

161. Stanislav Segert identifies a degree of shared horror at a dog's potential for desecration of holy places: 'Semitic Poetic Structures in the New Testament', in *ANRW* 2.25.2.1453.

162. RW Redding, 'The Vertebrate Fauna', in SC Herbert (editor), *Tel Anafa 1.i: Final Report on Ten Years Excavation at a Hellenistic and Roman Settlement in Northern Israel* (Ann Arbor: JRA Series 10, 1994), 289; contrast the Roman evidence: see L Allason-Jones, *Women in Roman Britain* (London: British Museum Publications, 1989), 167.

163. There is little difference from Homeric usage,—Greeks can hurl the epithet at each other as well as at the Trojans; the term also has a particularly abusive application for women. There is one notable

canem was not a warning to others from *behind* the protection of a chained dog; it was a prohibition against engagement with *any* dog.

Have Canis

There is no Jewish parallel to the honour of a dog that runs from Odysseus' old faithful Argus[164] past the time of Jesus.[165] This dog is a welcome and desirable member of the household, not even the terror at the threshold. This is Pliny's true friend, equalled only by the horse.[166] Domestication is now complete and the dog has become a prized accompaniment to the pleasures of life, indeed a contributor to them.

The dog becomes the object of exultation and praise, renowned for its breeding and training, its companionship and devotion. Epitaphs will be erected *in memoriam*;[167] cities will be given *in nominem*;[168] walls, furnishings and vases will abound *in decoraminem*;[169] sarcophagi through reliefs and contents speak of the intimate connections between hunter and companion hound.[170]

Literature constantly recalled the poignant, perceptive welcome by one solitary hound to the archetypal male hero, Odysseus.[171] This story was improvised numerous times in stories of the relationship between kings and canines.[172] Aristotle could thus assert, 'There is honour in

---

exception however: the use of 'dog' in abuse of a deity; see Lilja, *Dogs,* 22.

164. See Hom *Od* 17.292–327.
165. See *NDIEC* 4.158, Toynbee, *Animals,* 366n69.
166. *HN* 8.142; *cf* also Lucret *Nat Rer* 5.864–865, 6.1222–1223. Horses and dogs were often commemorated in Hellenistic epitaphs: see JM Snyder, *The Woman and the Lyre: Women Writers in Classical Greece and Rome* (Carbondale, IL: Southern Illinois University Press, 1989), 70, who cites G Herrlinger, *Totenklage um Tiere in der antiken Dichtung* (Stuttgart: W Kohlhammer, 1930), for details of epigraphy.
167. A number are collected in *GA* Book 7; *cf* Diod Sic 13.82, and the survey in Toynbee, *Animals*, 110–111.
168. Alexander the Great reputedly named a city after his favourite dog, Peritas (as also one after his favourite horse, Bucephalia): Plut *Vit (Alex)* 61.3.
169. For example, the wall-painting of a pet dog from the House of the Epigrams, now held at Museo di Napoli (inv 110877); *cf.* the great hunt painting on the royal tomb at Vergina: LC Reilly, 'The hunting frieze from Vergina', in *JHS* 113 (1993): 160–162.
170. Fox, 'Ancient Hunting', 140.
171. Hom *Od* 17.375–391.
172. For example, Ael *NA* 6.25; *cf* Plut *Mor* 969c–d.

being a dog.'[173]

Swiftness, the power of the sense of smell, perseverance in downing the enemy, the ability to see hidden things—these expressed the positive dimensions of the dog for the Greek and Roman.[174] The context was the hunt, which denoted the control of the hunter. The irony was that, even here, links with the female's propensity for wandering and attraction to the male were preserved—with bitches being regarded as better at tracking than male dogs.[175] The hand of the hunter was what enabled the bitch to be conformed to a positive goal.

Odysseus himself is the hunter-shepherd, whistling to signal the ferocious Diomedes who is caught in doggish (κύντατον) indecision.[176] And when rage had erupted within Homer's hero, like a bitch protecting her whelps from a stranger, yet he 'held it hard in leash, *submitted to his mind*'.[177]

Positive attributes of a dog might describe courageous, loyal men,[178] but this was the hound of the hunt. The lapdog rarely surfaced as a symbol of fidelity;[179] its domestication is so complete that it almost becomes contemptible and is allied with the feminine and the effeminate. The dog's sexual proclivities and gluttony have not been eradicated but merely shifted from the wild to the social. It is sometimes portrayed as almost parasitic in its consumptive habits,[180] and becomes proverbially tied to women: 'a lapdog takes after its

173. *Rhet* 2.24 (1401a). The reference is probably a play on 'Cynic' but the general maxim merely provides the opportunity for the pun.

174. Plat *Rep* 375a, 376a, Sext Emp *Pyrr* 1.64.

175. Pind fr 95, Soph *Aj* 7.

176. *Il* 10.502–506; *cf* Hector in *Il* 8.338–340, in a passage that develops the rabidness to a level that reduces Hector to the bestial; see JM Blakey, 'Canine Imagery in Greek Poetry' (PhD Thesis, University of North Carolina, 1972), 30–31.

177. Hom *Od* 20.5–24 (my emphasis). The force of this episode was felt by Plutarch to be an example of the power and virtue of control: *Mor* 475a. In general terms, baying dogs quieted by a man's voice is the illustration of self-control (465c).

178. Occasionally, as in the bitch protecting her whelps it may have a positive association *in connection with a mother*; see *GA* 30 (Gow and Page edition—Loeb edition 7.425).

179. *Vit Aes* 50; more often it was the hound used in hunting or military campaigns that was portrayed in these terms: see Ael *NA* 10.41, Plut *Vit* (*Them*) 10.10.

180. Eubolus fr 90, Mart *Epig* 5.44, 14.198; *cf* Plut *Mor* 472c.

mistress'.[181] Theophrastus dismisses the honouring of a lapdog as a sign of petty ambition.[182] Petronius, Martial and Juvenal all caustically satirised 'Pearl', 'Dolly', 'Issa' and 'Malchio' as gluttonous, frivolous, faithless, conceited, painted (as a prostitute), a sign of the corruption of Rome (as of other nations)[183]—the female names again suggesting the theme of descent occasioned by or through the female;[184] the male name likewise by its play upon μαλακός.[185] Even the emperor Claudius did not escape censure for 'the little white bitch' he petted.[186]

Preoccupation with the dog

As has been seen, the dog expressed both danger and devotion, disgust and desire, dirt and decency.[187] The preoccupation with the dog in the ancient world can be measured by the attention afforded to it in art, decoration and literature. Aristotle, Xenophon, Aelian and Pliny devote large sections of major works to dogs.[188] Proverbs and fables are filled with references to dogs and hounds, bitches, puppies, lapdogs. 'The dog in the manger' is one of the best known, cropping up everywhere from an Aesopic fable[189] to a logion of Jesus in the *Gospel of Thomas*.[190]

It would be a mistake however to deduce any static universality in the appreciation of dogs through the ancient world. The dividing line between pest and pet was fraught with potential breaches; it was a boundary demanding unswerving vigilance. The fetter or leash was a constant reminder of the need to subdue the unruly and keep it in close check. In the case of the rabbis, the recommended implement of control was the stick, used to keep the unruly at safe, purified

181. Plato is scathing in his expansion on the proverb: no discipline, arrogant sauntering, pushing against everyone: *Rep* 563c; *cf* Epicharmus fr 168, Diog Laert *Vit* 5.93. The proverb had an even more concise, but equally derisive (racially tarnished) neighbour: Μελιταίον κυνίδιον.
182. Theophr *Char* 21.9.
183. Athen *Deip* 518f.
184. Petron *Sat* 64, Mart *Ep* 1.109, Juv *Sat* 6.643ff; *cf* 9.60.
185. Mart *Ep* 3.82; *cf* Mt 11:8//Lk 7:25, *P Hib* 54.
186. (Ps?)-Sen *Ap*13.
187. This distinction between the desirable and the dangerous is reflected in the translations of ancient texts where 'hound' and 'dog' (or 'mongrel') are used for the same Greek word in an effort to convey the cultural distinctions evoked by the context.
188. See generally Hull, *Hounds and Hunting*.
189. Phaedr suppl §702 (Perry's edition).
190. *GT* 102.

distance.[191] Attitudes to dogs ran along the spectrum from Diana's exulted hunting companion to the disdainful rabbinical injunctions against providing board for dogs, Gentiles and students (especially if one were a widow).[192] These attitudes not only reflect cultural codes; they were recognised as indicating ethnic particularity—Aristotle, for example, thought Indians inter-bred dogs with tigers.[193] Even the Hellenistic translator of Proverbs felt that a Hebrew proverb needed to be changed to one more appropriate to an Alexandrian context — and so we gain the warning against grabbing a dog by its Greek tail rather than by its Hebrew ears![194]

The animal connections of human character

The invitation of fables, proverbs and larger treatises is to view the dog as far more than an object of scientific enquiry. The moral that frequently attaches to an Aesopic fable indicates that a different kind of 'cross-breeding' is being encouraged—a correlation between dogs and human life.[195] Differences in culture were occasionally noticed, though such differences were usually ascribed to 'nature'—the wild, dark peoples of India or the even more ferocious Chinese.[196]

Aelian's *On the Characteristics of Animals* is laced with interlocking observations about human affairs, pursuant to his claim that 'in all subjects Nature is an instructress without rival'.[197] Hierarchical relationships at mealtimes, for example, are justified by such an appeal:

> How could the noble son of Eunomos [that is, Lycurgus] seek to rival and compete with the laws of Nature . . .

191. b*Shab* 155b. Interestingly, there is a Hellenistic parallel—*GA* 11.153 (line 3).
192. b*Shab* 63a, b*Ab Zar* 18b.
193. *HA* 607a; noted also by Ael *NA* 4.19, 8.1, 16.20, 31, Poll *Onom* 5.43, Diod Sic 17.92, Strab *Geog* 15.1.37. Given proper training and constraint, such hounds were regarded as ideal for hunting: Xen *Cyn* 9.1. Herodotus wrote of Xerxes' invasion of Greece being supported by a multitude of Indian hounds: *Hist* 7.187.
194. Prov 26:17; see generally G Gerleman, 'The Septuagint Proverbs as a Hellenistic Document', in *Oud Stud* 8 (1950): 15–27.
195. See, for example, the state as a defence against the threat of the barbaric, in the fable in *Vit Aes* 97.
196. Grat 159 *cf* Plut *Mor* 499d on Hyrcanians and the use of dogs to devour their dead.
197. Ael *NA* 6.59.

> the young ones give way to the elders in feeding; they wait upon those that are weak in age; they guard them from danger; when they fall into pits the young ones will drag them out . . .[198]

The description of animals is frequently carved according to observations of human affairs, thus strengthening the links between the two worlds and increasing the possibilities for exchange.[199]

Not every writer was totally convinced of the probity of using the natural world to define and illustrate the human,[200] but even suspicious Plutarch could happily resort to 'nature' as reinforcing hierarchical distinctions between persons.[201] The appeal to nature was important for argument and ideology.[202]

However, where the supremacy of (hu)man(ity) might be challenged by such comparisons, the differences were asserted. Thus Porphyry's advocacy of a vegetarian diet works from a premise that animals are unlike humans and hence humans should cultivate actions which demonstrate their distinctiveness.[203] However, this is a variation rather than a critique of the use of animals to characterise humans.

The animal, woman and character portrayal

The use of animal behaviour and the natural world generally to facilitate observation, analysis, prescription, ideology and polemic in human life has a long and venerated history. Fortenbaugh regards Plato's use of dog imagery as 'drawing on a long tradition of likening

198. *Ibid*, 6.61.
199. Susan Cole notes that Aelian, though a Roman freedman, relies totally on Greek authors for his work, which thus becomes a clear compendium of Greek attitudes linking animal and human behaviour: 'Women, Dogs and Flies', 182. Compare also Oppian's *Cynegetica*.
200. Plut *Mor* 493b–c; *cf* Sen *Ir* 1.3.4f, 2.16.1.
201. Plut *Mor* 616b.
202. Thus Plato resorted to 'nature' to defend the use of the oral over the written (*Phdr* 274a–277a) and Dio Chrysostom argued that long hair and a beard were according to 'nature' (*Or* 33.64). Seneca denounced hot baths, potted plants and banquets after dark as 'against nature' (*Ep* 122.7–8). Aristotle claimed that political involvement and coupling 'by nature' belonged to a man, although the latter was even more 'by nature' than the former! (*Nic Eth* 1.7.7 (1097b), 8.12.7 (1162a).
203. *On Abstinence from Animal Food*. Aristotle notes that courageous men are often compared with wild animals in Homer, but he is careful to distinguish that wild animals react from pain, whereas men operate from 'the good' (τὸ καλόν—*Nic Eth* 3.8.11 (1117a)).

human behaviour to animal behaviour'.[204] It has been used with equal force and frequency in literature, religion, politics and science. Indeed, despite little explicit exposition in the standard ancient textbooks, it can be claimed as a classic rhetorical device. Certainly, as Edmund Leach observed, 'When an animal name is used . . . as an imprecation, it indicates that the name itself is credited with potency.'[205]

Classical rhetoric put great store on classification based on character and characterisation. It was crucial for the various genres of rhetoric, whether by way of appeal, argument or prosecution. However, when the actual characterisations are analysed, one discovers the virtual rather than argued assumption about the aptness of recourse to bestial terms. A classification under 'figures of speech' is unsatisfactory for it does not look to the larger issues governing the accepted use of animal epithets for human beings, especially women. This merits careful investigation, if only to avoid reinscribing the same assumptions.[206]

Aristotle recognised that slander of another went less to the substance of an argument than to the arousal of prejudice among those who decide,[207] even though the appeal be located in the *a priori* of 'nature'. And if there be warrant from 'the great Homeric spring', no dispute about the authority for such a comparison nor any quibbling over the content of the application appeared. Homer's frequent deployment of dog metaphors, especially in abuse, authorised the adoption and extension of such usage. Thus, for Longinus, an impudent fellow simply is 'Heavy with wine, with the eyes of a dog'.[208] Images and figures that drew upon animals were regarded as fit emotive pictures to enliven a piece of writing.

204. Fortenbaugh, 'Aristotle: Animals', 161n20, citing *Rep* 375e, 376a, 441b.
205. Leach, 29; *cf* 26.
206. E Schüssler Fiorenza, 'Challenging the Rhetorical Half-Turn: Feminism and Rhetorical Biblical Criticism', in SE Porter and TH Olbricht (editors), *Rhetoric, Scripture and Theology: Essays from the 1994 Pretoria Conference* (Sheffield: Sheffield Academic Press, 1996), 35, 44n42; *cf* JDH Amador, 'Not with Excess of Word or Wisdom. . .: Power and Rhetorical Criticism of the New Testament' (PhD Thesis, GTU, 1995).
207. Arist *Rhet* 1.1 (1354a).
208. Longin 4.4–5, citing, without (the need for) acknowledgement, *Il* 1.225.

If the metaphor was daring, the rhetoricians advised conversion to a simile.[209] Yet we find the linkage of women and dogs far more frequent as a metaphor than a simile, indicating that such an equation was *not* seen as daring. Indeed, if Aristotle's directions as to the use of proportional metaphor are to be followed, metaphors that operate within the same species or from species to genus are to be preferred[210] —a rhetorical indication of suspicions about the canine colouring of women.

The scientific and literary affirmation of the animal-human interface ensured that rhetoric had a firm grounding for an appeal to the bestial characteristics of a human being. The clearest authorisation from nature was held to be gender differentiation.[211] Confusion of gender was therefore unacceptable, and implied 'bad' character.[212] Gender distinction reinforced gender inequality—woman was, after all, 'the inferior thing' (τὸ χεῖρον) according to Aristotle.[213] Language and socio-cultural values overlap,[214] and both are funded by nature.

Women rarely figure in formal treatises on character, although other forms of literature certainly painted standardised types. Semonides' trenchant critique of the varieties of women became a standard reference, and certain women, such as Hecuba and Medea provided regular typologies.[215] Aristotle's *Nicomachean Ethics* concentrates on examples of men's characters, merely referring to women as counterfoil examples to his exposition of male virtues.[216] Elsewhere, Aristotle makes a general reference to female excellence lying in beauty and

209. Demetr *Eloc* 2.80, Longin 32.3–4. Aristotle saw a closer connection: *Rhet* 3.4 (1406b–1407a).
210. Arist *Rhet* 3.10 (1411a–b).
211. Malina, 'Circum-Mediterranean Person?', 70–71, JH Neyrey, 'What's Wrong with this Picture? John 4, Cultural Stereotypes of Women and Public and Private Space', in *BTB* 24 (1994): 78–82.
212. Arist *Poet* 15.4ff (1454a).
213. *Poet* 15.3 (1454a). On Aristotle's attitude, see N Demand, 'Women and Slaves as Hippocratic Patients', in SR Joshel and S Murnaghan (editors), *Women and Slaves in Greco-Roman Culture* (London: Routledge, 1998), 70–71. However, she overplays the contrast with Plato, for whom the body was inherently 'womanish', to be escaped from.
214. See P Trudgill, *Sociolinguistics: An Introduction to Language and Society* (Harmondsworth: Penguin, revised edition, 1983), 29. Hence, Aristotle included elements on character under both Ethics and Rhetoric.
215. *Cf Poet* 9.4 (1451b). See ML West, *Hesiod Works and Days* (Oxford: Clarendon Press, 1978), 160.
216. *Nic Eth* 3.6.5 (1115a), 5.6.1-2 (1134a), 5.9.16 (1137a).

stature, prudence and non-servile industry[217]—in other words, all that a male could want for the honour of his household.[218]

Praise and blame in the rhetoric of character definition

Abuse occupies a key place in Greek and Roman literature. The rhetorical handbooks devote considerable attention to the importance and methods of building praise or blame (Greek: ἐγκώμια or ψόγοι, Latin: *laudationes* or *vituperationes*).[219] Within this binary opposition were different grades and associated descriptions of the type of praise or blame available and the situations in which use was advised.[220] These organised arrangements of rhetorical practice[221] provided much of the theoretical undergirding of standard training in rhetoric. Exercises were frequently turned to the establishment of the character of a friend or opponent usually in epideictic display but also for forensic purposes.[222]

Probably, Ben Sira knew something of the discipline of this linguistic rhetoric. He was certainly aware of the social implications of the language of praise and blame (Sir 5:11–6:17, 8:5–7, 28:14, 39:4,6,10).[223] This is the ancient discipline of ethology (ἠθολογίαι) or

217. *Rhet* 1.5 (1361a).

218. EC Keuls, *The Reign of the Phallus: Sexual Politics in Ancient Athens* (New York: Harper & Row, 1985), 229.

219. *Rhet ad Her* 1.5.12f, Quint *Inst* 2.4, 3.4.12, Suet *Rhet* 1 See generally, R Webb, 'Poetry and Rhetoric', in SE Porter (editor), *Handbook of Classical Rhetoric in the Hellenistic Period 330 BC—AD 400* (Leiden: Brill, 1997), 356–359.

220. MA Grant, *Ancient Rhetorical Theories of the Laughable: The Greek Rhetoricians and Cicero* (Madison: University of Wisconsin Press, 1924), 75f, 128–131.

221. Whilst it is becoming clear that many of the ancient writers on rhetoric brought their political agendas into their analyses, this ought not sideline the importance of their observations on the mechanics of persuasive argumentation. They show great consciousness of actual practice and were often aware of the 'unconscious' awareness of rhetorical prowess: Arist *Rhet* 1.1 (1354a), Quint *Inst* 2.11–13. The description of the existing and accepted patterns of the use of rhetoric is therefore an inherently conservative, even an ideologically defensive undertaking: see C Glenn, *Rhetoric Retold: Regendering the Tradition from Antiquity Through the Renaissance* (Carbondale and Edwardsville: Southern Illinois University Press, 1997), 18–20, 33–36, 56–63.

222. Cic *Top* 83, Quint *Inst* 1.9.3, Suet *Gram* 4. See generally, DA Russell *Greek Declamation* (Cambridge: Cambridge University Press, 1983).

223. See S Freyne, 'Vilifying the Other and Defining the Self: Matthew's and John's Anti-Jewish Polemic in Focus', in J Neusner and ES Frerichs

character-drawing (χαρατηρισμοί), which could be utilised as much in oratory as in the writing of history (for example).[224]

Oratory was often quite restrained because of the necessity of maintaining the moral stance of the orator.[225] There are some levels of vituperation, for example, that oratory would eschew—for example, the obscene execrations that were to be found in the mimes,[226] the so-called *scurrae*[227] and certainly the biting destructive innuendo of the satirists. Such 'obscenity' (αἰσχρολογία) could undermine the persuasive authority of the orator.[228] Propriety dictated that the application of a term of abuse be carefully considered[229]—the implication being that when the orator (who operated from the presumed position of moral rectitude) assigned a piece of vituperation against another, it was apt. The gender dimensions of this presumption were obvious—orators, being male, favoured innuendo;[230] obscenity characterised women's festivals.[231] As Joy Connolly has shown, such distinctions

---

(editors), *'To See Ourselves as Others See Us': Christians, Jews, 'Others' in Late Antiquity* (Chico, CA: Scholars Press, 1985), 118; AA Di Lella 'Use and Abuse of the Tongue: Ben Sira 5.9–6.1', in AA Diesel *et al* (editors), *'Jedes Ding hat seine Zeit . . .' Studien zur israelitischen und altorientalischen Weisheit* (Fs D Michel), (BZAW 241), (Berlin: de Gruyter, 1996), 33–48.

224. Quint *Inst* 1.9.3. Compare Cicero's *In Pisonem* with some of the portraits in Tacitus or Sallust. See generally Christopher Gill, 'The Question of Character-Development: Plutarch and Tacitus', in *CQ* 33 (1983): 469–487.
225. See, for example, Quint *Inst* 2.12.4–5.
226. Roughly, mime is the ancient equivalent of vaudeville. Philo likens the abuse heaped upon the delegation to the emperor Gaius as akin to that characterising mimes: *Leg* 359. On the mime, see Grant, *Theories of the Laughable*, 48–51.
227. The sycophantic witticisms of the professional banquet parasite, so much part of the Roman scene (less apparent in Greek comedy).
228. Arist *Nic Eth* 4.8.6 (1128a); *cf* Plat *Gorg* 460c, Quint *Inst* 2.15.33–34. See T Reekman, 'Verbal Humour in Plutarch and Suetonius' Lives', in *AncSoc* 23 (1992): 230–231. Aristotle prefers It should be remembered that).
229. Defamation was a critical offence under the Roman *Twelve Tables*; Old Comedy was, at various times, outlawed by Greek city authorities: Grant, *Theories of the Laughable*, 97–98. Aristotle is conscious and approving of suchlike limitations: *Nic Eth* 4.8.9–10 (1128a).
230. Cic *Orat* 2.251.
231. See L McClure, *Spoken Like a Woman: Speech and Gender in Athenian Drama* (Princeton, NJ: Princeton University Press, 1999), 47–52.

lay in the label rather than linguistics—the hidden reality and rhetoric was the asymmetry of gender.[232]

Theorists of rhetoric knew well the range of possibilities available.[233] The orator could rely on this knowledge when presenting an argument, thus avoiding any charge of unseemliness or abuse and yet enlisting the support of the audience for his overall case because of their own (mental, though sometimes interruptive) provision of material at any specific instance. Thus the master attorney, Demosthenes, declaimed, '. . . I need not say anything ugly or unpleasant about him now; if I simply say that Philokrates brought back some women, you all know, and so does the crowd round the court, what followed'.[234] The exchange between orator and audience makes for a much larger presentation than either party provides alone. The attitudes and knowledge of the audience therefore become a key factor in determining the effectiveness and depth of the characterisation of individuals.[235]

Figures of speech as acceptable forms of abuse

Allusion, metaphor and simile are crucial to vituperation, for they hide and reveal at the same time. Metaphors have the capacity to attract associations that the substitute readily contains, and which, if asserted directly of the term which they replaced, might be held in certain situations to be overly confronting and offensive. Quintilian recognises this veiling dimension of figures of speech—they divert attention in the very act of attracting it.[236] Hence, not merely an additional context, but a *substituted* one, was provided which allowed a specific individual to be assessed totally by reference to that which was not present.[237]

232. 'Mastering Corruption: Constructions of Identity in Roman Oratory', in Joshel and Murnaghan, *Women and Slaves*, 136.
233. For example, Quint *Inst* 1.8.5–12. There were frequent exchanges between actors and orators as to techniques of voice manipulation, facial expressions and gestures (*ibid*, 1.11.1f). For an illustration at the highest level (the emperor Gaius), see Phil Jud *Leg* 204.
234. *Decl* 19.309.
235. For example, Quint *Inst* 2.17.28–29; *cf* Menand *Dysk* 1f, 45f, 194, 659, 666, *Peri* 7f, 47f, *Phasm* 19f.
236. Quint *Inst* 2.13.2; *cf* Arist *Rhet* 3.2 (1405a), 3.11 (1412a).
237. The presence and absence of values cultivated by figures of speech is explored by Adrienne Rich, *The Dream of a Common Language* (New York: WW Norton, 1978), H Michie, *The Flesh Made Word: Female Figures and Women's Bodies* (New York and Oxford: Oxford University Press, 1987), 139–149, and T de Lauretis, *Alice Doesn't: Feminism, Semiotics, Cinema* (New York: Macmillan, 1984), 3–8.

This was especially important for calling forth assessments of character based upon stereotypes. The readiness to dispense and elicit judgments based on generalised sweeps rather than particular discernment was all part of the skill in applying praise and blame.[238] Attention would be given to a stock range of features—origins, social background, status, appearance, virtues or vices (most especially to do with morality and levels of restraint), activities, progeny and their behaviour—all in stereotypical patterns and often using metaphor and associations to promote definite perceptions.[239] Within this general frame, animal metaphors were a key component.[240]

Proverbs also, given their frequent metaphorical base,[241] readily served such rhetorical purposes.[242] Their sheer longevity of usage resisted critique of any offence delivered. They were perceived as a truism—provided of course that the proverb, like a metaphor, was accepted as being proportional to the context to which it was joined.[243] But, if accepted, an additional context—'the hidden text of a proverb'—was down-loaded.[244]

In this sense, a boundary has been crossed. Metaphor can become so tied to a subject that it begins to stand for that subject; metaphor has become ossified into metynomy. Because of the readiness to inscribe woman as inferior to man, and animal as inferior to human, the pairing of woman and animal could breach the metaphor of comparison and become the metonymy of prescriptive description. Aristotle stands as representative of a dominant view that readily slid from the animal world to the woman.[245] True character (ἦθος) will out, and especially

238. See CJ Schlueter, *Filling up the Measure: Polemical Hyperbole in 1 Thessalonians 2.14–16* (Sheffield: JSOT Press, 1994), 97–103.

239. Quint *Inst* 3.7.19–22, Arist *Rhet* 1.9 (1367a).

240. RGM Nisbet, *Cicero: In L Calpurnium Pisonem: Oratio* (Oxford: Clarendon Press, 1961), 192–198.

241. Arist *Rhet* 3.3 (1406b), 3.11 (1413a).

242. See RP Honeck and JG Temple, 'Proverbs—The Extended Conceptual Base and Great Chain Metaphor Theories', in *Metaphor & Symbolic Activity* 19 (1994): 85–112.

243. Arist *Rhet* 3.7 (1408a); *cf* Sir 20:20.

244. See A Dundes, *Analytic Essays in Folklore* (The Hague: Mouton, 1975), 109–110.

245. *Eg Pol* 1.2.10–13 (1254b). I owe this recognition of the metamorphosis of metaphor into metonymy to Page duBois, *Sowing the Body: Psychoanalysis and Ancient Representations of Women* (Chicago and London: University of Chicago Press, 1988), 34–36.

when that character is revealed as defective, the haunts of the animal will be manifest, as surely as Helen's bestial treachery.[246]

The rhetoric of abuse

Rhetorical handbooks lack any catalogue of metaphors and the like which can serve the vilification or exaltation of a character. The full sweep of writing, from ethics to tragedy, from comedy to epic, from graffiti to edict, required descriptions and intimations of character to facilitate their respective purposes, though not all were transferable between forms. From street pantomime to high culture, character could be enhanced by non-verbal means—the masks of course, but also clothing, gestures, expressions, movements. Where these were absent, typical or standardised descriptions were the means of building a sense of character.[247]

Even the barest description could, by a latent store of stereotypical associations, provide an audience with an 'immediate' grasp of the character concerned. This characterisation might be corrected through an author's, orator's or performer's manipulative additions, but it provided the foundation. Outside of oratory, a much fuller range of figures and phrases was available for the indications of character.

Hence, the rhetoric of abuse must be explored in greater measure than the descriptive summaries of rhetorical handbooks (which are substantially directed towards oratory). A review of other literature unlocks a vast array of the language of blame and praise. It is here, for example, that we discover that dog-metaphors belong 'almost exclusively to character-speech', a Homeric usage that dominated later writing.[248] Characters usually on the receiving end of such abuse were slaves, brothel-keepers and other procurers, prostitutes, foreigners and men who act outside the parameters of convention (for example, a lascivious old man).[249] KJ Dover distils the standard foci of abuse, which

---

246. Aesch *Ag* 680–736. Helen is likened by the chorus to a lion, reared with love as a cub but who turns on its providers once full grown.
247. Even named characters frequently bore typical rather than individual features: Arist *Poet* 9.4–5 (1451b). See R Hawley, 'Female Characterisation in Greek Declamation', in D Innes, H Hine and C Pelling (editors), *Ethic and Rhetoric* (Oxford: Clarendon Press, 1995), 255–267.
248. Graver, 'Dog-Helen', 44.
249. See Lilja, *Terms of Abuse*, 11, 69, 84. On the stereotypical deviants in ancient society, see R Laurence, *Roman Pompeii: Space and Society* (London: Routledge, 1994), 70–87.

he suggests holds for both comedy and oratory:[250]

i) to impugn the ethnic and/or servile origins of an opponent;
ii) to revile the occupation of the opponent or her/his kin;
iii) to censure an opponent for being a prostitute (or brothel-keeper/procurer) or some other deviation from conventional sexual behaviour.

To this could be added, more specifically,

iv) to denigrate the gender of the opponent, either because she is a woman[251] or because he has behaved as a woman.

Such characters were often themselves the vents for invective—a certain reciprocity in abuse is found in Comedy.[252] Abusive speech was reinforced through the common or rough metre, the iambus, though not confined to it.[253]

Comedy rather than tragedy displays the most caustic abuse, especially in Old Comedy and mime. Saara Lilja notes the 'very great number of metaphors from the animal kingdom.'[254] Menander supplies the general, metonymous collation:

> πολλῶν κατὰ γῆν καὶ κατὰ θάλατταν θηρίων
> ὄντων κάκιστόν ἐστι θηρίον γύνη[255]

250. KJ Dover, *Greek Popular Morality in the Time of Plato and Aristotle* (Indianapolis and Cambridge: Hackett Publishing Co, 1974), 32–33. Dover concentrates on a comparison of the comic writers and Demosthenes' oratory for his conclusions. However, these elements of abuse remained substantially consistent into the Common Era: see EW Handley, *The Dyskolos of Menander* (London: Methuen & Co, 1965), 31.
251. *Eg* Antiphan *Miso* 159k, Menand *Dysk* 259ff, 384f.
252. Lilja, *Terms of Abuse*, 76–77.
253. Grant, *Theories of the Laughable*, 41–45. Russell and Winterbottom comment that iambic metre is the metre of lampoons: DA Russell and M Winterbottom (editors), *Ancient Literary Criticism: The Principal Texts in New Translations* (Oxford: Clarendon Press, 1972), 94.
254. Lilja, *Terms of Abuse,* 30.
255 Fr 422 'of the many beasts of earth and sea, woman is the worst.'

Most especially, animal metaphors were applicable where prostitutes or promiscuity were involved or suggested.[256] Dogs are prominent in such description. But they also figure for their wheedling, barking and biting, often applied to women to suggest their raspy garrulity and their avarice (often combined with their deceptiveness—fawning being followed by theft or destruction).[257] As Margaret Graver distils it:

> . . . metaphors drawn from the κύων group are a rather harsh form of abuse, one which labels its object as greedy and potentially cannibalistic in the domain of material goods, or of fighting, sexuality or speech.[258]

Such abuse in comedy is peppered with diminutives[259] — a model for characterisation emulated in other genres of writing, including oratory. A standard deprecation of a Greek by a Roman, for example, was to call him a 'little Greek' (*graeculus*) and mention his vacuous ramblings.[260] Juvenal was caustic in his disdain for the Greek and borrowed a further damnatory racial stereotype—that of the promiscuous Syrians—to add to his denunciations.[261] Thus diminutives and stereotypes frequently worked in combination to exacerbate the impact of the abuse.

This overview of the rhetoric of vituperation in the ancient world has indicated the potential and circumstances of the application of abuse to indicate character. Animal epithets are a key constituent of this arsenal though nuanced by reference to setting, genre of writing and especially the gender of the recipient. Missing from the rhetoricians' extrapolations, however, is the philosophical undergirding of the use of animal epithets. It is presumed.[262] There is little effort to *ex-*

256. Amphis *Gyn* 9k-a, Anaxil *Neot* 22k-a, Eubul *Kek* 53k-a,Timocles *Ep* 10k-a.
257. Aeschyl *Pers* 111–114, *Ag* 795-804, Menand fr 802, Plaut *Men* 714f.
258. Graver, 'Dog-Helen', 53.
259. DC Swanson recognised diminutives as arising from a comic background; comedy provides his constant reference in his 'Diminutives in the Greek New Testament', in *JBL* 77 (1958): 134–151. Tragedy officially refuted their use (Swanson, 134), though it appears that Euripides did use a diminutive—for which he was criticised by Aristophanes: Lilja, *Dogs*, 78.
260. Cic *De Or* 51.220; *cf* 22.99, *Orat* 1.102, Petron *Sat* 64.
261. Juv *Sat* 3.
262. Dover, *Greek Popular Morality*, 74, D Wiles, *The Masks of Menander: Sign and Meaning in Greek and Roman Performance* (Cambridge:

plain the adoption of the particular terms, such as the dog; certain persons were simply prone to that collation. The dog, as animals generally, were especially deployed in the characterisation of women when associations of gluttony, promiscuity, indifference to boundaries and the like, were required. The collation reinforced the inherent lack of control by the *logos* and the need for it to be imposed by one deemed to be more attuned to self-mastery: the male.

Parameters guiding the adoption of a methodology for critical analysis

This brief survey has accented a number of factors that are to guide the selection and appropriation of a methodology for my purpose. It is clear for reasons of contemporary accountability and the sheer absence of substantial treatment of the use of bestial epithets as such, that rhetorical analysis alone is insufficient for the task. The investigation thus far has revealed the pervasiveness of bestial epithets in ancient society. Steven Lonsdale finds that the use of animals in figures of speech is, in ancient Greek and Mesopotamian society, one of the earliest and most durable types.[263] Whether for positive or negative purposes (and these may have particular cultural emphases), such usage was more than literary. It reflects a scientific and religious view of the world. Given the importance of gender and its management in the ancient world, it is not surprising to discover that when gender is given a central place in guiding analysis, particular accents emerge. Indeed, the animal can join woman in a single broad category as *aloga*, irrational creatures. Consequently, a methodology is needed which can assist in the elucidation of the triangulation of gender, animal and reason, can remain informed by cultural specificities, and can be critiqued by a sociopolitical awareness. To this we now turn.

Cambridge University Press, 1991), 86; nevertheless, interest by the rhetorical schools in the natural sciences is clear: S Bartsch, *Decoding the Ancient Novel: The Reader and the Role of Description in Heliodorus and Achilles Tatius* (Princeton, NJ: Princeton University Press, 1989), 155.

263. Along with fire and other natural phenomena; see SH Lonsdale, *Creatures of Speech: Lion, Herding and Hunting Similes in the Iliad* (Stuttgart: BG Teubner, 1990), 103.

2

A Dog Returns to its Own Vomit
Ethological Constructions of Woman

Searching for an adequate methodology

Introduction

The exploration of the interrelationship of woman, animal and reason in the ancient world has revealed that the correlation of human beings and animals was a commonplace. The combination was frequently used to indicate character (*ethos*). However, the provision of invigorating metaphors was grounded not in literary inventiveness but in assumptions about invariables of nature. As John Matthews writes:

> This is more than stylistic affectation. We must also see it in the context of the Classical view of man's rational faculty as that which preeminently sets him apart from the world of animals.[1]

Ancient studies of animals were not only a demonstration of the supremacy of human reason. Through extensive taxonomies, they provided the assurance that bestial associations and implications based on gender, ethnicity and status were completely valid.[2] The validity ranged from medical to rhetorical usage, though a systematic, dedicated study of interconnections between the animal and human is lacking.[3] Even so, from comparisons of animal and human in the

---

1. J Matthews, *The Roman Empire of Ammianus* (London: Duckworth, 1989), 258.
2. *Contra* H Lloyd-Jones, *Female of the Species: Semonides on Women* (London: Duckworth, 1975), 29. Lloyd-Jones argues for a levity on the part of Semonides, with his metaphors linking types of women with species of animal nothing more than figures of speech. The combination of cosmology and satirical metaphor in one brief composition makes such an apologetic difficult to sustain. The naturalised value system is clear.
3. DM Balme reckons Aristotle's *Survey of Animals* comes closest to a descriptive collection of data but, whilst 'wide and perceptive', is 'surprisingly disorderly': 'Aristotle's Use of Differentiae in Zoology',

classical world one foundational tenet reigned: the separation of the sexes. All other comparisons, as well as logical and socio-political systems, flow from this supposed fundamental testimony of nature.[4]

The human as animal: modern ethology

The formal study of animals and their behaviour, with an interest in deductions for human life, is generally asserted to be a recent development.[5] This discipline betrays an ancient origin, however, even in its name: 'ethology'.[6] One of its foremost proponents, Edward O Wilson, has extended the formal implications of the comparative discipline into a grand schema for human knowledge.[7] Religion, ethics, anthropology and culture are all related to sociobiology; sociobiology, he claims, is the *sine qua non* for such knowledge.[8] The dependence

---

in J Barnes, M Schofield and R Sorabji (editors), *Articles on Aristotle 1 Science* (London: Duckworth, 1975), 183.

4. See RC Davis, *The Paternal Romance: Reading God-the-Father in Early Western Culture* (Urbana and Chicago: University of Illinois Press, 1993), 73–96; V Songe-Møller, *Philosophy Without Women: The Birth of Sexism in Western Thought* (London: Continuum, 2002), *passim*.
5. Konrad Lorenz, *The Foundations of Ethology*, translated by KZ Lorenz and RW Kickert (New York/Wien Springer-Verlag, 1981), 1.
6. Paolo Mantegazza, at the turn of the twentieth century, had recognised the ancients' comparison of man and animals and traced the practice from Plato through to the 'golden age' of physiognomy in the seventeenth century: *Physiognomy and Expression* (London: Walter Scott, 189–), 5–7. This is not to confuse ancient and modern ethology but it does note the importance of animal comparisons to both character definition on the one hand and human behavioural patterns on the other.
7. EO Wilson, *Consilience: The Unity of Knowledge* (New York: AA Knopf, 1998); see also M von Cranach, K Foppa, W Lepenies and D Ploog (editors), *Human Ethology: Claims and Limits of a New Discipline* (Cambridge: Cambridge University Press, 1977), xv, and RA Hinde, *Ethology* (Glasgow: Fontana, 1982), 201–269. Note, however, the roots of such totalising visions were established by the nineteenth century social evolutionists, Schiller and Spencer. See, for example, Karl Groos, *The Play of Animals: A Study of Animal Life and Instinct* translated by Elizabeth L Baldwin (London: Chapman & Hall, 1898), who draws correlations between animal behaviour and human culture, such as dance and the arts generally (293). The nineteenth century foundations of modern ethology are surveyed by WH Thorpe, *The Origins and Rise of Ethology* (London: Heinemann, 1979).
8. Wilson, *Consilience*, 142.

of the discipline upon evolution and ontogeny builds a sense of the determinacy of the observations.[9]

Accordingly, ethology may provide a theoretical *comparative* base for the present study, not in an anachronistic imposition on ancient materials, but as a means to expose some of their dynamics. Modern ethology's claimed objective observations about women, along with the contemporary problematisation of such rational results by feminist scholarship, reformulate the same triangulation as already propounded. That is, ethology and the critical assessment of its claims by feminist scholarship (especially) are configured around the interplay of nature/animal, gender and rational enquiry. These are the elements, albeit framed in contemporary language, that we have seen to be integral to an analysis of the story of the Syrophoenician woman.

If due recognition is given to the cultural materiality in the ancient text and its context (understood as variegated according to general and audiential values) so as to avoid anachronistic ethnocentric assumptions, the contemporary debates about ethology have potential to enable insights into the interpretation of this crucial story in Mark's gospel. Moreover, by approaching modern ethology in contest with feminist critique of sociobiological determinism, a hermeneutical check is supplied which, hopefully, will guard against a re-inscription of late antiquity's literary subjection and objectification of women. It will become apparent that the lines between ancient and modern ethology are not so fractured after all, and both are advisedly critiqued.

A critical excursion into ethology

Ethology is that field of modern scientific research where comparisons for human beings are made on the basis of and in conjunction with animal research. Certain 'homologies' or evolutionary biological similarities provide the warrant for such comparisons, though analogies also have their role indicating 'laws dependent on functions'.[10] Though Oskar Heinroth, Konrad Lorenz and Irenäus Eibl-Eibesfeldt are key figures

9. S Sperling, 'Baboons with Briefcases: Feminism, Functionalism, and Sociobiology in the Evolution of Primate Gender', in B Laslett, SG Kohlstedt, H Longino, E Hammonds (editors), *Gender And Scientific Authority* (Chicago and London: University of Chicago Press, 1996), 379. Ontogeny is the study of the course of physiological development of an individual member of a species.
10. I Eibl-Eibesfeldt, *Ethology: The Biology of Behaviour*, translated by E Klinghammer (New York: Holt Rinehart and Winston, second edition, 1975), 533.

in the development of the discipline, the far-reaching implications of ethology were signalled in Wilson's massive tome *Sociobiology*.[11] Wilson argued that all-important social behaviours were reducible to genetics. Even altruism and Wilson's own sympathy for socio-political change were but variations of the adaptation of the species seeking to maximise its own future.[12]

Ethology and gender

Highly significant for this study is the attention given to gendered behaviours, that is, behavioural observations and conclusions that are riveted in differences between male and female. This is the stock 'dimorphism' of gender. One example from Wilson will suffice:

> It pays males to be aggressive, hasty, fickle and undiscriminating. In theory it is more profitable for females to be coy, to hold back until they can identify the male with the best genes. Human beings obey this biological principle faithfully.[13]

The stereotypical modes of expression used here reflect socio-cultural attitudes about women and men. They are uncritically transferred to the animal world in order then to receive them back under a guise of objective, scientific observation. The antiquity of this practice is frequently overlooked.[14]

Wilson's linguistic dependence on a long-standing correlation between women's masquerades and procreative fecundity is illustrated

---

11. EO Wilson, *Sociobiology: A New Synthesis* (Cambridge, MA: Harvard University Press, 1975); but *cf* Konrad Lorenz's reflections on 'Cultural Ethology': *Foundations,* 344–346.
12. WD Hamilton, 'The Genetical Evolution of Social Behaviour', in *JTB* 7 (1964): 1–52, RL Trivers, 'The Evolution of Reciprocal Altruism', in *QRB* 46 (1971): 35–57, S Sperling and Y Beyene, 'A Pound of Biology and a Pinch of Culture or a Pinch of Biology and a Pound of Culture?: The necessity of integrating biology and culture in reproductive studies', in LD Hager (editor), *Women in Human Evolution* (London and New York: Routledge, 1997), 138, Wilson, *Consilience*, 258.
13. EO Wilson, *On Human Nature* (Cambridge, MA: Harvard University Press, 1978), 125, *Consilience*, 170.
14. See Winkler, *Constraints of Desire*, 22–23, who recognised, as but one example, Aelian's observance of elephants' concern for the sanctity of marriage as nothing more than men's anxiety over their wives' (potential) adultery.

by Karl Groos' quotation of the late nineteenth-century physiognomist, Paolo Mantegazza:

> Coquetry is not the exclusive prerogative of the human female. No woman ever born could surpass the abominable (*sic*!) refinement of cruelty displayed by a female canary in her pretended resistance to her mate's advances. All the countless devices of the feminine world to hide a Yes under a No are as nothing compared with the consummate coquetry, the deceptive flights, the bitings and the thousand wiles of female animals.[15]

Little wonder that ethology has been viewed by feminist political activists as an ideological tool of those structures resistant to greater justice for women.[16] Little wonder also that the genealogy of recent ethology seems to track easily to classical views, especially in the construction of a dualistic sequence anchored to the dimorphism of gender.

Contemporary sociobiologists have surrendered the nineteenth-century political battle against women's education, which sought scientific justification via biological differentiation for the mounting of barriers against access. However, other aspects have not been so easily dismissed. The interrelationship of scientific argument and social responsibility is patent in the appeal to what might be called ethical evolutionary principles. Here the assumption of the biologically-necessary, reproductive functions of the female demands, as a value, that the female sacrifice the possibility of rational equality (certainly superiority) for the sake of the fulfilment of maternity, requisite for the posterity and health of future generations.

Whilst these arguments were plentiful in the nineteenth century,[17] they have survived in their tenacity. Indeed, Irenäus Eibl-Eibesfeldt held that a biological stemma for ethics must be the preferred position

---

15. Unsourced quotation found in Groos, *The Play of Animals*, 285. Groos disputes the conclusions about the antagonism of the sexual impulse and the coyness but not the characterisation of 'the feminine world'. He goes on to express his sympathy for the male cuckoo: 'the poor fellow is fairly driven crazy' by the female's 'alluring laugh'.
16. See R Bleier, *Science and Gender: A Critique of Biology and Its Theories on Women* (New York: Pergamon Press, 1984).
17. See generally Janet Sayers, *Biological Politics: Feminist and Anti-Feminist Perspectives* (London/New York: Tavistock Publications, 1982), 7–42.

to the highly threatening alternative of cultural relativism.[18] Wilson deemed the price of setting social arrangements against the biological domain in order to garner sexual equality was too great.[19] Hence, nature was not merely something to which women *do* conform but was something to which they *must* conform—not merely for their own well-being but for the broader well-being of society.

Ethology and children

Consequently, a measure of culpability is attached to women where societal cohesion and especially paediatric development are disrupted. Women become responsible not only for having children but also for refraining from such activities as might compromise the wellbeing of their offspring.[20]

Moreover, the evaluation of responsibility reverts to the naturally invested dimorphism of gender. 'The bodies of . . . infants serve as sites where biological and cultural notions of gender clash.'[21] The infant becomes the criterion whereby the (adult) female is judged (by adult male!), as well as locating in itself the perpetuation of gendered differentiation. The infant is thus the battlefield where the dimorphic hierarchies are reinforced.[22]

Survival as dependent on universal, hierarchical dualism

Some adjustment to the politicising reductionism of sociobiology has followed critique.[23] Sociobiology has been reformulated on a gene-culture co-evolution where each has significant impact upon the other. However, this in no way compromises the survival quest. In fact, it intensifies it, or, as Wilson would have it, it has liberated 'deep pools of talent'. It fortifies the claim that universals or near-universals have emerged in culture.[24] These 'universals' he considers to be shaped

18. Eibl-Eibesfeldt, 501—thus revealing a value judgement as the basis for reputed scientific objectivity.
19. Wilson, *On Human Nature*, 148.
20. RL Trivers, 'Parental Investment and Sexual Selection', in B Campbell (editor), *Sexual Selection and the Descent of Man 1871–1971* (Chicago: Aldine, 1972), 174.
21. The Editors 'Introduction', in Laslett, *et al* (editors), *Gender and Scientific Authority*, 13.
22. See Sayers' criticism of the deposition of biological universalism on particularist human relations: *Biological Politics*, 60.
23. Wilson's recent work, *Consilience*, has one reference to feminism (215).
24. *Ibid,* 149, 216, 217.

substantially along the structuralist lines promoted by Claude Lévi-Strauss. Wilson imagines an extra-terrestrial visitor observing the parallels between animal and human behaviour, and recognising (agreeing!) that dominance-hierarchies are integral to both.[25]

There are direct correlations that flow from the insistence that dyadic polarisations are not merely cultural but biologically based—what he calls the 'dyadic instinct'.[26] The examples he provides are in-group and out-group, child versus adult, kin versus non-kin, married versus single, sacred and profane, heaven and earth, good and evil. As such, the taboos and rituals that reinforce the boundaries between these dualities are similarly coeval with universal biology.[27] Furthermore, they all have their fundamental expression in the male-female dichotomy. The implication therefore is that the differentiation of humanity must be hierarchically rather than cooperatively (or otherwise) arranged.

The control of space

For Wilson and Lorenz, the innate aggressiveness and physical strength of the male spawns and sustains this hierarchy,[28] (as also others, such as

25. *Ibid,* 259.
26. *Ibid,* 153. By contrast, the sociologist, Bryan Turner, credits bipolar thought to Christianity and industrialisation, and whether right or wrong, relativises the claims made for such structural patterns: *The Body and Society* (London: Sage Publications, second edition, 1996), 51. Note also Richard Bernstein, *Beyond Objectivism and Relativism: Science, Hermeneutics and Praxis* (Oxford: Basil Blackwell, 1983), who mounts a thorough critique of dichotomous thinking in scientific method.
27. Feminist responses to a binary epistemology vary. Some have rejected the schema entirely: see Schüssler Fiorenza, *Discipleship of Equals*, 362, V Plumwood, *Feminism and the Mastery of Nature* (New York: Routledge, 1993), 43. Others have seen the potential that alterity can hold as a starting point for the construction of alternative realities: see A Monro, *Resurrecting Erotic Transgression: Subjecting Ambiguity in Theology* (London / Oakville: Equinox, 2006), especially chapters 3–5.
28. K Lorenz, *On Aggression* (New York: Bantam Books, 1969), 44, Wilson, *Consilience*, 170, DR Omark, FF Strayer and DG Freedman (editors), *Dominance Relations: An Ethological View of Human Conflict and Social Interaction* (New York: Garland Press, 1980). Alison Wylie points out how this actually had implications for the academic sphere that provided these results; there is, she claims, a 'masculinist view of science' that affects the decisions as to what is studied, who studies and how, with direct implications for how women are characterised, who are in or wish to enter the field: 'Good Science, Bad Science, or Science

kin/tribe)[29] just as in the ancient world the polarity of strong/weak was predicated on male/female differentiation in nature. This had direct correlations in the territorial sphere, such that place became feminine space[30]—to be controlled, guarded and its fertility preserved against encroachment.[31] In his section 'Special Properties of Dominance Orders', Wilson repeatedly draws parallels between animal (especially primate) and human behaviours. The 'Xenophobia Principle', 'The Peace of Strong Leadership', 'The Will to Power', 'Social Inertia' and 'Nested Hierarchies' all have their human expressions, such that he can conclude:

> to dominate is to possess priority of access to the necessities of life and reproduction. This is not a circular definition: it is a statement of a strong correlation observed in nature . . . this power actually raises the genetic fitness of the animals possessing it.[32]

Wilson does not operate at mere description. There are political (and, he would argue, ecological) implications authorising resistance to certain practices or proposals. He announces the 'absence of any species that shows reversal of the sex roles, wherein females court the males, and then leave them to care for the young'[33] Feminist sociobiologists would question the sweeping claim providing the basic premise,[34] but the assumption of a universal and irrefutable *transtemporal* reality unmistakably lurks here. It has been called the 'naturalist' fallacy.

Unlike ancient ethology however, nature is not construed as subject to cosmic determination; rather the converse is asserted. Either way, religious and natural realities reinforce one another. The god(s) are inherently irresistible—the male simply illustrates this by relation to

---

as Usual? Feminist Critiques of Science', in LD Hager (editor), *Women in Human Evolution* (London: Routledge, 1997), 29–51.

29. Eibl-Eibesfeldt, 367.
30. M Franzmann, 'The City as Woman: The Case of Babylon in Isaiah 47', in *ABR* 43 (1995): 1–9.
31. Wilson, *Sociobiology*, 274–285.
32. *Ibid*, 286–287.
33. *Ibid*, 456.
34. Sperling, 'Baboons with Briefcases', 364–390, MS McDonald Pavelka, 'Sexual Nature: What Can We Learn from a Cross-Species Perspective?', in PR Abramson and SD Pinkerton (editors), *Sexual Nature: Sexual Culture* (Chicago/London: University of Chicago Press, 1995), 17–36.

the female. Patriarchy therefore becomes the inevitable consequence of 'natural' proclivities. This has economic, spatial as well as social implications—the ancient male preserve of the hunt (whether human or animal)[35] becomes transformed into wage-earning capacity:

> the women and children remain in the residential area while the men forage for game or its symbolic equivalent in the form of barter or money.[36]

The male and control of/by logos

Wilson seeks to reclaim the realm of the *logos* as belonging inextricably to the same realm as that of the aggressive male. In his claim that 'No barrier stands between the material world of science and the sensibilities of the hunter and the poet',[37] he privileges the control of the animal and of the literary as belonging together—just as in the ancient world, although differently configured.[38]

Thus he can even assert that metaphor becomes a crucial player in the continued survival and adaptability of the species precisely because metaphor opens up multiple possibilities and referents in its usage![39] On this understanding, metaphor (serving whatever purpose) becomes tied to male dominance as a guarantee of the future. The multiplicity of referents said to constitute metaphor allows decisions/adaptations to be made which narrow those referents to those lines of development favoured by those able to promote their own future. The connection between nature and language thus becomes forged, in this instance deliberately.[40]

Language, control and ethological confi/ormation

However, this connection had already been prepared through the incorporation of literary devices into scientific presentations, fudging

35. Instances of the female of the species as the primary hunter are dismissed as inconsequential to the general homology: see Sayers, *Biological Politics*, 78–79.
36. Wilson, *Sociobiology*, 553.
37. Wilson, *Consilience*, 237.
38. See the discussion of 'the Man of Reason' as a 'gendered' not 'generic' phrase by Susan Hekman, *Gender and Knowledge: Elements of a Postmodern Feminism* (Oxford: Polity Press, 1990), 33–39.
39. Wilson, *Consilience*, 218–219.
40. Support for the biological origins of language have been claimed from Noam Chomsky's linguistic studies (Lorenz, *Foundations*, 11), with associated claims to the universality of (gendered) grammar rules (Eibl-Eibesfeldt, 127).

boundaries whilst claiming unity and objectivity. Konrad Lorenz appropriated the proverb as reinforcing scientific observations about the mule: 'the mule is *proverbially* surefooted because it has inherited some of the donkey's capabilities.'[41] In this turn of phrase, literary inheritances and animal homologies 'naturally' bolster and 'prove' the other.[42] When stereotypes become written at the level of the essentials of nature therefore, the possibility of alteration is precluded. This is precisely the connection made by Paolo Mantegazza who finds in proverbs 'the first germs of the embryonic substance which later yield materials for a new science'.[43]

Eibl-Eibesfeldt sees language as conferring the basis for objective communication,[44] thereby buttressing such claims. One of the ironies of the discipline of ethology occurs right at this point. At the very heart of the discipline are weighty tomes, mountains of words defending the connections between human beings and animals. Even though the huge syntactical gap between the two is explicable in terms of the accelerant which language delivered to the evolutionary process,[45] the word remains the medium of control—'the record of the action of the spirit on matter, the record of the power of voice on matter'.[46]

Accordingly, revised modes of experimentation and observation will be insufficient to relativise the universal claims of much ethological writing. The challenge must also be made at the confusion between linguistics and phenomenalism—that is between the *statement* that it is so and that *it is so*.[47]

Exposing the role of language in ethology

Language therefore must be cited as a primary mechanism of control—both *Cave Canem* and *Have Canis* derive from the foundational power of naming, systematising and manipulating. It is no coincidence that one ancient analogy of the hierarchical relationship between male and

41. Lorenz, *Foundations*, 321 (my emphasis).
42. S Harding, *The Science Question in Feminism* (New York: Cornell University Press, 1986), 233–239.
43. Mantegazza, 2.
44. Eibl-Eibesfeldt, 532.
45. Lorenz, *Foundations*, 343.
46. E Scarry, *The Body in Pain: The Making and Unmaking of the World* (New York and Oxford: Oxford University Press, 1985), 196.
47. Paul de Man calls this confusion 'ideology' and, because it is cast in literary terms, requires as one instrument of refutation, a literary counter: *The Resistance to Theory* (Manchester: Manchester University Press, 1986), 11.

female was, respectively, the imprinting stylus and the *tabula rasa*.[48] The chain that accompanies the dog in one work of art and the absence of it in another *both* depend on the prior assertion of logocentric control. This language is not merely or even primarily the language of biological scientific enquiry. In fact, it is more likely that such enquiry is *subsequent* to another language,[49] governed by it in its driving concerns and values, and shaped thereby in its conclusions.[50]

Literary forms which carefully, aesthetically, and popularly inscribe such understandings, act as key mechanisms for the reinforcement of a passive acceptance of the inevitability of the description. They benefit from the exchange with nature in that nature-as-immutable is seen as reinforcing the literary form of which it is an allusive part. A further potency is added by the form's disappearance in the mists of antiquity: the inability to trace its genealogy only reinforces the appearance of natural order.

As Peter Berger points out, the ancient literary forms and stories—myths, legends, proverbs and maxims—are a key means of legitimation of a socially (and one might add here: biologically) constructed world. Moreover, where necessary, they provide a key mechanism for the restoration of that world when any disruption occurs.[51] The inclusion, within such forms, of elements from the natural world adduces the 'naturalness' and therefore the 'rightness' of both the resource and the agency of the form. Thus, from the earliest period, claims Seneca, 'we give children proverbs—what the Greeks call *chriai*—to learn off by heart, since a childish mind which cannot yet comprehend anything more can nevertheless grasp such proverbs'.[52] Nature thereby becomes colonised into the service of culture (yet again), or, as Wilson express it (in demonstration of my argument), Dionysian impulses are subjected to Apollonian control.[53]

48. See duBois, *Sowing the Body*, 130-166.
49. Just as Mantegazza suggested.
50. Angela M O'Rand, 'Scientific Thought Style and the Construction of Gender Inequality', in JF O'Barr (editor), *Women and a New Academy: Gender and Cultural Contexts* (Wisconsin: University of Wisconsin Press, 1989), 118.
51. *The Sacred Canopy: Social Reality of Religion* (Harmondsworth: Penguin, 1973), 13–14, 39–41.
52. Sen *Ep* 33.7.
53. *Consilience*, 216.

Communication besides language

However, the force of comparison of animal and human behavioural patterns expands the ancient questioning as to what if any intelligence lay in animals. The evolutionary significance of language, by a study of its progenitors in the broader animal world, has been complicated by careful mapping of gestures, expressions, movements and non-syntactical vocalisations. Functional analogies between humans and animals have been deduced,[54] frequently privileged with universalist claims.[55]

Whilst the level of modern analysis may be more systematic, the recognition of the connection between non-verbal and verbal realms *was* well-known in antiquity, not the least being the mystique that attached to certain animals' prescience of the future.[56] Rhetoric included more than the manipulation of verbal constructions, according to the handbooks,[57] and there appears to have been considerable exchange between actors and orators about gestures and expressiveness.[58] Even non-verbal vocalisations were noted as having an immense power to communicate.[59]

Dimorphism and communication

Ethology has reinforced the primary dimorphic analysis at the level of communication as well. Thus females mimic rather than invent;[60] females have a primary role in relation to the young, but not to the adult.[61] Eibl-Eibesfeldt unwittingly discloses the presumptions governing his detailed analysis. In his reference to the function of the smile in infants, he cites the legend of Cypselus, who became the ruler of Corinth. As a baby, Cypselus thwarted his ten assassins by smiling at them. Eibl-Eibesfeldt immediately follows this story with

54. Eibl-Eibesfeldt, 159. The role of gestures in the animal world was also noted and commented upon by the ancients: see *Gospel of Pseudo-Matthew* 36.
55. Eibl-Eibesfeldt, 455.
56. Plut *Mor* 975a–b.
57. Cic *De Or* 59.220, Quint *Inst* 1.11.15–19.
58. Quint *Inst* 1.11.1–14, 2.13.9–13, 2.15.7–9, 11.3.91; *cf* Arist *Poet* 17.3 (1455a).
59. Cic *De Or* 53.227, Lucret *Nat Rer* 5.1041–1090, Athen *Deip* 3c; *cf* Longin 39.1–3.
60. Eibl-Eibesfeldt, 487. This is a striking parallel to Xenophon's Isomachus who tells Socrates how he trained his wife in the management of his estate (*Oecon* 6.17–10.13).
61. Eibl-Eibesfeldt, 445f.

the comment: 'It is a fact that the smile releases delight in the mother, even those who initially were indifferent, and aids in the establishment of a strong emotional tie.'[62] He omits to say that the story has *male* assassins.[63] His appeal to an ancient literary account is designed to illustrate and buttress the subsequent claim, conveniently editing out any difficulties that the story might engender for his larger artifice. Writing and reading of 'the laws of nature [are] through the lens of social relations'.[64]

Moreover, the notion that there are essential differences between the sexes has remained, though not as rudimentary as denying innate reason to the female. Wilson has eagerly seized upon recent research that promotes the differences between male and female brains and intellectual processing as confirmation of biological stratification.[65]

Resistance of ethological enquiry to critique

This cursory sweep over the field of ethology has been guided by the demands for a methodology.[66] Nevertheless, the 'naturalness' of the natural order of things argued in ancient times has been seen as mirrored and strengthened by much contemporary ethological description.[67] 'Nature' therefore becomes a constraint on both analysis and behaviour because it generates the sensibility that material constituents and organic relationships are set.[68]

The inquiry that reaches conclusions demonstrating such immutabilities may be culturally or ideologically driven, but it remains opaque under the mask of the resultant 'universal reality', just as we have seen that certain animal epithets for women were taken

62. *Ibid,* 448.
63. Hdt *Hist* 5.92.4,5, Polyaen *Strat* 5.31t.
64. L Schiebinger, 'The Private Life of Plants: Sexual Politics in Carl Linnaeus and Erasmus Darwin', in M Benjamin (editor), *Science & Sensibility: Gender and Scientific Enquiry 1780–1945* (Oxford: Basil Blackwell, 1991), 123.
65. Wilson, *Consilience*, 215.
66. For further critique of sociobiology, the work of Edward Wilson and the scientific method, see Hekman, 118–135.
67. See generally, D Haraway, *Primate Visions: Gender, Race and Nature in the World of Modern Science* (New York/London: Routledge, 1989, reprint by Verso 1992), and her *Simians, Cyborgs and Women: The Reinvention of Nature* (London: Free Association Books, 1991).
68. Sharon McDonald, 'The Socialisation of the Natural and the Naturalisation of the Social', in S Ardener (editor), *Defining Females: The Nature of Women in Society* (Oxford/Providence: Berg, second revised edition, 1993), 189.

(asserted) as naturally applicable by male writers of late antiquity. Exposure would jeopardise the surety of the results.[69] Contingency and chaos may be in nature; they are not permitted to be present in the investigation of nature and in the conclusions drawn from its description. As Sandra Harding writes, 'The discipline of biology pays back with interest the support it borrows from the social order'.[70]

Thus cultural arrangements are made part of that 'continuous feedback process' whereby nature provides rationale and reinforcement.[71] The promethean claims of contemporary ethology over other disciplines signals a significant shift in the configuration of the nature-culture division of thought inherited from the ancient Mediterranean world. However, even as culture has been increasingly represented as subject to evolutionary and ontogenetic laws, the chief expository tool of culture—language and communication—has maintained its hegemony. The necessity of culture to articulate and thereby control nature remains, albeit now held to be subject to the same rules which it has imposed. The irony of this position is to posit an even greater immutability to the cultural expressions said to be in harmony with, and even derived from, the natural world.

Some preliminary conclusions of method

The portrayal of ethology in this section has been informed substantially by feminist responses. This is not to assume that feminist critiques have been uniform, nor that the results of ethological research and the sociobiology project have been uniformly repudiated. Early distrust from anthropologists, who were concerned to protect the 'august nature of humanity',[72] has had varied support from some feminist theorists. Both have yielded in some measure to the benefits that can be extracted from the discipline given critical suspicion, a necessary political awareness and a resistance to totalising and self-protective claims.[73]

Thus far, the survey of ethology has highlighted the significance attached to the dimorphism of gender, a differentiation that is played

69. Harding, 233–239.
70. *Ibid*, 128.
71. McDonald, 'Socialisation', 198.
72. Lorenz, *Foundations*, 338.
73. See Sayers, Hrdy *loc cit*, LB Slobodkin, 'Is History a Consequence of Evolution?', in PPG Bateson and PH Klopfer (editors), *Perspectives in Ethology, volume 3: Social Behaviour* (New York/London: Plenum Press, 1978), 233–255.

out upon the 'site' of the child. Particular characteristics and derived responsibilities are held to attach to male and female, related to the survival of the species in terms of reproduction, territorial defence, food provision and protection. Contemporary ethology, at least in the writings of one of the exemplars of the discipline, Edward Wilson, has claimed a biological base for dualistic frameworks, uses of metaphor, proverb and myth, the construction of language and the deployment of reason, a base which is anchored to the dimorphism of gender. These elements, whilst demanding (and receiving) critique, show considerable potential for guiding the analysis of the dynamics of the story of the Syrophoenician woman. There are two particular concentrations that remain to be discussed: the body and the significance of the child.

The animal and the body

Ethology does refocus attention to the importance of the body and the significance that is to be attached to the non-verbal elements of life and meaning. The problem of the dog(s) in the story may yet yield something positive precisely because, as we shall see, in the movement of the story material and bodily reality rather than the verbal, becomes privileged. As Bryan Turner writes:

> . . . images of the body as animal flesh, as artistic representation and as a forgotten narrative of religious exchange indicate the proximity of the body to metaphors of sociality.[74]

Contemporary research in many disciplines has begun to valorise the body as crucial for the understanding of identity, relationships and politics.[75] This can readily be hijacked to the conventional gendered perspective and, indeed, does suffer from a dimorphic reductionism in standard ethological discussion. Nevertheless, with careful negotiation, the potential for a different approach is offered precisely by the focus on the body as a *subjective* site for the construction of meaning.[76] But the shift must be from object to agent.[77] The body of and in itself

74. Turner, xiv.
75. See, *inter alia*, Scarry *loc cit*, E Grosz, *Volatile Bodies: Toward a Corporeal Feminism* (St Leonards, NSW: Allen and Unwin, 1994).
76. L Birke, 'Biological Sciences', in AM Jaggar and IM Young (editors), *A Companion to Feminist Philosophy* (Massachusetts and Oxford: Blackwell, 1998), 197–203.
77. McDonald, 'Socialisation', 202.

must 'speak' or, better, 'act' (which may include communication). If colonisation is not simply to be renovated by ascribing to the body through external inscription, the body must find its own mechanisms of communication.[78] Even partial success in material communicative positioning would undermine the hegemony of the word and words.

The body of the child

Secondly, the invitation to construct the site differently is extended by the figure of the daughter/child in the story. Ethology has made the infant a particular concern, if only from its commitment to the exploration of the maximisation of the 'gene pool' and its relationship to the evolutionary tenet of species survival. However, the relative ease with which comparisons and analogies can be made with animal behaviour has promoted this aspect of study, even though it *may* stand apart from the usual male/female dimorphism.[79]

There is no effort to recapture an innocence for the study of a gospel passage through the means of a child.[80] Rather it counters the mask of naiveté that has been attached to the image of the child, who yet staggers beneath the weight of both logocentric and now biocentric argument. It potentially will deliver a choice about the significance and signification of the child—the daughter in the story. Previously, in conventional and feminist studies alike, she has remained marginalised.

Problematising the word

The insights from ethology have been passed through a feminist critical grid to expose the cloaking of cultural and linguistic commitments. The combination of ethology and its critique has already suggested a means of dealing with the triangulation of nature, gender and reason. This triad has been identified as crucial to the interpretation of the story of the Syrophoenician woman (and daughter) in Mark's Gospel.

---

78. See the warnings of Veronica Brady, 'Towards a New Geography: Body of Women, Body of the World', in H Fraser and RS White (editors), *Constructing Gender: Feminism in Literary Studies* (Nedlands, WA: University of Western Australia Press, 1994), 287–301.

79. R Rorty, 'The Myth of the Given', in his *Philosophy and the Mirror of Nature* (Princeton: Princeton University Press/Oxford: Blackwell, 1980) cited by McDonald, 'Socialisation', 190.

80. Such trading in innocence has a distinct Herodian stench about it: Mk 6:21–28.

Moreover, contemporary ethology has been seen to have substantial ancient forebears.

The value-laden scientific method that presupposes and then proves a dimorphic structure to nature is substantially reinforced by the very cultural mechanisms that shape those values—the logocentric artifices of speech and writing. When animal behaviours and characteristics are found in other forms of writing, metaphorical description and behavioural comparison do more than serve homological interests. The parallel reference is taken as further proof of the natural relations and proclivities of the players. Hence, even in contemporary ethological enquiry, constant reference to cultural artefacts in ancient 'wisdom' strengthens scientific 'discovery'. Reflexively, scientific results bolster the literary legacy.

And yet, the very effort to reinforce the primacy of the *logos* by reference to nature exposes a potential fissure. The realm of the body, invaded for raw materials to build the edifice of culture and inscribed to authorise the colonisation, itself stirs a threat and alternative to the supremacy of the mind. The use of a natural metonymy (woman=dog) as a vituperative reminder of place and control signals the threat of resistance, precisely because so much attention is given to the body. Here a new justification for a review of Jesus' words is found: in the conjunction of a literary artifice with a 'scientifically' based order and in the potential for subversion because of its material focus and embodied delivery. The word of the woman may, paradoxically perhaps, lay the basis for the removal of the hegemony of the word and the establishment of the integrity and subjectivity of *two* women's bodies.

Preliminary testing of directions suggested by ethology

General considerations

The previous chapter moved from the animal comparisons in Jesus' words to the widespread use of bestial references for character vituperation. The ethological comparison directed in Mark 7:27 to the woman (αὐτῇ) and in reference to both her and her daughter (the plural τοῖς κυναρίοις), harbours particular menace. Unlike other words of Jesus in Mark's Gospel, this is the only occasion where an explicit equation of the animal and human realm occurs with apparent reproachful intent.[81] The contrast cuts more sharply when the contrasting laudatory simile of sheep in the first feeding story is recalled (6:34).[82] Aelian considered that the particular attribute of sheep is that they are taught by nature to submit to being ruled.[83] This coheres extremely well with the common Hebrew collation of King-Shepherd and Kingdom-Sheep. The reminder is prompted by the evangelist's own craft—that layered pastoral scene is evoked through the *Stichwort* (χορτασθῆναι 7:27 ἐχορτάσθησαν 6:42) and through the etymology of the word itself. Even at the end of the second century CE, χορτάζω retained its associations with feeding animals. 'Foddered' is one translation that captures the sense.[84]

Legion and the Syrophoenician woman

There is a more confronting contrast. There was a common (Jewish) collation of swine and dogs, as seen in Matthew 7:6.[85] If the

81. There may be negative bestial *allusions* however. Some have seen the name of the spirits possessing the demoniac—Legion—as a thinly veiled reference to the Roman occupiers of Syro-Palestine, which might then be connected with the herd of swine: JDM Derrett, 'Contributions to the Study of the Gerasene Demoniac', in *JSNT* 3 (1979): 2–17, and Ched Myers, *Binding the Strong Man: A Political Reading of Mark's Story of Jesus* (Maryknoll, NY: Orbis, 1988), 190–194. The 'den (σπηλαίον) of terrorists' in 11:17 may be metonymy for lions, serpents or other wild animals.
82. *Cf* Mk 14:27 = Zech 13:7.
83. Ael *NA* 7.27.
84. Athen *Deip* 96f, CB Gulick's translation in the Loeb edition. The context in Athenaeus suggests a comic intent, but this is not the only setting; *cf* Derrett, 'Law in the New Testament', 172–173n8.
85. Is 66:3 LXX, 1 En 89:42, b*Shab* 155b, GT 93, *P Oxy* 840, 2 Pet 2.22. This extended to the less literary realm: see J Naveh and S Shaked, *Amulets and Magic Bowls: Aramaic Incantations of Late Antiquity* (Jerusalem: Magnes Press, 1985), 200-201. AL Connolly adds a further link: ' . . . dogs are frequently mentioned in parallel with pigs and prostitutes.' (*NDIEC* 4.158.) Marc Philonenko sees in Matthew 7:6 a parallel with 4QMMT B 58–62, and finds the explanation in the imagery of the holy camp, outside of which prowl the dogs constantly threatening the purity of the sacrifices. It is not merely that the dogs are unclean of themselves, but that they actively menace the sanctity of the persons and practices of those within: '"Dehors les chiens" (Apocalypse 22.16 et 4SMMT B 58-62)', in *NTS* 43 (1997): 450. See especially, H von Lips, 'Schweine füttert man, Hunde nicht: Ein Versuch, das Rätsel von Matthäus 7,6 zu lösen', in *ZNW* 79 (1988): 180. The dog and pig were alike renowned for gluttony in Greek literature—see Aristoph *Pax* 24 *cf* Plat *Euth* 298d.

Syrophoenician pericope be interpreted as a mission aetiology,[86] and the woman is collated with a dog, then one might expect that the *first* venture into gentile territory in Mark 5:1–20[87] would have the supplicant characterised in porcine terms.[88] But Mark's narrative does *not* confer any homology between the person and the pig. The only commonality granted is at the level of uncleanness (the pigs, v 11, by correlation with Leviticus 11:7–8 *etc*, and the 'unclean spirit', v 2).[89] The demoniac himself is distinguished from swine, which are made to bear the double burden of their own (classified) nature and their demon relatives. Unclean spirits and unclean animals can be equated.[90]

---

86. Elizabeth Schüssler Fiorenza cites Matthew 7:6 as an important cross-reference for understanding the use of 'dogs' in the Canaanite/ Syrophoenician story: *In Memory*, 137.
87. Elizabeth Malbon recognises this earlier mission of Jesus into gentile territory, and the discomfort that this delivers to the standard reading of the Syrophoenician pericope; however she does not depart from the traditional mission reading, seeking merely to graft into it some element of gender (word plus faith): 'Fallible Followers: Women and Men in the Gospel of Mark', in *Semeia* 28 (1983): 37. Mary Ann Tolbert however, notes that the key distinctive between the Legion account and the Syrophoenician story turns on gender: 'Mark', in CA Newsom and SH Ringe (editors), *The Women's Bible Commentary* (London: SPCK, 1992), 269.
88. The collation was possible. Cicero reportedly retorted to the intent of Caecilius, a Jewish sympathiser, to prosecute Verres for his corrupt praetorship in Sicily, by asking, 'What has a Jew to do with swine?' The force of the witticism turns on a pun on Verres name—*verres* means male boar; see Plut *Vit (Cicero)* 7.6; *cf* Hom *Od* 10.235–243 where Circe turns Odysseus' men into swine. 'Pig' was readily turned to abuse for example, Plaut *Mil* 1058, Xen *Mem* 1.2.30.
89. Mark resolutely portrays evil throughout the Gospel by a socio-religious geography of pollution, sometimes awkwardly embellishing received traditions (such as 9:25); see my 'The Hermeneutics of Purity in Mark's Gospel: Considerations for the AIDS Debate', in *Pacifica* 5 (1992): 145–169.
90. Richard Bauckham's 'lesser of two evils' interpretation of the story is unsatisfactory, directed as it is by the interests of apologetics: 'the destruction of the pigs is preferable to the destruction of a human personality.' He wants to provide a christian expression for an animal liberation agenda, but does so by promoting an anti-semitic and ahistorical Jesus. Whilst his observations about the demonic needing a place to stay are generally accurate, he rides over the classificatory system of pollutions that shapes Mark's heuristics, and pays no attention to the dyadic homology infecting the gender subdivision of 'human superiority to animals'. In consequence, his criticism of Augustine's adoption of the Stoic division between rational humans and irrational

The collation does not (must not?) extend to the one possessed (τὸν δαιμονιζόμενον / ὁ δαιμονισθείς vv 15, 18).[91]

Any apologetic efforts to elide or mollify the offence of Jesus' words in Mark 7:27 must, in the light of this prior excursion beyond Judaic territory, falter at the shocking collation of *women* and dogs in this pericope. Legion is a *man* (ἄνθρωπος 5:2), confirmed by an ample distribution of masculine markers and gender specific participles. Gender identification now becomes a crucial element in this overall narrative section (4:35–8:26).[92] Jesus speaks to *him* (ἔλεγεν γὰρ αὐτῷ 5:8) and he speaks to *her* (καὶ ἔλεγεν αὐτῇ 7:27); the former is omitted from an animal homology; the latter receives a full bestial collation.

Male is preserved from the unclean (animal and demon); female is melded. The dualism is clear. Lurking in the background, though not mentioned by Mark, is the bestial collation between *pigs* and women that *resists* any confusion with the male. The evocation of the connection wandered the gamut from the metaphor of gluttony to the euphemism/metonymy of the pudenda.[93] The Latin pastoral poet, Varro, expressly equated pig with a woman's nature.[94] Hence, the pig, in Legion's story, is *counter* to the man.

---

animals returns to haunt his own solution: 'Jesus and the Animals I: What did he Teach?', in A Linzey and D Yamamoto (editors), *Animals on the Agenda: Questions about Animals for Theology and Ethics* (London: SCM, 1998), 47–48. For an alternate and more nuanced (though still ungendered) understanding of Jewish appreciations of animals, which recognises an equation between animals and humans (mainly Gentiles) see S Stern, *Jewish Identity in Early Rabbinic Writings* (Leiden: EJ Brill, 1994), 33–40.

91. The relation of a person to a demon does not necessarily attract a bestial epithet, especially when the possessed is seen as a victim or vicarious representative; compare P Hollenbach, 'Jesus, Demoniacs, and Public Authorities: A Socio-Historical Study', in *JAAR* 49 (1981): 572–582, especially 581–582.
92. Tolbert, 'Mark', 269.
93. See Prov 11:22, Athen *Deip* 650e, Epict *Disc* 2.4. ASF Gow and DL Page provided an extended note to the porcine associations of prostitution: *The Greek Anthology: Hellenistic Epigrams* (Cambridge: Cambridge University Press, 1965), 267 (see *GA* 11.363.5). See also JN Adams, *The Latin Sexual Vocabulary* (Baltimore: Johns Hopkins University Press, 1982), 82, 139, Keuls, *Phallus*, 353–357, and duBois, *Sowing the Body*, 156–157. 'Dog' could also be used in such a fashion (*GA* 5.105). These associations survived unchallenged in Christian tradition: see Grant, *Early Christians and Animals*, 6–7.
94. *RR* 2.4.9–10.

The singular reproach of the woman

Thus, (the) woman is isolated for reproach in two ways. Firstly, she is contrasted with the affirmative homology of men and animals in the figure of sheep. Whatever may be the semantic force of the opening phrase of Jesus' words in 7:27, the *Stichwort* χορτασθῆναι mentioned above invites an equation between τὰ τέκνα and the 5000 beneficiaries in 6:44—who are expressly designated: ἄνδρες. The benign *male* 'sheep' are suitable recipients for compassion (6:34); the woman is not. Indeed, the only narrative antecedent for τέκνον is ὁ παραλυτικός (2:5)[95]—also male, like the sheep of the first feeding.[96]

Secondly, the woman is implicitly set apart by the resistance to any negative equation between a man and beasts in the story of Legion. For this woman, there is no positive animal; any bestial connotation will be coloured with uncivilised and rank hues. Any challenge to this connection will be difficult, given the alliance between narrator and hero, as portrayed here. In the story, any resistance hangs on the woman's word and her daughter's act—but this is to signal an ethical challenge and political subversion unfolded in later chapters. For the moment, Mark's narrative falls under the overweening shadow of the deterministic and metaphysical conclusions of the discipline of ethology in its ancient expression.

Dimorphism and dualisms

The standard dimorphism in both ancient and modern ethology sets a foundation stone for an expansive dyadic classification, which privileges male over against female through a series of other valorised members of pairs.[97] The most potent pair as we have seen was rational

95. Robert Gundry rejects the suggestion that τέκνα in 7:27 refers to Jews generally (as from the first feeding), applying it rather to the disciples (*cf* 10:24). He argues that the preferred word for Jews would be υἱοί, a distinction unsupported by Pauline usage and a highly dubious proposition for Mark (see 2:5, 10:29, 12:19, 13:12). That he even finds the disciples present in the Syrophoenician pericope reflects the continued influence of Matthew's version on Markan interpretation (in spite of Gundry's own repudiation of such contamination); see his *Mark: A Commentary on His Apology for the Cross* (Grand Rapid: Eerdmans, 1993), 373, 375.

96. Duncan Derrett cites, approvingly, RL Lindsey's translation of Mark as distinguishing 'sons' in Jesus' words from 'children' in the woman's reply: 'Law in the New Testament', 165n5.

97. For Aristotle, 'male' and 'female' are the primary example of a binary opposition (*Meta* 1.5 (986b)); he draws on an ethological base for the decision. There is a neat summary of Stoic dyadic classifications in Plut

and (versus) irrational, *logos* and (versus) *thêr* (beast). In the ancient world, the divine bond with reason was unassailable. In this quite rigid dichotomous system, female was formatted on the underprivileged side, that is: Legion and (versus) the Syrophoenician woman. Through this perspective, it may be offensive that the woman was collated with a dog; it is thoroughly explicable within the cosmology of Jesus and the evangelist.

Once this is allowed, there can be no room for dogmatic and apologetic approaches which can only forge Jesus' salvation by repudiating the world of his day—admittedly so often the basis for christian apologetic. Bill Loader's recognition of a conservative Jesus accents that Jesus was formed by the value systems of his day.[98] However the value system runs beyond a racial antipathy; attitudes to females and animals are caught into the knot binding the woman and the dog.

Gender difference as primary in ethology

The use of the animal world to construct a natural order, which securely situates the woman in a position that she is expected passively to accept, remains unaddressed. The collation of the *woman* and the dog needs to be confronted. The presumed, and oft-repeated, reviling of gentiles as 'dogs' by Jews is an 'axiom' built on sand anyway.[99] It owes more to subsequent centuries of christian anti-semitism than a concern to reconstruct first century attitudes. This is not to dispute that gentiles, even as a group, could be labelled as dogs (and probably with racist overtones) but rather to question the assumption of exclusive congruency between the two in Jewish slander. Not only could 'dog'

Mor 960b-c. Jewish constructions agreed: Jos *C Ap* 2.201. The tenacity of this organising methodology is shown in its continued operation in contemporary societies: see Bennett, *Belted Heroes*, 138n64, referring to a rural Greek village.

98. W Loader, 'Challenged at the Boundaries: A Conservative Jesus in the Markan Tradition', in *JSNT* 63 (1996): 45-61; *cf* L Schottroff, *Lydia's Impatient Sisters: A Feminist Social History of Early Christianity* translated by B and M Rumscheidt (London: SCM, 1995), 15. The danger of slipping into an historicist reading of a 'conservative Jesus' too early, however, is that Mark's literary artifice may be prematurely stymied.

99. A-J Levine, *The Social and Ethnic Dimensions of Matthean Salvation History* (Lewiston: Edwin Mellen, 1988), 147–150.

connote more than merely gentile; 'dog' could also be used of Jews and by Jews, of their own.[100]

Some have allowed the racial denigration to remain either by arguing that Jesus is a type of a later ecclesiology resistant to gentile claims upon the gospel (thus avoiding the particularity of the female-engendered text) or by accenting the personal growth of Jesus through the boundary-crossing encouraged by others. Again, there is a failure to address the difficult problem raised by the shift from a discussion of a request by a woman for release for her daughter to that about dogs eating bread. Indeed, to make the story operate in such a fashion allows both anti-semitism and misogyny to collaborate. Thus John Chrysostom affirmed gentile supercessionism as the main emphasis of the story, but unrepentantly found dominical approval for his contention that the woman *was* a dog and her daughter, a dog of a dog.[101]

Ethology seeks ancient (literary) authority

The primacy of gender to the story, which an ethological perspective highlights, does not preclude other factors that have received more elaborate attention—such as race, territorial transgression, self-preservation and survival. These are all encompassed within ethology. Nevertheless, the fundamental assertion of ancient and modern ethology is the division of the sexes.

---

100. The demur by I Abrahams *Studies in Pharisaism and the Gospels* (Cambridge: Cambridge University Press, 1924), volume 2, 195, and CG Montefiore *The Synoptic Gospels* (New York: KTAV reprinted second edition, 1968), 167 has not been widely heard. But see WD Davies and DC Allison *A Critical and Exegetical Commentary on The Gospel According to St Matthew* (ICC), (Edinburgh: T&T Clark, 3 volumes, 1991), volume 1, 675 who suggest that 'dog' was a *general* term of contempt. Consequently, efforts to draw on the *Targum Neofiti* on Exodus 22:30 where gentile and dog are likened, as a generic first century formula, are suspect. Jesus is taken as changing his attitude (if he ever really held it)—that attitude being interpreted as being forged in his Jewish environment rather than in his own person: see R Le Déaut, 'Targumic Literature and New Testament Interpretation', in *BTB* 4 (1974): 247.

101. John Chrysostom *The Canaanite* 52.457.43, *On the Spread of the Gospel* 51.319.56. Does Chrysostom allude to a proverb in his assignment of additional dialogue to the woman: 'you call me a dog, as I keep a dog?' Gerald Downing reframes the entire Chrysostom homily as a Cynic exchange, failing to recognise the ethological background: *Cynics and Christian Origins* (Edinburgh: T&T Clark, 1992), 293.

Thus, however useful may be Gerd Theissen's exposition (prompted by the reference to Tyre in Mark 7:24) of Jewish-Tyrian relations in the first century CE, his concentration on militaristic and economic interests is flawed from an ethological perspective. Such factors are *ancillary* to the primary dyad, that of gender. He makes no reference at all to Tyrian women, whether by stereotypical or historical analysis.[102]

By its very existence as an intellectual discipline, ethology authenticates itself in connection with this primary division. Thus, at the level of reason, language and communication, the exponents of ethology privilege their own position within their discipline. Given that the ancient pedagogy and much of the rise of modern ethology lay in the hands of men, it comes as no surprise that the primary division was unequal, for *logos* and speech were joined to the male.

The appeal to the natural world did not gain its primary weight *from* the world of nature but *by the logocentric construction of nature*. In this sense, the order of nature owed as much to its explication as to any intrinsic systematics. Of course, this lies at the heart of feminist criticism of contemporary ethological determinism; but, in ancient constructions, this was both asserted and assumed without embarrassment.

Accordingly, alongside the exposition of the animal world, the ancients readily made observations about human society and spliced literary quotations into their scientific teachings. Such evidence of the force of their *logos* was made the more authoritative when longevity was attested, for antiquity bore witness to the atemporal universality of any assertion. Hence, stereotypes (the frequent anchor for anyone or anything in the ancient world[103]) and familiar forms and constructions of language (the persuasive edge of communication[104]) were far more than mere adornment of a scientific work—they demonstrated the veracity of the writer and his (*sic*) analysis.

102. *The Gospels in Context: Social and Political History in the Synoptic Tradition* translated by Linda M Maloney, (Minneapolis: Fortress Press, 1991), 61–75. This is not from want of a variety of evidence, as subsequent chapters will show.

103. BJ Malina and J Neyrey, *Portraits of Paul: An Archaeology of Ancient Personality* (Louisville, KY: W/JKP, 1996), 169–174.

104. See BH Fowler, *The Hellenistic Aesthetic* (Madison WN: University of Wisconsin Press, 1989), 110–136, on the interconnection between the artistic and the scientific.

. . . and authority is repaid
Conversely, a handbook on oratory and rhetoric could regularly contain appeals to nature to demonstrate recommendations about good style. On the one hand, art and civilisation were celebrated as cultivating nature to a level of productivity that it would never achieve by itself. Oratory, claimed Quintilian in hyperbolic eloquence, was essentially the civilisation of nature.[105] On the other, certain structural and rhythmical elements were regarded as correct and persuasive precisely because they were in accord with nature. Again, Quintilian betrays the ethological foundation of his enterprise when he writes of 'another order [of words] which is natural (*est et alius naturalis ordo*)' and hence to be preferred to the reverse sequence. His examples unveil the standard, emphatic, gendered, dyadic formula: 'man and woman, day and night, rising and setting'.[106]

Recognising an ethological perspective in the words of Jesus

An awareness of an ethological perspective, combined with a suspicion of ethology's technique of reliance upon literary reinforcement as part of its defence of dominant cultural and political values, restores a sense of the critical importance of the saying of Jesus. This might appear to perpetuate the analysis of the modern period that has so strongly concentrated on the word(s) of Jesus. However, an ethological perspective demands that behavioural comparisons be noted which might warrant the (stereotyped) equation of the woman and the dog. Conversely, a suspicion of ethology's techniques alerts us to ask questions of the saying of Jesus (its form as well as its content) that may be designed to bolster the force of the saying in the narrative context.

Four constituent elements of enquiry
Subsequent chapters (3 to 5) will explore four constituents, suggested by the ethological analysis previously outlined. These offer some potential for interpretation of the saying of Jesus and the Syrophoenician woman in relation to its narrative and cultural contexts. They are:

i) the conjunction of scientific/philosophical axioms with cultural values reinforced through long-standing literary expression,

105. *Inst* 9.3.3–4.
106. *Ibid,* 9.4.24.

ii) the moral implications which attach to the inferior partner categorised in any hierarchical exchange,
iii) the territorial boundaries which afford spatial protection for dominant and submissive entities, and
iv) the socio-political conclusions which assert a foundation in the natural order.

These four elements will guide much of the analysis of Jesus' words and the woman's reply. However, two further identifications have been made through the critique of previous scholarship on the Syrophoenician woman and through elements that contemporary ethology raises that will need to be addressed, namely, a focus on the role(s) of the body and the child in the story. These provide a caveat on this renewed though different concentration on the word (of Jesus and/or the woman). That caveat ultimately becomes a caveat on the universalist 'lunge' of the word, precisely because the body demands a situated perspective having its own expression. This understanding of the body stands against its reduction to a site for encryption by *logos* fantasies and logocentric controls (such as motherhood and childhood). Rather it challenges the promethean ambition of the word to exist supreme over, and apart from, the body.

3

Dog in a Manger
The Ethological Words of Jesus

Introduction

Four constituent elements of enquiry from the perspective of ethology were isolated in chapter 2 as pertinent for the analysis of the saying of Jesus. These are:

i) the conjunction of scientific/philosophical axioms with cultural values reinforced through long-standing literary expression,
ii) the moral implications which attach to the inferior partner categorised in any hierarchical exchange,
iii) the territorial boundaries which afford spatial protection for dominant and submissive entities, and
iv) the socio-political conclusions which assert a foundation in the natural order.

These will guide the analysis in the chapters of this section. This chapter concentrates on the first of these elements—the conjunction of science and culture through literary reinforcement. The ethological foundation of dimorphism is established from the beginning of the Markan narrative for the delivery of the proverb. This gendered dynamic must guide the analysis of the saying given to Jesus, even in its detail. The recognition of the fundamental form—proverb—provides a deliberate, traditional adjunct to the appeal to nature ('dogs') contained within the saying and adds considerable authority to an unimpeachable judgment. As Foley observes, a proverb 'embeds the specifics of a particular situation in the overarching traditional network that informs all individual moments. It builds a bridge between the particular and the generic, the momentary and the tradition.'[1] The intricate analysis

1. JM Foley, *How to Read an Oral Poem* (Urbana: University of Illinois Press, 2002), 106.

of the proverb and the additions given to it establish that Jesus' words are uncompromisingly abusive of the Syrophoenician and dismissive of her request.

The valorisation of a literary form

Observations about the fundamental form and its embellishment in the saying of the character, Jesus, are not designed to perpetuate the familiar, atomistic concerns of form criticism. Rather, the object is to expose the attempted coherence between intellectual disciplines (such as literature and ethology or physiognomy), which posits a unified witness to/from the cosmic order. Scientific theory thus becomes 'ideologically linked with non-scientific views in earlier texts',[2] each reinforcing the other, the political dimensions never far away.

Since ancient and modern ethology seek to cultivate a tonal register of almost metaphysical antiquity about the discipline, the use of any long-attested characteristic conducive to ethological assertion is strategically appropriate. Thus the identification of forms, rhythms and literary complements enables us to perceive the encompassing nature of the argument in 7:27 and better prepares us to assess its place in the narrative. The very breadth of aspects touched in such a brief saying itself promotes the sense of universal reality which the ethological comparison of woman and animal assumes and replicates. In this sense, the narrative introduction directs the comparison, since it rests on the cosmic authorisation of the male.

A man addresses a woman

The first-century Roman lecturer on oratory, Quintilian, stated: 'Language is based on reason, antiquity, authority and usage.'[3] The proper province of the human male is in the exercise of *logos*—language. Quintilian's four pillars for language circumscribe an utterance of a man living according to the *logos* that imbues the natural world. At the same time, the very act of utterance distinguishes man from the animal, which is a non-articulate participant in that natural world.[4]

2. Gillian Clark is scathing: Aristotle provided 'a reassuringly scientific explanation for common prejudices . . .': *Women in Late Antiquity*, 121.
3. Quint *Inst* 1.6.1: *sermo constat ratione vel vetustate, auctoritate, consuetudines.*
4. Colish, *Stoic Tradition,* 1.56. Quintilian claimed the power of speech distinguishes man from animal: *Inst* 12.1.2.

The collation of the woman and the dog is a reminder of (who holds) the power of language and who else, therefore, ought be submissive to it. Whilst this observation ventures to an examination of the interaction of context and proverb,[5] it nonetheless asserts that the very foundation of the proverb form and, in this case, its ethological content is, properly in ancient conception, the province of man.

The male connection with *logos* was a commonplace in ancient texts. Perictione's advice to young ladies, probably written by a male Neopythagorean disciple under a female pseudonym,[6] intoned:

> If things are sweet or bitter to her husband, she will go along with his leading; *otherwise, she would be out of harmony with her entire state*.[7]

Xenarchus tied this to the natural order: 'Are not the male cicadas a happy lot? Their females haven't a bit of voice in them.'[8] Even Plutarch and Musonius Rufus' commendation of education for women was designed to divert them from untoward conduct (such as dabbling in spells and the like)[9] to the better management of their households. Quintilian aligned the mastery of language and the well-ordered household.[10]

John Winkler warns that these renditions are little more than male 'wishlists'.[11] However, their repetition in certain biblical texts (for example, 1 Cor 14:35, 1 Tim 2:11–12) indicates how widespread such conventions were and how adoption and promotion of them by a minority group was designed to secure a place within wider, often-suspicious society, by accepting the control and the ideological justification for it grounded in *logos*-articulated nature. The proverb was one succinct expression.

---

5. See chapter 4.
6. This is Sarah Pomeroy's judgment: *Goddesses, Whores, Wives and Slaves: Women in Classical Antiquity* (New York: Schocken, second edition, 1995), 134.
7. ἢν μὴ ἀναρμόνιος ἐς τὸ πᾶν ἔῃ: *apud* Stob *Flor* 4.28.19.84–85 (my translation).
8. *Apud* Athen *Deip* 559a. The observation on cicadas is also found in Ael *NA* 1.20.
9. Plut *Mor* 145c-d, Mus Ruf fr 3 (*That Women Too Should Study Philosophy*).
10. *Inst* 10.3.9, and compare the extension of the metaphor in 11.2.20.
11. Winkler, *Constraints of Desire*, 4–5.

Alan Dundes has cautioned against seeking the meaning of a proverb without reference to the protocols of usage.[12] Peter Seitel's research on the social use of metaphor delineated gender, status, location and situation (at least) as significant for the analysis of proverb meaning and use.[13] This 'ethnography of speaking' provides the necessary detail for the general commitment to context as the determinant of meaning. The construction and reinforcement of the dynamics of gender, however, is more than a contingent contextual matter, according to ethology. Its fundamental dimorphic taxonomy assumes and enforces the inseparable alignment of the male with speech.

The primary address in the Syrophoenician's story is from a man to a woman: καὶ ἔλεγεν αὐτῇ (v 27).[14] Familiar structural breakdowns of v 27 overlook the significance of this opening.[15] The evangelist marginalizes the initiating speech of the woman by making it indirect (v 26b, unlike Matthew 15:22). The evangelist, in full adherence to logocentric conventions, emphasises that Jesus—the male—delivers the opening sortie.

The assignment of the privilege and priority of direct speech to Jesus is constraining. It establishes a hierarchy (similar to that contained within the saying itself: πρῶτον) that builds on the ethos of virtue already established in the larger narrative (note especially Mark 7:14–23). It initiates an expectation of truth-telling with the audience. And it authorises the aptness of any rebuke that such speech may contain as it enters a (narrative) setting.[16]

Annabel Patterson observes that literature, in its most basic form, is always spoken to unequal power relations.[17] This functions at two levels. Firstly, the literature itself constructs a power relationship that is designed to reinforce audiential acquiescence in standard

12. A Dundes and E Ojo Arewa, 'Proverbs and the Ethnography of Speaking Folklore', in *Analytical Essays in Folklore*, 36.
13. P Seitel, 'Proverbs: A Social Use of Metaphor', in *Genre* 2 (1969): 144–147.
14. The syntactical superfluity of the αὐτῇ is corroborated by its omission from a few manuscripts (1, 209, 28, 90*, c).
15. Apart from the use of καί as a contribution to the elucidation of the overall structure of the pericope, according to the proposal of B Flammer, 'Die Syrophoenizierin', in *ThQ* 148 (1968): 464.
16. See Shawn Carruth, 'Strategies of Authority', in JS Kloppenborg (editor), *Conflict and Invention: Literary, Rhetorical and Social Studies on the Sayings Gospel Q* (Valley Forge, PA: TPI, 1995), 98–115.
17. A Patterson, *Fables of Power: Aesopian Writing and Political History* (Durham: Duke University Press, 1991), 11, 15–16.

understandings. A dimorphic hierarchy is the accepted foundation for these standards. As Heather McKay writes, '. . . latent sexual agendas stimulate extra engagement with the narrative and anaesthetize the reader to the persuasive and normalizing intentions of the authors'.[18] At this point in the pericope, the narrator's androcentricity is patent.[19]

Secondly, the gender of the characters in the story is significant for an appreciation of the use of a proverb. The power relationship implied in the direct speech here is that the man holds power above the woman, and likely over her. The imperfect (ἔλεγεν) may reinforce this—the 'fore-grounding' of attention wrought by the tense is again in marked contrast to the Matthean parallel (ὁ δὲ ἀποκριθεὶς εἶπεν, 15:26).[20] Matthew switches ἔλεγεν to the woman to accent her effort to prosecute her claim from Jesus and his disciples (even if through a liturgical formula). *If* the imperfect possesses a progressive or continuous meaning[21] for the Matthean story (ἔκραζεν, προσεκύνει), then, in application of the same notion to Mark's story, Jesus is repeatedly trying to get something through.[22] He is authorised to do so by his maleness, his initiating speech and the conferred appropriateness of this in the cultural backdrop that infuses the audience of the time.

That a proverb is contained within the speech by the (authoritative, virtuous) male to the female, is no coincidence. The effort to get something through, to assert, to dominate, to socialise, is, according to an ethological perspective, not only to be expected. It is, effectively, to be *required* if the male is to operate according to the biological impulse which pursues arrangements that will provide the optimum conditions for his own future. The proverb is the distilled wisdom of human

18. HA McKay, 'She Said to Him, He Said to Her: Power Talk in the Bible or Foucault Listens at the Keyhole', in *BTB* 28 (1998): 45.
19. The distinction between author and narrator here is important. McKay tends to blur the distinction. It will be shown in chapters 6 and 7, that Mark's purpose as author may be to manipulate (presumed) cultural assumptions of the audience, so that the narrative reversal of v 29 becomes the more explosive.
20. See S Porter *Idioms of the Greek New Testment* (Sheffield: Sheffield Academic Press, second edition, 1994), 302 for this aspectual analysis of the present-imperfect tenses.
21. *Ibid*, 21f, 34-5. Ulrich Luz accented this force of the imperfect in Matthew 15:22: *Matthew 8–20*, translated by E Crouch (Minneapolis: Fortress Press, 2001), 339.
22. This suggests that the δέ of v 28 (the introduction of the woman's reply) is not merely adversative but interruptive.

society *which has survived*,[23] and is therefore taken to demonstrate the validity of arguments based on dimorphism.

Speech, in this constructed context, therefore acts as a mechanism of dimorphic reinforcement of male superiority, necessary, so it is argued, for biological (and consequently, cultural) survival. Therefore, *of all forms of speech*, the proverb is the most fitting to be spoken by a male adhering to a restrained strategy of constraint. And in a curious circularity, the fitting quotation of a proverb reinforces the audience's positive assessment of the speaker.[24]

Heather McKay has alerted us to the potential for sexual dynamics being involved in gender dynamics. The potential is realised in this pericope (though McKay does not explore them) once the cultural significance of the metaphorical transfer of 'dog' to the woman is appreciated. Only if these dynamics are allowed, does the use of the diminutive κυνάρια (*and* in the plural) become explicable. The diminutive cannot be explained in lexicographical isolation from its narrative and cultural context. It is to the diminutive therefore that I turn.

The force of a diminutive

The diminutive in the saying of Jesus has attracted considerable interest. Montefiore considered the term κύων / κυνάριον improper to Jesus' speech and suggested it 'swum' across from the woman's reply.[25] He was not blaming the woman as the source of Jesus' abusive words. Rather, having accepted that κυνάριον indicates a house dog, he recognised the cultural incongruity of a Jew being 'at home' with a house dog.[26] By contrast, some have reasoned that κυνάριον repre-

23. Aristotle wrote a treatise on proverbs which appealed to the mythology of a lost civilisation. For all a proverb's common, universal convention, they are, according to Aristotle, created by an ancient philosophy. Fragments of this philosophy survived a cataclysmic disaster because of their concise, adroit form, enabling them to pass into common memory and usage. Ironically, his treatise only survives in fragmentary form (*Philo* fr 13). See J Russo, 'Prose Genres for the Performance of Traditional Wisdom in Ancient Greece: Proverb, Maxim and Apothegm', in L Edmunds and RW Wallace (editors), *Poet, Public and Performance in Ancient Greece* (Baltimore: Johns Hopkins University Press, 1997), 52.

24. Arist *Rhet* 2.21.11 (1395b), Quint *Inst* 5.11.37.

25. TR Glover, *Conflict of Religions in the Early Roman Empire* (London: Methuen, 1909/1918), 127n1.

26. CG Montefiore, *The Synoptic Gospels* (New York: KTAV reprint, second edition, 1968), 167; so also JI Hasler, 'The Incident of the

sents a diminution of the force of the abuse compared to the use of κύων,[27] or even that the term is used in a hypocoristic sense.[28] Either way, Jesus is in some measure exonerated.

JK Elliot argued that diminutives had lost their diminutive force by New Testament times and are virtual synonyms of the prime nouns from which they are formed.[29] There certainly is some support for this view in the common language of commerce and family exchanges in the papyri.[30] Quintilian knew of such harmonised usage, *but repudiated* it,[31] which, given his date, raises questions about Elliot's sweeping claims. The abundance of diminutives in the woman's reply (as indeed in the whole pericope) strengthens these doubts.[32]

Syrophoenician Woman (Mt xv.21–28; Mark vii.24–30)', in *ET* 45 (1933–34): 460. Montefiore left unrecognised the 'spatial' dimensions imagined by the proverb.

27. CEB Cranfield, *The Gospel According to St Mark* (Cambridge: Cambridge University Press, 1959), 248, V Taylor, *The Gospel According to St Mark* (London: Macmillan, second edition, 1966), 350, J Camery-Hoggatt, *Irony in Mark's Gospel: Text and Subtext* (Cambridge: Cambridge University Press, 1992), 150, D Rhoads, 'Jesus and the Syrophoenician Woman in Mark: A Narrative Critical Study', in *JAAR* 62 (1994): 356–357.
28. A number describe Jesus as 'playful': TR Glover, *The Jesus of History* (London: SCM, 1917), 48–49, Hasler, "Incident", 459–460, D Smith, "Our Lord's Hard Saying to the Syrophoenician Woman", in *ET* 12 (1901): 320. SE Johnson expressly rejects such a description: *A Commentary on The Gospel According to St. Mark* (London: A&C Black, 1960), 137; *cf* Gundry, *Mark*, 373: 'The diminutive would ill suit the woman herself, grown mother that she is.'(*sic*!)
29. JK Elliott, 'Nouns with Diminutive Endings in the New Testament', in his *Essays and Studies in New Testament Textual Criticism* (Cordoba: Ediciones el Almendro, 1992), 79–85; so also CH Turner—see JK Elliott, *Language and Style of the Gospel of Mark: An Edition of CH Turner's Notes on Marcan Usage Together with Other Comparable Studies* (Leiden: EJ Brill, 1993), 126, GP Shipp, *Modern Greek Evidence for the Ancient Greek Vocabulary* (Sydney: Sydney University Press, 1979), 432, N Turner, *A Grammar of New Testament Greek Volume 4: Style* (Edinburgh: T&T Clark, 1976), 28. None of these writers investigates the contextual factors attending usage, such as gender and status.
30. *Eg P Oxy* 10. 1299 l.7 τὰ χυρίδια (pigs), l.11 has πιπεράδιον (pepper), but note that this papyrus is dated to the fourth century CE.
31. Quint *Inst* 1.5.46.
32. David Rhoads is also struck by the prevalence of diminutives: 'Jesus and the Syrophoenician Woman', 356–357, 366–367; see also C Focant, 'Mc 7.24-31 par Mt 15.21–29. Critique des sources et/ou étude narrative", in C Focant (editor), *The Synoptic Gospels* (BETL 110), (Leuven: Leuven University Press, 1993), 56, 66.

In any case, the result of Elliot's assertion is to leave the abuse undiminished. The proposal that the abuse is *compounded* by the use of the diminutive, has rarely been made,[33] even though its deployment for contempt is noted by some grammarians.[34]

i) Diminutives as small versions

Diminutives *can* indicate a reduced form, for example, βοίδιον ('little ox'), ῥοίδιον ('little pomegranate')[35] or the ἰχθύδια ('little fish') of Mark 8:7. Aelian writes of a bitch producing a number of puppies (σκυλάκια).[36] Yet, even in an innocuous use of a diminutive, a hierarchy of relation is present. It is deemed a diminished instance of the norm, the template. As Dionysius of Thrace, the grammarian, taught: 'A diminutive is the reduction of the prototype, incomparably signified.'[37]

ii) A hypocoristic use

Diminutives were also used in an affectionate or intimate sense. Familial relationships readily attracted diminutives, regardless of who is the elder.[38] It was a short move from this to diminutives as pet names,[39] or the use of a diminutive form of a person's name.[40] The diminutives, κυνάριον and κυνίδιον, were sometimes used to

33. EK Broadhead, to my knowledge, is the only one to have suggested this reading. He does not test the suggestion and is content with seeing the logion in terms of Jewish antagonism to Gentiles: 'The Role of Wundergeschichten in the Characterisation of Jesus in the Gospel of Mark' (PhD Thesis, Southern Baptist Theological Seminary, 1986), 283n41.
34. For example, HW Smyth, *Greek Grammar* (Cambridge, MT: Harvard University Press, 1956), §856.
35. Athen *Deip* 650e; *cf P Oxy* 10.1299 ll.5–7, 10–11.
36. Ael *NA* 9.5. Aelian proceeded to prove female inferiority to the male: 'nature appears to pursue reason in setting the male which sows above the female which receives.'
37. *Ars gram* 1.1.28 l.5 (my translation); *cf* Arist *Rhet* 3.2.5 (1405b). See *PUG* 50.8–9 (third-fourth century CE) for an apt example.
38. Juv *Sat* 6.390, Cic *Att* 1.2.1 (both *filiolus*), Plut *Mor* 858c (μαμμιδιον), Luc *Deo Con* 8 (μειράκιον).
39. The nickname for the Spartan Zeuxidamus was Κυνίσκος: Hdt *Hist* 6.71. The female form is also found: *GA* 13.16.2.
40. Mart *Epig* 8.43, 11.90 (*Chrestilla* and *Chrestillus*) Interestingly, Paul, the contemporary and guest of Prisca, only ever refers to her by that name (Rom 16:3, 1 Cor 16:19; *cf* also 2 Tim 4:19). Luke however uses only the diminutive, Priscilla (Acts 18:2, 18, 26). This would suggest either that Luke had a more intimate relationship with this early patron

accent pet-dogs (or 'lap-dogs') which might also be given names in diminutive form.[41]

However, this context was relatively confined and readily lent itself to other agendas, including parody,[42] and manipulative flattery. A woman's advice on how to address a person in order to extract a favour includes, in Menander's language, πατρίδιον ('little daddy').[43] There may be a demeaning sense here, even a trivialising. Certainly, the jump from a lap-dog to a 'petty whore' was no effort.[44]

iii) Diminutives as abuse

Diminutives were frequently turned to demean a person or context (λοιδαρία),[45] and thereby indicated the superiority of the person making use of the form. The ridicule or debasement of race, status, gender, and occupation was often assisted by the deployment of diminutives. If a diminutive could attract another meaning, depraved or not, this compounded the defaming pungency. One piece of graffiti from Pompei has:

> *Oppi, emboliari, fur, furuncule*:
> Oppius, clown, thief, petty crook![46]

This particular graffito is saturated with double barbs: the diminutive *furunculus* also meant an irritating boil.[47]

---

and teacher in the Christian movement (though note that Acts 18 does not contain 'we' passages) or that he was subtly diminishing her status.

41. Gow and Page claim diminutives were usual for lap-dogs: *Greek Anthology* 2.555.
42. Luc *Deo Con* 5.
43. Menand *Dysk* 499.
44. Thus κυνίδιον refers to a low-grade harlot in Aristoph *Ach* 542–543 (following Lilja, *Dogs*, 69); *cf canicula* in Plaut *Curc* 598.
45. One scholiast to Aristoph *Eq* noted τινὲς δέ ὀνειδισμῶν καὶ λοιδοριῶν (Scholia 100a; see also 100b-c, Suda N§574).
46. *CIL* 4.1949.
47. Moreover, *fur* was such a stereotyped description of a slave that it had become a synonym: Ter *Eun* 776, *cf* Mart *Epig* 11.54. And *emboliaria* alludes to the second-rate actress who provided entertainment in intervals and breaks between plays: Verg *Ecl* 3.16, Pl *HN* 7.158. Again the female compounds a vituperative slur. There may even be a deliberate allusion to the 'three-letter man', a caustic proverb built on the practice of signalling status by abbreviating one's three names into initials; Plaut *Aul* 325–326 ties the three letters to F-U-R (*cf* Juv *Sat* 5.126–127).

Any stereotype of a foreigner could be debased further by a diminutive. Plutarch has Gorgo, daughter of king Cleomenes, warn her father about Aristagoras of Miletus, '. . . the miserable foreigner (τὸ ξενύλλιον) will be your ruin if you don't get him out of the house pretty soon!'[48] Cicero's typically Roman insecurity about Greek culture was countered by belittling the contemporary Greek position: *graeculus*.[49] The Greeks as readily demeaned other races.[50]

Status components could be added to those races who, having been conquered, were assumed to be slaves. The standard name for a Syrian slave was Σύρος or Σύρα—demeaning enough to lose one's identity to the name of one's country of origin.[51] Such degradation could be accented by the use of a diminutive, as in Συρίσκος.[52] Other diminutives could be similarly dumped. Simiche, in Menander's *Dyskolos*, is described as οἰκουρὸν γράδιον ('the little, old housekeeper').[53] The very use of a diminutive often suggested an address or a description of slaves. Παιδάριον may indicate little about age or size, but a great deal about station (and a person's attitude to it).[54] Thus the hyper-diminutive, ὠτάριον, in Mark 14:47 is linguistically 'apt' to the position of the victim (δοῦλος), given the status differentials that language communicates.[55]

48. Plut *Mor* 240d.
49. Cic *De Or* 51.220; *cf* 22.99, *Orat* 1.102.
50. The 'little bun-eating Boeotian' (κολλικοφάγε Βοιωτίδιον): Aristoph *Ach* 872.
51. See the clear collation in Luc *Tox* 28.
52. So used in the non-extant play, *The Well*, by the character Anaxippus *apud* Athen *Deip* 486f.
53. This could be reinforced by the description of her appearance, designed to demonstrate her degraded position. Julius Pollux, in his description of comic masks, assigned her mask number 30—'snub-nosed [that is, like a pig?], with two teeth in each jaw.' (*Onom* 4.1).
54. Menander's character Smikrines, uses the term to deprecate 'one born of a whore' (*Epit* 645); elsewhere it is more of a general term for a household servant treated with contempt (*Thras* 989). The reality of this lower status is found in the statement of payments (early fourth century CE) on *O Mich* 34.1.102 (Inv 4427) where, it would appear, a group of πεταρία (read παιδαρία) are paid substantially less than others (the number of actual slaves is unknown).
55. It has nothing to do with the size of the severed ear or Mark's supposed 'fondness' for diminutives, as Charles Turner speculated! See *'Notes on Marcan Usage'*, 125. Elsewhere in the gospel οὖς is used, in contexts without mention of slavery (Mk 4:9, 23, 7:16, 7:33, 8:18).

The label 'dogs' was readily applied to slaves, as to anyone who could be accused of being kept.[56] In this sense, to suggest that someone was a lap-dog (whether κυνίδιον, κυνάριον, κυνίσκον or σκυλάκιον or the latin equivalents: *canicula*, *catellus*) was damning.[57]

iv) Diminutives and (little) women

Diminutives proliferate in the area of gender (and sexuality). The methodological insight of Maurice Olender has yet to infiltrate New Testament studies: namely, that since male and female roles are not equivalent in the ancient world, words and gestures cannot be expected to align symmetrically.[58] The supposed natural hierarchical division between male and female was reinforced by the diminutives. Women were characterised as possessing diminished intelligence and petty emotions. Livy has Valerius say that depriving men of honours 'could wound the spirits of men; what do you think it could do to the spirits of our little women (*mulierculae*) whom even small problems disturb?'[59]

A woman could readily be slandered by averring to a disparaged profession. Here diminutives conveyed a more pronounced, abusive tone. Cicero, for example, cannot abide a woman philosopher—this is enough to denounce the little prostitute (*meretricula*) Leontion of the Epicureans.[60] Such abuse is prolific and more coarse in farce and mime. The description of a group of women as χοιριδίων θυγατέρες in one first century fragment[61] melded the infantilising and execrating dimensions of invective; clearly, no hypocoristic intent is present.

56. Aristoph *Vesp* 682, 704f. (Here slaves and dogs act as synonyms in the denunciation of jurors who are kept, trained by power-hungry politicians.) *Cf* Pl *Euth* 298d, e, *Rep* 539b.

57. Mart *Epig* 1.83, 3.82, 14:198. *Canis* can also be used of a kept person *eg* Cic *Verr* 2.1.48 §126, 2.3.19 §40, 2.5.56.§146, *Att* 6.3.6, *Pis* 10.23.

58. 'Aspects of Baubo: Ancient Texts and Contexts', translated by R Lamberton, in DM Halperin, JJ Winkler and FI Zeitlin (editors), *Before Sexuality: The Construction of Erotic Experience in the Ancient Greek World* (Princeton, NJ: Princeton University Press, 1990), 103. Olender was applying the principle to the interpretation of obscenity, but the methodological caution is generally pertinent. Note also Greg Horsley's brief aside of similar import in *NDIEC* volume 2, 103.

59. Liv 34.6–7. For Juvenal, woman encapsulated vengeance, the desire of a 'little, weak and petty mind': *Sat* 13.189–192.

60. Cic *ND* 1.33.93. A similar use of a diminutive for 'prostitute' is found in Menand *Peri* 340 (πορνίδιον) and his *Epit* 984 (ἑταιρίδιον).

61. *P Oxy* 3.413 l.38. The fragment has been variously dated between the first century BCE and the first century CE: see G Harrocks, *Greek: A*

While not as vilifying, the frequent use of diminutives for the names given to prostitutes, hetaerai and drunken nurse-maids functioned to remind the bearers of their diminished status. Mark Golden sees the use of neuter diminutives as names as contributing 'to a tendency to depersonalise and objectify women, to present them as things—and rather insignificant things at that'.[62] The use of a neuter suggests the descent of the woman to a non-human realm,[63] a sense which is reinforced when the diminutive is bestial, as, for example, Δόρχιον[64] and Περιστέριον.[65] Sarah Pomeroy reports a graffito from Pompei: 'Sucula ['little sow'] asks you to make Marcus Cerrinius aedile'.[66] This particular name carried a further obscene connection—it was one of a range of animal euphemisms for the female pudendum.[67]

v) Diminutives are not neutral

This survey of the use of diminutives leads to an inescapable conclusion: the diminutive in Jesus' words to the Syrophoenician woman *aggravates* the abuse. It does not ameliorate it or leave it unmodified.[68] Moreover, the diminutive can intensify the severity

---

History of the Language and Its Speakers (London: Longman, 1997), 56.

62. Σειληνίδα was apparently proverbial as a name for a female drunkard: *GA* 11.409. *Chrestilla* (Mart *Epig* 8.43), and Ἀθήνιον (*GA* 5.138) are well-known names given to hetaerai though not confined to them: Gow and Page, *Greek Anthology*, 237.
63. *Children and Childhood*, 24.
64. *GA* 5.192, 194, 12.51, *IG* 2.3.3639; *cf* Lucret *Nat Rer* 4.1161.
65. Menand *Mer, apud* Athen *Deip* 654b. Of the almost 400 names of hetaerai collected by K Schneider, 'Hetairai', in *RE* 8.1358–1371, 42 are neuter diminutives, frequently bestial. Other diminutives (and animals) also occur.
66. Pomeroy, *Goddesses, Whores*, 201, commenting on *CIL* 4.159.
67. Thus Antisthenes writes of hetaerai: 'For those women must feed their little pigs (δελφάκια) whether they will or no.' *The Expert in Physiognomy apud,* Athen *Deip* 656f. The use of animal metaphors for male and female genitalia was frequent in the ancient world, drawn by the sense that the passions of sexual behaviour were more to be aligned with the bestial than the human realm, especially when control was absent: Adams, *Latin Sexual Vocabulary*, 29–34, 82.
68. The deprecation that resides in various degrees in the use of diminutives may well lie behind a singular reading of the text of Mark 7:27. Codex Ω (045) has τοῖς κοιναρίοις 'petty commoners'. The assonance between κυνή and κοινή allowed for such word-plays: see *P Mich* 5.244.13 l.6, *SB* 12.11012.2.1; *cf* Rev 21:27, 22:15.

of abuse with lewd associations.[69] The woman is thereby reminded of her inferiority (to men, if not the male speaker)—an inferiority which may be compounded by racial stereotype, her connection with the non-human state (through the neuter form as well as the bestial association), and, as will be tested more extensively in the next chapter, her sexually untamed nature. John of Damascus made no attempt to side-step the vilification, calling Jesus' words ὄνειδος and, through the Syrophoenician's voice, responding: ὑβρίζεις με.[70] Both these classifications are drawn from the rhetorician's lexicon of abuse.

Moreover, the woman is generalised through the use of the plural κυνάρια, not merely infantilising her with her daughter, but also removing any particularity about her (and her request for her daughter's healing). A gender perspective on the question dramatically changes the appreciation of the use of the diminutive in Jesus' saying, and highlights the abusive aspect of the ethological ascription. Moreover, the diminutive plays an important role in the structure of Jesus' saying. To this, we turn.

The structural components of the saying

The words given the man Jesus to speak to the Syrophoenician woman have three sections.[71] Each can stand as a phrase in its own right.[72] At the same time, the scalpel must not dissect each part permanently. Overall function and form must also be achieved.

α ἄφες πρῶτον χορτασθῆναι τὰ τέκνα
β οὐ γάρ ἐστιν καλὸν
γ λαβεῖν τὸν ἄρτον τῶν τέκνων καὶ τοῖς κυναρίοις βαλεῖν.

Succeeding analysis will further justify this division. To achieve this, it will be profitable to commence with the final phrase. Sensitivity to linguistic structures as found in practitioners and commentators of antiquity will necessarily inform the analysis, without requiring that

69. Mart *Epig* 14.198, *P Oxy* 3.413 l.38.
70. *Sacred Parallels* 95.148.41–45.
71. In agreement with J-F Baudoz, *Les Miettes de la Table: Études synoptique et socio-religieuse de Mt 15,21–28 et de Mc 7,24–30* (Études Bibliques (ns) volume 27), (Paris: J Gabalda et Cie, 1995), 246.
72. This conforms with Aristotle's understanding of a phrase (λογός, with yet another meaning): Arist *Poet* 20:11–13.

the evangelist (or Jesus) be trained in such usage. Their observations are reflections, albeit not disinterested, upon how language operated as a key component of societal interaction and cohesion.[73]

γ λαβεῖν τὸν ἄρτον τῶν τέκνων καὶ τοῖς κυναρίοις βαλεῖν

i) The structural and stylistic significance of the infinitives

In the structure of this section, the two infinitives (λαβεῖν and βαλεῖν) dominate. Infinitives appeal to the universal. The universal appeal of the general saying is accentuated by the pluralising of terms—here τέκνα and the diminutive κυνάρια. Aristotle noted that the use of the plural for the singular was a means, drawn from the poets, for adding *gravitas* or impressiveness to a saying.[74] Any particular referent is thereby subjected to a larger claim,[75] precisely the operation of a proverb. The section has a narrative integrity that enables it to stand alone with a measure of meaning, but sufficient imprecision in isolation as to allow/require specific application in diverse contexts. In this case, the woman and her daughter are the referents, made subject to the proverb.

The combination of the two infinitives forges a remarkable symmetry, assonance and phonemic quality. The metathesis of λαβεῖν—βαλεῖν has sometimes been noted by contemporary commentators,[76] though with little exposition. Its importance lies in the phonemic quality (*paronomasia*)[77] wrought tensively by the

73. Arist *Rhet* 1.1 (1354a); *cf* Quint *Inst* 12.10.74, 80.
74. Arist *Rhet* 3.6 (1407b); *cf* Longin 23.2–4, *Rhet ad Her* 4.33.44–45.
75. Arist *Rhet* 3.7 (1408a); see Russell and Winterbottom's comments to this effect: *Ancient Literary Criticism*, 144.
76. J Gnilka, *Das Evangelium nach Markus* (Zürich: Benziger Verlag, 1978), 1.249, Baudoz, *Les Miettes*, 249–250 (who sees an antithetic parallelism), and EA Russell, 'The Canaanite Woman and the Gospels (Mt 15.21–28; *cf* Mk 7.24–30)', in EA Livingstone (editor), *Studia Biblica 1978 II: Papers on the Gospels* (Sheffield: JSNT, 1980), 2.263 (who wonders about its mnemonic value). Robert Gundry thinks that the assonance and chiasm (!) of infinitive placement emphasize the contrast between Jesus' disciples and Gentile children, although how this might occur remains opaque. He finds the disciples to be present (having tagged along from 7:17) and ciphered under the τέκνα of Jesus' saying to the woman: *Mark*, 373.
77. A minor argument about definitions runs amongst contemporary grammarians: compare GB Winer, *A Treatise on the Grammar of New Testament Greek*, translated by WF Moulton (Edinburgh: T&T Clark, eighth edition, 1877), 793–796, F Blass and A Debrunner, *A Greek Grammar of the New Testament and Other Early Christian Literature*,

shift of consonants and the contribution that it makes to the sense of balance in the saying. Demetrius argued that the impact of words that sound similar, generated a sort of clash (σύμπληξις) that arrested attention more vividly than could otherwise be achieved (by a prosaic description).[78] Quintilian warned against overuse.[79] Even so, the λαβ–βαλ connection is a common ornament amongst Greek writers, and is found from Homer[80] to Gregory of Nazianzus[81] and beyond.[82] As Seneca wrote, 'single maxims sink in more easily when they are marked and bounded off like a line of verse'[83]

The careful placement of the infinitives enables them to function as boundary markers for the key concerns of the saying. The saying, so highlighted, possesses an impulse of its own meaning even though it will require a context to demonstrate how meaning will be extrapolated. Winton speaks of a proverb's 'syntactic completeness'

edited and translated by RW Funk (Chicago: University of Chicago Press, ninth to tenth edition, 1961), §488. AT Robertson, *A Grammar of the Greek New Testament in the Light of Historical Research* (Nashville, TN: Broadman Press, 1934), 1201, CW Davis, *Oral Biblical Criticism: The Influence of the Principles of Orality on the Literary Structure of Paul's Epistle to the Philippians* (Sheffield: JSOT Press, 1999), 79, SG Green, *Handbook to the Grammar of the Greek Testament* (London: Religious Tract Society, Revised. edition 1907), §413. Note that the *Rhetorica ad Herennium* (4.21.29) allowed a wide range of candidates for the category of paronomasia.

78. Demetr *Eloc* 2.105–106; *cf* Cic *De Or* 4.29. Mark uses the device elsewhere, in 4:39 (γαλήνη μεγάλη) and perhaps 7:24 (ἤθελεν–λαθεῖν). Here, I suspect the total segment is pre-formed.
79. *Inst* 8.5.13–14, 20.
80. *Od* 21.359.
81. *Poems of His Own Life* 1270.5 (in a section almost self-consciously full of the device).
82. See Arist *HA* 611b, Plut *Mor* 442d, Ps-Gal *Rem* 3.461.12–13, Alex *Ther* 2.467.24. The twelfth century bishop-grammarian, Eustathius, made the obvious but nevertheless confirmatory comment: παρηχοῦσι γάρ πως αἱ τοιαῦται λέξεις, καὶ γίνεται οὕτω κοινῶς κάλλος φρά σεως, ἰδίως δὲ ἐν τῷ λαβὼν καὶ βάλε. ἀναγραμματισθὲν γὰρ τὸ λαβεῖν ποιεῖ τὸ βαλεῖν (*Comm Il* 3.166.3), 'Such-like words were held together and thus commonly become a fine phrase just as in the expression "λαβὼν καὶ βάλε". For by transposition "λαβεῖν" becomes "βαλεῖν".' (my translation).
83. Sen *Ep* 33.6. The reference to 'a line of verse' (*carminis*) is telling and will be explored below.

which, whilst not confined to a proverb, is a necessary element for its identification.[84]

This symmetry of syntactical arrangement contrasts with Matthew's, who rearranges the proverb into a parallelism with each infinitive heading its own clause:[85]

> Λαβεῖν τὸν ἄρτον τῶν τέκνων
> καὶ
> βαλεῖν τοῖς κυναρίοις

Mark's syntagmatics seal the arrangement more strongly than Matthew's, though Matthew's arrangement adheres to Aristotle's recommendations for the positioning of such words in each member,[86] and for the positioning of a rhythmic paeon at the end of a line.[87] Too much ought not be made of structural propriety. Plutarch engineers the infinitives into a central *hinge* for a balanced sentence bearing a complex phonemic play.[88] Whatever arrangement is adopted, the symmetry in Jesus' words indicates that a discrete formal element is present. The analysis here is, of necessity, confined to visual patterns. The power lies in what Eric Havelock called 'acoustic responsions'[89] — not sight of a text but hearing of a performance.

---

84. AP Winton, *The Proverbs of Jesus: Issues of History and Rhetoric* (Sheffield: Sheffield Academic Press, 1990), 34, citing D Zeller, *Die weisheilichen Mahnsprüche bei den Synoptikern* (Würzburg: Echter Verlag, 1977), 18.
85. The shift of accent to the sound κ and ρ in Matthew echoes the woman's κράζει (15:23). It may attempt to make *her* speech the barking eloquence of a dog! Certainly the shift in word order places an accent on τέκνων and κυναρίοις; so EM Wainwright, *Towards a Feminist Critical Reading of the Gospel According to Matthew* (BZNW Volume 60), (Berlin: Walter de Gruyter, 1991), 240.
86. Arist *Rhet* 3.9 (1409b).
87. Arist *Rhet* 3.8 (1409a) followed expressly by Demetr *Eloc* 2.38–39; see the discussion by DF McCabe, *The Prose-Rhythm of Demosthenes* (New York: Arno Press, 1981), 16–21.
88. Plut *Mor* 38e.
89. EA Havelock, 'Oral Composition in the Oedipus Tyrranus of Sophocles', in *NLH* 16 (1984): 183, cited in C Bryan, *A Preface to Mark: Notes on the Gospel in its Literary and Cultural Settings* (New York: Oxford University Press, 1993), 78.

ii) The phonemic quality of the saying

The structures in Matthew and Mark also neatly divide into two equal parts (*isocolon*), defined by the parallelism of sound in the infinitival endings (*paromoiosis*).[90] The balance combines with multiple phonemic qualities to operate psychagogically, bolstering the appropriateness of both metaphor and proverb beyond the mere communication of content. James Russo makes a telling observation on such constructions:

> A certain amount of jingle or echo may be used here to contribute to the total effectiveness of parallel structure in highlighting similarities or opposites. An apparent word-magic is at work here, in the non-rational suggestion that sheer phonemic parallels help ensure that the realities named will also proceed along the course indicated . . .[91]

The resonances of the striking letters within the saying in Mark have their own force and significance. In the words bounded by the paranomatic infinitives, the dominating sounds are ρ and κ:

λαβεῖν τὸν ἄρτον τῶν τέκνων καὶ τοῖς κυναρίοις βαλεῖν

These letters draw on harsh expulsions of noise. β and λ contribute to this pungency as well. The former was long recognised as a rough sound;[92] the latter was tied to the ρ.[93] In fact, the Greek letter ρ and

90. For further explication of *isocolon* and *paromoiosis*, see R Dean Anderson, *Glossary of Greek Rhetorical Terms* (Leuven: Peeters, 2000), 90–92.

91. Russo, 'The Poetics', 124. Quintilian gives a telling exposé of the psychagogic influence over an audience: *Inst* 8.3.1–6. The danger however is the loss of the rational—significantly, Quintilian aligns this 'fault' with women (*ibid,* 10.7.12). Herein lies a fissure in the reign of *logos*.

92. Demetr *Eloc* 3.176, Quint *Inst* 12.10.32.

93. Quint *Inst* 1.11.5, Luc *Iud Voc* 4. Compare Demetrius' similar analysis of the mimetic qualities of words conveying lapping dogs, based on a passage from Homer: *Eloc* 4.220. Both rho and lambda could separately be regarded as euphonic letters—so WB Stanford, *The Sound of Greek: Studies in the Greek Theory an Practice of Euphony* (Berkeley: University of California Press, 1967), 52–53. However, in certain words and combinations they approach a cacophony: *ibid,* 112–113.

Latin *r* were designated the 'dog-letter' (*canina littera*)[94] so-called because of the barking or threatening growl that it made.[95] Ovid uses it for the archetypal dog-woman, Hecuba; Homer for Helen.[96]

The shaping of the saying to emphasize sound-qualities reinforces the linguistic communication of its content.[97] The caustic rasp of a crushing retort demolishes any claim that the woman advances.[98] Jesus is neither speaking humorously nor didactically for the woman's encouragement or development. And his sonorous denial has another menace. The ethological connections between woman and dog were seemingly supported by the similarities of sound between κ and γ. Γυνή readily blurred into κύνη / κυνῆ / ἡ κύων. This type of word-play was a common-place.[99]

iii) The metre of the proverb

There is a further inner resonance of structure to the proverb which carries psychagogic effect. This is metre. Aristotle observed that metaphor was most suited to be expressed in iambics,[100] just as iambics was the prime metre of/for common conversation.[101] Hence, it should come as no surprise to discover that iambics are the foundational rhythm in Comedy (especially Old Comedy) and its close relative, Mime,[102] with common conversation frequently spiced with crudity. Plutarch, for example, allies mime with prostitution ('bad art and bad taste').[103]

In fact, base language, scornful abuse, bitter tone, and sexual license were so caught into the meaning of iambic, that David Gerber suggested that iambic was not just a metre but a style.[104] Comedy

---

94. Pers *Sat* 1.109–110.
95. Varro *LL* 6; *cf* Lucil *Sat* 3–4, Plaut *Capt* 485.
96. Ov *Meta* 13.567–579, Hom *Il* 6.344; *cf* Dio Chr *Or* 33.59.
97. See Williams, 'Power of Form', 39, 44–47.
98. On the harsh κ sound, see Stanford, 112.
99. Menander, for example, played on 'old woman': Πολὺ χεῖρον ἐστιν ἐρεθίσαι γραῦν ἢ κύνα. 'It's far worse to stir up a hag than a dog' (my translation). Menand fr 258 (Meineke) *apud* Stob *Flor* 73.46.
100. Arist *Poet* 22.19 (1459a).
101. Arist *Rhet* 3.8 (1408b).
102. Arist *Poet* 4.13 (1449a).
103. Plut *Mor* 706d.
104. DE Gerber, 'Introduction' to the LCL *Greek Iambic Poetry*. The name derives from Iambe, Demeter's (in)famous servant-girl, 'remembered' (blamed?) for her cutting and vulgar humour: Lloyd-Jones, *Female of the Species*, 13, Olender, 'Aspects of Baubo', 89–91.

was its literary province,[105] and two of its favourite devices were metaphor[106] and diminutive.[107] It is frequent also in prose satire,[108] and the vilification of an enemy in oratory. Plutarch for example describes Cato:'betaking himself to iambic verse, he heaped much scornful abuse upon Scipio, adopting the bitter tone of Archilochus.'[109]

Metre used in a proverb has an evocative as well as mnemonic function. It arranges and identifies sound.[110] Thus, where a metre is incorporated, a much larger universe is projected. This demands neither developed training nor circumspect attention. The socio-rhetorical world that formed people and enabled them to communicate, meant that access to these associations was as close as the air that was breathed.[111] Aristotle could even speak of nature (φύσις) showing the right metre to use.[112] Some have wanted to remove metre from the gambit of New Testament prose, claiming that any occurrence is simply fortuitous. This fails to recognise how proverbs often gained a power of remembrance and application.[113]

In Greek, the syllable not the word functions as the basic linguistic unit.[114] This explains why metre has 'power' beyond simple lexical progression. As Plutarch observed: 'poetry adds to the prose meaning,

105. 'The natural metre for invective is the iambic …': FM Cornford, *The Origin of Attic Comedy* (Gloucester, MT: Peter Smith, 1968), 101–102.
106. Arist *Poet* 22.19 (1459a).
107. Lilja, *Dogs*, 78.
108. Athen *Deip* 445b.
109. Plut *Vit (Cato)* 7. Plutarch tried to save Cato's standing by adding that he 'avoided his [Archilochus'] license and puerility'. Archilochus is similarly credited with the pungency of iambics by Hor *Ars Poet* 79; *cf* Catullus' threats to unleash his iambics on an opponent (*Poet* 40.2, 54A, Fr 1).
110. Plat *Phil* 17b.
111. Cic *De Or* 3.191, 195.
112. Arist *Poet* 24.12 (1460a).
113. Charles Dodd had identified an iambic pentameter in John 4:35: *Historical Tradition in the Fourth Gospel* (Cambridge: Cambridge University Press, 1965), 394. Even though Raymond Brown was prepared to acknowledge the presence of a proverb, he regarded any metrical structure as an accident: *The Gospel according to John 1–XII* (Anchor Bible) (New York: Doubleday, 1966), 174. The careful (poetic) lexical structure in that proverb, as also the one in John 4:37, more readily suggests and accommodates the use of metre than denies it and it draws attention to its traditional status as a proverb.
114. Arist *Poet* 20.5 (1456b), 'but *also* (ἀλλὰ καί) these sounds belong to the theory of metre.' So also Quint *Inst* 1.7.31.

the delights of song and metre and rhythm'.[115] This 'Aesthetic Field Framework'[116] deals with that realm that belongs between the idea and its speaking, namely the realm of combinations of rhythm and phonetic sound. The aural evocation from oral or textual performance elicits 'a broader or more abstract reality' to be brought to bear upon the compact content of a few lines.

In this sense, *embodiment* is the source of speech—'rhythm and thought are one'.[117] This has enormous implications for one who does not speak in the Markan pericope, yet embodies communication (namely, the daughter).[118] For the moment, it is important to emphasise that there is a common network of sound, sense and rhythm whenever a surface structure evokes a certain commonly understood *gestalt*.[119] It may take an audience weaned on a traditional referentiality to appreciate this potential fully. But this is precisely the point: 'all ancient literature was intended to be spoken or read aloud and the ears of the speakers and hearers had become highly sensitive to the various possible effects.'[120] The metrical form of a saying augments the sense of order and communication working upon, in and through words, shaping the tone and modulation of the delivery.[121] Dan Ben-Amos neatly sums up the argument: '. . . the existence or absence of a metric substructure in a message is the quality first recognized in any communicative event . . .'[122]

115. Plut *Mor* 769c.
116. The phrase is taken from Elizabeth C Fine, *The Folklore Text: From Performance to Print* (Bloomington: Indiana University Press, 1984), 68ff. It is this aspect which makes a substantial addition to Vernon Robbins 'tapestry' of interacting modes of engagement with a text: see generally, his *Tapestry of Early Christian Discourse*. And it reinforces and extends the analysis of Mark in terms of its oral patterning made by Christopher Bryan *loc. cit*. The whole field of rhythmical patterns and their rhetorical function in the prose writing of the gospels awaits exploration.
117. AB Lord, *The Singer of Tales* (Cambridge, MA: Harvard University Press, 1971), 32.
118. The importance of embodiment as a necessary factor in speech and as possessing its own communication is explored at length in chapter 7.
119. MS Kitts, 'Oath-Making in the Iliad' (PhD Thesis, Berkeley: University of California/Graduate Theological Union, 1994), 55–56, referring to the work of Michael Nagler, *Spontaneity and Tradition: A Study in the Oral Art of Homer* (Berkeley: University of California Press, 1974).
120. G Kennedy, *Quintilian* (New York: Twayne Publishers, 1969), 90.
121. Quint *Inst* 1.7.2–3.
122. D Ben-Amos, 'Analytical Categories and Ethnic Genres', in D Ben-Amos (editor) *Folklore Genres* (Austin: University of Texas Press,

A return to the infinitival boundary-markers is revealing. The inherited metathesis possesses its own distinctive rhythm. Λαβεῖν—βαλεῖν yields an iambic foot, and when this hint is applied to the whole saying, the rhythm is found to dominate:

λαβεῖν τὸν ἄρτον τῶν τέκνων
˘ — ˘ — ˘ — ˘ —
(καὶ)
—
τοῖς κυναρίοις βαλεῖν
— ˘ ˘ ˘ — ˘ —

The first line is an iambic dimeter.[123] The second continues the use of the iambs delivering half an iambic trimeter.[124] The καί is superfluous to both rhythm and meaning, and when omitted, cultivates a purposive function to the second infinitive.[125] Even if it is included, the overall impact is little affected, the whole proverb being dominated by iambics.[126] As Demetrius observed, a 'general metrical character' will produce the desired effect.[127] Certainly, if κύσιν (˘ –) rather than

---

1976), 228. Dio Chrysostom recognises the same: *Or* 12.71.

123. Compare Aristoph *Ran* 449—following the scansion of JW Halporn, M Ostwald, and TG Rosenmeyer, *The Meters of Greek and Latin Poetry* (London: Methuen & Co, 1963), 46. Note that τέκνων is scanned as τε.κνων as recommended *inter alia* in the late third century BCE text on syllabic breakdowns: *P Cair* 65445, col 1, l.8 (A.KNWN), as well as evidence of scansion in identified poetic writings.

124. As in Bacchylides 17.3, again as per Halporn, Ostwald and Rosenmeyer, 35.

125. Smyth, *Greek Grammar*, §2009 notes that the infinitive of purpose is especially used after verbs meaning, *inter alia*, 'take'. In doing so, the thrust of the proverb is made more univocal. When combined with the sententious introduction, the charge might be interpreted to be two-fold rather than singular that is, *both* taking the bread *and* giving it to dogs.

126. In fact, if Quintilian's observation of a 3:2 ratio of beat for a paeon holds (*Inst* 9.4.47), then the καί could be retained without disturbing the iambic measure. The whole saying would then be an iambic trimeter with a laudatory cretic ending (– ˘ –), which stalls any straying into versification proper (*Inst* 9.4.104, 107, substantially following Cic *De Or* 3.183). The recommendations and discrediting of metrical substructures for prose rhythms continued to be observed in later centuries, albeit with (rhetorical) protestations about plain speaking; see SM Oberhelman, *Rhetoric and Homiletics in Fourth-Century Christian Literature: prose rhythm, oratorical style and preaching in the works of Ambrose, Jerome and Augustine* (Atlanta, GA: Scholars Press, 1991).

127. Demetr *Eloc* 3.181.

κυναρίοις is used,[128] the καί (¯) can happily contribute to the scansion. In either case, the relationship between the textual manifestation and a recognisable oral-aural performance is plain.

Matthew's inversion of elements scans as a trochaic foot with a final paeon. Significantly, both the iamb and the trochee were regarded by Aristotle as not conducive to dignity.[129] Moreover, Quintilian criticises a succession of short syllables in the middle of a sentence, 'as this would cause a sound similar to that of children's rattles (*paene puerilium crepitaculorum*)'.[130] He complains that this fault is common in his day.[131] The metaphor is arresting—the rhythm (˘ ˘ ˘)[132] in κυναρίοις reinforces a diminutive that infantilises those receiving the abuse.[133]

Given how readily κύσιν can enter the rhythmic structure to produce an even succession of iambs, the disruption of the metrical evenness therefore highlights the word. That this word—κυναρίοις—has preoccupied the attention of commentators from the beginning testifies to how effective this rupture was. It was intended to offend,[134] semantically and rhythmically,[135] and it has! Jesus, at this juncture,

---

128. As found in Basil of Caesarea *Feria Homilies* 28.1049.3–4, and the *Pseudo-Clementine Homilies* 2.19. If the pristine form of the proverb did read κύσιν, the article likely was ταῖς, given the predominance of the feminine of dog we have noted: thus, Arist *HA* 574a, Theoph *HP* 9.8.4, Xen *Cyn* 7.6,12, 10.8, Arr *Cyn* pref, 5.7, 15.2, 20.2, 28.1, 2, 31.2.
129. Arist *Rhet* 3.8 (1408b-1409a). Compare also Longin 41. Quintilian noted Aristotle's comments, but argued that the iambic was unavoidable at times—what was important was to surround the common with the superior! See *Inst* 9.4.87–91.
130. Quint *Inst* 9.4.66, himself adopting the rhythm that he criticises to make the point!
131. Cretic-paeonic rhythms are found in Aristophanes but very rarely in tragedy: see ML West, *Introduction to Greek Metre* (Oxford: Clarendon Press, 1989), 55. Aristoxenus *Theory of Metre* is not so scathing about its use, though the reserve remains: see *P Oxy* 9.4.
132. Sometimes called the tribrach: see McCabe, 16.
133. A similar intensification of abuse by infantilising occurs in the tale of Charition, the barbarian woman hunter, who, along with her friends, is slandered as a 'little swine' (χοιρίδιον): see *P Oxy* 413 (l. 38).
134. Quintilian considers iambics to be filled with bitterness (*acerbitas*): *Inst* 10.1.96.
135. Such offences occur in many poetic forms, whether Hebrew (for example, Ps 137:4) or Homeric (for example, *Od* 4.688), as (mis-) quoted by Longin 27.4. Longinus claims to find a number of such faults: 33.3–4.

flows in the stream of invective hurled against women since that most pungent of exponents, Semonides.[136]

A range of aspects has been analysed—the use of a non-identical (cross-species) metaphor, the syntactically self-contained saying, the phonemic and metrical arrangement which evokes expanded realities and excites memory, the succinct appeal to the universal through generalisation and pluralisation. The case for this part of the saying of Jesus to be recognised as a proverb is substantial.[137] Shirley Arora's dictum that the more markers, the greater the recognition and remembrance of a proverb is well-satisfied.[138] The special focus on assonance and metrical structure of the proverb provides reasonable grounds for discounting the suggestion that the proverb, in the form in which it appears here, owes its origin to a Jewish matrix.[139] A complexity is thereby introduced into the analysis—namely the use of a Greek proverb by a Jew. This emphasises the need to test how such a form operates within the narrative context as well as solicit a search for parallels. First however, the remaining two parts of the saying need to be examined, especially given that there is no formal introduction of a quotation (such as τὸ λεγόμενον), the γάρ being formally a constituent of the second part of the saying rather than a signal for the proverb.

β οὐ γὰρ ἐστιν καλόν

i) Providing the value judgment of a maxim

There is a potential danger in the use of universalising statements—the audience may not share the same values, or, at least, not be clear that

136. See Semonides of Amorgos *On Women* where the bestial denigrations find their first (extant) elaboration, much of which is also in iambics. The text is found in E Diehl, *Anthologia Lyrica Graeca* (Leipzig: Teubner, third edition, 1949–52), fr 7; Sarah Pomeroy provides an English translation: *Goddesses*, 49–52.

137. Certainly, all these features are given by Arland Jacobson as indicative of proverbs: AD Jacobson, 'Proverbs and Social Control: A New Paradigm for Wisdom Studies', in JE Goehring *et al* (editors), *Gnosticism and the Early Christian World* (Sonoma, CA: Polebridge Press, 1990), 82.

138. Arora, 'The Perception of Proverbiality', in *Proverbium* 1 (1984): 1–38, reprinted in M Meider (editor), *Wise Words: Essays on the Proverb* (New York: Garland Press, 1994), 13. The markers she expressly names are, *inter alia*, traditionality, appropriateness and currency (on which see further below in relation to contextual referents), metaphor, rhyme, metre, assonance, parallelism, repetition, grammatical and syntactical features offering contrastive distinctions.

139. *Contra* Theissen, *Gospels in Context*, 75n45.

they do! Whilst the rhetorical impact of a universal appeal is made all the more persuasive by the empathy operating between performer and spectator, many rhetoricians recognised that this alliance sometimes had to be assisted. This carried the advantage of magnifying the authority of the speaker. The sound moral character of the speaker is conjoined to the general moral effect of the maxim.[140] The pronouncement of a value gave and received a moral weight to/from the conventional wisdom expounded in the proverb.

Hence, the addition of οὐ (γὰρ) ἐστιν καλόν sequesters one form of speech into another. When Demetrius writes of this practice, it is noteworthy that the form that is the product of change is a precept.[141] The result is a value judgement followed by an infinitive—the main form that is found in many gnomological collections, as elsewhere in the New Testament.[142] This is exactly what has happened to the proverb in the declaration of Mark's Jesus: it has been appropriated as a maxim.[143]

Καλόν, therefore, does not have the comparative force it bears in the collection of *Tobsprüche* in Mark 9:42–50.[144] Rather, it stands on

140. Arist *Rhet* 2.21 (1395b); see, generally, S Carruth, 'Strategies of Authority: A Rhetorical Study of the Character of the Speaker in Q 6:20-49', in JS Kloppenborg (editor), *Conflict and Invention: Literary, Rhetorical and Social Studies on the Sayings Gospel Q* (Valley Forge, PA: TPI, 1995), 98–115.

141. Demetr *Eloc* 5.296.

142. For example, Rom 14:21, 1 Cor 7:1, 26.

143. So strongly was this felt in the course of the transmission of the text of Matthew that the οὐκ ἔστιν καλόν was hardened into οὐκ ἔξεστιν in some manuscripts—moral goodness had become legislated! (*cf* Lk 6:4, 20:22). Of the witnesses, D and Origen (to Mt 11:17) are the most famous. There is also Old Latin and Syriac support. Elaine Wainwright takes up Duncan Derrett's suggestion that there is a legal debate occurring here: *Feminist Critical Reading*, 240 and n74. One manuscript (1293) went further, turning the maxim into a direct instruction addressed not to the woman but to the disciples: '*she* is not to take . . .', omitting καλόν, found also in Tertullian and Eusebius. Robert Gundry holds that, in any case, the woman is not being addressed in Matthew's version until v 28: *Matthew*, 308. This minuscule, at least, supports his reading. Regardless of the addressee, Gundry recognised a maxim (314).

144. *BDF* §358.1 rightly recognise these and others like them (for example, Mt 18:8, Mk 14:21) as different from this instance—they are akin to 2 Pet 2:21.

its 'self-evidencing power',[145] as in Mark 14:21b.[146] Robertson held, 'The good is sometimes more absolute than better or even best'.[147] Consequently, it is eminently suited to fund the appeal to public allegiance that lies at the heart of a maxim's form and function. It not only expects universal support but, as Demetrius writes of maxims, it comes ἀλλὰ μηχανῆς ('but from the pulpit').[148] Here lurks the transcendental reinforcement of ethology.

The effect therefore is to turn the proverb into a sententious moralism—still appealing to the universal, but now narrowing the indeterminacy of the metaphorical reach of the proverb. The audience is to be left in no doubt as to the value appended to the saying.[149] The gnomic turn relies upon the empathy of the audience but won't risk leaving unstated the training in convention that spawned such empathy. Hence, maxims were frequently deployed to conclude an argument or situation, in other words, to bring a discussion to an end—a *sententia clausula*.[150]

The negative expression highlights the direction of this moral turn—it is the negation of the woman, her request and her daughter. This coheres with the preliminary discussion of invective,[151] which operates as the negative face of epideictic rhetoric—the exposé of the dishonourable.

ii) A post-positive problem

The discussion thus far has been oblivious to the presence of the post-positive conjunction, γάρ. Matthew is satisfied without it.[152] Mark appears to introduce the γάρ on the basis of the preceding phrase.[153]

145. *VGT* 318.

146. The maxim in Mark 14:27b also bears the stamp of antiquity: see Bacchyl 5.155–156 *cf* Job 3:3 LXX.

147. Robertson, *Grammar*, 276. The construction is found in semitic and classical Greek usage; *cf* K Beyer, *Semitische Syntax im Neuen Testament* (Göttingen: Vandenhoeck & Ruprecht, second edition, 1968), volume 1, 78–81.

148. Demetr *Eloc*. 4.232. The image he conjures is of the god who spoke words of warning or rebuke in the lofty stage-machine from which a solemn λόγος προτρεπτικός was felt to be more appropriate. Quintilian used another image: 'speaking with the authority of a judge' (*Inst* 8.5.8).

149. Just as Aristotle recommended: Arist *Rhet* 2.21 (1394b).

150. Quint *Inst* 8.5.2, 13–14.

151. See chapter 1.

152. And a very few manuscripts of Mark that is, g^2 sy^s.

153. Focant, 'Mc 7,24–31 par Mt 15,21–29', 50.

The conjunction would otherwise not be required. Its introduction shifts the value judgement, expressed in negative terms, from a moralising maxim standing alone, to a rationale. This is different from a narrative expansion, such as in the use of γάρ in some readings of v 25.[154] Rather it *curtails* development.[155] All that is required for clarity, then, is a premise for this rationale.

α ἄφες πρῶτον χορτασθῆναι τὰ τέκνα

The imperative singular ἄφες that opens Jesus' words, is unique in Mark's gospel.[156] An immediate, pointed focus is given. The rhetoric of the maxim appeals to the global, but its particular application is plain. The effort to 'impose one's will on another'[157] is transparent. Hence, it is difficult to see Jesus offering the Syrophoenician anything other than a conclusion to the encounter.

This highly particularised injunction stands in marked contrast with the general intertexts commentators collate with this phrase, namely Romans 1:16, 2:9.[158] Whether it is Tertullian's supercessionist reading of repudiation of Jews ('first' = prior but no longer)[159] or a more contemporary egalitarianism of Jew and Gentile ('first' implies a 'second'),[160] a Paulinist reading of Mark's phrase has been

154. Aland's Majority Text supports ἀκούσασα γὰρ γυνή.
155. Following SH Levinsohn, 'Some Constraints on Discourse Development in the Pastoral Epistles', in SE Porter and JT Reed (editors), *Discourse Analysis and the New Testament* (Sheffield: Sheffield Academic Press, 1999), 333; see also ML Stirewalt, *Studies in Ancient Greek Epistolography* (Atlanta, GA: Scholars Press, 1993), 58–59.
156. The plural imperative is found at 10:14, 11:25, 14:6, 15:36.
157. RA Young, *Intermediate New Testament Greek: A Linguistic and Exegetical Approach* (Nashville, TN: Broadman & Holman, 1994), 141.
158. *Cf* Acts 3:26, 13:46, 18:18, 28:28.
159. Tert *Fug* 6.3 (*cf C Marc* 4.7), often repeated: see H Alford, *The Greek Testament* (London: Rivingtons, 4 volumes, 1856), volume 1, 340–341.
160. RA Guelich, *Mark 1–8:26* (WBC), (Dallas, TX: Word, 1989), 386, J Jeremias, *Jesus' Promise to the Nations* translated by SH Hooke (London: SCM, 1958), 30. John Kloppenborg however warns that 'egalitarianism' is a special interest of *ours* [his emphasis] that needs both to be declared and controlled carefully' lest apologetics obscure historical and rhetorical analysis: 'Egalitarianism in the Myth and Rhetoric of Pauline Churches', in EA Castelli and H Taussig (editors), *Reimagining Christian Origins: A Colloquium Honoring Burton L Mack* (Valley Forge, PA: TPI, 1996), 260.

determinative.[161] Both operate to exonerate Jesus. He, it is concluded,[162] intended all along to 'feed' the woman, given that the children (the Jews) had already been satisfied (in the first bread miracle).

This line of interpretation requires caution:

i) It assumes that the woman's hearing about the healer/exorcist (Mk 7:25) included hearing of the wonder of the loaves and credits her with the interpretative skills to recognise that this was the meaning of Jesus' curt response to her request. The confusion between character and audience is patent.

ii) The Pauline and Lukan phrases are general statements,[163] as also the distinctive Matthean formulation of the lost sheep of the house of Israel (Mt 15:24). They lack the sharp, pointed function of Mark's imperative. Mark's rationale (οὐκ ἔστιν καλὸν . . .) carries no temporal or sequential meaning. Effectively, commentators have substituted their own Paulinist rationale. The presumption is that Mark either knew the Pauline formula (Rom 1:16, 2:9) and accepted it without question, or that it reigned unchallenged

161. Baudoz is indicative: 'Par conséquent, si Marc, dans la péricope de la S-P, ajoute un logion, dans lequel figure l'adverbe πρῶτον, il est dans mouvance du paulinisme, dont nombre d'auteurs se plaisent à souligner l'influence sur le deuxième évangile.' Baudoz, *Les Miettes*, 279; *cf* J Marcus, *Mark 1–8* (ABC), (New York: Doubleday, 2000), 74–75, 462.

162. The blatant psychological play of nineteenth and early twentieth commentary constructed Jesus as concerned either for the woman's growth in faith or at his own struggles to find a way to proceed compassionately: see H Cowan, 'Syrophoenician Woman', in J Hasting, JA Selbie and JC Lambert (editors), *A Dictionary of Christ and the Gospels* (Edinburgh: T&T Clark, 1906), volume 2, 693, Hasler, 'Incident', 460–461. More recent commentary has distanced the person of Jesus by the use of the literary construction of a 'quest story' or 'obstacles to success': R Pesch, *Das Markusevangelium* (HTKNT), (Freiburg: Herder, 2 Volumes, 1976), 1. 391, J Painter, *Mark's Gospel* (London/New York: Routledge, 2001), 114, Gundry, *Matthew*, 314. Nevertheless, the effect continues to exonerate Jesus.

163. Robert Guelich calls them principles and schematics (*Mark 1–8:26*, 386).

in earliest Christianity.[164] (The Matthean formula alone undermines this). Few have suggested that the triumph of the woman might be a repudiation of the totality of Jesus' saying, even with its supposed 'Pauline' flavour.[165]

iii) No effort has been made to interpret the force of ἄφες in its address to a woman. Here the interpretative dominance of ethnic and missiological concerns and gender invisibility, reaches its zenith.

iv) The intertextual relations forged between Mark and Luke-Paul have deftly sidelined analysis of other instances of πρῶτον in different sources. J Murphy O'Connor notes the use of πρῶτον in Jn 1:41 for example.[166] Here, there is no 'second' (δεύτερος) action,[167] though he surmises that Andrew also called others. One or two commentators have read this part of Jesus' saying similarly in Mark as implying exclusivity.[168] The sense of pre-eminence

---

164. The fact that πρῶτον is omitted in Romans 1:16 by B G and some Sahidic manuscripts shows that an alternate view was possible in early Christianity, even if, as TA Burkill suggests, this betrays Marcionite influence: 'The Historical Development of the Story of the Syrophoenician Woman (Mark 7:24–31)', in *NovT* 9 (1967): 162n1.

165. Elisabeth Schüssler Fiorenza decentres the emphasis on the Paulinist model of mission by placing the Gentile woman as the critical gatekeeper, whilst maintaining the missionary perspective: *But She Said*, 97. Hal Taussig ignores the Pauline dimensions altogether, seeing the language of 'first' as belonging to the earliest stage of the tradition relating to table hierarchies. 'Dealing under the Table: Ritual Negotiation of Women's Power in the Syro-Phoenician Woman Pericope', in Castelli and Tausssig, *Reimagining Christian Origins*, 265.

166. 'John the Baptist and Jesus: History and Hypotheses', in *NTS* 36 (1990): 362; *cf* Mt 5:24, 2 Cor 8:5.

167. *Cf* Jn 4:54. Murphy O'Connor considered that it was edited out.

168. Guelich, *Mark 1–8:26*, 387, though he does so by removing πρῶτον from the original saying, perhaps unnecessarily, if one reads πρῶτον as exclusive, as does Dieter Lührmann, *Das Markusevangelium* (Tübingen: Mohr, 1987), 131. The influence of a Pauline reading has persuaded many that πρῶτον is late Markan redaction. Occasionally, it is read as entering the tradition before final redaction: L Schenke, *Die Wundererzählungen des Markusevangeliums* (Stuttgart: Katholisches Bibelwerk, 1974), 256–257, Jeremias, *Jesus' Promise* 29n2, Taussig,

rather than sequence is found in pseudo-Pauline usage as well (1 Tim 5:4; *cf* 2:1).[169] Certainly, pre-eminence is not excluded from Mark's usage (for example, 9:11, 10:31, 44). Markan usage has not received parity of analysis. The temporal priority of πρῶτον is certainly indicated in Mk 3:27, though the inevitability of the sequence is not demonstrated.[170] The same applies in the sequence of the growth of corn/wheat in Mk 4:28, the coming of Elijah (9:11, 12) or even, perhaps, the coming of Jesus himself or world anarchy (13:10). Πρῶτον is a priority, not necessarily a sequence.[171] Certainly Mark's adjectival use emphasises rank and hierarchy (for example, 6:21, 9:35) and may offer nothing in terms of race. The noted desire of some Jewish leaders for the 'pre-eminent couches' (πρωτοκλισίαι Mk 12:39) is a clear example of this understanding.

v) Whilst Duncan Derrett applies the Jew-Gentile grid to the Sarepheth story, he avoids a Heilsgeschichte perspective, looking to ancient (Jewish) legal prescriptions on acceptable hospitality for Gentiles.[172] The emphasis on eating in the gospel sayings and Elijah's preamble (1 Kgs 17:13) suggests that we are dealing with Christian struggles over the etiquette and rationale for dining (not missionary) practices. This remains dominant in the woman's reply, and, it will be argued, in the action of her daughter. The

'Dealing under the Table', 265. Vincent Taylor argued for the authenticity of the adverb: *Mark*, 350; *cf* K Kertelge, *Die Wunder Jesu im Markusevangelium. Eine redaktionsgeschichtliche Untersuchung* (StANT Volume 23), (München: Kösel, 1970), 153, R Kampling, *Israel unter dem Anspruch: Studien zur Israelthematik im Markusevangelium* (Stuttgart: Katholisches Bibelwerk, 1992), 136.

169. As elsewhere: Eur *Bac* 20, Acts 28:7.

170. That is, there is no necessity that the plundering of the house follow on the binding of the strong man. This would be, in Aristotle's terms, a false deduction *Rhet* 2.24 (1400b–1402a).

171. *Contra* Marcus, *Mark 1–8*, 463.

172. Derrett, 'Law in the New Testament', 166–167.

> accent on ecclesial disputes ought not quarantine analysis from general eating conventions in the ancient world, whether this be from an historicist or audiential perspective.[173] Indeed, if the proverb micro-narrative be allowed its concise application, there is no consent that the dogs be fed at all nor that they be fed the same food as the members of the household.[174] Certainly, even in (Greco-Roman) households that included dogs, there were sometimes scruples about allowing dogs to share the same food as the masters. Distinctions in food—of kind, amount, order of distribution, manner and place of dining—served a larger semiotic: the distinction of species.[175] As a familiar Pompeian graffito has it: 'The one with whom I do not dine, is a barbarian to me.'[176] And if my earlier suggestion holds, that τέκνα in Mark has a monandric as well as ethnic reference,[177] then πρῶτον may be limited to practices within Jewish households. These households made no interior provision for dogs.[178]

Consequently, the presence of πρῶτον does not require a missionary sequence or even a shared table fellowship. It may simply indicate prominence.

173. Hal Taussig and Kathleen Corley are the only writers, to my knowledge, who have raised such a suggestion: see Taussig, 'Dealing', 272–274, K. Corley, 'Jesus' Table Practice: Dining with "Tax Collectors and Sinners," including Women', in *SBLSP* (1993): 445.

174. Ps-Luc *As* 33 is instructive. The master plans to slaughter an ass. The entrails would be given to the dog, but the prime cuts were reserved for the master's men.

175. Distinctions of species could variously deal with race, age and status. See generally Plut *Mor* 635b–638a, and Pedar W Foss, 'Kitchens and Dining Rooms', 45–56.

176. *At quem non ceno barbarus ille mihi est* (*CIL* 4.1880).

177. 'The Singular Reproach of the Woman' in chapter 2.

178. See further chapter 4. Such houses did pursue a hierarchy of eating practices, an interpretation recognised though not endorsed by Schüssler Fiorenza, *Sharing Her Word*, 127.

An enthymeme?

The saying of Jesus in Mark 7:27 cannot remain dismembered, either syntactically or ideologically. Γάρ networks the words. In fact, the totality of the saying enhances the assertion of universal reality.

ἄφες πρῶτον χορτασθῆναι τὰ τέκνα
οὐ γάρ ἐστιν καλὸν
λαβεῖν τὸν ἄρτον τῶν τέκνων καὶ τοῖς κυναρίοις βαλεῖν

The connection between maxim and enthymeme was long recognised by the rhetoricians.[179] Paul Holloway can speak also of an 'enthymematic proverb'.[180] The relationship was not so much formalistic as rhetorical or functional. Part of the power of both proverb and maxim is the appeal to a universal or general truth. The invocation of convention, custom or universal admission is deemed to control the use of a metaphor,[181] preserve a proverb across time,[182] ground a maxim,[183] and provide the basis for the construction of an enthymeme.

The appeal to convention accessed an arena of reasoning that supported the enthymeme. Usually, a premise, though sometimes a conclusion, might be left unstated.[184] A maxim could supply either.[185] In Aristotle's view, it was not always wise to leave something unspoken (as we saw above in regard to the moralising introduction in some maxims). However, the level of persuasion was the more successful

179. Arist *Rhet* 2.20–21 (1393a–1394a), Quint *Inst* 8.5.4, 9–10.

180. PA Holloway, 'The Enthymeme as an Element of Style in Paul', in *JBL* 120 (2001): 335n42, citing Sen *Ep* 85.4: *Non est bona valitudo mediocritas morbi* ('good health doesn't mean middling illness'). Lane McGaughy notes Aristotle's bipartite division of rhetorical proof collated maxims and proverbs under enthymemes: 'Pagan Hellenistic Literature: The Babrian Fables', in *SBLSP* (1977): 211n1.

181. Demetr *Eloc* 2.86. A risk rides in a daring metaphor (2.80). Seneca advised against such use (*Ep* 59.6).

182. 'The wisdom of a people, the wisdom of the world' (Demetr *Eloc* 4.232).

183. Even those which are well-worn: Arist *Rhet* 2.21 (1395a).

184. V Robbins, 'From Enthymeme to Theology in Luke 11:1–13', in RP Thompson and TE Phillips (editors), *Literary Studies in Luke-Acts: Essays in Honor of Joseph B Tyson* (Macon, GA: Mercer University Press, 1998), 191. Aristotle certainly allowed for the latter: *Rhet* 2.23 (1400b). In fact, he noted that such premises were frequently resistant to conscious propositional formulation: *Inc* 702b.

185. *Rhet* 2.21 (1394a).

if the performer had rightly adduced the wisdom of the audience,[186] precisely because audience and performer become collaborators in this 'speech event.'[187] The audience, in a sense, provides the 'missing' part of a syllogism. Demetrius calls it an addition to speech.[188] Its compactness, empathy and forcefulness of presentation[189] avoided the danger besetting the trained logician of losing the audience in the obscurity and prolixity of a major proposition.[190]

Vernon Robbins expands on the power of the enthymeme: 'A proposition plus a rationale presents an enthymeme (a syllogism with a premise),'[191] the more influential when it is framed in terms of a contrary or negative, that is of advocating one course of action over against another.[192] This had the effect of exposing the inadequacies not only of an action but of someone who appeared to be in pursuit of such a course—as in the case of the Syrophoenician woman. And it invited the audience to make their 'wise judgement'.

The exemplary enthymeme is built therefore on a dualistic contrast. In fact, Jeffrey Walker's list of the 'emotively significant oppositions' that delivered an enthymeme's power begins to look disconcertingly familiar: human/animal, wise/foolish, cultured/ignorant and so on. One might have added the familiar ethological foundation of male/

186. Arist *Top* 1.1.101b, *Rhet* 1.1 (1355a). Quintilian even calls the enthymeme the syllogism of oratory(!)—*Inst* 9.4.57; *cf* the more standard appraisal in 5.14.24. Jeffrey Walker tackles the problem from another angle, arguing that 'syllogism' in ancient Greek bore a meaning beyond that of logical progression. It encompassed an intuitively derived inference more familiar in the ordinary currency of life: *Rhetoric and Poetics in Antiquity* (Oxford: Oxford University Press, 2000), 170–183.

187. 'The truth of the conclusion is dependent upon the truth of the premises as acknowledged by the interlocutors . . . ': D Hellholm, 'Enthymemic Argumentation in Paul: The Case of Romans 6', in T Engberg-Pedersen (editor), *Paul in his Hellenistic Context* (Minneapolis: Fortress Press, 1995), 128. On Aristotle's recognition of the role of audience, see *Poet* 17.1–3; *cf* Longin 41.2–3.

188. Demetr *Eloc* 1.32.

189. The summary description of Jeffrey Walker, *Rhetoric and Poetics*, 176.

190. This is exactly Cicero's criticism of Stoic orators (*De Or* 2.157–159, 3.78–79).

191. 'Progymnastic Rhetorical Composition and Pre-Gospel Traditions: A New Approach', in C Focant (editor), *The Synoptic Gospels: Source Criticism and the New Literary Criticism* (BETL 110), (Leuven: Leuven University Press, 1993), 125.

192. Anaximen *Rhet* 1430a. See the discussion in Holloway, 'The Enthymeme', 330–335.

female.[193] The appeal therefore to an audience's presuppositions is grounded in *and* reinforces familiar sociobiological stru(i)ctures.[194]

A proposition with a rationale, reinforced by a negative quite succinctly breaks down parts α and β–γ of Jesus' saying in verse 27:

Proposition: α ἄφες πρῶτον χορτασθῆναι τὰ τέκνα
Rationale (by contrary):[195] β οὐ γάρ ἐστιν καλὸν
(γ) λαβεῖν τὸν ἄρτον τῶν τεκνων καὶ τοῖς κυναρίοις βαλεῖν

The proposition functions, given the imperative, as a rule. Framed in such a fashion, the saying possesses a similar structure to that recorded of Aesop:

> When a certain man had been torn by the bite of a vicious dog he dipped a piece of bread in his own blood and tossed it out to the evildoer, because he had heard that this was a remedy for such a wound. Then said Aesop:
>
> (*Proposition*) 'Don't let any more dogs see you doing this,
> (*Rationale*) lest they devour us alive when they learn that guilt is rewarded in this way.'[196]

Vernon Robbins advocated that to distinguish enthymemes from formal logic, as well as to discern how an individual enthymeme is crafted, the language of major/minor premise and conclusion should be adjusted to rule, case and result.[197] According to this frame, the rule is the proposition expressed as an imperative, the case is the rationale and the result, expressed as a moralism by contrary, is deduced by the editor, acting for the audience: 'The success of the wicked lures many others into evil ways.'.

---

193. Walker, *Rhetoric and Poetics*, 178.
194. Walker, *Rhetoric and Poetics,* 184.
195. One subset of Aristotle's demonstrative enthymeme: *Rhet* 2.23 (1397a).
196. Aes *Fab* 2.3 (Phaedrus).
197. See generally, 'Enthymeme to Theology'. Robbins relies upon RL Lanigan, 'From Enthymeme to Abduction: The Classical Law of Logic and the Postmodern Rule of Rhetoric', in L Langsdorf and AR Smith (editors), *Recovering Pragmatism's Voice: The Classical Tradition, Rorty, and the Philosophy of Communication* (Albany, NY: SUNY Press, 1995), 49–70.

Following this suggestion, we may frame the syllogism of Jesus' words to the Syrophoenician woman as:

Rule: Let the children first be fed
Case: Taking the children's bread and throwing it to
the dogs (is not good . . . therefore)
Result: The request by a dog for food is (to be) denied.

The result or conclusion is left unstated but an audience, sharing (or invited to share) the same value, supplies the muted element of the enthymeme by deduction. It is here that the sententious introduction to the proverb invites the result.[198] Of course, this demands an appreciation of the context that induces this empathetic judgment. For the enthymeme to work rhetorically, the equation of woman/daughter and dog must operate within an agreed conventional assessment. Accordingly, the narrative must provide sufficient clues, with linkages to the cultural conventions of the audience, to invite acceptance of and contribution to the reasoning portraying itself as customary.

The question of a shared hold upon cultural conventions is the shadow that haunts ancient rhetoricians. Accordingly, they advise speakers, by foreknowledge and/or flattery, to close the gap between themselves and their hearers.[199] For the moment, it is important to recognise that each form mounts a claim to universal verity: the aggregation of proverb, through maxim, into enthymeme becomes almost unassailable. Tones of antiquity, nature and literature have become one in witness to the logocentric order of the cosmos.

The sanctity of the antiquity of the forms

Shirley Arora writes:

> Probably the most consistently accepted generalization concerning proverbs, in virtually any language, is that they are 'traditional', and that it is their traditionality—the sense of historically-derived authority or of community-sanctioned wisdom that they convey—that makes them 'work'.[200]

198. So Arist *Rhet* 2.21 (1395b).
199. Quint *Inst* 3.7.23–24, 3.8.14, 15, Arist *Rhet* 1.9 (1367b).
200. Arora, 'Perception of Proverbiality', 4.

In a society which placed a high premium on antiquity,[201] the use of proverbs in speech laid claim to their evident truths, to one's own place in the continuum from that ancient time when such truths were carved, and to one's exemplary place in a community that held to such values. Scriptural citation and allusion operate similarly, as does a reference to a revered authority (such as Homer 'the Poet').[202] They are universal, they are ancient, and they reserve a standing.

In this sense, according to Arora, a community's *perception* of proverbiality operates in the same way: if enough of the phenomenological markers are present, even a coinage may receive the honorific status that attaches to proverbs. Even so, in the discipline of paroemiology, textual research for prior instances was a necessary, though not absolute, part of the testing of antiquity.[203] As will be seen, each part of Jesus' saying satisfies the tests of antiquity and currency.

α ἄφες πρῶτον χορτασθῆναι τὰ τέκνα

When granted the opportunity to be viewed from the perspective of an appeal to antiquity, this part of the saying draws its authority not from a response to a novel issue, but by a fitting application of an established principle. This section of the enthymeme relies upon a recognised table hierarchy (males before women and children before slaves, concubines and dogs). Pedar Foss has provided a detailed analysis of age, gender and status divisions at meal-times.[204] Whilst he has concentrated upon elite Roman arrangements, he has demonstrated how ingrained was the concern for conventions about eating. Ancient writers noted etiquette differences between cultures—for example: whether, when and in what circumstances wives and children would eat with the main male of the house (and his friends).[205] But the concern for hierarchies of dining was constant.

---

201. Quintilian, for example, equated antiquity and sanctity: *Inst* 1.6.1 (*vetus, religio*); *cf* his appeal to antiquity when a matter is in dispute: 12.1.36; also Longin, 7.4, 13.2–4, Pl *Ep* 1.16, 22; *cf* Lk 5:39.
202. For example Plut *Mor* 617c.
203. Arora, 'Perception of Proverbiality', 7.
204. See generally P Foss, 'Kitchens and Dining Rooms'; see also K Corley, *Private Women, Public Meals: Social Conflict in the Synoptic Tradition* (Peabody, MT: Hendricksen, 1993), 24–34, 100n82.
205. See, for example, Plut *Mor* 613a in the debate over whether and where philosophers should be placed at meals. Some did not host them: 'and the pretext they very solemnly employ is that philosophy should no more have a part in conversation over wine than should the matron of

Hence Sarah does not eat with Abram when he entertains the three companions (Gen 18:1–9) just as Herodias does not infringe the men's domain at Herod's party (Mk 6:24).[206] Sarah's role is in the preparation of food.[207] Children by age (or by another determinant, as is the force of τέκνα) may or may not eat with the leader (either by seating arrangement, allocated dining quarters, or time of eating), depending on the nature and purpose of the meal (*cf* Gen 27:15–29). Jesus groups worked out diverse, gradated arrangements related to seating.[208]

The order of seating also flowed into the receipt and quality of food. The slide down the status scale meant that slaves often were fed the leftovers of the leftovers.[209] All these arrangements could 'become a sinister instrument of power and exclusion.'[210] However, the primary grounding of eating practices lay in the subtle combination of recognition and imposition of order in/upon nature. In the debate over the taxonomy of seating arrangements in Plutarch's *Table Talk*, Plutarch's father, the signifier of antiquity, argues strongly for the careful and appropriate designation of respective places.[211] He

---

the house. They commend the Persians for doing their drinking and their dancing with their mistresses rather than with their wives.'

206. Note the spatial differentials indicated in the daughter's 'going out' (ἐξελθοῦσα) to speak to her mother.

207. The singular imperative ἄφες, in verse 27, given the gendered context constructed by αὐτῇ, may carry this further dimension—that of the domestic responsibilities of woman, ordained by ancient custom, for the preparation of food in a household: Ov *Med Fac* 16–17, *Fast* 4.697–698, Hor *Epod* 2.39–48, Mart *Epig* 12.18, Prov 31:15. This is distinct from food '*for* a household' which was the responsibility of a κυρίος, if present. This 'guardian' could be father, brother, eldest son or husband, or indeed, one person fulfilling all these roles—see Ter *And* 295.

208. Compare for example Lk 14:7–10, 17:7–9 and Jas 2:1–4. Christians were simply entering familiar philosophical territory of debate: see C Osiek and DL Balch, *Families in the New Testament World* (Louisville, KY: WJKP, 1997), 195—199.

209. Mart *Epig* 12.48; *cf* Hor *Sat* 2.8.10–13, Mart *Epig* 2.37, 3.23, 60, Juv *Sat* 8.40–44. Even in an elite male dining setting, the quality of food betokened status differences: Juv *Sat* 5.67–88. For a detailed analysis of food and status in Palestine, see G Hamel, *Poverty and Charity in Roman Palestine, First Three Centuries CE* (Berkeley: University of California Press, 1990), 8–39.

210. E Gowers, *The Loaded Table. Representations of Food in Roman Literature* (Oxford: Oxford University Press, 1993), 131, P Veyne, 'The Roman Empire', in P Veyne (editor), *A History of Private Life I: From Pagan Rome to Byzantium* translated by A Goldhammer (Cambridge MA: Belknap Press, 1987), 186–188.

211. Plut *Mor* 616b.

clinches his argument by the appeal to a proverb: 'Myconos Equality'. The proverb hangs as the denouement of the argument; it is assumed that it is understood in the context. Strabo provides us with the necessary explanation. It refers 'to those who bring under one title those things which are *by nature* (τῇ φύσει) separate'.[212] Antiquity, universal wisdom, and a subtle appeal to nature, rightly interpreted, have combined to clinch the argument about the right ordering of table fellowship.[213] In the Markan story, the syntax of eating is intimated by Jesus' opening command, one which is long-established and widely-acknowledged.

β οὐ γὰρ ἐστιν καλόν

The phrase adopts the familiar beginning of a 'sentence'—a type of moral maxim that simply asserts 'it is good/not good, wise/not wise, better/worse'. Christian and non-christian sources attest its popularity.[214] The proverb devolves into a perfunctory axiomatic sentence, its summary endorsement of conventionality intended to close debate without dispute.

The formulaic beginning is not only widely attested in Hellenistic and biblical writings across a variety of genres; it is ancient as well. The use of the formula in the mouths of the enemy troops in Judith 10:19 hints at the cross-cultural use of the formula. The maxim is found with and without the copula in Homer;[215] and there is the striking parallel to this introductory formula in the opening biblical book. Genesis 2:18 reads: Οὐ καλὸν εἶναι τὸν ἄνθρωπον μόνον. Commentators have occasionally aligned the texts.[216] The intertwining of the claim upon the divine and the use of a maxim reiterates the cosmic foundation of universal governance.[217] Considerable doubt might attend whether Mark (or the tradition) intended the allusion. However, whilst God is not explicit in Jesus' saying, lying in the background is the long-standing rule of 'the good', virtually synonymous with the divine.[218] The notion was particularly influential upon the array of Judaisms

212. Strab *Geog* 10.5.9.

213. The opposing, egalitarian view is put by the idealistic younger brother of Plutarch; Plutarch himself provides the final word, which reinforces convention. On a similar combination of an appeal to reason, antiquity and nature, see Vitr 2 pref 5.

214. See, for example, *The Sentences of Sextus*.

215. Hom *Od* 18.287, 20:294.

216. Baudoz, *Les Miettes*, 252.

217. Charond *Leg* preface.

218. Phil Jud *Spec* 2.6, Sen *Ep* 66.12.

in the Hellenistic period. The *Testament of Naphtali* provides an illuminating example:

> If you practise the good, my sons, humans and angels will bless you; and God will be glorified through you among the gentiles. The devil will flee from you; wild animals will fear you and the angels will secure you.[219]

Here the ethological dimensions of the pursuit or non-pursuit of 'the good' are transparent. Hence, to stand against the good runs counter to the divine and cosmic order, undercuts honour (*cf* Sir 41:16) and warrants collation with the anarchy of wild animals.[220]

The particular wording of a sententious formula found in Mk 7:27 is not fortuitous or coincidental. It lays claim to the systemic arrangement of the *logos* to provide the necessary grounding for the ethological collation that follows. The use of γάρ merely reinforces an acceptance of such traditional verities.[221]

γ λαβεῖν τὸν ἄρτον τῶν τέκνων καὶ τοῖς κυναρίοις βαλεῖν

In Mark's pericope, the repetition of γυνή (Mk 7:25, 26; *cf* Mt 15:22 only) descends into talk of dogs. This metaphorical connection not only reinforces the suggestion of a proverb but also promotes the ethological comparison of women with beasts.[222] A short essay by David Smith,[223] long-forgotten in commentary on the Syrophoenician woman's story,[224] pointed out a proverb in Erasmus' sixteenth century collection which had remarkable similarities to the words of Jesus:

219. *TNaph* 8:4 (my translation); *cf T Benj* 11:1.

220. See also the collation of bestial, demonic (and female form) in Aristotle's allusion to Lamia in *Nic Eth* 7.5.2 (1143b).

221. This probably lies behind the addition of γάρ in a number of manuscripts of *TNaph* 8:4.

222. Recalling Aristotle's 'proverbs are metaphors from one species to another': *Rhet* 3.11 (1413a); *cf Poet* 21.7–8 (1457b).

223. 'Hard Saying', 320. Smith apologetically applied his discovery to ameliorate the ferociousness of Jesus' words. He deployed the supposedly softer Hellenistic response as an alternative to the hard-hearted Pharisaical reply, which he felt had characterised previous interpretations of Jesus' words. The anti-semitic heuristic device is clear. Further, he takes no account of the cultural transfer of a proverb. There are good grounds for considering the Jewish use of a Hellenistic proverb to a Hellenic woman as fomenting stronger abuse.

224. But see Derrett, 'Law in the New Testament', 172n5.

σεαυτὸν οὐ τρέφων κυνας τρέφεις, (*non alenste, alis canes*), loosely translated 'Being unable to feed yourself, you yet feed dogs'. In the form αὑτὸν οὐ τρέφων, κύνας τρέφεις, it is recorded by Diogenes the second century CE (?) paroemiographer in his examples of proverbs in trochaic metre.[225]

i) The currency, antiquity and protean manifestations of the proverb

The currency of the proverb is as widespread as it is variegated in form. It is usually recorded in the proverb collections as a fragment of comedy.[226] Ferdinand Orth considered that the proverb lay behind the servant's cry τοιουτονὶ τρέφειν κύνα ('fancy keeping such a dog') in Aristophanes' *Wasps* (835).[227] That dog's name, Labes, is a play on λαβεῖν, and relies on the traditional association of greed with a dog—nothing in the kitchen is safe.[228] Stealing bread is a dog's proclivity.[229]

The shame that attached to the dog in this regard was transferred to any who took food from another.[230] The frequency of the cry οὐκ ἐκφορά ('do not carry it off') in literature and inscription[231] may confirm the prevalence of the problem, but it also signals the dominant convention. Plutarch calls the breaking of it 'low and vulgar'.[232]

Xanthias' opening exclamation in the scene from the *Wasps* is crucial to our understanding, for it plays upon the despised nature of

---

225. From A Schottus, *Paroimiai Helllenika Adagia sive proverbial Graecorum ex Zenobio seu Zenadoto, Diogeniano & Suidae Collectaneis* (Antwerp: officina Plantiniana apud viduam & filios Ioannis Moreti, 1612), 642–643.
226. Comica Adespota *Fragmenta incertarium poetarum* 639.
227. Orth, 'Hund', *RE* 8.2572; Saara Lilja doubts the connection: *Dogs*, 73n13. However, the association of the dog with the thief Laches, through both onomastic assonance and narrative (the comic trial of the dogs), makes the connection clear.
228. Aristoph *Eq* 1022–1025; *cf Ach* 1159–1160, Ps-Luc *As* 26.
229. So strong was the dog's instinct to snatch bread, that the comic writer Diphilus used it to accent a woman's ugliness: 'from whom a dog would not take bread' (fr 91.2).
230. See the snide comments of Mart *Epig* 5.50. It may be that clients received a food supply from their patron; however this does not remove the shame of doing so. Shame here operates as a status differential, reminding clients of their dependency and lack of autonomy: see S Robinson, *Juvenal: Sixteen Satires on the Ancient Harlot* (Manchester: Carcanet New Press, 1983), 82.
231. *Eg* Aristoph *Plut* 1138, Plut *Mor* 660b, *CIL* 4.7698.
232. Plut *Mor* 660b.

the dog—the scavenger. Xanthius bellows: βαλλ' ἐς κόρακας, 'chuck it to the crows', an imprecation of particular relevance here, for both crow and dog were the carrion-foragers of the ancient world.[233] The household was no place for them. But there is another edge: carrion suggested a dishonourable death (*ie* without burial).[234] In the play, the familiar oath becomes an ironically prophetic curse on the human thief, Laches. The entire scene of the taking of food is metaphorical.

The proverb is also well-known in Latin: *Te ipsum non alens canes alis*. Tertullian fell into its form, when alluding to Jesus' words to the Syrophoenician in his teaching on the Lord's Prayer. However, his accent was on the father feeding his sons, woman and daughter being completely elided.[235] The acceptance of the proverbial background of the dominical word is indicated in the Greek fathers. John Chrysostom, for example, implants additional dialogue into the Syrophoenician's address of Jesus: 'you call me a dog as I keep a dog' (κύνα με καλεῖς ὡς κύων τρέφομαι). The key terms, κύων τρέφομαι, come from the pristine proverb. The expanded dialogue assumes that a dog is kept.[236]

ii) The proverb as basis for a declamatory exercise

First century schooling in oratory was underpinned by declamatory exercises. Jeffrey Walker notes,

> the focus of declamation in this period was on the invention and deployment of memorable, penetrating, epigrammatic *sententiae*, which did in fact serve as a crucial weapon of 'rhetorical attack' (and defense and

233. Luc *Dem* 60.
234. For example, Hom *Il* 23.182–183, Aeschyl *Sept* 1014, Sen *Contr* 1.7.2, Eus *DE* 4.10.2.4–5.
235. Tertullian writes, 'Does a father take away bread from his children and hand it to dogs?' and goes on to comment, 'For he [the Lord] shows what it is that sons expect from their father.' (*Orat* 6.3). If this is an allusion, even an intended quotation of a part of the story (which part Tertullian calls a parable), then Tertullian has completely restructured the story to make the father the provider of bread and the sons the recipients, even though the 'parabolic saying' of Jesus has a woman and her daughter as the referents of the saying. The triumph of the gospel for Tertullian meant that it was no longer Jewish and no longer female.
236. *Can* 52.457.42–46.

> counterattack) in actual political life and in the courts . . .[237]

These exercises not only drew on actual cases but mined potential topics for disputation from poetry, mythology and history.

One of the stock declamation themes hung on the ancient obligation to support one's parents.[238] Quintilian states the law bluntly: 'Children shall support their parents under penalty of imprisonment.'[239] Declamatory exercises were constructed on whether such an obligation had any legal or conventional limits. Quintilian refers to one testing of this obligation familiar from his youth, although no longer enamoured of its contemptuous style. It drew on a poetic origin. *Etiam canem pascis* is the Latin equivalent[240] of the proverbial allusion in Aristophanes' *Wasps* already quoted: 'Fancy keeping such a dog!' The debate is played against the command: *da patri panem.*[241] The same declamatory maxim is found in Seneca the Elder's *Controversiae*, though given a twist: 'Don't you give your father the bread you give your dog?'[242] Various arguments were tested for and against the two sides—defending the well-being of one's family or justifying the suspension of such an obligation.

The proximity of this declamatory exercise to the issues and even the language in Jesus' saying is remarkable. The proverb warning about

237. *Rhetoric and Poetics*, 97.
238. Such domestic concerns go to the heart, argues Jeffrey Walker, of the deeper social issues of the Roman elite: *Rhetoric and Poetics* 98. They were also 'the backbone of adolescent education': Connolly, 'Mastering Corruption', 137.
239. Quint *Inst* 7.6.5. Quintilian makes constant use of illustration and argument based on this obligation; see 7.1.52, 7.7.9, 11.1.58–59, 62, 66. It frequented declamatory exercises: see Sen *Contr* 1.1, 1.6, 7.4, Ps-Quint *Decl* Bk 5. Lurking in the background is the ethos of the Twelve Tables which, whilst not specific, was taken to adjure filial responsibility (see especially, Tables IV, XII); *cf* Plat *Leg* 930a–932d, Sir 3:1–16. Whilst normally focussed on fathers and sons, the same issue arises in Plautus' *Asinaria* of a mother and daughter, the limits here tested by the mother's prostitution of her daughter.
240. *Pasco* provides the Latin translation, *inter alia*, for τρέφω. Although not found in the Old Latin or Vulgate in Mark 7:27, it is sometimes listed as the translation for χορτάζω: see, for example, C Schreveli, *Lexicon Manuale Graeco-Latinum et Latino-Graecum* (London: Rivington, 1831), sv.
241. Quint *Inst* 8.3.22.
242. Sen *Contr* 1.7.17–18.

the maintaining of a dog is sharpened (οὐ κάλον). The obligation to one's own is expressed in terms of τέκνα. The question of how to understand the referent of τέκνα may be at issue if we draw too close a parallel with the terms of the standard exercise of declamatory training. Matthew certainly draws the connection between the 'children' and 'the lost sheep of the house of Israel' (15:24,26),[243] and it might be argued that this was synonymous with fathers. The terminology operates clearly enough within a Jewish framework. However, the slight adjustment in language creates an ambiguity that the woman will later exploit in the shift to παιδία. However τέκνα be understood, the proverb is dispensed as their privilege and protection. Accordingly, the deployment of the proverb as a reminder of responsibilities has found another arena, one scored by contest.

iii) Origins in the hunt?

The proverb concentrates on the dog's lack of social propriety and its disturbance of conventional obligations.[244] The origin of the proverb may derive from the dangers that beset the hunter. The borderlands of the hunt were the bestial. A sign that a breach of boundaries had occurred was a collapse of proportion—the household was sacrificed for the sake of the hounds. The Byzantine lexicon, the *Suda*, applied the proverb to the status exchanges of meals: 'concerning those without resources who yet announce the feeding of others.'[245]

The proverb's flexibility is shown in its indication of greed, not by the animals themselves but by the one who kept them. The paroemiologist, Macarius, made this clear in collating this proverb with another, δειλὸν ὁ Πλοῦτος ('vile is the god of wealth') explaining it as those who secure their houses and keep dogs.[246] Philo displayed complementary Jewish disdain, castigating the gluttonous extravagances wrought by desire, comparing its debauched devotees to greedy κυνιδία sneaking around banquet halls.[247] But greed could give way to poverty, where the dogs themselves were lost.[248] Seneca

243. On 'children' (τέκνα) as primarily indicating adults, see Osiek and Balch, *Families*, 163–165. On the importance of the debate in early christianity, *cf* 2 Cor 12:14b, 2 Cor 6:13, 1 Tim 5:8, 2 Tim 3:2.
244. It was allied with a similar proverb: 'Who feeds a stranger's dog' (Isocrat *Dem* 29, *cf* Luc *Fug* 16, *Nigr* 21, Dio Chr *Or* 31.114, Phil Jud *Gig* 35).
245. *The Suda* A§4513 (my translation).
246. Macarius 3.27, *cf* Diod Sic 13.82, Athen *Deip* 123f.
247. Phil Jud *Spec* 4.91.
248. Tzetzes *Comm Il* 37.8.

dispenses a further maxim that proceeds in this direction: 'Those who do not support their own go hungry.'[249]

The array of contextual applications and variegated manifestations of the proverb (fraudulent greed, abdication from social and familial responsibility, abject poverty) coheres with observations of the semantic flexibility and genre promiscuity of proverbs. But the antiquity and currency of the proverb is confirmed.

Conclusion

Every part of the saying of Jesus in Mark's story lays claim to traditional wisdom. The proverb owes its origins to a Greek (rather than Jewish) formulation,[250] or at least to one which has been shaped by a Greek comic metre. Its deployment, far from ameliorating the abuse (as David Smith wanted), in fact compounds it. The edifice of hallowed antiquity, transmitted through its literary traditions, towers over the woman and her daughter. To have the female-bestial collation confirmed by a conjunction of scientific/philosophical axioms and literary/cultural expression, is to privilege, even require, that the confirmation be declaimed by that monument to a logocentric universe: a man.

The very structure of Jesus' words to the Syrophoenician woman, not simply their content, reasserts the fundamental dimorphic alignment that lies at the heart of ancient and modern ethology. The saying is invested with a political agenda, cloaked under a 'traditional referentiality' of prized forms (proverb, maxim and enthymeme) and incorporates a fundamental ethological comparison that places the woman in an inferior position. The inevitable diminishment of character flowing from this dualism is grounded in the requisite gender privilege attached to the speech of a man. It is intensified by the psychagogic aspects of the intricacies of the saying's construction and the deliberate and potent use of a diminutive. In my assessment, there can no longer be any equivocation about the nature and intent of Jesus' words to the woman: it is vituperative abuse, designed not merely to deny the woman's request but to cast a damning judgment upon her identity (*ethologia*). Any exoneration is to be repudiated as complicit in the

249. *Contr* 1.1.16.

250. *Contra* Burkill, 'Historical Development', 172, Pesch, *Das Markusevangelium*, volume 1, 390, P Pokorný, 'From a Puppy to The Child: Some Problems of Contemporary Biblical Exegesis Demonstrated from Mark 7:24–30/Mt 15:21–8', in *NTS* 41 (1995): 324.

same valorisation of the male that lies at the foundation of ethology, and of the particular male speaker in this Markan pericope.

In the course of this analysis, it has been impossible to avoid reference to context. However, this has been muted. There are both scholarly and political dangers in any attempt to treat words in isolation (whether those of Jesus or a commentator). Any notion that the word can stand apart from interrelationships with (material) context[251] denotes a privileging that reflects not only the ideological commitments of particular approaches, but also, opaquely, reinforces the very dyadic hierarchy that structures ethology. The following chapter therefore takes up the remaining three elements of ethological enquiry: the moral discrediting of the inferior, the correct(ive) provision of territorial boundedness, and the socio-political reflections of/for the natural order. These bring contextual matters to the fore, and enable us to assess the function of the Jesus words within the context of the Markan pericope and its wider cultural setting.

251. Such interrelationships will always be multifaceted: Note the important analysis of Vernon Robbins, 'Progymnastic Rhetorical Composition', 113–114, citing RM Fowler, *Linguistic Criticism* (Oxford: Oxford University Press, 1986), 85–101.

4

The Scent of a Dog
The Ethological Words of Jesus in Context

Introduction

The significance of the form and structure of Jesus' saying has been explored in detail in the previous chapter. This chapter investigates the level of appropriateness of the saying of Jesus to the context given to it. The Markan Jesus in this pericope is found to be an ideologue for the conventional stratification of gender. The proverb relies upon a larger world of order that utilises shaming stereotypes, careful regulation of space and a cultural representation of nature to impose a judgement upon and about the Syrophoenician woman.

Moral implications: exposure and shame of inferior behaviour

The conventional role of abuse

The study of form, metre, diminutive, the claim to antiquity and the gendered context of Mark 7:27 has lead to the inescapable conclusion that the metaphor in the proverb delivers an abusive, ethological assessment of the woman. The *performative function* of the saying exposes the threat to order in a real or conceptual situation, and induces shame so that the threat might be defused by a restoration of and (renewed) commitment to right behaviour.

Comedy and satire, frequently the sources or exemplars of such sayings, fulfilled a strong, conventional role. They pointed out with impunity the faults of those 'worse than ourselves.'[1] There were occasional strictures on targets on which/whom Comedy could wield its sword.[2] But the street theatre of the market-places was less constrained by such niceties.[3] Pliny affirmed the proper role of both

1. See S Halliwell, *Aristotle's Poetics* (London: Duckworth, 1986), 269–270.
2. Arist *Poet* 5.1–2 (1449a), Plat *Rep* 606c–d, *Phil* 48a–50b, *Leg* 935b–e).
3. See IC Cunningham's introduction to *Herodas Mimes* (LCL), 204, R Meiggs, *Roman Ostia* (Oxford: Clarendon Press, second edition, 1973),

by reference to the now-familiar dualism: the praise of virtue and the attack on vice.[4] Quintilian too defended the iambics of the street against Aristotle's demeaning (as he saw it) by arguing that the orator ought to know the invective vocabulary of the coarser class, just as he needed to learn the appropriate occasion for its use.[5]

The performance of abuse in Jesus' words would have been completely familiar to a first-century Mediterranean audience, even if many of them had never been inside a theatre.[6] Mime, scrawlings of crafted graffiti,[7] street-performers (*cf* Mt 11:16–17),[8] public orations in the agora,[9] ensured that a trained ear was not required for its recognition.

The question then becomes an assessment of the appropriateness and purpose of Jesus' words in Mark. The semantic force of Jesus' words *within* Mark's narrative context rivets moral judgments to a woman of a particular race, geopolitical connection and status. The shame that attaches here is exacerbated by the inability to nurture, protect and heal one's offspring. The moral assessment able to be read from the narrative frame *appears* to warrant Jesus' words.

421–423.

4. Pl *Ep* 6.21; also Sen *Ep* 8.8.
5. Quint *Inst* 9.4.88; *cf* 1.4.4 yet warning against the use of vilification (12.9.9–13).
6. Sepphoris near Nazareth in Galilee contained a 4000–5000 seat building. More populous cities, such as Ephesus, Antioch and Jerusalem, boasted even larger edifices. Household slaves accompanied their owners, and seats were graded according to position and cost, indicating that a range of the populace attended (from the guild of tanners to the municipal clerk, as at Aphrodisias). Both gospel writers and probably Jesus seem quite familiar with the stage (especially as in the use of the term ὑποκριτής—see Mt 23:13, Mk 7:6). Some have suggested that Mark's gospel itself was designed to be performed: see A Stock, *The Method and Message of Mark* (Wilmington, DE: Michael Glazier, 1989), 26.
7. Some graffiti reveal traces of verse: J Ward-Perkins and A Claridge, *Pompei AD 79* (Sydney: Australian Gallery Directors Council, 1980), 59, citing *CIL* 4.1520; see further, J Lindsay, *The Ancient World: Manners and Morals* (London: Weidenfeld and Nicholson, 1968), 246–247.
8. Metics and other wanderers frequently exhibited their thespian abilities in the marketplace, hopeful of an evening engagement at some aristocrat's dinner party (Plut *Mor* 712c; *cf* Pers *Sat* 1:131–134). The common knowledge of plays provides the satirical edge to the opening of Lucian's *Hist* 1.
9. One of Dio Chrysostom's public orations is spent on a comparison of a common subject addressed by three playwrights (*Or* 52).

And that woman was a Greek,
a Syrophoenician by birth

i) The woman

a. framed by male language

The third century CE sophist, Athenaeus, showed the continued life of the sentiments of the fifth century BCE tragic poet, Carcinu: 'O Zeus, why need one say evil of women in detail? It were enough if you say merely woman.'[10] The sixth century CE encyclopaedist, John Stobaeus, is still reiterating Semonides' misogyny from over a millennium before.[11] This literary oligarchy promoting such views includes Jewish representatives. Philo reckoned that the pouring of the golden calf was made possible from the earrings of women, *not* of men 'for to entertain such trash [that it could be a god] is the work of an effeminate and sinew-less soul'.[12] Here lies the usual pattern of epideictic rhetoric that moulded characters according to virtue or vice,[13] grounded in man and woman. In a narrative construction incorporating two characters, one of whom is a male authority figure (Jesus), and the other a woman, the 'other' must, almost necessarily, be presumed a worse character.[14] This simply repeats the assymetry of characterisation grounded in the standard sexual dimorphism.[15] The milder sentiment of Pseudo-Aristotle's *Physiognomics* adjudged: 'it is a good thing to refer all the signs which have been mentioned both to natural conformity and to the male and female sex; for this makes the most complete classification, and the male sex has been shown to be juster, braver, and speaking generally, superior to the female.' Menander gave this its abusive edge: 'Woman is one great bestiality.'[16]

---

10. *Deip* 559f; similarly, Plaut *Curc* 591–593, Ter *Hec* 198–204.
11. The encyclopaedist John Stobaeus is still drawing together Semonides and other exponents of the abuse of women in his *Florilegia* in the sixth century CE (§§67–74).
12. Phil Jud *Post C* 166. The presence of sinews is a mark of the male: Ps-Aristotle *Phys* 810b.
13. See Arist *Poet* 2.1 (1448a).
14. Aristotle embellished this basic distinction in *Rhet* 2.11 (1388b).
15. *Phys* 814a.
16. Fr 488, translated by Anne Carson, 'Putting Her in Her Place: Woman, Dirt and Desire', in Halperin, *Before Sexuality*, 144. The Physiognomics author devolved to this also: *Phys* 809b.

b. required to be silent

The collation of the woman with a dog prevented any noise she uttered as being worth attention. Speech, as was noted in chapter 1, is the communication arm of reason, the confirmation that reason has been endowed. The nature of dogs is to bark, snarl and whine, not speak. The shaming therefore goes to the very identity of the creature approaching Jesus. This is no overstretching of a metaphor. The pungency of the metonymic collation stands in the mythological tradition of Hecuba, Hecate and Skylla, and the literary resilience of Semonides' 'yapping' woman.

The context for Jesus' saying to the woman shifts the actions of falling at the feet of Jesus (προσέπεσεν πρὸς τοὺς πόδας αὐτοῦ—v 25c) and the request (ἠρώτα—v 26b) from an indication of piety and status acknowledgement[17] to the archetypal fawning.[18] As AL Boegehold notes, 'Almost any single gesture can be ambiguous, even in the course of a conversation that is being conducted in spoken words'.[19]

Sycophantic behaviour was inherently untrustworthy. Philo calls it venomous (ἰοβόλος), thereby adding a demonic dimension to the behaviour. The poison lurks behind calm, mild language.[20]

17. This interpretation can be allowed of the actions of the man Jairus (Mk 5:22, Lk 8:41; *cf* Jn 11:32, Acts 5:10, 10:25, Rev 19:10, 22:8, *P Lond* 6.1926, *P Sakaon* 1.37). Even so, MB O'Donnell distinguishes προσκυνέω and προσπίπτω, suggesting that the latter does not indicate full submissiveness: "Translation and the Exegetical Process, Using Mark 5.1–10, "The Binding of the Strong Man" as a Test Case", in SE Porter and R.E. Hess (editors), *Translating the Bible: Problems and Prospects* (Sheffield: Sheffield Academic Press, 1999), 176.

18. So, H Kinukawa, *Women and Jesus in Mark: A Japanese Feminist Perspective* (Maryknoll, NY: Orbis, 1994), 54; Amy-Jill Levine recognises the problems of interpreting the gesture of the Canaanite woman, arguing on the basis of analogous 'women-with-a-petition' stories in the Hebrew Scriptures, that it is a blocking movement: 'Mathew's Advice to a Divided Readership', in DE Aune (editor), *The Gospel of Matthew in Current Study* (Grand Rapids: Eerdmans, 2001), 36. The spatial difference in Mark's narrative precludes such a reading here, but the point about the interpretation of gesture remains.

19. AL Boegehold, *When a Gesture is Expected: A Selection of Examples from Archaic and Classical Greek Literature* (Princeton, NJ: Princeton University Press, 1999), 17. A good example is the low-crouching of slaves and satyrs, the former indicating subservience, the latter a variety of sexual practice: see F Lissarrague, 'The Sexual Life of Satyrs', in Halperin, *Before Sexuality*, 56–57.

20. Phil Jud *Prob* 90.

Consequently, even should a woman be eloquent, this could be taken as confirming her canine proclivities. Better, said Euripides' *Hippolytus,* that a woman be untalented: through lack of intelligence she stays clear of folly.[21] Plutarch's recommendation was silence, with a dose of blushing thrown in![22]

For a woman, *not* speaking is what brings her closest to the classification 'human', a category otherwise (for males) defined by 'speech' (the evidence of *logos*). The 'no man's land' of the Tyrian provenance (v 24),[23] now symbolises the Syrophoenician woman's quandary—speak and she is not human; silence and her daughter has no chance of healing.[24] Either way she is locked into bearing shame, for, as we shall see, the demon-possession of her child is likely *the mother's* shameful responsibility. Her apparently unaccompanied movement *in public* confirms that shame. The moment that the woman seeks to answer (ἀπεκρίθη v 28), she has confirmed the stereotypical and metaphorical assessment that has been laid upon her. Two arenas—spatial location and language—are critical to the assessment of the woman. Peter Stallybrass comments, 'The signs of the 'harlot' are her linguistic 'fulness' and her frequenting of public spaces'.[25] Both are apparent here.

It might be countered that the woman could withstand the negative implications of her public, unaccompanied travel and her unannounced breach of the boundaries of privacy, on the grounds of extreme emergency,[26] comparing the story of the haemorrhaging woman. Yet, that woman was bounded by a crowd (a complex

21. Eur *Hipp* 638.
22. Plut *Mor* 154b; also Sen *Contr* 2.7.3; *cf* Sir 26:24b.
23. The geographical liminality is accented by the variant to ὅρια in v 24: μεθόρια (A, Maj Text), which, for a time, held sway as the accepted reading. The distancing of the woman from the cities actually accentuates her diminished status: see Dio Chr *Or* 31.116; *cf* Jn 1.46, 7.52.
24. The dilemma is similar to that named for women generally by Rosemary Radford Ruether: 'emancipation through identification with a misogynist male rationality or identification with a concept of "nature" and "feminity" which ever returns them to powerless, inarticulate subjugation'. (*New Women/New Earth: Sexist Ideologies and Human Liberation* (New York: Seabury, 1975), 194.)
25. 'Patriarchal Territories: The Body Enclosed', in MW Ferguson (editor), *Rewriting the Renaissance* (Chicago: Chicago University Press, 1986), 127; see Aristoph *Eccl* 1101.
26. On which see section 3 below.

relationship, admittedly)[27] and she only spoke when required to do so. Up until Mark's analeptic insertion pinning the woman (in v 26), an ambiguity hangs over her, but it is temporary. Mark's manipulation of audiential engagement is apparent as the evangelist withholds the detail until *after* the request has been made.[28] The moment that she is announced not as 'mother' (*cf* Mk 5:40) but as 'woman' (compounded by the further qualifiers), a decision is made. Even her address, κύριε, becomes suspect.[29]

ii) Her birth

a. problems in contemporary interpretation

Before interpreting the additional descriptions in v 26, the expression τῷ γένει ('by birth') needs clarification. Recent scholarship has taken it as the woman's *racial* identity: Syrophoenician.[30] The choice has implications for the meaning of 'Hellene'. The Vulgate's translation of Ἑλληνίς as *gentilis*, compounded by the commitment to the Pauline interpretation of v 26a, has meant that 'Hellene' is taken as Gentile, even if improvised as pagan,[31] or given a religious/cultural affiliation.[32]

---

27. Mk 5:24b–37, *cf* Mk 5:35, 38, Jn 11:31; *cf* 11:19. Compare Philostr *Vit Apol* 3.38 where a woman, seeking the exorcism of her son, is accompanied by a group. Mary Lefkowitz recognises the importance of surrounding, protective crowds for women from mythological stories: *Women in Greek Myth*, 45.
28. *Cf* Mk 10:17–22, where the key element about the rich man is withheld until the last two words. Such control of audience reactions was a staple of oratory and play alike. At the extreme, it was deemed to be a form of magic. The designation of one type of actor in Mime, the magodist, comes from his perceived power to manipulate an audience's responses: see Athen *Deip* 621d.
29. Compare the obscene sense of *dominus* in Mart *Epig* 2.18, 11.70, 12.66, and the armoury of address cultivated by the flatterer in Menand *Dysk* 487–497. Courtesans especially were renowned for the turning of conventions of address and formalities of deference to their own advantage; see Corley, *Private Women*, 98.
30. The explanation is not itself particularly new: see JJ Wettstein, Η ΚΑΙΝΗ ΔΙΑΘΗΚΗ*: Novum Testamentum Graecum editionis receptae cum variantibus . . .* (Amsterdam, 1751–1752), volume 1, 590, who saw the reference as meaning '*natione, gente, patria*'.
31. TA Burkill, *New Light on the Earliest Gospel: Seven Markan Studies* (Ithaca: Cornell University Press, 1972), 72, EA McNamara, 'The Syrophoenician Woman', in *AER* 127 (1952): 362.
32. So Theissen, *Gospels in Context*, 66–72, Marcus, *Mark 1–8*, 462. Curiously the Latin of the 'Celtic Gospels' (LJ Hopkin-James, *The Celtic Gospels: Their Story and Their Text* (London: Oxford University

But it has not been taken as indicating the woman's ethnicity.[33]

There are problems with this interpretation:

i) Another division gains a minor mention in Paul's writings: Greeks and barbarians (Rom 1:14). Jewish and christian studies are socialised to the axiomatic pairing of Judaism and Hellenism. In the world of late antiquity, 'Greek' was opposed not only to 'Jew' but also to a number of other nationalities, especially after Alexander the Great. Adherence to national distinctiveness was a concern not only amongst the colonised. Greeks also were concerned at the possible contamination that might occur to all things Greek amongst their people in a foreign country. It wrought a process of 'othering'.[34] Thus, in Egyptian-Greek contact, the stock division was just that: 'Greek and Egyptian'.[35] 'Roman and Greek' was an intriguing long-running battle. Even more telling is the division *between* Greek and Syrophoenician that is made by Lucian.[36] All this raises the question of the perspective of the group that is both naming

Press, 1934), 128) has *sero poecisa* for *Syrophoenissa*, making the phrase 'late a Greek but Phoenician (?) by birth'. *Poecisa* appears to be a mistake in transcription (for *phoenicissa*?).

33. HB Swete's comment that Ἑλληνίς indicates a 'Greek-speaker' merely focuses the cultural interpretation: *The Gospel According to St Mark* (London: Macmillan, second edition, 1902, (1898)), 156–157. He overlooks the Greek chauvinism that was happy to dispense the denigration 'barbarian' to any Greek-speaker who did not pronounce Greek correctly. Others have allowed the possibility of 'Greek-speaking': Cranfield, *Mark*, 247, Russell, 'Canaanite Woman', 269. Codex Δ uses Ἕλλην—a rare but not unparalleled use with γυνή· see Philem *Paidar* fr 1—incontestably indicating Greek ethnicity.

34. Schüssler Fiorenza defines 'othering' as establishing 'identity either by declaring the difference of the other as the same or by vilifying and idealising difference as otherness. It justifies relationships of ruling by obfuscating structures of domination and subordination as 'naturalised' differences.' 'Paul and the Politics of Interpretation', in RA Horsley (editor), *Paul and Politics* (Harrisburg, PA: TPI, 2000), 45. It ought to be noted however that the politics of othering can also occur as a defensive, resistant and cohesive strategy by those who are oppressed.

35. *P Tebt* I.5.

36. *Deor* 4; *cf* Juv *Sat* 8.159.

and receiving the information. To an Egyptian, Greek did not mean gentile, nor to a Roman or a Syrophoenician.[37]

ii) If Hellene means only 'gentile' then Συροφοινίκισσα is tautologous. Taylor seeks to combine them.[38] Focant described it as 'pleonastic'.[39] The myopia of seeing only Jew and Greek (=Gentile) misses the import of another ethnic dispute, involving Jews and Phoenicians. Certainly, given that, at least according to Josephus, the Tyrians (one of the city-states described as Canaanite/ Phoenician) were the Jews' bitterest enemies.[40]

iii) Mark's clear preference in referring to 'gentiles' is ἔθνη (10:33, 42, 11:17, 13:10; *cf.* 13:8). If 10:33 is to be informed by Mark's subsequent narrative, the primary demonstration of 'Gentile' is not Greek but Roman.

iv) The seventeenth century commentator, John Lightfoot, offered another suggestion, which has not been tested. He claimed that Συροφοινίκισσα τῷ γένει designated the woman's place of habitation.[41]

Clearly then, the two expressions, Ἑλληνίς and Συροφοινίκισσα τῷ γένει have been interpreted in isolation from one another or blended.

b. reading Ἑλληνίς and Συροφοινίκισσα τῷ γένει as a unit

The vast movements of people around the Mediterranean for diasporan

37. John Stambaugh and David Balch move towards recognising the variety of dualistic prejudices: *The New Testament in its Social Environment* (Philadelphia: Westminster Press, 1986), 113.

38. Taylor, *Mark*, 349.

39. 'La Fonction Narrative des Doublets dans la Section des Pains: Mc 6,6b–8,26', in F van Segbroeck *et al* (editors), *The Four Gospels 1992: Festschrift Frans Neirynck* (Leuven: Leuven University Press, 1992), volume 2, 1050. There is even debate over whether 'Ἑλληνίς' is a later addition: see Focant, 'Mc 7,24–31', 48–49; *cf* Pesch, *Das Markusevangelium*, volume 1, 388.

40. Jos *C Ap* 1.70.

41. J Lightfoot, *Horae Hebraicae et Talmudicae* (Oxford at the University Press, 1658), 229, 230. Guelich views it similarly, as a reference to her citizenship: *Mark 1–8*, 38.

or colonising reasons, demanded careful distinctions by authorities so that clear racial identifications and affiliations could be made.[42] Double references clarified ethnic origins as well as geopolitical ties.

When only *one* point of designation was provided, racial origins appear to be implied.[43] Thus in a fourth-century account of a hearing of a property dispute between a woman and a certain Syrus the Libyan,[44] the *logistes* was uncertain as to whether Λίβυς indicated birth or place of residence. Accordingly, he asked, Λίβυς δὲ τῷ γένει εἶ; A clear answer did not come. Syrus simply acknowledged he did not *live* within the jurisdiction of this *logistes*.[45] Accordingly, the *logistes* may have needed to refer the case elsewhere.

In one fragment of the second-century *Acts of the Pagan Martyrs*,[46] the advocate appearing for the Alexandrians before Caesar is noted simply as Παῦλος Τύριος τῷ γένει which at least implies he is a Tyrian national.[47] The advocate for the Jews is Σώπατρος Ἀντιοχεὺς τῷ γένει.

There *was* an unequivocal way of expressing the ethnicity of birth. Lucian provides an example: 'Demonax was Cypriot by birth (ἦν δὲ τὸ μὲν γένος Κύπριος).'[48] This formula is also found in the papyri.[49] Ethnic origins could also be shown by adjectival qualification.[50]

42. For example, Pausan 1.5.5. I am not suggesting these efforts were always successful—there is considerable evidence, for example, that the lower levels of the military regularly partnered and, where possible, married 'native' women in the places where they were stationed.
43. For example, Gal 1:14, Plut *Vit* (*Cim*) 4.9. Τῷ γένει could sometimes be used to infer the status of a person (which may or may not necessarily be distinguished from location). Thus Caesar accuses Hermaisci of taking advantage of his birth (τῷ σεαυτοῦ γένει) in the *Acts of the Pagan Martyrs*: *Acta Hermaisci* (*P Oxy* 1242 *l*.44); *cf* of bastards, *Ps-Clem Hom* 8.18.2.
44. *P Oxy* 54.3758.
45. *Ibid*, 167.
46. *P Oxy* 1242 (*Act Herm*).
47. Musurillo considered him to be a Greek. A Paulus of Tyre is listed as a rhetor in the Suda (P§809). His volunteering his services for the Alexandrians is taken as an indication of the strong ties binding Greeks across the Mediterranean: HA Musurillo (editor), *The Acts of the Pagan Martyrs: Acta Alexandrinorum* (Oxford: Clarendon Press, 1954), 174.
48. Luc *Dem* 3.
49. See, for example, *UPZ* 121 (=*P Par* 10) 1.4 cited in *NDIEC* 8.11.
50. Whether simple ethnic adjective or compound word with –γενης, for example, φοινικογένης (Eur fr 475a).

Τῷ γένει may be a reference to *place* of birth only.[51] Certainly, when the place of birth *supplemented* a reference to ethnicity, then the τῷ γένει formula expresses geopolitical location. For example, Barnabas, Aquila and Apollos are first confirmed by race or tribe[52] and then located by place of birth using the τῷ γένει formula.[53] This holds in non-biblical references as well. Lucian writes: 'We are Syrians, Damascus men by birth (Σύροι μέν ἐσμεν, ἐκ Δαμασκοῦ τῷ γένει).'[54]

Therefore, the primary affirmation of the 'Syrophoenician' woman is that *she is a Greek*, born outside of the homeland.[55]

iii) Stereotyping the woman

Elisabeth Schüssler Fiorenza has commented a number of times that the description of the woman in Mark 7:26 delivers the painfully-familiar stereotyping of women—that is, by gender, race and class.[56] Whilst she consciously proceeds from the rhetorical and political stance of contemporary feminism, her notice is extremely pertinent for the text in its sociocultural realities. As a simple communication of 'gentile', v 24a is sufficient, especially given the widespread recognition that the section 7:24–8:10 is 'A Ministry to Gentiles'.[57] Verse 26a is far more than a concern that we do not miss the point. It is designed to awaken a range of perceptions and expectations, a set of universals conjured precisely because the brevity of description provides no nuanced qualification.[58] Here, one cannot subsume gender under ethnicity, quite contrary to David Rhoads and others who hold that gender 'is

51. As in *P Oxy* 3023.
52. The use of tribe as a designator is found also in *P Oxy* 42.3054 §10.
53. Acts 4.36, 18:2,24.
54. Luc *Pod* 265; *cf* Pausan 1.5.5.8. One epigram clearly removed any ethnic ambiguity: *GA* 7.162.
55. The Old Latin manuscript, a, may capture the meaning with its reading: *natione Syraphoenissa*.
56. Occasionally religion is added; see E Schüssler Fiorenza 'Introduction', in E Schüssler Fiorenza and MS Copeland (editors), 'Violence Against Women', in *Concilium* 1994.1, xi; *cf* Kwok, *Discovering the Bible*, 74.
57. Bryan, *Preface to Mark*, 97.
58. 'The pre-existing beliefs of the authorial audience become apparent when the narration presents information in a straightforward manner without resorting to explanations, definitions or redundant attempts to modify the pre-existing content of the frames evoked by particular words.' P Danove, 'The Narrative Rhetoric of Mark's Ambiguous Characterisation of the Disciples', in *JSNT* 70 (1998): 24–25.

not essential for the story to work'.[59]

a. stereotypes in the ancient world

Stereotypes in the ancient world delivered far more than one basic trait. They enabled a person to be located within the ordering of a rational universe. Stephen Halliwell's observation is particularly pertinent:

> The strong tradition of literary stylization . . . marks a significant divergence from the kinds of individualism familiar to us in our own dominant literary forms, and involves a countervailing tendency towards the understanding and evaluation of people by reference to wider ethical categories and standards;[60]

For Mark's audience, a simple narrative description awoke a set of understandings and judgements that enabled other elements in the narrative to be understood and interpreted. 'The ancients used such information to determine status and degrees of social interaction.'[61]

Stereotypical characterisation was seen as a positive authorial attribute, especially in Comedy. The appeal to the universal was deliberate. Name, ethnicity, occupation and the like, conveyed character merely by their mention.[62] The more trigonometric points of general reference, the more likely that the plotting of character would be considered true.[63] These stigmatising stereotypes were more than a literary fiction and operated powerfully in mundane relationships, which only strengthened the sense of reality in literary

59. Rhoads, 'Jesus and the Syrophoenician Woman', 367, Mary Ann Beavis, 'Women as Models of Faith in Mark', in *BTB* 18 (1988): 6.
60. S Halliwell, 'Traditional Conceptions of Character', in CBR Pelling (editor), *Characterization and Individuality in Greek Literature* (Oxford: Clarendon Press, 1990), 57.
61. D Neufeld, 'Jesus' Eating Transgressions and Social Impropriety in the Gospel of Mark', in *BTB* 30 (2000): 24. To dismiss the verse as nothing other than a parenthesis (Gundry, *Mark*, 372) is seriously to emaciate the reading of the total pericope.
62. SH Butcher, *Aristotle: Theory of Poetry and Fine Art* (New York: Dover, 1951 (1894)), 376–377.
63. Ps-Arist *Phys* 807a. This was sometimes turned to authorial advantage to construct a surprise based on the disruption of stereotypes. Almost always this was in a direction that raised the status of the character, as in the Romance novels predicated on an undisclosed noble birth.

characterisations.[64]

b. the problem of the anandrous woman

The first element of the categorisation in v 26 is that the person is a woman. It reiterates the emphasis on gender in the constructed setting of v 25, but adds significant qualifications: 'Greek, a Syrophoenician by birth.'[65] This is compounded by a voluble silence in the text. The woman is anandrous. Commonly in the papyri, γυνή will be followed by a man's name, decisively indicating that the meaning is 'wife'.[66] A similar syntax is followed in Mark (6:17).

Up to this point in the Markan narrative, women have been located in some measure by reference to a male. Peter's mother-in-law, Jesus' mother and sisters, the wife and daughter of Jairus, the wife and (step-) daughter of Herod, and even the haemorraghing daughter *of Abraham* are defined in the text by reference to a male. The mother of the seven martyred sons similarly proclaimed her own virtue by reference to father, husband, son and boundedness to their households.[67] And in each Markan instance, a buffer-zone of communal connectedness reinforces that the women are contained and constrained.[68] For these, a group exists that can avow that the person is 'with us' (πρὸς ἡμᾶς—Mk 6:3; *cf* 3:21, 9:38).

The only bracketing for the Syrophoenician compounds her *dis*connection—she has a daughter.[69] Both women therefore occupy 'no man's land', situated only by reference to one another. The absence of a father and/or a properly constituted marital relationship is

64. For example, *CPJ* 2.411 1.7, *P Oxy* 1639, *BGU* 4.1142, *P Col Zen* 66; *cf* Gen 31:14–16, 1 Cor 14:11.
65. The *interplay* of the physiognomic features conveyed by these descriptions and founded upon gender dimorphism is crucial. Bruce Malina's helpful survey leaves this element undeveloped: Malina, 'Circum-Mediterranean Person?', 66–87.
66. See, amongst many examples, *P Oxy* 24.2421.
67. 4 Macc 18:6–9.
68. For Peter's mother-in-law there is a town, a household and a group of her son-in-law's friends; for Jairus' wife, there are the household domestics, the status connections of the synagogue, and the town. Stuart Love's suggestion that the crowds around Jesus 'open a real but limited alternative for women' may have a measure of validity, but the converse is that the crowd provide the demographic zone in which conventional, societal (and audiential) values were located (*cf* Mk 10:48): see SL Love, 'The Place of Women in Public Settings in Matthew's Gospel: A Sociological Inquiry', in *BTB* 24 (1994): 62.
69. The fear of a woman's father was an unmarried pregnancy (Sir 42:10).

a manifest justification for the repudiation of a person.[70] They are open to the pejorative, 'unclean', as Paul seemed unperturbed to dispense (1 Cor 7:14b).[71]

The awkwardness of a religious text recounting contact between Jesus and an unbounded woman needed explanation. One strand of tradition,[72] witnessed in both textual transmission and narrative retelling, reassigned the woman to a place of pity (and Jesus, thereby, to a place of compassion). Thus, the *Pseudo-Clementine Homilies* not only conferred a righteous identity upon the woman in naming her 'Justa'; it exemplified her sanctity by 'widowing' her.[73] A male connection was, as it were, ghost-written into the story.[74] The intertextual relationship forged with the widow of Sarepheth (2 Sam 4:8–37) had already found intratextual support.

The sanitising attention to the woman in these instances, demonstrates that it is not 'Greek' and 'Syrophoenician' in general that must be factored. These qualifiers must be anchored to the emphatically named, and isolated, 'woman'.

c. the stereotype(s) of the (unbounded) woman

The repeated reference to women in the *Acts of the Pagan Martyrs* provides an interesting comparison with Mark's usage. Highly abbreviated references to female gender, race and class provided a stock of abuse supporting the main agenda of arguing a case in an all-

70. For example, Athen *Deip* 577a-b, Ter *And* 468–470.
71. See OL Yarbrough, 'Parents and Children in the Letters of Paul', in LM White and OL Yarbrough (editors), *The Social World of the First Christians* (Minneapolis: Fortress Press, 1995), 129.
72. The dominant tradition of interpretation sought sanctuary in the gentile mission as the explanation (or compensation) for the woman's anandrous state.
73. *Ps-Clem Hom* 2.20. Here however, widowhood is occasioned by the woman's conversion, a path her husband is apparently unwilling to follow. Hence widow and divorcee are made synonymous. See my 'What's in a Name? The Tenacity of a Tradition of Interpretation [Justus/a and the Clementine Homilies]', in P Lockwood (editor), *Festschrift for Victor Pfitzner* in *Lutheran Theological Journal* 39 (2005): 218–239.
74. One Syriac manuscript has the woman as a Phoenician widow (sy[s]). Modern interpretation has echoed: P-L Couchard, 'Notes de critique verbale sur St Marc et St Matthieu', in *JTS* 30 (1933): 120f, G Schwarz, 'ΣΥΡΟΦΟΙΝΙΚΙΣΣΑ–ΧΑΝΑΝΑΙΑ (Markus 7.26/Matthäus 15.22)', *NTS* 30 (1984): 626–628.

male hearing. One example will suffice:[75]

> *Claudius Caesar*: 'Isidorus are you really the son of an actress?'
> *Isidorus*: 'I am neither slave nor actress's son, but gymnasiarch of the glorious city of Alexandria. But you are the cast-off son of the Jewish Salome!

In another fragment of these Acts, Hermaiscus says to Caesar, 'So even the word 'Jew' is offensive to you?'[76] The insults behind these statements can only be discerned from the standardised perceptions operating in the ancient world.[77] Isidorus' response reflects the three basic roles for women found in literary sources: courtesan, respectable wife and slave.[78]

The unboundedness of the Syrophoenician woman is exacerbated by the macro-identifications. These compound her as 'other', providing far more information than a racial group or a cartographical location. They convey character, deliberately undifferentiated and presumed to be negative.[79] Joy Connolly noted how a 'confusion of spheres' occurs when a given group or person becomes constituted according to a dominant stereotype: foreignness, womanliness and servility all become bound together, each one accented according to the demands in any given situation.[80] Put bluntly, the woman will look, smell, talk, gesture and walk differently.[81] Her difference makes her a 'spoiled identity' to use Erving Goffman's expression. Her capacity to construct a positive impression will be handicapped.[82]

---

75. *Acta Isid* Rec A Col iii.
76. *Acta Herm* (*P Oxy* 1242 l.45).
77 Tcherikover and Fuks partly miss the point of such abuse by concentrating on the literal issue of the emperor's (il)legitimacy: *CPJ* 2.156d notes to lines 11, 12.
78. Robinson, *Juvenal*, 99; for a clear example see Mart *Epig* 3.33.
79. See R Brown, *Group Processes: Dynamics Within and Between Groups* (Oxford: Basil Blackwell, 1988), 231–239.
80. 'Mastering Corruption', 150n2, citing, for the general notion, P Bourdieu, *The Logic of Practice* translated by R Nice, (Cambridge: Polity Press, 1990), 86–87.
81. So Malina, 'Circum-Mediterranean Person?', 69.
82. E Goffman, *Stigma: notes on the management of spoiled identity* (New York: Simon and Schuster, 1986).

Goffman's stress on the importance of visibility for the processes of stigmatisation to operate is pertinent.[83] Mark makes the woman highly visible by stalling the narrative flow to insert the defining/confining description, even as she has been isolated in public space intruding on private space (Mk 7:25).[84] Her foreignness and gender compound the woman's transgression and draws the stereotypical labelling mechanism that is the linguistic reinforcement of proper boundary maintenance.[85] Jesus' abrupt, acerbic adjuration provides just this.

The stigmatisation of woman is already given a preliminary invitation, given the ethological assumptions upon which the society is constructed. Hence, in the absence of stereotyped honorific expressions,[86] in the absence of a male in whom the woman might be embedded, and, by contrast, in breached presence before an authoritative male, the shameful associations of the woman come to the fore.

Already, without detailed analysis of the qualifiers added to her as 'woman', her character is severely compromised in the narrative. Ancient *literati* dotted their writing about women with stereotypes. When their subject was a prostitute or woman accused of sexual misdemeanors, '. . . her historical specificity and individuality are minimized.'[87] The storehouse of stereotypes was visited, in order to fix the person in this episode; they prompt recognition of her character. Philo is one who raided the supply:

> Her gait has the looseness which her extravagant wantonness and luxury has bred; the lascivious roll of her eyes is a bait to entice the souls of the young; her look speaks of boldness and shamelessness; her neck is held high; she assumes a stature which Nature has not given her; she grins and giggles; her hair is dressed in curious and elaborate plaits; under her eyes are pencil lines; her eyebrows are smothered in paint; she revels perpetually in the warmth of her bath; her flush

---

83. *Ibid*, 5.
84. The variant εἰσελθοῦσα (ℵ L (D) 700 892 lat) makes the implication of the text clear.
85. See SK Stowers, *A Rereading of Romans: Justice, Jews and Gentiles* (New Haven: Yale University Press, 1994), 271.
86. Such as frequent public inscriptions and epitaphs in honour of exemplary women; see for example *NDIEC* 6.3.
87. Hawley, 'Female Characterisation', 261.

> is artificial; her costly raiment is broidered lavishly with flowers; bracelets and necklaces and every other feminine ornament wrought of gold and jewels hang around her; her breath is laden with fragrant scents; a strumpet of the streets . . .[88]

Perhaps the comic mask or the mimic display of the courtesan filled the imagination.[89]

d. a resistance to essentialising

A word of caution is needed. Analysis of characterisation needs to be aware of the audience and the genre wherein characterisation operates.[90] Moreover, hegemonic (male) presumptions generally undergird stereotypes used in characterisation.[91] An appeal to universal acceptance may be compromised by non-adherent hearers. This sensitivity enables us to resist essentialising the woman according to the stereotypes that are conferred upon her, whether or not she has engaged in prostitution. Indeed, we may need to watch for a narrative strategy that is intended to subvert the stigmatisation that could be presumed from the audience as they heard the demarcations of character in v 26. This will be developed in the next chapter.

iv) The Hellene

For the woman to be described as a Greek without any other qualifier, would, in many parts of the world, have been taken as honorific. There appears to have been a strong network of support amongst Greeks

---

88. Phil Jud *Sacr* 21 *cf* Luc *Bis* 31–32, Xenarchus fr 4 *PCG*, Prov 5:14–17.
89. In the list of forty-four comic masks provided by the second century writer Julian Pollux, there are five masks for *hetairai*, presumably indicating different accents and aspects of such characters: see the survey in Wiles, *Masks of Menander*, 177–184, TBL Webster, *Monuments Illustrating New Comedy* third edition revised and enlarged by JR Green and A Seeberg (London: Institute of Classical Studies, 2 volumes, 1995), volume 1, 44–49. Masks were so standardised that they communicated character wordlessly.
90. See E Schütrumpf, 'The Meaning of ἦθος in the Poetics—A Reply', in *Hermes* 115 (1987): 180, drawing especially on Arist *Rhet* 2.12 (1389a) *cf* Quint *Inst* 6.22.8.
91. So E Stehle and A Day, 'Women Looking at Women: Women's Ritual and Temple Sculpture', in NB Kampen (editor), *Sexuality in Ancient Art* (Cambridge: Cambridge University Press, 1996), 101.

across the Mediterranean.[92] Musurillo developed an assessment of being Greek in the Roman Empire.[93] He based his observations on a comparison of the *Acts of the Pagan Martyrs* with ancient novels. I have drawn upon and extended his conclusions:

> a. There is a general pride in Greek birth, and an attribution of good qualities to the Hellene in contrast with the alleged inferiority of barbarian races.[94] Hence, to begin an oration with a compliment about Greek identity would almost guarantee a positive reception.[95]
>
> b. This pride could extend to one's name, even if a prostitute. Athenaeus records the shame of a courtesan bearing a Phrygian name, especially should she come from the very centre of Greece (that is, Athens).[96]
>
> c. Language and its pronunciation were cause for inflation, as also was dress,[97] to the extent that where a Greek person was recognised, the expectation was that Greek would be spoken in an exchange.[98]
>
> d. There was a mutual sympathy between Greeks of different countries.[99]
>
> e. There is a concern for religious piety directed towards local divinities.

Nevertheless, there were gradations of status even within the array of people called 'Greek'. Ionians were regarded as the most promiscuous,[100] Boetians the most obtuse.[101] More significantly, Greeks who lived in colony or diaspora were treated suspiciously as

92. Luc *Imag* 15.
93. Musurillo, *Pagan Martyrs*, 253.
94. *Charit* 5.11.6, 7.3.8–10.
95. So, Dio Chrysostom in Tarsus: see *Or* 33.
96. Athen *Deip* 578b-c.
97. Heliod *Aeth* 2.21
98. Luc *Pseud* 14. On status elements in the use of Greek, see Harrocks, *Greek*, 79–86.
99. *Charit* 2.5.8, *Heliod* 1.26.
100. Athen *Deip* 524f–526d, 620e; *cf* Hor *Od* 3.6.21.
101. Compare Tert *Anim* 20, who parades a list of 'proverbial' national characteristics.

being leached of their Greek identity under 'foreign' influence. Indeed, Ionians' promiscuity was explained by their permeability to 'barbarian rulers'.[102]

Whatever may have been the level of 'fusion' with the native population, effort was made to champion one's Greek heritage, both in relation to the locals and in relation to the 'homeland', whether regarding burial[103] or employment of wet-nurses.[104]

v) Syrian and Phoenician contamination of the Greek

In the symposia debates of the third century sophist, Athenaeus, one of the speakers, a Greek from Tyre (Ulpian) is variously called a Syrian and a Phoenician and is accused of polluting Greek purity in both customs and language—at one stage he is contemptuously called a 'Syro-Atticist'.[105] Almost a refrain through the writing, it indicates the stereotyped stigma blaming Syrian and Phoenician for degrading Greek identity.[106]

In Euripides' *Phoenician Women*, the Chorus comments that Phoenicia acted like a wet-nurse, a nanny fostering the women descended from Cadmus (280–1). This is not necessarily a ringing endorsement and casts a shadow on any positive affirmations[107] that were made about Greek descendants linked with Syria and Phoenicia.

102. Athen *Deip* 624d; *cf* 632a, Plat *Men* 245d, Eur *Troad* 764: 'Greeks from barbarians finding evil ways.'
103. See MR Lefkowitz and MB Fant, *Women's Life in Greece and Rome: A source book in translation* (Baltimore: Johns Hopkins University Press, second edition, 1992), §333; *cf* Mart *Epig* 9.30, *GA* 7.76, 79, 280, 281, 560, 569, 660, 715.
104. Favorinus in Aul Gell *Att* 12.1; *cf* Soran *Gyn* 2.12.19, Tacit *Germ* 19.
105. There is an additional stock slur of being a glutton: immediately after the address (Συραττικέ), he turns to eat his fill of pudding: Athen *Deip* 126f. These coinages of double referents sometimes had loose administrative functions: Φοινικαιγυπτίος and Ἑλληνομέμφιτος in *PSI* 5.531 §1; Ἀρσενοφοίνικος in *P Lond* 4.1419 §§1285, 1290. But they also were prone to diminish status among either group that made up part of the doublet.
106. See, for example, 121f, 126e, 346c; compare the discrediting of cities in Syria by Dio Chr *Or* 31.163. See EL Wheeler, 'The laxity of Syrian legions', in DL Kennedy (editor), *The Roman Army in the East* (JRSs 18), (Ann Arbor, MI: JRS, 1996), 232–46.
107. As appears in Eur *Phoen* 214f, Dio C *Hist* 13.54.3, Pausan 5.25.12.

vi) To play the Syrian and/or the Phoenician

The reductionist racism that used proverbs euphemistically to indicate vices,[108] did not overlook either Syrian or Phoenician. Both are laden with licentious overtones. Συρίζω[109] and Φοινίζω were thrown about as a description or warning about sexual proclivities.[110] 'To play the Syrian' was particularly cutting as it included an association with the lascivious god, Pan, and his pipe-playing.[111]

Similarly, 'to play the Phoenician' conjured associations of the phallic palm as well as the prostitute's colour (φοῖνιξ), red.[112] It swathed Dionysius[113] and other gods of the area.[114] The Wisdom of Solomon's scathing dismissal of idolatry (13:14), especially in its combination with sexual license, gives considerable attention to the paint colour.[115]

The devastating attack by the satirist, Lucian, upon a critic of his work, includes the Phoenician innuendo: 'In the name of the gods, tell me how you feel when the rabble call you names derived from Lesbos and Phoenicia.'[116] Dio Chrysostom after enticing the people of Tarsus to give him a hearing by appealing to their Greek identity, turned on them: 'Would anyone call you Greeks, or the most licentious of Phoenicians?'[117] Hesychius the lexicographer defined σκύλαξ (young dog) as an erotic posture of the kind adopted by Phoenicians.[118] The

108. Adams, *Latin Sexual Vocabulary*, 202.
109. It also occurs as τυρίσδω (Theocrit *Id* 1.2). Racial stereotypes frequently occur in graffiti; see for example Τύρια λασθῆ (*CIL* 4.2319 l), *Turia percisa* (*CIL* 4.2319).
110. See Dio Chrysostom's scathing denunciation of a Phoenician man, marked by innocuous origins, a depilated body, and who wears stays! (*Or* 31.116). The sexual incontinence of the Phoenicians, along with their greed and theft, goes back to Hom *Od* 15.416–471.
111. The combination of Tyre, promiscuity and Pan is found in Mart *Epig* 4.28. Tyre was popularly a haven for prostitutes: Herodas *Mime* 2.16.
112. Mart *Epig* 2.39.There was an even more sordid association, that of cunnilingus and menses.
113. Pausan 2.2.6.
114. *Sib Or* 3.589, Pl *NH* 33.36. The phallus charm was frequently painted red: one Pompeii sculpture has retained the colour: see M Grant, *Eros in Pompeii* (New York: Stewart, Tabori and Chang, 1997), 111.
115. Pottery and painting remains tend to confirm the Phoenician propensity for red: see PM Bikai, *The Pottery of Tyre* (England: Aris & Philips, 1978), 75, MGA Guzzo, 'Painting', in S Moscati (editor), *The Phoenicians* (Milan: Bompiani, 1988), 448.
116. Luc *Pseud* 28.
117. Dio Chr *Or* 33.41.
118. Hesychius §1164.

spectre of disease hung over these foreign reprobates as well: Greeks called leprosy 'the Phoenician disease.'[119]

vii) Contemptible servility

Slavery is a clear feature of the Hellenistic period. Alexander's cracking of the Tyrian defences had fired the trade—thousands were sold into slavery.[120] Later, we find an edict of Ptolemy II Philadelphus (dated April 260 BCE) which clearly connects the trade in slaves to Syria and Phoenicia.[121] Fergus Miller commented on the particular liability of a native population to slavery and to being *assumed* to be slaves.[122] Cicero's sweeping gratuity 'Syrians and Jews, nations born to slavery'[123] provides ancient, dismissive and stereotyped witness.[124]

A typical name for a slave in Greek comedy is Suros/Sura.[125] It indicated not only slave status (by reference to the geographical source of the slave)[126] but also the associations of the area. A Syrian female was held to be promiscuous and untrustworthy,[127] a standard recipient of blame for the sexual license of banquets.[128] The biblical tradition is little different. The Septuagint provided a wife for Manasseh (Gen 46:20). She is tellingly described as a Syrian prostitute or concubine

119. Not unlike Victorian England's characterisation of syphilis as 'the French disease': see MD Grmek, *Diseases in the Ancient Greek World* translated by M and L Muellner, (Baltimore and London: Johns Hopkins University Press, 1989), 167.
120. Diodorus Siculus claimed the figure was 13,000 (17.46.4); Arrian suggested 30,000 (*Anab* 2.24.5).
121. *COP* 22.
122. F Miller, 'The Problem of Hellenistic Syria', in A Kuhrt and S Sherwin-White (editors), *Hellenism in the East: The interaction of Greek and non-Greek civilizations from Syria to Central Asia after Alexander* (Berkeley and Los Angeles: University of California Press, 1987), 119–120.
123. Cic *Prov Con* 10.
124. Arist *Pol* 7.6.1 (1327b), Mart *Epig* 8.51, 9.2.
125. See, for example, Apollodorus fr 8. Menander *Epitrepontes*, *Dyskolos, Dis Exapaton, Georgos*, Plautus *Cistellaria*; *cf P Oxy* 7.1062.
126. Athen *Deip* 108e. Gow and Page note that the line between name and national origin is frequently blurred for slaves: *Greek Anthology* 2.96. Lucian in fact provides confirmation: 'His [*ie*. Antiphilus] slave, Syrus by name and Syrian by nationality' (*Tox* 28).
127. Athen *Deip* 335d, Plut *Mor* 748e–771e.
128. Slaves and dwarfs were often presented as ithyphallic in literature, performance and pictorial representation.

(ἡ πολλακὴ ἡ Σύρα).[129]

The familiar tirade of Juvenal echoes throughout: the polluted waters of the Syrian Orontes pouring in distortions of language, morals and music in the alluring form and rapid tongues of prostitutes.[130] The satirist alerts us to one apparent exception to the denigration of a slave's speech:[131] the courtesan (who was often a slave . . . a particular type of slave). Yet this commodified, witty accompaniment to a meal merely confirmed the courtesan's status. Her speech was nothing more than a wheedling tongue in search of food and sex.[132] The combination of sexual decadence, gender, servility and race gains papyrological confirmation.[133] Indeed, 'slave' was frequently a metonym for brothel.[134]

129. John Wevers states, 'Nothing further is known of her, and the origin of the tradition is obscure.' *Notes on the Greek Text of Genesis* (Septuagint and Cognate Studies 35), (Atlanta, GA: Scholars Press, 1993), 782. The tradition recurs in 1 Chr 7:15. Philo denigrates her in typical fashion, contrasting her with the exemplary wife of Ephraim: *Hypoth* 40–43. The use of Συρα (Sura/Syria) in many manuscripts of Mk 7:26, sometimes separated from Φοινί(κι)σσα (B E F G H M S* V* X Ψ Γ Σ Ω f^{13} 700 1010 1278 *pm* || U W 5 6 *pm* a q vg), in the light of Gen 46:20//1 Chr 7:15 LXX, raises an intertextual possibility quite different from the 'widow' previously encountered!

130. *Sat* 3.62–65. Their named mentor, Isaeus, is significant—he was an ancient Assyrian rhetorician.

131. Slaves were variously represented as incomprehensible, seditious, seductive and destructive in their speech: see Herodas *Mime* 6. Syrians were singled out for comment: Luc *Merc Con* 10 comments on a doorman with a vile Syrian accent; *cf* Aes *Paroem* §97.

132. Madeleine Henry rightly underscores that the admission of a courtesan's wit in male writing was nothing other than a permutation on women existing for men's pleasure. The abdication of responsibility for this objectification is achieved by the suggestion that such women are filled with insatiable (and untrustworthy) sexual appetites; see 'The Edible Woman: Athenaeus's Concept of the Pornographic', in Richlin, *Pornography*, 263–265.

133. *P XV Congr* 22.iv.13–14 (=*P Duk* inv G177).

134. Hipponax 69. Taverns and inns, a common venue for female slaves, were popularly, and in Roman law, connected with prostitution and procuring: see JE Grubbs, *Law and Family in Late Antiquity: The Emperor Constantine's Marriage Legislation* (Oxford: Clarendon Press, 1995), 206–207, 290–291, JF Gardner, *Women in Roman Law and Society* (London: Croom Helm, 1986), 251. Slaves, as property, were frequently leased. *P Wisc* 5 (186 CE) rents a female slave to a weaver, but with retention of certain 'rights' by the owner, including calling her during the night to 'make bread' for him—probably a

viii) Occultic foreigners

There is a further significant aspect. 'Sura' was a familiar name for the Syrian slave well-informed in the magical arts.[135] The Syrian witch rivalled Thessalian women for the ability to 'pull down the moon', the stock caricature of occult ability.[136] Her incantations covered the range from healing, to procuring, to divining, even exorcising.[137] Such a 'Sura' even became consort-diviner for Alexander in his conquests.[138]

Plutarch provides the conventional distrust of foreign practitioners of magic, with warnings against learning evil ways from foreigners.[139] The aptitude, propensity and potential for witchcraft were made the peculiar province of women, whatever their ethnicity.[140] It was not just being a Syrian but being a *female* Syrian that 'demonstrated' the danger.

ix) Combining the Syrian and the Phoenician

Overall, three basic stereotypes attach to Syrians. They are slaves, licentious, and practiced in the magical arts. A Phoenician connection confirmed the promiscuity.[141] The standard denigrations of slave compound these broad brush-strokes: thieving, unfaithful, gluttonous.[142] Tyre itself provided a focal-point, with Europa, the Tyrian bride[143] one of its leading exemplars.[144]

---

euphemism reflecting sexual exploitation. On the use of bread with sexual connotations, see Athen *Deip* 112c, 698e, Mart *Epig* 14.69.

135. Luc *Dial Mer* 4.4; *cf* Arr *Anab* 4.13.5.
136. For example Aristoph *Nub* 749, Plut *Mor* 145c, 416f, Juv *Sat* 6.610–611. *Lucian* held that the moon has a number of transformations, beginning with a woman and ending with a whelp (σκύλαξ): *Philops* 14.
137. Luc *Philops* 16; *cf* Mart *Epig* 7.54.
138. Arr *Anab* 4.13.5; *cf* Plut *Vit* (*Mar*) 17.1–3.
139. Plut *Mor* 166a.
140. See M Bar-Ilan, 'Witches in the Bible and in the Talmud', in HW Basser and S Fishbane (editors), *Approaches to Ancient Judaism* (Atlanta, GA: Scholars Press, 1993), Volume 5, 7–32, who links accusations of witchcraft to the socio-political division of male and female (19).
141. Dio Chr *Or* 31.116, 33.41.
142. See the stereotypes coalesced about foreign slaves by Pl *HN* 33.26–27; *cf* Pl *Ep* 1.21.
143. Nonn *Dion* 8.363.
144. The story of the rape of Europa of Tyre by Zeus had lead to a transfer of culpability for the despoiling to the women of this region. Europa is 'the most yielding of kidnap victims': Bartsch, *Decoding*, 54. See the second-century (BCE) poem of Moschus 'Europa and the Bull' (*Poems* 2.108–130) and Arist Tat *Leuc* 2.30. The callous irony is that women in the ancient world were generally presented as non-violent

The combination of Syrian and Phoenician compounded rather than reduced the stereotypical presumptions. Thus, as distinct from a geographical, administrative or sepulchral reference, meaning operated at an evocative rather than a reductionist level.[145] Hence, the use of *Syrophoenix* in Pliny the Elder's treatise on the medical properties of plants,[146] or in epitaphs noting the geopolitical origins of the deceased,[147] is far from Mark's intent.[148] The context must influence the assessment of the intent and function of a given terminology.[149]

Lucian's use of the term in his *Council of the Gods* is more pertinent. The writing debates the adverse affect on a community (in this case the community of the gods) when foreign persons and customs are admitted. Dionysius becomes the first test-case. The opening description lays down the stereotypical formulae:

> It is this peerless Dionysus, who is half human; in fact, on his mother's side he is not even Greek, but the grandson of a Syrophoenician (Συροφοίνικος) trader named Cadmus.

Again, the dispute about Cadmus comes to the fore, but the Greek connection is severed. This is less a denial of the ancient connection as a demonstration of the pollution that has occurred through mercantile

---

and compliant (as here)—a male fantasy that enabled both desire and blame: see Stehle and Day, 'Women Looking', 106 and n.24.

145. Certainly, the observation that Mark was making a distinction from the Phoenicians of Carthage or Libya merely reinscribes Roman bureaucratic mentality: Alford, *Greek Testament*, 1.340, Taylor, *Mark*, 349, JR Donahue and DJ Harrington, *The Gospel of Mark* (Sacra Pagina), (Collegeville, MN: Liturgical Press, 2002), 233. Burkill's suggestion that Mark distils Tyre and Sidon from the reference to Syrophoenician is similarly reductive and misses entirely the narrative function of the delayed stereotypical description in v.26: 'The Syrophoenician Woman: The Congruence of Mark 7:24-31', in *ZNW* 57 (1966): 35.

146. *HN* books 24–27. The reference to *Syrophoenicas* occurs at 7.201.

147. For example, *CIL* 9.1718, *AE* (1916) 0093, (1987) 1123.

148. For Mark, it has long been recognised that space conveys a wider meaning than mere cartography. See RH Lightfoot, *Locality and Doctrine in the Gospels* (New York and London: Harper, 1938), ES Malbon, *Narrative Space and Mythic Meaning in Mark* (San Francisco, CA: Harper & Row, 1986), MF Trainor, *The Quest for Home: The Household in Mark's Community* (Collegeville, MN: Liturgical Press, 2001).

149. So, B Winter, *After Paul Left Corinth: The Influence of Secular Ethics and Social Change* (Grand Rapid: Eerdmans, 2001), 115.

contact with the foreign. The Syrophoenician contrast designs a negative appraisal, which is then unfolded:

> Inasmuch as he has been honoured with immortality I say nothing of the man himself —either of his hood or of his drunkenness or of his gait; for you all, I think, see that he is womanish and unmanly in his character, half crazy, with strong drink on his breath from the beginning of the day.[150]

For a monotheistic group antithetical to idolatry these associations register the demonic. Justin Martyr's use of ἡ Συροφοινίκη becomes significant here.[151] It emerges as a passing comment on the contemporary designation (λεγομένη) of a geographic area. He aligned Damascus to the region and held that it had been under the control of a particular evil demon (from Is 8:4).[152] The connection of the demonic with Syrophoenicia adds a Judaic/Christian edge to the vilified woman whose daughter is the lodging of an unclean spirit.

x) Jewish and Christian confirmation of stereotypes

This survey has drawn upon a broad range of sources from across the Mediterranean world in order to build a sense of the stereotypical construction given to the woman in the Markan pericope. Whether or not the gospel registers a Roman, Alexandrian or Syrian provenance, the stereotypes are attested through all these regions, in both elite and more populist evidence. The stereotypes stigmatise the woman.

When a Judaic perspective is brought more strongly into play, the Greek element impugns the woman. The rampant license of the Greeks comes under frequent attack from Jewish writers,[153] just as the equation of Tyre-Sidon with harlotry is a biblical standard (for example, Is 23). The combination of harlotry and magic and idolatry is epitomised in Jezebel of Sidon (2 Kgs 9:22). Just as Tyre was blamed for polluting Greek standards, so Jews blamed it for funnelling Greek pollutions into Israel (Joel 4:6 LXX).

150. *Deo Con* 4. The prosecutor, Momus, proceeds to link Dionysius with Pan, Satyrs and Silenus.
151. *Dial Tr* 78.10.
152. *Ibid*, 78.9.
153. For example, *Sib Or* 3.185f, 545f, 595f, 732f, Wis 13–15, Rom 1:18–32, Joel 3:4–8 LXX.

This continued in second century Christian fantasies about the arch-heretic Simon Magus. His consort is used to paint in stark relief his promiscuity, infatuation with the esoteric and infidelity. She, significantly, is named Helen. Like the archetypal Helen, she is 'the Aegyan bitch',[154] incapable of anything but whoring.[155] Harlotry stalks the one designated Ἑλένη, a small 'lamdakismic'[156] jump to the Ἕλλην or Ἑλληνίς.[157]

The conventional Jewish attitude was to blend harlotry with the dog (Deut 23:18), not that this was absent from the Hellenistic environment, as the name for a brothel-keeper attests: κυναλώπηξ.[158] Similarly, the apocryphal gospel fragment found at Oxyrhynchus has Jesus castigating the Pharisees for washing in waters in which dogs and pigs have wallowed; within a line this is transferred to an accusation of being anointed by prostitutes and flute-girls. François Bovon conjoins the two phrases.[159]

xi) The Syrophoenician prostitute

'Dog', as conferred on a woman, bore all the detested characteristics of the animal. The stereotypes bend back to the primordial woman as constructed by Hesiod: the spirit of a bitch, the temperament of a thief, all muddied by lies, greed and deceitful words delivered with occultic artistry.[160] The arsenal that Mark raided is loaded against the Syrophoenician. It does not affect the argument that the woman is, seemingly, from the hinterland. Prostitutes are connected with villages as well as cities.[161] Her actions and words will be adjudicated

---

154. Lycoph *Alex* 850; *cf* Dio Chr *Or* 11.54; *cf* Mart *Epig*. 1.62
155. Hippol *Ref* 6.19.3; *cf* Just M *Apol* 1.26.1–3, Iren *C Haer* 1.23.2; see S. Haar, *Simon Magus: The First Gnostic* (Berlin / NY: Walter de Gruyter, 2003), 263-66.
156. Quint *Inst* 1.5.32 comments on the Greek propensity to invent names.
157. The jump from Hellene to Helen is precisely the one executed by Aristoph *Thesm* 907–909. It carries a sexual innuendo of licking (for example, Aristoph *Pax* 855) sometimes connected onomatopoetically with the letter *lambda*: see Auson *Epigr* 87, Mart *Epig* 12.58 with its assonantial play on the letter l, and 12.59 with its suggestion of a consequential sexually-transmitted disease. A similar connection of Helen and the Greeks occurs in *Ps-Clem Hom* 2.25.
158. Lilja, *Dogs*, 77.
159. F Bovon, 'Fragment Oxyrhynchus 840, Fragment of a Lost Gospel, Witness of an Early Christian Controversy over Purity', in *JBL* 119 (2000): 717.
160. Hes *Theog* 570–602; similarly, Phil Jud *Agr* 73.
161. Dio Chr *Or* 5.25.

as shameful on the grounds that the stereotypes that have fostered a prior prejudice, have been confirmed not rectified by the metonymous canine labelling. Alice Dermience's conclusion directs us well:

> . . . on peut en déduire que le féminin évoquait une femme peu recommandable, voire une prostituée.[162]

Kathleen Corley may be right in noting that the suggestion of a 'prostitute' may be no more than an indication that a woman is behaving outside accepted boundaries,[163] much like Cicero's treatment of Clodia.[164] Mark's stigmatising literary artifice is clear in its portraiture. In any case, we must avoid the trap of distancing Jesus from prostitutes or the suggestion of prostitutes, if that means uncritically reinscribing a sanitising concern of the developing church.[165]

The sketch in v 26 induces a satisfaction of, if not a justification for, the denigration dispensed by the proverb. The proverbial use of 'dog' is appropriate to the context in ancient conventional terms. The implication of lack of sexual restraint, the associations of pilfering, infidelity, gluttony and unrefined speech, and the suggestion of involvement in the dark, uncontrolled forces of magic, all attach to the stereotypical statements of v 26a. The vice list of vv 21–22 may have found an exemplar.

Marginal variations in these stereotypes occurred, depending on whether a Greek, Jew, Syrian or Roman provided the perspective. It suggests that, as in comedy and mime, those who are so stigmatised belong to an *other* class or group. An audience would feel confirmed that they were *unlike* those categorised. *Their* honour is enhanced as others are shamed.

162. 'Tradition et rédaction dans la péricope de la Syrophénicienne: Marc 7,24-30', in *RTL* 8 (1977): 23; so also Corley, *Private Women,* 166, Osiek and Balch, *Families,* 136, Love, 'Jesus, Healer', 17.
163. 'Were the Women around Jesus Really Prostitutes? Women in the Context of Greco-Roman Meals" in SBLSP (1989): 520-521; *cf* J. Lieu, 'The "Attraction of Women" in/to Early Judaism and Christianity: Gender and the Politics of Conversion', in *JSNT* 72 (1998): 20.
164. *Cael* 15.36, 25.61.
165. See S Matthews, *First Converts: Rich Pagan Women and the Rhetoric of Mission in Early Judaism and Christianity* (Stanford, CA: Stanford University Press, 2001).

And she 'begged' him to expel the demon from her daughter

We have already seen the importance attached to a mother's nurture and protection of her child. This domestic responsibility is configured in popular and literary evidence. The moment the Syrophoenician woman seeks the healing of her daughter by Jesus, an aggregation of shame occurs. In the story, the metaphor of bread and its provision controls the perspective for the woman and her request. Previously, the narrative had hinted at the importance of bread. Jesus instructed the parents of another girl in need of healing: εἶπεν δοθῆναι αὐτῇ φαγεῖν (5:43). The expression recurs in the first feeding miracle when Jesus instructs the disciples to take responsibility to feed the crowd: εἶπεν αὐτοῖς δότε αὐτοῖς ὑμεῖς φαγεῖν (6:37). The basic provision is bread.

Bread was often taken as a source of healing and a confirmation that healing had begun.[166] Bread is a manufactured cultural testament to the advantages of wisdom over and against ill-formed nature (Sir 15:3).[167] Bread speaks of the proper ordering between the domestic interior and the agricultural exterior.[168] Bread is what the Syrophoenician lacks; bread bears witness against her; bread is the solution to her distressed wandering. Accordingly, the metaphor alleges:

(i) that she and her own nation are (now) powerless to bring healing
(ii) that she has failed in her duty of care
(iii) that she is not able to provide for her daughter and has to scrounge from others.

The exploration of this triple shaming follows.

---

166. Plut *Mor* 694d, *GA* 7.57. There was even, in some festivals, a bread called Σωσίβος—'Health': Athen *Deip* 115a. Similar understandings were held in Judaism: see AJ Bledstein, 'Was habbiryâ a Healing Ritual Performed by a Woman in King David's House?', in *BR* 37 (1992): 15–31.

167. The long disquisition on bread in Athen *Deip* (109b–116a) is a testimony to the mark of culture; *cf* Alex Tral *Ther* 2.217.16–23.

168. Hom *Il* 11.638–641, Xen *Oecon* 7.3–6, 35–40, Pl *HN*18.107. Spinning, carding and weaving were even stronger emblems of the domestic ordering of women. On the division of labour as a reinforcement and an expression of sexual dimorphism, see Sallares, *Ecology*, 83.

i) The failure to heal

Pride in local deities and local expressions of widely known deities is evident through the ancient world. Whether it be 'Great is Artemis of the Ephesians'[169] or 'The One God ... Great Kore',[170] the acclaim is part of the strengthening of identity for the population in a particular area. Demons and evil spirits were similarly deemed to observe geographical boundaries as much as gods did,[171] as implied by Justin Martyr's reference to the demon of Damascus previously mentioned. Lucian was bemused that demons answered exorcists in the geoethnic language of the sufferer.[172]

The disorder and anarchy that demonic possession wrought was expected to be dealt with by the god(s) of that region. This deity was the primary focus of votive and thank offerings, gravitating around the charism that developed with that local expression—whether oracles, healings, protection or whatever. Courtesans and prostitutes were as likely to be clients of such cults as anyone else, as the inscriptional evidence attests. Many of their dedications were related to healing.[173]

For a member of the Tyrian population, the temple to Herakles-Melkart, renowned as a healing centre, was the focus of supplication.[174]

---

169. Acts 19:28.

170. *NDIEC* 1.68, an inscription dated second and third century BCE, found at Samaria.

171. Some adjuration formulae in magical texts use 'by the places in which you dwell': *P Lon Hay* 10391, 10414. Demons however (unless otherwise 'bound') could be summonsed by the appropriate spell to another place for a specific task. Mark's demons, at least in 5:1–20, have a geographical connection (see v 10); compare Mt 12:43, Tob 8:3, Bar 4:35, 4 Macc 18:8.

172. Luc *Philops* 16.

173. MB Skinner, 'Nossis Thêlyglôssos: The Private Text and the Public Book', in Pomeroy, *Women's History*, 24–27, Catherine J Gaster, 'Epicurean Hetairai as Dedicants to Healing Deities?', in *JGRBS* 23 (1982): 51–57.

174. Herodotus claimed, 'the temple of the god was founded when Tyre first became a city and that was two thousand three hundred years ago.' (Hdt *Hist* 2.44). Archeological excavations lend support: see Bikai, *Pottery,* 72. A sister temple was sited on the mainland as well, perhaps to service the wider Tyrian hinterland: Curt Ruf 4.2.4, Just Hist 11.10.11. There is some evidence of the progress of the Heraklean influence into northern Galilee: EM Meyers, JF Strange and CL Meyers *Excavations at Ancient Meiron, Upper Galilee, Israel 1971–2, 1974–5, 1977* (Cambridge, MT: ASOR, 1981), 152. Herakles figures in a number of panels in the floor mosaic from the House of Dionysius at Sepphoris: Meyers *et al Sepphoris* (Winona Lake, IN: Eisenbrauns, 1992), 44–45.

Alternately, resort could be made to the Syrian goddess Semiramis (the courtesan-become-queen-become-divinity sometimes blended with the age-old Ashteroth of various names)[175] and, from early Hellenistic times, Demeter and Kore.[176] Mark provides no indication which god may have attracted the Syrophoenician's devotion, although male writers frequently allied women with goddesses and reserved gods for men.[177]

The popularity and influence of these deities caught the attention of writers of the period and provided the devotional focal point for other rungs of society. Those who were (self-)appointed to the maintenance of social cohesion (including such satirists as Juvenal) often viewed with suspicion the desertion to other gods, especially if ritualistic practices incited a collapse of order. 'Our traditional faith is good enough,' says Plutarch through the voice of his father.[178] Similarly, male Jewish resort to magical amulets was blamed for a defeat in battle (2 Macc 12:40).

One interpretation, therefore, of the Syrophoenician's movement to seek out Jesus, as informed by society's *literati*, is a desertion of her (requisite) allegiance. The action blurred her ethnocultural distinctives, though it tacitly acknowledged that those distinctives had failed to serve her well-being.[179] It bordered on barbarian fickleness.

---

175. There is some suggestion that the Syrian god/dess Semea, known from magical papyri (for example *PGM* III.29, V.429, *PDM* 14.214), is to be identified with Semiramis: see HD Betz (editor), *The Greek Magical Papyri in Translation* (Chicago and London: Chicago University Press, second edition, 1992), 24.
176. Susan Harvey claims that the emphasis on the feminine in early Syrian Christianity derives from the prevalence of female deities in the pre-Christian period: SA Harvey, 'Women in early Syrian Christianity', in A Cameron and A Kuhrt (editors), *Images of Women in Antiquity*, (London: Croom Helm, 1983), 288–298.
177. For example, Juv *Sat* 6.434–456.
178. Plut *Mor* 756b; *cf* Tac *Hist* 5.5.1, 2.
179. Compare the reassessment of Rahab's action: JE McKinlay, 'Rahab: a Hero/ine?', in *BibInt* 7 (1999): 44–57. Significantly, however, there is some evidence in the non-literary papyri that a lack of reciprocity from gods might justify a defection: see *P Oxy* 7.1065, *CPJ* 2.442. Here perhaps is evidence of the gap between popular appraisal and dominant literary prescription. These papyri involve women; a male threat of defection is found in *P Par* 47 (=*UPZ* 70).

Thus, while it may be understandable that such a woman might turn to a foreign resource,[180] it pulled down considerable suspicion of her motives—both at home and abroad.[181] Such stigma was difficult to shake. What is more, it threatened to embroil Jesus in borderless action—one of the most serious indictments against magic in ancient convention.[182] Magic notoriously had nil- or ill-regard for boundaries.[183] Mark's setting of the pericope in the liminal zone of the Tyrian hinterland provides the spatial semiotics for a suspicious encounter.

Mark seems careful to preserve Jesus' honour by the provision of insight into Jesus' will: he wanted to escape notice (7:24b). This has traditionally been interpreted as part of the 'messianic secret' but it may have a more pointed purpose. Mark is concerned elsewhere to shift a categorisation of Jesus away from 'magician'.[184] The addition in the Greek translation of the Aramaic words in Mark 5:41 is pertinent.[185]

180. There is a tradition of interpretation that claims that Jewish healers/exorcists had a widespread reputation in the ancient world (*cf* Luc *Philops* 16). Certainly, magical papyri bear ample testimony to the use of Hebrew names for God (see Tcherikover, 'Introduction', 110–111). But this has never been critically tested. Magical amulets from across the Roman empire do not appear to privilege the Jewish connection above any other potentially helpful formula: see R Kotansky, *Greek Magical Amulets* (Opladen: Westdeutscher Verlag, 1994); *cf* E Schürer, *The History of the Jewish People in the Age of Jesus Christ* (Edinburgh: T&T Clark, 1986), 3.2.353–354n23.

181. From a Greek (and Roman) viewpoint, such a quest was not only a betrayal but irrational: Arist *Pol* 8.6.1 (1327b) and Juv *Sat* 3.62–65 are but two examples among many. A dimorphic asymmetry about travel, as about speech, also governs such attitudes—Galen declaimed as an honorific emblem the amount of travel he'd undertaken in pursuit of knowledge and excellence in healing: *Anat* 2.217–218.

182. The Emperor Augustus ordered the burning of magical books in 13 BCE (Suet *Aug* 31.1).

183. Betz, *Magical Papyri*, xlvi-xlvii, E Schüssler Fiorenza, 'Miracles, Mission and Apologetics: An Introduction', in E Schüssler Fiorenza (editor), *Aspects of Religious Propoganda in Judaism and Early Christianity* (Indiana: University of Notre Dame Press, 1976), 13.

184. A similar scruple is evident in the Acts of the Apostles: see C de Vos, 'Finding a Charge that Fits: The Accusation against Paul and Silas at Philippi (Acts 16.19–21)', in *JSNT* 74 (1999): 51–63, SR Garrett, *The Demise of the Devil: Magic and the Demonic in Luke's Writings* (Minneapolis: Fortress Press, 1989), 98–99.

185. It is completely obliterated by the NRSV, which seems to want to correct Mark's poor translation by giving an 'accurate' rendering (*cf* the NRSV rendition of Mt 9:18).

The expression Ταλιθα κουμ, standing alone, could easily be construed as the necessary incantational formula for the healing/raising.[186] The insertion of σοὶ λέγω into the translation of the Aramaic is Mark's attempt to underscore that the healing is tied to Jesus, not reducible to the formula—the words are inseparable from the speaker. In 7:24b, Mark uses a hidden sojourn to defend Jesus' respectability, and so tries to avoid the lack of boundedness that characterises (womanly) magic.[187] His proverb, as we have seen, can be used to warn against being caught into loss and ignominy. Such an application appears eminently suited here.

ii) The failure in a duty of care

A woman's responsibility for a child ranged from its conception and sex at birth to its growth, early education and wellbeing.[188] In particular, a mother was expected to avoid exposing the child to situations where the darker, chaotic forces of life could disturb and threaten.[189] Safeguards included apotropaic devices designed to guard the child from night-demons,[190] to deflect the bewitching evil eye (ὀφθαλμὸς πονηρός;

186. D Aune, 'Magic in Early Christianity', in *ANRW* 2.23.2 (1980): 1534–1535. Gerd Theissen considered the command to secrecy as applying to the words of the formula: *The Miracle Stories of the Early Christian Tradition* translated by F McDonagh, (Philadelphia: T&T Clark, 1983), 140–152.

187. John Pilch's folk therapist, practiced in magic and exorcism, is characterised, *inter alia*, by treatment *outside*: 'Sickness and Healing in Luke-Acts', in JH Neyrey (editor), *The Social World of Luke-Acts: Models for Interpretation* (Peabody, MA: Hendrickson, 1991), 199–200. David Aune drew attention to the emphasis on confidentiality in the healings of Mark 7:31–37 and 8:22–26 as related to a construction of magic as a socially deviant practice ('Magic', 1537–1538).

188. See the touching yet conventional recitation of a wife's responsibilities in *CIL* 6.1527 and the fulsome exposition (including the implication of the wife's responsibility for a lack of conception) in *NDIEC* 2.8; *cf Ass Mos* 11:12.

189. ES McCartney, 'Praise and Dispraise in Folklore', in A Dundes (editor), *The Evil Eye: A Folklore Casebook* (New York: Garland, 1981), 12.

190. This '*bulla*' was often in the shape of a heart and was worn by the girl until maturity. (Boys also wore them.) See Ps-Mart *Epig* 13, 14. In protective amulets, the mother's name is often found: J Naveh and S Shaked, *Amulets and Magic Bowls: Aramaic Incantations of Late Antiquity* (Jerusalem: Magness Press, 1985), 74. The distinction between prevention and deliverance is sometimes difficult to differentiate in the extant materials: R Kotansky, 'Incantations and Prayers for Salvation on Inscribed Greek Amulets', in CA Faraone and D Obbink (editors),

cf Mk 7:22),[191] or to ward off ailments.[192] Maintenance of purity and protection of person and house were required.[193] A woman could invite possession of her child through her own actions; in one instance, she was deemed culpably responsible because of her perverse disrespect for her dead husband.[194] More generally, accession to lust or any kind of incontinence exposed progeny to attack.[195]

A child, at liminal zones, was deemed to be most vulnerable to attack from evil powers. This is why women took/were given responsibility to guard the thresholds of their homes.[196] The space of entry-exit was a physical site that had larger metaphysical significance.[197] Physical liminality concretised other liminal zones: where young girls, for example, were held to be most liable to possession—at birth, at night, at the onset of puberty, or when travelling.[198]

Hence, daughter and mother, child and woman became sites to express a society's particular values.[199] Their limited and fragile connection with the fundamental logocentric arrangement of society meant that they were the ones most prone to the chaotic, the rebellious and deviant.[200] In particular, where disruption and social tension

---

Magika Hiera: Ancient Greek Magic and Religion (New York: Oxford University Press, 1991), 120.

191. Children were most susceptible to the evil eye: Plut *Mor* 680d.
192. Naveh and Shaked, *Bowls*, 82–84.
193. *Sent Sext* §348: 'Unclean demons lay claim to an unclean soul.'
194. She remarried too soon! See Philostr *Vit Apol* 3.38.
195. *Clem Recog* 9.9; see also T Ilan, *Jewish Women in Greco-Roman Palestine* (Peabody, MA: Hendricksen, 1996), 109–110.
196. Sometimes incantation bowls contain the names of the children of the house: see Naveh and Shaked, *Bowls,* 2, 3, 10. These bowls could be for general or specific protection, healing or exorcism. Such vessels and jewellery containing apotropaic formulae have been discovered throughout the Mediterranean area, including in Palestine and Tyre. They indicate not only that these were regularly resorted to but also that they were expected to be.
197. SI Johnston, 'Defining the Dreadful: Remarks on the Child-Killing Demon', in M Meyer and P Mirecki (editors), *Ancient Magic and Ritual Power* (Leiden: EJ Brill, 1995), 363.
198. Heliodorus writes of a beautiful young girl who took part in a religious procession. She became sick and retired to her room. Her condition was attributed to the evil eye: Heliod *Aeth* 3.7.
199. See SS Sered, *Priestess, Mother, Sacred Sister: Religions Dominated by Women* (New York: Oxford University Press, 1994), 275–276.
200. *Cf* Bennett, *Belted Heroes*, 136-142, Winkler, *Constraints of Desire*, 74.

increase, the child became the receptacle open to colonisation by the demonic.[201]

The supreme but understandable irony, is that the Greek child-killing demons, Mormo, Lamia and Gello, and the most famous Semitic demon (Lilith) were female.[202] These were women who had broken the ordered confines of society through uncontrolled grief, envy or revenge and became transmuted into a perpetuation of their irrationality.[203] 'Their femaleness is linked with their earth-born status, their attack on the mind and their habitation in darkness.'[204] Moreover, as part of the reinforcement of negative stereotypes based on race, the geographical origins of these demons were frequently cast as *other*. That is, the chilling female Greek demons originated elsewhere: in Libya, in Tyre, in Egypt, anywhere but 'home'.[205]

Thus, mothers bore within themselves both proximity to the demonic and responsibility to ensure that the demonic was kept in check.[206] The absence of a male guardian in the arrangement of the Syrophoenician's life was part of her culpability, and certainly part of the explanation for the state of her daughter. The 'fierce father' was the 'natural foe to vice',[207] as well as the ultimate boundary marker for the female.[208] The Syrophoenician had breached more than one boundary when she travelled to petition Jesus.

Of interest in the specifics of Mark's pericope is the designation of the daughter as θυγατρίον, a 'little daughter' (7:25). This opening term for the child is parallel to the opening identification of Jairus' daughter (5:23), whom, we learn, is twelve years' old (5:42), the age

201. PW Hollenbach, 'Jesus, Demoniacs and Public Authorities: A Socio-Historical Study', in *JAAR* 49 (1981): 573.

202. Pomeroy, *Goddesses, Whores*, 138.

203. Indeed, many demons were female, and men suffering adversities often blamed them (for example, the Furies, the Sirens) for their distress; see *TSol* 4.1–11, 15.1–11.

204. R Padel, 'Women: Model for Possession by Greek Daemons', in Cameron and Kuhrt, *Images of Women*, 4.

205. Johnston, 'Defining the Dreadful', 379–380.

206. Sarah Johnston argues that the demonic functioned with terrifying negativity to reinforce the acceptable positive female roles: 'Defining the Dreadful', 366–367.

207. Menand *Dysk* 382–390.

208. Plutarch, along with other free male writers, advises the restriction of women indoors. Even when exemplary women are permitted to come to the doorways, for example to witness a marriage procession, the passage is described as between males (father to husband): *Mor* 677a, citing Hom *Il* 18.495f.

typical for the onset of sexual maturity and availability for marriage.[209] But it was also the time, according to the medical treatises, when a girl-become-woman was most prone to become hysterical and suicidal,[210] and open to possession.[211] Where there was no father, the opportunities for the demonic were increased; the boundaries were more fluid and less policed, and the inclinations to transgression unchecked.

From these male iterated conventions, the woman is clearly culpable. The possession of the daughter 'proves' that the mother has not provided the necessary ordering to protect the daughter; she has failed in her duty of care for her daughter. In effect, she has sacrificed her daughter to the demon (*cf* Ps 106:36).

So the stigmatising, shaming assessment expands. Contemporary commentary on this passage sometimes reinscribes the same judgement. The woman is to blame for the state of her child, whether because of her idolatry, her (s)mothering or other psychological constriction.[212] Hence, Jesus' enthymemic, sententious proverb is warranted, calling to account the presumed shameful neglect by a mother. It does not matter that the ancient world was frequently capricious in its injury of others. Because injury occurred, a perception of transgression was induced (*cf* Lk 13:4, Jn 9:2).

iii) The inability to provide for one's own

Bread as a metaphor is widely attested throughout the ancient world in popular and élite circles.[213] We have seen already the role of bread in the cultivation and preservation of health. Accordingly, there is little surprise in finding the metaphor of bread in Jesus' words to the

---

209. Ilan, *Jewish Women*, 65–69 distinguishes between the halakhic ideal and the actual practice of marriage, which shows a somewhat later age for the marriage of young women. The first century doctor, Soranus, places puberty at about fourteen years: *Gyn* 1.24.

210. See the Hipp *Virg* 8.468. Monika Fander explores the connection of the putative age of the child with menstruation as the connective point with the discussion of pollution in the previous pericope: *Die Stellung der Frau im Markusevangelium: Unter besonderer Berücksichtigung kultur- und religionsgeschichtler Hintergründe* (Altenberge: Telos Verlag, 1989), 181–206, 285.

211. *NDIEC* 4 §114.

212. Derrett, 'Law in the New Testament', 185 ('distress amongst children . . . is due to open or hidden disturbance in their guardians'); *cf* D and P Miller, *The Gospel of Mark as Midrash on Earlier Jewish and New Testament Literature* (Lewiston: Edwin Mellen, 1990), 196 (a fracture of the generations causes psychological disturbance).

213. For example, Mart *Epig* 8.16, 9.2, 10.59, 14.69.

woman. The provision of health for the children through the medium of bread is testimony to the honour that Jesus possesses. Conversely, a failure to (be able to) provide, figured in the metaphor of bread, is shameful.[214] Seeking bread from a provider other than oneself, denoted parasitical or beggardly behaviour.

The dog was renowned not only for its gluttony but for its dependence on others for food. A privileged position as Greco-Roman house-dogs, or the contemptible subsistence as rubbish-collectors in any ancient Mediterranean city, did not alter this assessment. Here, the contrast with the human was pronounced. It was a mark not only of honour, *but of being truly human*, to provide food for one's own. The problem of poverty was not merely the absence of food but the absence of honour consequent on being dependent on another.[215] The dog was a pariah, in this sense even when collared.

The honour of independent means is extolled in several Judeo-Christian texts.[216] Working with one's own hands expressed the sentiment.[217] The honorific value is echoed in a Greco-Roman context.[218] The notion of being unencumbered by any sort of debt is related. A letter from a young man to his mother declaimed, 'Don't you know that I would rather become a cripple than owe a man even an obol?'[219] Women also were extolled, as one epitaph states, if they 'lived well and owed no one anything!'.[220] This value carried into early Christianity (Rom 13:8 *cf* 2 Thess 3:10); reliance on another's bread is not exemplary (2 Thess 3:8). The contempt of the parasite looms behind such sentiments.

The male in Mark's story (Jesus) is confirmed as the bringer of civilisation by pronouncing the proverb. He shames the woman by accenting her proximity to the dog and her need to observe the teaching that a male—the authority figure in a dimorphic framework—offers. As a Greek, she 'ought' to be familiar with the proverb and/or its

214. Luc *Paras* 58.
215. This appears to have been drilled into the young: see (Ps-) Plut *Mor* 12e.
216. Sir 40:28–30, Ps-Phoc 156–157, Phil *Quis rer* 103, *Spec* 2.106, *Flac* 64.
217. *Gospel of the Nazarenes apud* Hier *Comm Mt* 12.13; see AFJ Klijn, *Jewish Christian Gospel Tradition* (Leiden: EJ Brill, 1992), 88–90 for parallels; *Ps-Clem Hom* 12.13.1–5
218. A proverb captured it: 'I would rather buy than beg'; *cf* Plut *Mor* 694d.
219. *BGU* 2.846.
220. *IGR* 1.104.

societal values. Correction by a foreigner intensifies the rebuke of the failure to provide for one's own.

The woman has assaulted conventional morality on manifold fronts. Ethnic differences modulate but do not expunge the interpretation of her offence. In this framework, the proverb has been carefully selected, both providing an interpretation of the woman's action and drawing from the narrative portrait to justify its usage.

Spatial Dimensions: Boundary Marking and Territorial Protection

The signification of spatial order

The key to the ordering of nature for protection against the ingress and egress of the uncontrolled and disorderly is the erection and maintenance of appropriate boundaries. From house design to the layout of cities to the administration of the empire, zoning was crucial. Space and place are not merely physical entities: they bear a symbolic capacity which illuminate and reflect concern for the dominance of culture over nature and the proper handling of that which is natural.[221] Decor, according to the first century master-writer on architecture, Vitruvius, was equally about decorum as decoration. Ordered houses were the mark of the ascent of man from the primeval birth of animals.[222] Any breach of conventional barriers shifted a woman from civilised life to the realm of the bestial. A fragment of Menander captures the spatial signification, but compounds it by reference to a woman's speech and a canine connection:

> You transgress the boundaries of the household, woman, with your chattering. The front door is the authorised boundary for a civilised woman's life. To engage in hot pursuit, running around trading insults in the street, is the trademark of a dog.[223]

The context of Jesus' saying is laced with issues of space, place and movement. These are key ingredients of the culture-nature exchange.

---

221. See A Wallace-Hadrill, 'The Social Structure of the Roman House', in *Papers of the British School at Rome* 54 (1988): 43–97.

222. Vitr 1.2.5, 2.1.1f, 3.1.1.

223. *Apud* Stob *Flor* 74.11 (my translation) reading διὰ τὴν λαλιάν for τὴν αὐλίαν with A Körte and A Thierfelder in their edition *Menandri Quae Supersunt* (Leipzig: BG Teubner, 1959), 191.

The occupation of private space by Jesus, the journey in public space first by Jesus and then by the woman, the Syrophoenician's transgression of the barrier between the man and the woman ('and he would not have anyone know') highlight the problematisation of the spatial. Geography, household and body are woven together in the pericope.

The proverb incorporated into Jesus' saying itself carries spatial implications in the movement from one space ('taking') and transfer to another ('throwing'). 'Throwing to the dogs' implies an outside,[224] a lack of boundaries and therefore a nature uncontrolled by culture. It is the place of dishonour, the demonic, the pariah.

The scavenging pests 'outside' preyed upon the unsuspecting, the exposed and the dregs of society (*cf* Lk 16:21). They were the lice upon the refuse that spilled from ordered boundaries. Hence, the most dishonourable death in the Greco-Roman and Jewish world was to be flung outside the walls of a town to be mauled by the feverish canine rodents that roamed the fringe zones.[225] Whether a Jezebel (2 Kgs 9:30–37) or an Acteon,[226] the dishonour is executed upon those who have acted dishonourably by the agents of dishonour—the dogs. The irony in the instance of Acteon was that the dogs had been subjected to the rule of the *logos*.[227]

Lap-dogs, guard-dogs, even the hounds of the hunt, could make the transition to the place where the *logos* reigned, that is, the 'inside', at least in a Greco-Roman context. Nevertheless, constant vigilance was required, especially where food was concerned. Hence, animals at or near human dining attracted considerable scruples. Reinforcement of the hierarchy of position within the household was paramount, whether by different places for feeding and/or differences in food portions—dogs frequently received the debris of household fare.[228] But, for prized hounds or pets, beneath the table at which the master dined, and sharing at least something of *his* meal, was common.

224. So Donahue and Harrington, *Mark*, 234.

225. Hom *Il* 8.379, 23.183. Throwing a traitor to the dogs outside the city walls was sometimes not considered good enough—the cadaver had to be cast beyond the limits of the territory: Thuc 1.138b.

226. Callimachus *Hymn* 5.109–116, Ov *Meta* 3.131ff, Poll *Onom* 5.38.

227. As mentioned in chapter 1, the wolf-like nature remained in the dog as anarchic potential. In the story of Acteon, he was turned into a stag, the now-bestial master unrecognisable by his hounds.

228. For example, Aristoph *Eq* 414.

'Throwing to the dogs' in a Greco-Roman context could therefore entertain both the wild and the domestic. It was simply a matter of distance from the central control, the logocentric heart of the household. If the wild outside edged too close to the domestic, a barrage of boundary maintenance was needed—the hurling of rocks, sticks and the requisite torrent of abuse. Prostitutes, musicians, actresses, and even high-cultured courtesans were always in danger of receiving this response. They were painted as wall-leaners, dwellers in the shadows, door-lurkers, road-rampagers,[229] thereby inviting correspondences with the parasite and the beggar.[230] (Even more pitiable were those free-born who took up these positions outside the house of a courtesan.)[231]

The Jewish emphasis

For a Jew however, the philosophical and practical distinction between wild and domestic varieties of dog never found acceptance, certainly as regards the household. Richard Weymouth stated bluntly: 'dogs are not domesticated animals in Palestine.'[232] The dog consistently is an external marauder in the Hebrew Scriptures, a border pest to be fed dishonour—namely, that which cannot be accommodated within ordered society. Hence, Jezebel, defiled meat,[233] and polluted 'dog-dough'[234] were to be despatched to the dogs.[235] Even the quite exceptional dog of Tobit (Tob 11:4), and the (negative) reference to shepherds' dogs (Job 30:1) place the animal *outside* the house.

Certainly, rabbinical injunctions reinforced the rejection of dogs, though their arguments suggest that there were some who were non-observant. Eating with a dog was idolatry, a dog is a kind of wild animal, feed a dog with a stick—such summary sayings dot the rabbinical collections.[236] Archeological evidence lends some support. Village houses at this time incorporated enclosed open-air

229. Mart *Epig* 1.34, 7.79, 11.104, 12.27, 32. Martial calls prostitutes 'wives of the walls' in *Epig* 3.82; *GA* 5.7, 5.150.
230. Luc *Nigr* 22; Mart *Epig* 12.32; *cf* 6.77, 10.5.
231. *GA* 5.164, 167, 189, Mart *Epig* 10.13.
232. Cited by Hasler, 'Incident', 460. Universal Hebrew contempt for dogs is repeated most recently by E Firmage, 'Zoology', *ABD* 6.1143–1144.
233. Ex 22:31, Jer 15:3.
234. Wendy Cotter points out the distinction between 'children's bread' and the nigh-inedible 'dog-dough' mentioned in the Mishnah (*Hallah* 1.8): *Miracles in Greco-Roman Antiquity: A Sourcebook* (London: Routledge, 1999), 242–243.
235. Ex 22:31, 3 Rgns 16:4, 22:38.
236. See, for example, m*Kil* 8.6, *Hull* 4.2, b*Shab* 63a, 155b, *Abod Zar* 22b.

courtyards,[237] which were largely allocated to cattle. Dogs were banned from these enclosures unless chained.[238] Certainly, fauna profiles from the Tel Anafa site (north-east Israel) during the Hellenistic and early Roman period, reveal negligible evidence of dogs in the samplings of domestic remains, either as canine bones or canine gnawings on other bones.[239]

The prevention of species confusion

Philo condemned hunting because hunter and hound shared the same food—a disregard for the boundaries between species.[240] Concern about the distinction of species, where food marks the boundaries of race, is the reading of the Syrophoenician's story offered by the *Pseudo-Clementine Homilies*. Jesus, here, offers a more fulsome rejection of the woman's request:

> It is not lawful to heal the Gentiles, who are like dogs on account of their using various (διαφόροις) meats and practices, while the table in the kingdom has been given to the sons of Israel.[241]

As Aseneth in the romance, *Joseph and Aseneth*, distanced herself from an indiscriminacy of diet by tossing her usual (unclean) foods to 'strange dogs',[242] so the Syrophoenician woman in the Clementine retelling, earns the healing of her daughter by 'having changed what she was, by living like the sons of the kingdom'. Lifestyle meaning is discerned by reference to table practice.

---

237. S Dar, *Landscape and Pattern: An Archeological Survey of Samaria 800 BCE–636 CE* (BAR Interpretation Series 308) (Oxford: BAR, 1986), 84, S Guijarro, 'The Family in First-Century Galilee', in H Moxnes (editor), *Constructing Early Christian Families* (London/New York: Routledge, 1997), 46–55.
238. m*Nez* 7.7.
239. RW Redding, 'The Vertebrate Fauna', in SC Herbert (editor), *Tel Anafa 1.i: Final Report on Ten Years Excavation at a Hellenistic and Roman Settlement in Northern Israel* (Ann Arbor: JRA Series (10), 1994), 289.
240. Phil Jud *Spec* 4.120. This indicates that the prescriptive comparison in *Pirqe Rabbi Eliezar* 29 ('Whoever eats with an idolater is like a man who eats with a dog') has an earlier foundation. An example of dog and master sharing the same food is found in Babr *Aes* 128.
241. *Ps-Clem Hom* 2.19.
242. *Jos Asen* 10.13.

The proverbial reinforcement of boundaries

The breach of another's household is simply another aspect of the dog that is evoked by the woman's action. She is uninvited. Unlike 'those whom he desired' who are 'called to him' (Mk 3:13), this woman is ἄκλητος, 'not invited'—a traditional designation of the beggar and parasite who force themselves upon a banquet (*cf* Mt 22:2–13).[243] The anandrous occupation of external space by the Syrophoenician woman in Mark's story combines with the transgression of the boundaries of the household, and the personal boundaries of a 'foreign' man. A compromising situation is constructed.[244] The chaotic is at hand. The dog needs to be dealt with.

The proverb fits. It is tailored to a despised fringe-dweller from the same space and time as the demonic and the dog.[245] This is the existing spatial expanse for the woman—completely at the mercy of the untamed (and hence able to be possessed by it). She is a 'public woman' (γυνὴ πάγκοινη), that is, a whore. Her place is the outside 'where the refuse is dumped'.[246] Her action, let alone her request, represents the outside threatening the inside.[247]

The locative elements of Jesus' saying presuppose and re-impose the division of inside and outside. The language re-establishes the priorities indicated by enclosed space, bounded place. The woman is re-directed to the importance (for her) of the provision and preparation of food—a primary instruction required of a free man to the women for whom he has responsibility (mother, sister, wife, slaves, even concubines). The very suggestion of abuse indicates that the woman has fallen outside properly bounded modesty and dignity.[248] The

243. Stark, 'Who Laughs at Whom', 102–104.
244. Joanna Dewey rightly perceives the ethnic-sexual overtones in the breach of boundaries in Mark's story: 'Jesus' Healings of Women: Conformity and Non-Conformity to Dominant Cultural Values as Clues for Historical Reconstruction', in *BTB* 24 (1994): 127. By comparison, Amy-Jill Levine denies 'any hypothetical sexual coding' ('Matthew's Advice', 27), possible only by denying the stereotypical gender characterisations triggered by ethnic and narrative cues.
245. Compare J-Y Thériault, 'Le Maître Maitrise! Matthieu 15, 21–28', in A Chené *et al* (editors), *De Jésus et des femmes. Lectures sémiotiques* (Montréal-Paris: Editions du Cerf 1987), 25–27 who applied a structural analysis to the clash of geosocial entities.
246. P Bird, 'The Harlot as Heroine: Narrative Art and Social Presupposition in Three Old Testament Texts', in *Semeia* 46 (1989): 121.
247. *PA* 5.150 indicates that the usual movement is for a hetaira to come to a man's house.
248. Liv *Hist* 34.1.

hierarchical ordering of mind over passion, man over woman, order over chaos all coalesce in the world of Jesus' saying.

The gender dimensions of speech operate to 'place' Jesus as well. The man has properly protected his own honour (even in private), under scrutiny by the (public) audience. He has demarcated boundaries not just for the woman but *between* woman and man. The proverb, in this sense, is self-protective (of his own reputation at least):

> Deft broadcasting of a man's temperate relations with women served to contain the plausibility of whatever insinuations his competitors could serve up,[249] as they strained to infer from his private life an intemperance which might compromise the fulfilment of public duty.[250]

Gender dynamics therefore become a prime mechanism for (male) self-protection as also, relatedly, of boundary maintenance.

Thus, the proverb protects and reinforces existing spatial arrangements and boundary markers. Since it is likely that a *Greek* proverb shames the woman, it carries the implication that it is a piece of universal wisdom that she as a Greek should have known. The migration of the proverb into another culture intensifies the spatial order implicit in the proverb itself.[251] Just as Aristotle saw it as a mark of shame for a (Greek) house to be *bereft* of a dog, so Jewish teaching at the time of Jesus took it as a mark of shame for a house to *keep* a dog. In Jewish hands, the accent must be on *throwing to* the dogs—a tossing out (βαλεῖν) that has no connotation of τρεφεῖν (which consistently conveys the sense of nurture or support).[252] Any such 'keeping' fractures the distinction between species/race and the spatial buttress to that distinction. Ethnic distinctives reinforce that dogs belong *outside*, food *inside* the boundaries. The woman has offended those boundaries and needs to be re-ordered.

249. See Mt 11:19, Lk 7:39, Jn 8:41.
250. K Cooper, 'Insinuations of Womanly Influence: An Aspect of the Christianisation of the Roman Aristocracy', in *JRS* 82 (1992): 153.
251. A similar intensification appears to occur with the proverb of taking a stick to the dog. Compare b*Shab* 155b and *GA* 11.153.3.
252. Gen 32:18, 3 Rgns 18:13, Isa 33:18, Jer 26:21; compare also *TJob* 10.3, 14.2, *PsSol* 5.9,11; *Sib Or* 3.130, 134, 254. It could extend to domestic animals (Is 7:21) but, as expected, dogs are not mentioned, unlike Greco-Roman texts. Note especially Lk 23:29.

Resocialisation by reference to the natural order

We have seen that rhetoricians recognised the power of the appeal to a universal and the force of a general maxim applied to a particular situation. The words of Jesus are totally in accord with these sentiments. Gerd Theissen, by contrast, identified the scandalous offence of Jesus' reply to the woman's need:

> How can we avoid being caught in the contradiction that children are given a higher value within the image presented, but in reality a suffering child is being denied help?[253]

Metaphor operates to *deflect* as well as address a particular issue. By the use of the metaphor, both the woman and her daughter are denied a particular place, a *human* identity.[254] They are made invisible by the use of one species to define another (to replay Aristotle's notion of metaphor). Against a confusion of species that might be thought to result, a deeper collation of 'like with like' occurs. Thus, at the very moment of acknowledging the presence of the *woman*, the saying insists on her absence.

The spatial implications within the saying have already been noted. However, this functions also at the level of the *literary* figure adopted in the saying. 'In speaking,' said Quintilian, 'there are certain things which have to be concealed . . . '[255] Significantly, this touches both players. The allusiveness protects the honour of the speaker and diminishes that of the target.[256] The asymmetry of the characterisation and gender is preserved.

The very act of concealing denies any specific or recognizably distinct place for the woman as (a) woman or for her daughter. The collation of the Syrophoenician and her child into the metaphor, uses the content of the metaphor to show her her place. She belongs in the same realm as the dog. Both dog and woman belong to nature, rather

253. Theissen, *Gospels in Context*, 65.
254. Michie, *Flesh Made Word*, 139, citing A Rich, *The Dream of a Common Language* (New York: Norton, 1978).
255. Quint *Inst* 2.13.12.
256. See S Montiglio, *Silence in the Land of Logos* (Princeton, NJ: Princeton University Press, 2000), 130–133. Her suggestion that silence was often used rhetorically to bolster the virtuous authority of the speaker whose subsequent utterance is thereby characterised as an unpleasant necessity has substantial implications for the interpretation of Matthew 15:23a.

than to the culture indicated by eating bread inside; both lack reason, which can supply the order of a household and the artifice of a literary form; both are devoid of the communication that is the emblem of reason.

The shaming of the woman, through the metaphor which makes her invisible, is designed to make her just that—invisible. This is the imposition of reason and order upon her. Any dignity that a woman could have was to be found in what the contemporary ethologist, Edward Wilson, called 'nesting'—a return to what nature had ordained for her. In this sense, the wisdom of the proverb has no other function than the (re)socialisation of the woman.[257] It operates to enforce a social control upon her and does so through an appeal to a universal moral truth reinforced by an ethological perspective. Space is aligned with literary artifice that is further aligned with the argument from nature.

All in all, the enthymemic, sententious proverb is designed to reinforce conventional boundaries regulating space, movement, gender and relationship. The debt to the natural order in Jesus' words is also a debt to cultural representation of that nature, intensified by racially-defined attitudes to dogs. The adoption of a proverb reinforces the notion of the timelessness of definitions of space. Thus nature 'becomes' unchangeable, as do the deductions to be made from nature for culture, and the need for culture to exert its influence over nature. This is the work of the proverb.

First conclusion (Jesus's saying)

The words of the Markan Jesus deliver an ethological response to a specific encounter with a suppliant woman. In the evangelist's narrative frame, the saying in both content and form uses the natural to reinforce contemporary conventions, especially as touch upon gender. The woman is exposed as offending culture and manifesting the disturbing disorders of unruly nature.

Jesus' command of language in Mark's story transcends racial divisions, and highlights that he, as located in properly ordered space, holds the hierarchically superior position. That position is set off against the grovelling, fawning woman and demands that

257. AD Jacobson, 'Proverbs and Social Control: A New Paradigm for Wisdom Studies', in JE Goehring, CW Hedrick, JT Sanders, with HD Betz (editors), *Gnosticism and the Early Christian World* (Sonoma, CA: Polebridge Press, 1990), 81–83.

he restore the very order that her unruly behaviour has threatened. The combination of elements in his saying—table/food hierarchy, enthymemic appeal to convention, sententious pronouncement and the ancient proverb that elicits the support of a witness from the natural order—are a masterly application of the tools and techniques given to his position. Jesus *is* the 'Lord' of the house (7:28—understood without any christian revisionism). As controller and articulator of its life, he takes responsibility for the harmonious ordering of the complex mosaic of nature and culture. He reinforces it by using it and thereby acts as a tool of that socio-political heritage which relies upon a (pseudo-) scientific ideology for its support. A Jew utilizing a Greek proverb merely accentuates the universality of that wisdom grounded in abiding nature. There can be no mistaking that Jesus has assumed the authority to pronounce upon and for this woman. If she is to rejoin or at least link with the human realm she must learn from the natural as tempered by the cultural.

5

The Hair of the Dog that Bit You
The Ethological Word of a Woman

Four main areas were previously isolated as important for the analysis of the saying of Jesus in Mark 7:27 from the perspective of ethology. These were:

i) the conjunction of scientific/philosophical axioms with cultural values reinforced through long-standing literary expression,
ii) the moral implications which attach to the inferior partner categorised in any hierarchical exchange,
iii) the territorial boundaries which afford spatial protection for dominant and submissive entities, and
iv) the socio-political conclusions which assert a foundation in the natural order.

The response of Mark's Jesus to the woman's request for her daughter's deliverance has been found to rely upon, apply and perpetuate constructions of the woman (and her daughter) that are grounded in an ethological framework.

The woman does not evade Jesus' brutal rebuttal of 'piddling dogs'.[1] She retains the κυνάρια from Jesus' sententious pronouncement, recognising that ethological associations are the crux of his repudiation. Accordingly, if we acknowledge the weight of Mark's unique, introductory formula in 7:28,[2] the woman's words demand analysis as a specific answer to Jesus. To appreciate the power of her reply, the same framework that was adopted to evaluate the ethological dimensions of Jesus' words will be applied. As we shall see, every facet of Jesus' humiliation of the woman is adroitly countered. In the process, a total reassessment of ethological comparison occurs and the

1. This translation is an effort to capture the denigration in Jesus' words.
2. Mark's use of a double indicative rather than a participle with indicative is found only here.

foundation is laid for the destabilisation of the hegemony of *logos*.

The valorisation of literary form

The structural components of the saying

i) The significance of the omissions

The woman's answer to Jesus is noteworthy not only in what it contains but also in what is absent. Her reply eschews any sententious formula. There is no value judgement added to the metaphor in her saying that might narrow and exact the appropriate, probative response. And there is no evidence of an enthymemic structure.[3]

Both these absences are important. Certainly, she does not trespass into linguistic forms that were sometimes denied to women.[4] But their omission also highlights the part of Jesus' speech that is seen as crucial, at least for the woman. After all, this was where the abusive metre and metaphor were summonsed.

The suggestion that the opening command of Jesus is a redactional addition to an earlier traditional exchange is unnecessary to this interpretation.[5] The woman, as Mark presents her reply, does not demand: 'Let my child be fed/healed.' Further, she avoids the temptation to speak *ex cathedra*, as is the characteristic of the maxim.[6] There is no attempt to usurp the authoritative position that has been demonstrated by a male (Jesus). Quintilian expressed the power of status differentials thus:

> Who would tolerate a boy, or youth, or even someone of low birth (*ignobilem*) who presumed to speak with all the authority of a judge and to thrust his precepts down our throats?[7]

At the same time, as we shall see, the shift of attention to the

---

3. The addition of γάρ in A L f^1 Maj Text lat sy^h is interesting however, for it directly recalls the γάρ in Jesus' words. On this reading, the woman has changed the 'case' in the enthymeme, which has the potential to change the result. This does not negate what follows in the text here, as the content of the 'case' is still crucial. However, it *may* modify the argument as to antiquity of form.
4. See further below: 'Proverbs and Women'.
5. In agreement with Gundry, *Mark*, 378.
6. *Contra* Derrett, 'Law in the New Testament', 172, who has confused maxim and proverb.
7. Quint *Inst* 8.5.8.

proverb alone actually realigns the story's dynamics, compelling Jesus to take responsibility for his *own* decision in a specific context, rather than rely upon a judgment ostensibly delivered 'from the beyond'. The problem of reliance on maxims was identified by the author of the *Rhetorica ad Herennium*—they become a substitute for arguing a case.[8]

There is one further absence. No infinitive is to be found. No recourse to an ethereal universal is ventured. There is no construction that would invite an audiential supplement, by way of an 'infinitive of exclamation' or 'predicative nominative', drawing an ethical judgement: 'is foolish / not good' for example.[9]

This does not rule out the presence of a proverb in her words. Rather, it *grounds* the encapsulation of narrative wisdom and narrows the contest of form. Her wisdom is hammered out in the observation of (domestic) human practice. This saying is diluted of moral caution. Put bluntly, it is the difference between a realistic and an idealistic wisdom saying. The folklorist, Alan Dundes, distilled the distinction as between 'summing up a situation' and 'recommending a course of action'.[10] This distinction of proverbs is admittedly functional, and not designed to be secluded from other analyses. A functional orientation can generate an awareness of the contexts in which particular proverbs might be used and how they are being deployed.[11]

Of course the underlying reinforcement of prescription by description characterises much ancient observation. But the observer is, in this case, a woman, and the power to turn her observation into persuasion, let alone legislation, is, in ancient convention, unlikely.[12]

8. *Rhet ad Her* 4.17.25.

9. See WC Green, *Aristophanes: The Wasps* (London, Oxford and Cambridge: Rivingtons, 1868), 84n, SE Porter, *Idioms of the Greek New Testament* (Sheffield: Sheffield Academic Press, 1992), 195.

10. 'On the Structure of the Proverb', in W Mieder and A Dundes (editors), *The Wisdom of Many: Essays on the Proverb* (Madison, WN: University of Wisconsin Press, 1994 [1981]), 45. The distinction was familiar to the ancients: see Arist *Poet* 9.2–3 (1451b), 25.1–13 (1460b), *Rhet ad Her* 4.17.24.

11. Alan Winton distinguished Jesus' *contrastive* proverb and the woman's *identificational* one, that is, the children are removed from (τέκνα) and connected (παιδία) with the dogs: *Proverbs of Jesus*, 47.

12. Cato's speech against women's ability to influence the affairs of state may be one extreme of contempt but its sentiment was long remembered, even (for example, seeking the instruction of husbands at home) in early Christian circles; see Liv *Hist* 34.1, (similarly, Publ Syr *Max* 365); *cf* 1 Cor 14:34–35, 1 Tim 2:8–15.

Rather, her venture into verbal contention risks annihilation. The absences in her answer, by comparison with the words of Jesus, render any moral assessment oblique, enhancing the subtlety of her response.

ii) A structural analysis of the saying

It is time for a closer examination of the saying of the woman:

καὶ τὰ κυνάρια ὑποκάτω τῆς τραπέζης
ἐσθίουσιν ἀπὸ τῶν ψιχίων τῶν παιδίων

Further contrasts from Jesus' proverb are apparent: word order, hiatus and euphony, the lexical choice for the verb, the plural, diminutives and metre.

a. The arrangement of the saying

The structural arrangement of the sentence turns the emphasis from assessment of the action (taking-throwing) to those who are affected by actions (dogs-children). The double universal expressed by the two infinitives is replaced by the single connective of an indicative verb. There is no parallel to the common ornament of phonemic metathesis found in Jesus' words in v 27 (λαβεῖν – βαλεῖν).[13]

Nevertheless, the placement of words is critical. Quintilian noted that words stamp themselves on the hearer when placed at the close of the sentence.[14] In the middle, they are obscured by their surroundings,[15] even though the verb may hold antecedent and subsequent phrases together.[16] The assignment of the verb to the middle of the woman's reply adds emphasis to the earlier part of the sentence.[17]

There is a further structural impact. Eloquent style recommended a crescendo in vividness from the opening to the closing.[18] This vividness could be conferred by imagery but also by the proper value of things. Thus stronger or more highly prized notions belonged to

13. Quintilian complained of the frequency of such simple word-plays in his day: *Inst* 8.5.13–14, 20.
14. This is not merely the influence of Latin on his thinking; compare Demetr *Eloc* 2.50.
15. Quint *Inst* 9.4.29.
16. *Rhet ad Her* 4.27.38.
17. BDF §472, Porter, *Idioms*, 295–296.
18. Demetr *Eloc* 2.50–51.

the end of a period[19] or sentence.[20] Here, a marked hierarchy in the sentence hinges on the verb, with the 'dogs under the table' inferior to the children (with their crumbs) syntactically (as culturally). Even in unadorned prose style, word order and choice were still important, if only to avoid (or suggest?) obscenities.[21]

b. Lexical selection: eating not 'foddering'

We have noted that the verb ἐσθίουσιν secures a muted emphasis in the sentence structure. Yet, it gains attention by a comparison with Jesus' χορτασθῆναι in v 27. Both words are found in Mark's feeding miracles.[22] However, χορτασθῆναι is a lexical item drawn from animal husbandry.[23] The woman prefers a word in ordinary usage, thereby achieving a greater clarity and simplicity.[24]

However, the word 'made ordinary by custom'[25] invites a subtle reconsideration of the place of dogs and perhaps also of Jesus' ethological equation of τέκνα with πρόβατα (Mk 6:34).[26] The bestial connotation of χορτάζω is clear in Revelation 19:21 where birds (crows?) tear at the flesh of slain men. In Luke 16:21, Lazarus joins the dogs and longed to be fed (χορτασθῆναι).[27] The exchange is aptly captured in Luke 15:16 where the one who has fallen to the state of the pigs is described as desiring to 'fodder' (χορτασθῆναι) on what *they* were *eating* (ἤσθιον). The word change accents the demise from his humanity.

By contrast, in Mark's story, the animals can 'eat' as the children 'eat', albeit of 'crumbs'. A connection is forged through ἐσθιεῖν not

19. Strictly, periods are rare in the New Testament. BDF §464 cite only Lk 1:1–4, Acts 15:24–26, Hbs 1:1—2a, though 'periodic sentence structure' has a few more representatives.
20. Quint *Inst* 9.4.23.
21. Quint *Inst* 8.3.45, 9.4.33; *cf* Arist *Rhet* 3.3 (1406b). Quintilian does not deny that word order and rhythms are to be found in ordinary speech. He was particularly concerned that obscenity be avoided.
22. Mk 6:36,37,42, 8:2,4,8. The use of ἐσθίω by the woman is a more encompassing Markan *Stichwort*.
23. Note the pastoral setting given to the first feeding miracle (Mk 6:34).
24. Aristotle compared the lexical choice of Aeschylus and Euripides for 'eating'. He deems Aeschylus' ἐσθίει eminently more suitable than Euripides' θοινᾶται in their otherwise identical iambic trimeter.
25. As Aristotle holds: εἰωθότος γλῶτταν: *Poet* 22.13 (1458b).
26. The word χορτασθῆναι had not lost its agricultural connections; see Athen *Deip* 96f.
27. *Like them* is the connotation, made the more poignant because the dogs lick him.

simply with the feeding miracles but with Jairus' daughter.[28] Her parents are instructed to feed her (φαγεῖν–5:43). The word change mounts a subtle challenge to the ethological degradation.

The text uses the plural verb for the dogs' eating. Grammarians disagree about the origin of disparity in number between verb and neuter plural subjects.[29] Mark has instances of both singular and plural verbs with plural neuter subjects.[30] The metrical difference between ἐσθίουσιν and ἐσθίει[31] may have governed the morphology; but there may be a further nuance. In Mark 4:32, there is a partial quotation from Psalm 103(104):12. The Septuagint has the singular κατασκηνώσει with the neuter plural τὰ πετεινά. Mark changes the singular to the plural κατασκηνοῦν.[32] This suggests that the plurality of subjects is being specifically respected in the choice of verb ending, so that *each*, not merely the undifferentiated, collective 'all', is in view.

c. The pleasing sound of the saying

The saying of the woman is a masterpiece of inventive, rhetorical finesse. Integral to its polish is not the counter-proposition of the content, but the phonemic resonances worked into the lexical choices and arrangements. The harsh rasp that dominated the proverb of Jesus is temporarily and partially echoed in the opening. But these give way to a predominance of 'vowel harmonies'[33] which soften the sound of the woman's reply. The harsh sounds (κ, ρ) belong to the first half

28. The matching of the words used for both young girls is striking: θυγάτριον 5: 23, 7:25; θυγατήρ 5:35, 7:26; παιδίον 5:41a, 7:30.
29. The three interpretations are that the plural indicates a reference to each of the constituents in the plural, that it respects the designation of persons or animates (including such entities as δαιμονία), or that the only 'rule' is a general freedom: Porter, *Idioms*, 74, BDF §133, Robertson, *Grammar*, 403–04.
30. Plural neuter with plural verb: 1:25*, 34*, 3:11, 4:32, 5:13, 7:28, 10:34*, 14:27 (asterisk indicates a derivative neuter subject from a previous clause); plural neuter with singular verb: 3:28, 4:8, 4:37, 7:4, 7:15, 7:23, 9:3, 13:30.
31. The reading of A K N Γ 1010 Maj Text.
32. No support comes from the Hebrew. Psalm 104:12 (MT) has a collective noun with a singular verb.
33. Joseph Russo takes up RA Rothstein's term ('The Poetics of Proverbs', in Ch E Gribble (editor), *Studies Presented to Professor Roman Jakobson by his Students* (Cambridge, MA: Slavica Publishers, 1968), 273), explaining that vowel harmony is more subtle than simple assonance, involving the repetition of vowels or diphthongs restricted to a narrow range: Russo, 'Poetics', 129n3.

of the saying (indicated by single underlining in the following) and are compounded by successions of short vowels (double underlining), hiatus (bold dots) and hissing[34] syllabic echoes (ordinary dots):

Καὶ τὰ; κυνάρια ὑποκάτω τῆς τραπέζης ἐσθίουσιν

The hiatus between κυνάρια and ὑποκάτω is likely deliberate. Hiatus causes a 'break of time between two vowels, as though there were a pause.' This can be harnessed, suggested Quintilian, for rhetorical effect.[35] It draws attention to what follows. If this is the case, then a surprising element of redefinition occurs. 'The dogs ... the ones beneath the table ...'[36] shifts the territorial environment from public to private space, from the wild to the domestic. Moreover, at the conclusion of an unusual adverbial preposition, ὑποκάτω, a phonemic change occurs—'under the table' becomes measured and weighty under the stabilising constraints of long syllables:

ὑποκάτω τῆς τραπέζης

The agitated rapidity of the opening gives way to a calming emphasis that reinforces the re-direction marked by hiatus. As will be seen below, this is a crucial strategy in taking rhetorical control of the dispute.

The verb marks a transfer in the euphony. Long vowels and diphthongs which began to surface in the first half, now control the woman's saying:

ἐσθίουσιν ἀπὸ τῶν ψιχίων τῶν παιδίων

Such sounds were regarded as softer, more measured, and persuasive. Their gentleness evoked a positive emotional response, according to

34. Jerome avowed that hissing noises were a mark of barbaric nations (*Ep* 130.5). Petronius' character Plocamus uses the 'whistling' jibe about Greek speech: *Sat* 64, clearly an 'othering' linguistic turn.

35. Quint *Inst* 9.4.36–37; also Demetr *Eloc* 2.72; Dion Harl *Comp* 23. For an overview of the use of hiatus in ancient writers, see McCabe, *Prose-Rhythm of Demosthenes*, 21–29.

36. One manuscript (P^{45}) adopted, or perhaps engineered, a reading identical to my translation, by the addition of τά before ὑποκάτω (*cf* 6:11). This however may have the additional suggestion of the 'subordinate kind, of the table': see Arist *Top* 4.2.4, 6.5.5. Alternately, the scribe may have tightened an alleged allusion to Jdg 1:7 LXX (where τά *is* included before ὑποκάτω).

the instructors on language. Where a range of synonyms was available, it suggested that a choice had been made.[37]

Demetrius singled out Sappho, who demonstrated the ability to style language so artfully as to achieve a desired effect.[38] Lucian extolled the voice of Panthea, a favourite of the Emperor Verus, as 'delicious and winning, that gently steals into the ear, so that even after she has ceased, the sound abides, some remnant of it lingering and filling the ears with resonance.'[39] This 'music and harmony of speech'[40] can tame agitation, please the ear and elevate even the most ordinary topic.[41] The bridge between Sappho's writing and Panthea's mellifluous eloquence is the intricate weave of sound and silence in the composition of words. Longinus' analysis of a line of Demosthenes noted that the quality of its expression is as much due to its musicality (ἁρμονία) as its thought (διανοία). He proceeded to unlock the line's metaphor, rhythm and the impact of syllabic placement and length.[42]

The craft of song and accompaniment inextricably influenced the formation of language. Gorgias recognised clearly the psychagogic element of *logos*: fear, grief, pleasure, pity could all be invoked by its delivery. Moreover, its subtle power could influence opinion.[43] Jeffrey Walker argues that the epideictic inheritance from ancient sung epic imbues every aspect of Greek, regardless of the classification of disciplines. Any persuasive or performative intent drew on the psychagogic force of language.[44]

However, this may cast a shadow. As Joy Connolly points out, the very mechanisms and structures of linguistic arrangement on which Quintilian conferred fancy technical terms as recommendations for oratorical performance were in constant danger of being repudiated

37. Quint *Inst* 8.3.16. He endorsed euphony as the determinant when synonyms were available (9.4.58). The shift from τέκνα to παιδία and from κλασμάτα (the choice of narrator and Jesus in the feeding stories, Mk 6:43, 8:8,19,20) to ψιχία is a euphonic shift, whatever theological significance may be attached.
38. Demetr *Eloc* 3.166–167.
39. Luc *Imag* 13.
40. Demetr *Eloc* 2.71. Many writers draw parallels with music and song when describing the use of such constructions for example, Arist *Poet.* 6.5–7 (1449b), Longin 39.14, Quint *Inst* 1.8.2–3.
41. Quint *Inst* 1.10.32–33, 9.4.9–12, Demetr *Eloc* 2.70–74, 3.183–185.
42. Longin 39.4.
43. Gorg *Hel* 8–11.
44. Walker, *Rhetoric and Poetics*, 128.

with abusive epithets when the performer was woman(ly).[45] Sappho and Panthea might have gained male accolades, but these may prove exceptional rather than characteristic. Aesthetic excellence might, given other factors (such as gender and status), be construed as magical incantation;[46] it could become irrational, a corruption of *logos*.[47]

d. Metrical influences

The diminutives and use of long vowels and diphthongs impact the rhythm of the woman's saying. A slow-down affect/effect is achieved as the saying unfolds, moving from an almost staccato-like agitation to a calmer, more even flow. This differs markedly from the blatant versification of Jesus' proverb, even though iambics are probably the least alien to everyday speech and prose rhythms.[48] The woman's speech shows a remarkable poetic complexity and rhetorical purpose.

Cicero understood that whilst the majority of people had no knowledge of 'the science of rhythm and metre' nevertheless everyone was influenced by the 'skilful arrangement of words' and recognised the rhythms that were used. He saw this as the connection between learning and nature—art merely giving the learned man the ability to utilise in particular what nature had bestowed generally. Moreover, this capacity enabled a speaker to 'rouse us up to excitement, and smooth and calm us down'.[49]

This is precisely what we find in the word of the woman. Unlike the comparatively uncomplicated metre of abuse pulsing from Jesus' mouth, the woman's speech unfolds a sophistication that makes his words seem almost rustic. Her word takes the agitation of the paeonic, demeaning diminutive[50] and melodically weaves a poesis of calm and perspective into the picture. Whether understood as exemplary of prose rhythms which commend the adoption of different metrical feet in its construction,[51] or as imitative of the Sapphonic brilliance

45. Connolly, 'Roman Oratory', 135–137.
46. See E Schiappa, *The Beginnings of Rhetorical Theory in Classical Greece* (New Haven, CT: Yale University Press, 1999), 127.
47. Quint *Inst* 10.7.12.
48. Quint *Inst* 9.4.76.
49. Cic *De Or* 3.195–197; *cf* Quint *Inst* 1.10.32–33. Menander reputedly placed his esteem here: 'The plot is worked out, but I have to add the spell of the verses'—cited by FH Sandbach, *The Comic Theatre of Greece and Rome* (London: Chatto & Windus, 1977), 76.
50. Longinus regards short syllables as promoting weak and agitated rhythm, superficial dance-hall stuff! (41.1).
51. Quint *Inst* 9.4.52–53.

in combining variations of metra in verse,[52] the woman's reply is as remarkable in its structure as in its content.

The scansion of the woman's saying delivers some options in metrical structure. Particularly in prose rhythm this is neither a problem nor even undesirable.[53] The musical quality is clear:

(καὶ)

τὰ κυνάρια ὑποκάτω τῆς τραπέζης

˘ ˘ ˘ ˘˘ ˘ ˘ ˘ — — ˘ ˘ —

ἐσθίουσιν | ἀπὸ τῶν ψιχίων | τῶν παιδίων

— ˘ — ˘ ˘ ˘ — ˘ ˘ — — — ˘ —

The short rhythms to begin could be suggestive of a Sotadean obscenity or emotional violence,[54] but then the ruse departs, and the rapids yield to a deep-rolling stream. The entire first line is revealed in its lyrical quality as a dactylic tetrameter.[55] This may explain the use of ὑποκάτω, which, quite properly, holds the bridge within itself. The requirement would be breached with ὑπό by causing the gap between words to fracture the line.[56]

The lyric dactyl resurfaces in the second line between a trochee and an iambic foot, a delightful combination quietly suggestive of a measured movement or melody. This is designed to please (and appease?) and calm—it is the 'noblest of rhythms' claimed Longinus.[57] The dignity and weight of the woman's saying reaches its elevation in the aggregation of long syllables to conclude her word,[58] especially

52. See Glenn, *Rhetoric Retold*, 21–23 for ancient assessments of Sappho's poetry. Rhetoricians debated the line between prose rhythms and full-blown verse though as readily broke or excused transgressions: see *Rhet ad Her* 4.32.44, Dion Harl *Comp* 4, Cic *De Or* 1.151, Quint *Inst* 9.4.52–66.

53. Quint *Inst* 9.4.49–51.

54. The Sotadean metre was regarded as the most effeminate and obscene: see West, *Greek Metre*, 74. Quintilian held that the short feet of Sotadean and Galliambic metres indicate wildness (*Inst* 9.4.6).

55. It may be open to scansion as anapaests or an ionic trimeter catalectic. The balance however with the second half of the saying favours the designation as lyric dactyls. Quintilian recognised the openness to different scansions: *Inst* 9.4.90.

56. Halporn, Ostwald and Rosenmeyer, *Metres*, 17.

57. Longin 39.4.

58. *Cf* Quint *Inst* 9.4.91, 93, Demetr *Eloc* 2.39, 44.

since there is 'the concurrence of the same long vowels.' In fact, as Demetrius goes on to say, this carries the suggestion of a song.[59]

The woman has not merely spoken to Jesus. She has woven into her reply the carriage and bearing of cultivation and training that leaves Jesus' crude abuse wallowing in its wake. The saying ought not be reduced to a clever joust of metaphors. Even if a proverb, it is shaped with such singular skill that mnemonic concerns (whether of the proverb itself or the wisdom it contains) are surpassed by sheer, epideictic beauty.[60] It breathes a soothing accompaniment that advances the prospects for the reception of the word. The embodiment of the idea has become essential to the possibility of a positive response—it is this, said Cicero, that 'gratifies the ears of humanity'.[61]

The sanctity of the antiquity of the form

i) The currency, antiquity and protean manifestations of the proverb (a reprise)

Shirley Arora has provided the helpful umbrella lens of 'traditionality' to assist in the recognition of proverbs. She acknowledges that contemporary inventions can function as proverbs because they bear the marks of 'traditionality'—'the sense of historically-derived authority or of community-sanctioned wisdom that they convey.'[62] The markers include appropriateness and currency, metaphor, rhyme, metre, assonance, parallelism, repetition, grammatical and syntactical precision. The answer of the Syrophoenician woman qualifies on almost every count, thus confirming the decision of a number of commentators.[63] It remains to test for the currency of the proverb. As expected, the proverb manifests in a variety of ways and with variations in its meaning.

a. The proverbial position of humiliation

Sometimes the distilled, narrative brevity of the woman's proverb has

---

59. Demetr *Eloc* 2.73–74.
60. Jeffrey Walker argues the advance of writing did not supplant oral performance; it meant that the *mnemonic* concerns of poetic style and structure were no longer as important. *Writing* became a supplement to memory. Thence, aesthetics became even more important: *Rhetoric and Poetic*, 21–27.
61. Cic *De Or* 3.185.
62. Arora, 'Perception of Proverbiality', 4.
63. Winton, *Proverbs of Jesus*, 132, EK Broadhead, *Teaching with Authority: Miracles and Christology in the Gospel of Mark* (Sheffield: JSOT Press, 1992), 130.

been collated with a number of stories of subservience known in the ancient world. Storch, for example, drew an equation with Adonibezek's fate in Judges 1:5–7. Eating scraps under the table displayed defeat and humiliation.[64] A similar story was recounted by Athenaeus about a Parthian subject who 'sits on the ground while the king reclines above him on a high couch; he eats dog-fashion (κυνιστί) what the king tosses to him.' Floggings and enforced obeisance accompanied the feeding.[65]

Clearly, sitting[66] on the ground to receive food is 'the dog's place'. Seneca expressed his horror at the wise man 'at a king's banquet being ordered to take a place beneath the table . . . to eat with the slaves assigned to the most disreputable service'.[67] One can only speculate at the nature of the humiliation of this 'disreputable service'. A similar disregard is found in Aristophanes' *The Clouds* in a form closer to that of the Syrophoenician's. Strepsiades addresses Socrates 'Then am I to snap up wisdom much as a dog snaps up a morsel?'[68] To be dog-like, therefore, was to be 'beneath another'. In the context of eating, it was a reminder of the governing hierarchy. It guided the gibes at Cynics as they were fed scraps from the table,[69] though this is far from the only context of such insult.

The clearest parallel to the Syrophoenician's proverb is said to be found in Philostratus' *Life of Apollonius of Tyana*. The connection had been argued *de novo* by David Smith in 1901,[70] long after John Wettstein first noted it (1751);[71] it has been repeated a number of times since.[72] Apollonius' long-time companion and recorder, Damis, was accused of behaving 'parallel to the practice where dogs feed

64. W Storch, 'Zur Perikope von der Syrophönizierin. Mk 7,28 und Ri 1,7', in *BZ* 14 (1970): 256–257.
65. Athen *Deip* 152f–153a, attributed to the historian Poseidonius (*FGH* iii.254).
66. Sitting itself, as distinct from reclining, indicated a subordinate position Luc *Sat* 2.27.
67. Sen *Const* 15.1.
68. Aristoph *Nub* 491–492.
69. For example, Mart *Epig* 4.53.
70. Smith, 'Our Lord's Hard Saying', 320–321.
71. The citation had been included in Wettstein's notes to Mt 15:27 (Η ΚΑΙΝΗ ΔΙΑΘΗΚΗ 1.425). Wettstein also includes a reference to the fragment of Euripides found in Athen *Deip* 97a, mentioned below. Oddly, this reference has never, to my knowledge, been pursued.
72. Derrett, 'Law in the New Testament', 172n6, G Petzke, *Die Traditionem über Apollonius von Tyana und das Neue Testament* (Leiden, EJ Brill, 1970), 145, Winton, *Proverbs of Jesus*, 132–133.

on what spills from a feast'.[73] Damis made a clever rejoinder about retaining every piece of divine ambrosia that falls from the gods, thereby reversing the standard convention demeaning the retrieval of things that had fallen from the table.[74] Even so, the status differentials remained unchallenged, despite the argument for an exemption. Living off the edges of another's fare drew on the familiar associations of the fawning sycophant. The image received the castigating bite of criticism in mime and satire.[75]

We do not find the proverb in either its pristine distillation[76] or the refined beauty of performance of the Syrophoenician woman. However, the parallels are clear. One meaning of the proverb, then, is to reinforce and express the hierarchy of eating by reference to the table and to the type of food which someone 'beneath' the table would receive. Yet, this is not the only possible application of the proverb.

b. An assured place in the hierarchy of eating

Moulton and Milligan observed that 'beneath' (ὑποκατω) can also bear the sense of 'belonging to'.[77] Here, even though the hierarchy remains unchallenged, the notion of humiliation fades in the light of the assured place that everyone in the household has. This certainly was the perspective on Persian practice given by Athenaeus. One of his symposium 'participants', Eustrophus, contributed to the discussion:

> Did people think that they ought always to leave something from dinner for the slaves and the slaves' children? They enjoy not so much the taking from as the partaking with us. So too the kings of Persia (they say) not only always send their portions to their friends and officers and bodyguards, but even see that the slaves' dinner and the dogs' dinner are served from their table, insofar as this is feasible, considering all who serve them sharers in table and hearth.

Significantly, he solicits a gnomic saying to clinch his argument:

73. Philostr *Vit Apol* 9.
74. *Ibid*, 1.19 *cf* Arist *Frag Cat* 5, Aristoph *apud* Diog Laert 8.34, Aristoph *Pax* 854.
75. Herodas *Mime* 6.5-8; *cf* Juv *Sat* 5.1–10, Luc *Herm* 11.
76. The closest is probably that found in a fragment of Euripides' *Cressae*, on which see below.
77. *VGT* 657.

'For by passing out food even the most sullen of wild beasts can be tamed.'[78] Here food distribution signals control of the bestial.[79]

This sense of combining acknowledgement of status difference with a measure of common participation in a household is seen in Arsenius' epigrammatic dedication in honour of a hunting dog:

> I am thy dog and thou my master art
> So do I bark and wish for my dog-food
> O lion-hearted king feed thou thy dog (τὸν κύνα τρέφε).
> I see thou huntest the barbarian beasts.[80]

The consistent metaphor, however, is giving crumbs to dogs, a common cultural practice in the Mediterranean. According to Athenaeus, the name given by Spartans to food from the table was κυνάδες ('dog-bits').[81] These dog-bits were the fragments of bread used to wipe the hands after the meal was ended,[82] sometimes called a duty.[83] This appears to provide the descriptive foundation for the proverb in its most succinct encapsulation: 'throwing crumbs to the dogs' (λείψαν' ἐκβάλλειν κυσίν)[84] and a dog living on crumbs' (*canis*

---

78. Athen *Deip* 703d; also Plut *Mor* 703d. Perspective is all-important. Athenaeus refers to the same Persian practice elsewhere but restores the emphasis to hierarchical levels of honour (*cf* Sen *Const* 15.1). The Athenian Timagoras is incensed that, although receiving food sent from the table of king Artaxerxes, the Spartan Antalcidas received food from the king's own hand, and one Entimus is actually invited to eat at the table with the family: Athen *Deip* 48d–f; *cf* 146f, and compare 143c–e where Cretan meal hierarchy is reviewed. The use of food to tame a dog is related by Ael *NA* 7.20–23.
79. This may also lie behind an ancient custom of guests taking some fragments with them for the journey home in the evening. The morsels were intended to be thrown to the night demon, Hecate, who came at them in the form of a dog; see Athen *Deip* 149c, Petron *Sat* 63.
80. Knox's translation in 'Fragmenta Choliambica' in the LCL *Theophrastus' Characters* 353.
81. Athen *Deip* 409d.
82. The ἀπομαγδαλίαι: Aristoph *Eq* 415, Plut *Vit* (*Lyc*) 12. The authority of Homer springs to the fore: *Il* 22.69; *cf Od* 17.309–310. Certainly this is the explanation proffered by Eustath *Comm Od* 2.192.3; *cf* Hesych A§6475, Suda A§3432, Athen *Deip* 149c, 409a,d. Gundry's question, 'where is the evidence that crumbs were so used?' (*Mark*, 381) is thus amply answered.
83. Petron *Sat* 64.8–9; *cf* Athen *Deip* 97a, Mart *Epig* 7.20.
84. Eur *Cress* (fr 469) *apud* Athen *Deip* 97a. Lilja (*Dogs*, 67) finds an intensification of the proverb in another anonymous fragment from

vivens e magdalis).[85] Both forms shift the sense of the dogs' eating from 'taking' to 'partaking'.

The flexibility of lexical choice, meaning and rendition of proverbs is evident again in this brief testing of the currency and variable manifestation of the 'dogs eating crumbs'. The proximity of these literary excerpts to the Syrophoenician woman's answer to Jesus corroborates the 'traditionality' which can be recognised in her words.

The sharpest distinction in contextual usage of the proverb lies between denigrating those who survive on another's provision and recognising a (regular, invited or subjugated) member of a household. Even so, no challenge is mounted against the hierarchical inequalities that govern access to food.

This problematises any suggestion that the woman is removing the force of Jesus' opening command because dogs (so it is asserted) eat *at the same time* as the children.[86] Whether the eating is contemporaneous or not, there is no suggestion that dogs sit with the 'children', eat the same portions (or cuts), or expect the same courtesies. Humility and/or acceptance of humiliation run through the proverb standing by itself. The ethological heart of the proverb reinforces the disparity between (hu)man dispensation and bestial deference.

ii) The Antiquity of 'Two Words'

a. recalling the function of a proverb

The woman's reliance on a proverb refocusses our assessment of form. Proverb becomes set in Mark's story as the primary means by which the woman dares to enter a debate with Jesus. Even so, the woman's effort is no mere imitation of Jesus' use of a proverb. There is more to her reply than meets the eye. The appeal to an antiquity of form goes beyond the citation of a *single* proverb.

As we have seen, the appeal to antiquity in the form of the proverb or maxim is an effort to solicit the authority of universal reality—the wisdom of all people, everywhere, throughout time. When this conjoins an ethological element, an added *gravitas* is granted. The proverb's introduction into a situation is designed to bring an authoritative comment or decision to bear.

Its compact, metaphorical consistency is intended to aid not

---

tragedy (fr 118.4 Nauck); *cf* Strab *Geog* 11.11.31.

85. The Latin is given by the Loeb editor (Charles Gulick) of Athenaeus' *Deipnosophists* (note to 149c).

86. So Guelich, *Mark 1–8:26*, 387.

merely memory but to *sound* authoritative in its utterance. 'This is an instrumental part of the proverb's strategy. But this does not mean that proverbs state absolute truths. Proverbs are just supposed to sound like they do.'[87] The use of a proverb therefore exerts a powerful socialising function. The introduction of another proverb into the same situation formalistically advances the same general claims to traditionality and universality. Of course, it may enjoin a similar summation or advice, in which case, authority is added to authority, each bolstering the other.

b. introducing an alternate perspective

When a second proverb introduces an alternate interpretative frame to a situation compared with the first proverb, a substantial disruption of the general aspiration and function of a proverb occurs. A clash of inherited 'universal' wisdom destabilises the very reason for the appeal to the ancient word. The proverb's autonomy is undermined, and a perspective (perhaps ideological) is isolated. No longer can the proverb automatically resolve a situation, precisely because a clashing pair calls for a decision to be made *between* competing visions. It no longer inherently conveys the judgment. In this sense, the woman independently *contributes* to the assessment of a situation. Another view is offered.

The irony is that this introduction of alternate assessments of a situation is itself of ancient attestation. It occurs in a number of genres. The *kommoi* one-line dialogue exchanges in tragedy (and sometimes in comedy) are often found between a man and a woman using allusive reference rather than direct dialectic.[88] They deploy short, pithy statements, sometimes called *kommata*. Demetrius regarded gnomic sayings as the best illustration of the *komma* for they compressed 'much thought in a little space'.[89]

Declamatory exercises also were frequently arranged by reference to two conflicting principles. Plutarch saw a number of advantages in placing antithetical propositions together. The conjunction offered a 'two ways' option to a person, to invite a person to the better side or to be revulsed from the worse;[90] it enabled a person to see truth expressed

87. B Kirschenblatt-Gimblett, 'Toward a Theory of Proverb Meaning', in *Proverbium* 22 (1973): 821.

88. See Raven, *Greek Metre*, 18.

89. Demetr *Eloc* 1.9.

90. Plut *Mor* 20c, e, 21d, Arist *Rhet* 2.25 (1402a–b). One papyrus records a declamatory exercise in dialogue form, each partner taking one of the sides: *P Hamb* 167.

in different genres (such as poetry and philosophy); and it provided a means of refining the skill of argumentation. Whole debates could be constructed by the presentation of positive and negative arguments, sometimes decided by announcement of a victor,[91] sometimes resolved by a synthetical 'third way'.[92] Indeed, the Pythagorean emphasis was that every question was capable of two answers: *duo logoi*,[93] a recognition given much embellishment by the Sophists.[94]

Of particular interest for our purpose, is the contribution to the variety of 'the two words' by gnomological collections. Indeed, this appears to have been one of the reasons prompting the compilations. Here *antilogia* are often found: *the conjunction of a saying with a contrary*, such as an antithetical conjunction of praiseworthy and culpable prescriptions.[95] Or they may offer couplets of discrete conflicting advice on the assessment of any given action. The example above of Damis' picking up left-overs from the king's fare is a good illustration of the latter, albeit resolvable by drawing in the distinction between general assessment (humiliation) and exceptional circumstances (treasuring ambrosia).

This structural arrangement is not confined to Hellenistic compilations.[96] In the Hebrew bible, the book of Proverbs, for all its authoritative conservatism, contains pairs of clashing wisdom. These couplets group together diametrically opposed assessments (for example Prov 17:27–28, 26:4–5).

Such pairings fragment the easy certitude conveyed by one proverb standing alone. The introduction of a counter-proverb shifts the focus from the authority of the proverb itself to the responsibility for making a choice between proverbs, a decision that presumably is forced to consider the merits of the situation at hand. A conflicting pair

---

91. For example, Ps-Luc *Amor*.
92. So the general precept of Sophocles fr 783 applied in Plut *Mor* 985c.
93. See generally, P Gordon, *The Critical Double: figurative meaning in aesthetic discourse* (Tuscaloosa: University of Alabama Press, 1995).
94. Not all were enamoured of the ability to see two sides of every argument. Aristophanes was especially scathing, considering that this destabilised the young as to what they should pursue: see J Barnes, 'A New Gnomologium: With Some Remarks on Gnomic Anthologies, II', in *CQ* (ns) 1 (1951): 3–4.
95. A similar pattern is found especially in Proverbs 10–15: see S Weeks *Early Israelite Wisdom* (Oxford: Clarendon Press, 1994), 25–26.
96. Barnes points out that the form is extremely resilient, running substantially unchanged from the early Hellenistic period to the late Byzantine period ('New Gnomologium', 2).

of proverbs shifts the reference from the universal to the contextual. Whatever restoration of social reality is to flow, the responsibility must be borne by participants, rather than hidden behind a surrender to an anonymously authored saying.[97]

Thus, an element of contest is introduced into the issue. The content of the woman's proverb may adopt a (semblance of) humility/humiliated position. Yet, when positioned adjacent to a proverb already delivered, the form and function change. An agonistic exchange is established through the contest of proverbs. This is not a battling for honour[98] but simply for the desired result—the healing of a young girl.[99] The suggestion of an alternate assessment through the oblique metaphor of another proverb invites a release from conventional constraints and a freedom of action that was not conceivable when only one perspective was on offer.

The brilliance of the woman's rhetorical strategy is that she has imitated the foundational form of Jesus' words, a 'compensation' for her refusal to be silent. She has ushered into the encounter another form of similar and related antiquity to that utilised by Jesus: the contest of 'two words', the clashing of wisdom. This is not a repudiation in a challenge/riposte agonistic exchange[100] but a destabilisation. Any decision about the particular case remains suspended at this point in the interchange, but a pre-emptive, magisterial denial has been thwarted. Moreover, the decision must now either offer a synthesis of the two claimants or choose one word over the other. A destabilisation has been introduced into the expected unfolding of Mark's story.

Woman addresses man

Arland Jacobson's important methodological essay on the socialising function of proverbs contains a one-line observation: 'proverb usage is associated not only with men but with women as well.'[101] It leaps

---

97. This qualifies the analysis of proverbs made by Alan Winton, *Proverbs of Jesus*, 132.
98. Compare the battles in Luke 11:27–28, 1 Corinthians 6:12–14, 8:1, 10:23.
99. See generally BB Whaley, 'When "Try Try Again" turns to "You're Beating a Dead Horse"—the Rhetorical Characteristics of Proverbs and Their Potential for Influencing Therapeutic Change', in *Metaphor & Symbolic Activity* 8 (1993): 127–139.
100. Which, however, *may* characterise the Matthean version: E Wainwright *Women Healing / Healing Women: The Genderization of Healing in Early Christianity* (London: Equinox, 2006), 153.
101. Jacobson, 'Proverbs and Social Control', 83.

unheralded from his text generating a conception of the gender dimensions of social control; but it remains undeveloped.

As we have noted in the analysis of Jesus' proverb, a key factor in determining the function of proverbs is the identity and status of both speaker and hearer. A proverb in the mouth of a man of significant authority is charged with the air of finality, of sententious pronouncement that is (meant to be) conclusive of a situation or argument. That the woman replies at all, let alone with a proverb, cannot be assessed without reference to the gender and status dimensions of the relationship of speaker and hearer. The next two sub-sections examine the significance of a woman speaking a proverb, and addressing it to a male accorded status above her in the narrative.

i) Proverbs and women

When Juvenal berated a woman for trespassing into the literary forms he deemed to be a male preserve,[102] or when Aristotle criticized Euripides for undercutting Menalippe's character with dialogue that was too 'manly or clever',[103] a convention of acceptable women's speech lies in the background as the standard of appeal. The span of time covered in these two examples (from the fourth century BCE to the second century CE) may attest the tenacity of women's resistance to naturalised determinations made by men. But it also builds the scenario where a woman, intent on gaining a persuasive voice on a male platform, may need to rely on a subtlety of construction to overcome or suspend convention. Without limiting women's actual deployment of language, it is important to recognise what recommendations on the conventional use of language by women were dispensed.

The linguistic cartography of the ancient world generally accommodated women's participation in speech at the margins, or what William Beardslee calls 'a prediscursive form of thought'.[104] Male hegemony mapped speech as an assertion of control. It displayed its skill in manipulating patterns of speech into higher credited systematisations of language, such as rhetoric and philosophy.[105] By contrast, women were charged to know, speak and teach the elementary

102. Juv *Sat* 6.434ff.
103. Arist *Poet* 15.4, 8 (1454a); *cf* 13.10 (1453a).
104. WA Beardslee, 'Uses of the Proverb in the Synoptic Gospels', in Mieder and Dundes, *The Wisdom of Many*, 165.
105. See Connolly, 'Roman Oratory', *loc cit*.

language constructs,[106] possibly as a derivation of the biological determinism attached to child-rearing.

Proverbs were one of the forms of language that enabled communication across status divisions, acceptable because status positions could be preserved through the deployment of oblique rather than direct language and by display of different levels of ability in manipulating such forms. Judgment on the application or appropriateness of an oblique form was generally reserved to a male authority figure. But there was a limited admission of women's speech. Here, potentially, lay the opportunity to argue for certain ends, provided that acceptable forms were observed.

ii) A woman speaking a proverb to a man

Peter Seitel has demonstrated how important it is to recognise the participants in a proverb exchange. Whilst he does not concentrate on the place of gender in the use of proverbs, his general observations are pertinent. A proverb in the mouth of a person of high status can function differently from the proverb spoken by a metic,[107] just as we have already seen how the same proverb can be turned to different meanings.

The status differentials inherent in relationships in which gender is a factor similarly impact upon the function and interpretation of a proverb. Whilst all the examples given previously are dominated by a male-constituted world, a comparison of the elements of power, status differentials and dependency can be made. The proverb uttered by a high-status male to a demeaned woman, especially including a key species metaphor, functions as dismissive abuse of the suppliant. However, the adoption of a form acknowledged as appropriate to women's speech, and especially in which the same species metaphor is imitated, secures a humble position in which a modest request can be made. As one ancient scholiast commented: 'It is not good for slaves to speak plainly to their masters, as if equal.'[108] Κύριε in the woman's opening address clearly signals the relative footing being enacted by the woman to position her answer, perhaps offering the

106. One mark of the honourable woman is that, precisely because she was bounded and thus less affected by changes in verbal fashion, she provided continuity with the ancient patterns: Cic *Orat* 3.45.

107. Seitel, 'Proverbs: A Social Use', 150.

108. Scholion to Aristoph 952.

necessary palliative to gain acceptance for what follows.[109]

The woman has therefore linked acceptable language form and content (as appropriate to her gender and position)[110] to her inappropriate behaviour of, *inter alia*, daring to speak in and against an indication of closure. Nevertheless, however glossed by her artistry of word, address and gesture, the refusal to be silent in passive acceptance of the superior's decision remains. A subtle challenge is delivered not merely to the pontifical words but to the speaker himself.

The woman's artistry extends to marginalising status differentials in the *content* of the proverb. The patron-client and master-slave relationships that govern the use of the proverb in the instances we have noted, disappear in the proverb's narrative world as improvised by the woman. Matthew's revisionism highlights the Syrophoenician's inventiveness. The *Canaanite* woman emphasises the largesse of the dogs' *masters* (τῶν κυρίων αὐτῶν: Mt 15:27). Mark, however, bypasses the language of dominance by accentuating the domestic, indeed, juvenile scene (τῶν ψιχίων τῶν παιδίων: Mk 7:28).

Without necessarily endorsing that the domestic was *the* place for women controlled by men,[111] the Syrophoenician has turned the arena *of view* from the outside to the inside, to the very place where her daughter and, significantly for the argument, the dogs dwell. Hence, the woman's proverb in response to a male utilizes a range of distinctives that acknowledge gender and status. These appear designed to secure a standing, a hearing. And yet, at that very moment, she engineers a subversive and challenging rearrangement of perspective upon her request. The dimensions of that rearrangement will be explored in sections 2, 3 and 4. However, one remaining point of analysis of the saying remains—the preponderance of diminutives.

109. As recommended in *Rhet ad Her* 4.37.49. However, it should be remembered that these rhetorical handbooks were observations on the actual use of language spiced with occasional indications of authorial preference and prejudice. There is no direct connection between the rhetorical training provided by these handbooks and the shaping of Mark's intent. However, Martial's satirical observations of first century life in Rome admit that natural or native cunning had a measure of rhetorical agility.

110. In terms of characterisation, the recommendations in *Rhet ad Her* are exactly fulfilled, namely, that dialogue should be appropriate to character (4.43.55).

111. For all the male writing on the household, the actual experience of women and the assertion of a power and freedom in such a context must be kept distinct.

The diminutive of endearment

The presence of three diminutives in one short saying has rarely drawn comment. David Rhoads understood the woman to be adopting a self-deprecating stance in relation to Jesus, effectively accepting the abuse. He mollified this position by accenting the hypocoristic use: 'the woman is 'least' on behalf of her daughter', thus replaying the nineteenth century notion of her exemplary maternal humility.[112]

Rhoads is correct in drawing attention to the conjunction of diminutives in this saying and in the pericope itself. Such a proliferation must be deliberate and designed for particular, if not startling, effect.[113] Certainly, the diminutives are adroitly positioned in the sentence structure to shape the rhythm of the saying.

But the interpretation of the diminutives is subtly changed from the motivation/effect we encountered in Jesus' saying, in part because they are spoken by a woman.[114] A more irenic engagement is being attempted by the woman (as suggested by the euphonic shift in the saying). Accordingly, the two diminutives in the second half of v 28 are likely not the same in operation as Jesus' use of κυνάρια. Moreover, even the repetition of κυνάρια in the woman's opening words is substantially qualified by the addition of ὑποκάτω τῆς τραπέζης.

There is a gender dimension to the use of diminutives. A status distinction is alerted by Mark in the addition of αὐτῷ in the introduction to her words, just as it had been clearly indicated that the male is addressing a woman in v 27 (αὐτῇ).[115] Given the other structural indicators, the woman is unlikely to be using diminutives in an abusive fashion. Rather, there is the indication of affection and intimacy that some commentators, in the past, have wanted to attach

112. Rhoads, 'Jesus and the Syrophoenician Woman', 366–367; Barnabas Flammer noted the diminutives as a style characteristic of Markan redaction but, following CH Turner (*'Notes on Markan Usage*', 126) discounted any significance: 'Die Syrophoenizerin', 464.

113. It is unparalleled in the New Testament.

114. Jim Perkinson develops David Rhoads' observation more creatively, calling the exchange 'a kind of "politics of diminutives"', played out between their "pejorative sense" and "a second meaning of "littleness"': 'A Canaanitic Word in the Logos of Christ; or the Difference the Syrophoenician Woman makes to Jesus', in *Semeia* 75 (1996): 75–76. This is similar to the argument developed here, though his argument attends less to the gendered dimensions.

115. Recalling that the gender markers are omitted in the Matthean rendition (Mt 15:26–27), apart from the precursor addition to the story (αὐτῷ Mt 15:25).

to Jesus' words.

Athenaeus cites a play by Mnesimachus.[116] It illustrates how the diminutives can ameliorate a request, especially in an exchange between unequals, and thereby increase the chances of success. The man says to a young ascetic:

> A. Make your demands moderate.
> B. But good heavens sir, how could they be more moderate?
> A. How? Fool me by using diminutive terms. Call fishes little fishes; if you speak of any other dainty, call it a little dainty.

This is exactly the ingratiating language recommended for a sycophant positioning him/(her?)self to secure some advantage.[117] It is a shopkeeper's phrasing in cultivating a sale.[118] Trygaeus' daughters in Aristophanes' *Peace* relied on diminutives to prise something from him.[119] Abusive diminutives would destroy any such purpose.

The gender of the speakers in this last reference is significant. Euripides delivered a similar sentiment without the conniving even obscene suggestions that stain Aristophanes' depiction. In the *Suppliant Women*, the character Iphis reflects:

> There is nothing more joyful to an aged father than a daughter. Boys have greater courage, but are less given to sweet endearments.[120]

The relationship between the Syrophoenician woman and Jesus may be different. Yet Mark Golden went so far as to assert that 'girls were especially fond of diminutives.'[121] This may uncritically re-inscribe ancient characterisations of female speech,[122] but the Syrophoenician

116. *The Peevish Man apud* Athen *Deip* 359c.
117. As for example Menand *Dysk* 495–500.
118. See Herodas *Mime* 7.111, 125.
119. Aristoph *Pax* 127, 140.
120. Eur *Supp* 1101–1103.
121. Golden, *Children and Childhood*, 211n72.
122. Contemporary socio-linguistics has observed the conjunction of diminutives and lack of abuse in feminine speech; at least one writer has drawn parallels with ancient literature. See L McClure, *Spoken Like a Woman: Speech and Gender in Athenian Drama* (New Jersey: Princeton University Press, 1999), 33, citing R Lakoff, *Language and Woman's Place* (New York: Harper & Row, 1975). However, this descriptive work must be problematised by attention to both transmission of women's

woman is certainly *presented* according to this understanding.

The line between endearment and ingratiation may be thin, especially given the context that shapes the meaning of the proverbs. Nevertheless, the colour and function of the diminutives *have* shifted along with the protagonist's gender and status. There is no hint of abuse in the woman's triple toss, and the move from the acerbic syllables of Jesus' terse censure to the Syrophoenician's mellow reminder of her dependant's need, resolutely delineates the contrast. Without claiming any absolute rule, gender and rhetorical distinctives are operating here in the use of diminutives.

Overall then, the aesthetic winsomeness of the woman's reply has retrieved attention from general conceptions to the immediacy of the encounter between Jesus and the Syrophoenician and to the absent presence of the woman's daughter. Now Jesus and his saying are unveiled for examination and for decision. A reappraisal of the dynamics of honour and shame in the story becomes imperative, a focus that turns now to the repudiating words of Jesus.

Moral implications: exposure and shame of inferior behaviour

Honour and shame in ancient (and modern) Mediterranean societies operate primarily as a male-reflexive beneficial value, grounded in a reinforcement of sexual dimorphism. The ideology and legislation of honour and enclosure were differentially assigned to women and were persuasive and pervasive (sometimes forcefully imposed). But to assume that women thought, promoted and acted upon this value without qualification merely reinscribes ancient justifications.

Janet Bauer's studies have shown that Iranian women are able to discuss and show preference for moral interpretations alternate to the dominant male construct, even though they may have little opportunity to implement their choices.[123] Michael Herzfeld has noted also the differences in patterns of relating between men and women in Mediterranean culture depending on whether the context is public

---

speech and cultural socialisation. Nevertheless, some Romans blamed the introduction of certain diminutives on lower-class, Greek-speaking prostitutes: Adams, *Latin Sexual Vocabulary*, 32–33, 173.

123. J Bauer, 'Sexuality and the moral "construction" of women in Islamic society', in *AQ* 58 (1985): 120–129.

or private and whether the connection with an observer is intimate or distant.[124]

There is some evidence in ancient texts of trickster or brave women exploiting the dominant male schema to call men to account. The infamous courtesan-queen, Semiramis, had her tomb inscribed with the invitation to any king in need of money to break in. Inside however, instead of treasure, the Persian king, Darius, supposedly found another inscription: 'If you were not an evil man and insatiably greedy, you would not be disturbing the rest of the dead.'[125]

Plutarch recounts a tale of Persian women confronting their men returning in flight from battle. Running outside the city walls into the path of potential slaughter, they lifted their garments, and berated the retreatants for wanting to slink back inside the womb. Mortified at the (double) exposure, the soldiers rallied and routed their enemy.[126] In such instances, the burden laid upon women for the avoidance of shame is transferred (back) to the male. Plutarch might be using the figure of women to make the point sharper. And yet, the stock culpability applied to women is qualified.

In Mark's story, the man Jesus, the mode in which his saying is cast, as well as his assessment of the woman and her request are all implicated by her answer. The question of shame now indicts Jesus. To this we turn.

The indecency of abuse

The contrast in tenor between Jesus' saying and that of the woman is striking. It sets in stark relief the abusive defamation in the cast and content of Jesus' words. A reversal of judgment is now invited. The initial evocation of approval from the audience for Jesus' words— an appropriately sharp response after 'proper' evaluation of the woman— is now less confident. The caveat will remain muted until the opportunity for a final adjudication be given, delivered in v 29. But it does invite a re-examination of the tone and pertinence of Jesus' response in Mark's story.

Here the wariness of rhetoricians about abuse surfaces. Quintilian warned that some orators 'fill up the gaps in their case with abuse

124. M Herzfeld, 'Within and Without: The Category of "Female" in the Ethnography of Modern Greece', in J Dubisch (editor), *Gender and Power in Rural Greece* (Princeton, NJ: Princeton University Press, 1986), 215–233.

125. Plut *Mor* 173b.

126. Plut *Mor* 246a–b.

of their opponents'. He counselled against its use, calling it 'a dog's eloquence' which opens 'the prospect of being targets for like abuse themselves ...'[127] Gregory Nagy draws together instances in the poets Pindar and Bacchylides where purveyors of abuse are depicted as biting or feeding on the corpses of heroes.[128] Abuse might be expected of lower classes, but 'the impudence of a dog'[129] was a dangerous commodity for one of higher or aspiring-to-higher status.[130] Indeed, Plato wanted to remove abuse entirely from his ideal city.[131]

Pindar, in particular, eschewed 'nasty-tongued Archilochus keeping his misery fat with insult and hatred.'[132] The missile of Archilochus' invective was the iambic,[133] precisely the metre and style employed in Jesus' saying. A similar protest is found in an anonymous epitaph in the *Greek Anthology*. His 'floods of abuse' set in 'scandalous iambics' are blamed for misrepresenting those who through gender and death are unable to answer, save of course in the very epigram that honours them.[134]

Modesty and reserve were the unsurpassed marks of character and authority. Quintilian extolled both and advised against abuse being part of a teacher's armoury.[135] Threats, said Chilon, were 'womanish'.[136] Menander put it succinctly: 'A man's character is known by his speech.'[137] Hence, any abuse that might flow from an orator would normally be prefaced by a claim that it had been drawn unwillingly from his lips.[138] Early Christian groups concurred in the promotion

127. Quint *Inst* 12.9.8–9. Demosthenes refused to join a reviling match, arguing that the victor comes off worse than the vanquished: cited (approvingly) by Phil Jud *Agr* 110, Stob *Flor* 19.4.
128. G Nagy, *The Best of the Achaeans* (Baltimore: Johns Hopkins University Press, 1979), 224–231. The image is familiar. The Pseudo-Aristotelian *Physiognomics* deemed abuse as common to dogs (808b).
129. So Jos *C Ap* 2.85 (here the charge is an effort at status reduction rather than status recognition).
130. Luc *Rhet* 22.
131. Plat *Leg* 934e–935b, 949b.
132. Pind *Pyth* 2.54–56.
133. Hor *Epod* 2.79.
134. *GA* 7.352. The epigram is sometimes attributed to Meleager.
135. Quint *Inst* 2.2.7, 8.3.38–39.
136. Cited by RP Martin, 'The Seven Sages as Performers of Wisdom', in C Dougherty and L Kurke (editors), *Cultural Poetics in Archaic Greece: Cult, Performance, Politics* (Cambridge: Cambridge University Press, 1993), 118.
137. Menand fr 72k.
138. Montiglio, *Silence*, 129–131; see Phil Jud *Leg* 141.

of exemplary speech (Jas 3:5–10; *cf* Wis 1:11, Sir 20:18–23). The assessment of abuse is clear. Abuse characterises the dog.

The woman's entry into speech may have recapitulated the stereotype attached to her—she is no compliant, silenced woman. Yet, she secures the positive value of refusing to adopt abuse in the exchange.[139] Subtly then, shame shifts onto abusive style and turns of phrase. The *kurios* is in danger of becoming a cur!

The retreat from public space

One of the difficulties in Mark's pericope is the expression οὐδένα ἤθελεν γνῶναι in v 24 combined with the indication that Jesus wanted to be hidden: καὶ οὐκ ἠδυνήθη λαθεῖν. Robert Gundry tried to explain the phrase not simply by the oft-used comparison with the similar expression in 9:30, but by imaginatively reconstructing a journey into the Tyrian hinterland *with* his disciples.[140] Jesus' purpose is thereby slickly transferred from a desire for privacy to an interest in instructing his disciples, as is the case in the narrative of 9:30.[141] The old tendency to assimilate Mark to Matthew's re-telling survives here. It ignores Mark's own careful return of the disciples in 8:1, where Jesus calls his disciples to him (as in 3:13).[142] Moreover, the generalising of the verse into the messianic secrecy category runs the risk of trivialising the woman's word. To claim that the hiding motif is designed to highlight

139. Montiglio, *Silence*, 91.
140. Gundry, *Mark*, 373, 380; so also WL Lane, *The Gospel According to Mark* (Grand Rapids: Eerdmans, 1974), 262, S van den Eynde, 'When a Teacher becomes a Student: The Challenge of the Syrophoenician Woman (Mark 7.24–31)', in *Theology* 103 (2000): 275. A similar mention of the desire for distance from others occurs in 5:37. The inclusion of disciples (Peter, James and John) is explicitly mentioned rather than left to a reader to provide. One can only assume that if Mark had wanted the disciples to accompany Jesus as either witnesses or students, they would have been noted.
141. Heikki Räisänen is diametrically opposed to Gundry, emphasising that the two verses do not express the same idea, that formally similar statements in Mark can have a different function, and that context is more reliable than form for interpretation: *The 'Messianic Secret' in Mark's Gospel*, translated by C Tuckett, (Edinburgh: T&T Clark, 1990), 167 and n85.
142. Baudoz sees the expression εἰσελθῶν εἰς οἰκίαν (7:24) as one of a number of unique expressions in this pericope, because here Jesus enters the house *without* any group! (*Les Miettes*, 350.)

Jesus' charismatic power[143] is simply a more sophisticated rendition of the exonerating explanation that Jesus intended all along to heal the child.[144]

Rather, the narrative notice of Jesus' enclosure stands in marked contrast to the occupation of public space by the woman in her travels and by the dogs with whom she is compared. The reply of the woman destabilises both narrative and the word of Jesus. She underscores the *private* space occupied by the dogs ('beneath the table').

Private space is where Jesus is, the very place where, implicitly, she is meant to reside if honour is to be upheld. There is no indication that public status and function have brought a modification of private boundaries such as we find in Mark 2:1–4.[145] Rather, the gender dimorphism so central to the story becomes the key determinant of public and private, house and territory. Quite simply, there is something wrong with the picture.[146] The politics of spatial arrangement that infused society attached honour and shame to the gender allocations of space. If a woman is prone to be denigrated for her occupation of public space, then similarly a man is suspect for his enclosure in private space. This is precisely the cultural dynamic Plutarch highlights about the Persian women's barbs against their fleeing men mentioned in the previous section.

The lead-up to the withdrawal into the Tyrian hinterland is marked by a series of battles fought in public space. But the travels, as with the engagements, are generally honourable, witnessing to the authority of Jesus and his willingness to be public. Jesus' own barb to his captors turns on just this value—he attests to his openness in his teaching and movements, unlike the veiled night-action of his opponents (Mk 14:48–49). Moreover, shame attaches to those who flee from him (Mk 14:50, 52).

Manliness in the ancient world is associated with being public. Even the organization and conduct of a man in a household was to be

143. So Marcus, *Mark 1–8*, 467, Donahue and Harrington, *Mark*, 232–233; *cf* Gnilka, *Markus*, 1.291.

144. *Cf* the criticism by Guelich, *Mark 1–8:26*, 384.

145. Trainor, *Quest for Home*, 94–96. On the variegated operations of the division between public and private in the signification of Roman households, see Wallace-Hadrill, *Houses and Society*, 8–14.

146. The dynamics of the arrangement and the interchange are a counterpoint to the story of the Samaritan woman which is located in public space: see JH Neyrey, 'What's Wrong with this Picture? John 4, Cultural Stereotypes of Women, and Public and Private Space', in *BTB* 24 (1994): 77–91.

modelled on the state, where confidence in and protection of ingress and egress were his responsibilities, and where openness to public affairs was exemplary (so Mk 2:1–2).

The failure to leave a house brought an indictment against a man[147] as surely as the failure to be bounded shames a woman. To be closed off was equivalent to the death of the man.[148] This failure contaminated a man with womanly ventures, whether honourable wool carding,[149] or shameful gluttony.[150] Nature was judge, 'Nature who has distinguished male and female so that each performs his/her own proper duty and office.'[151] Male fear of woman was that she would undermine a man's public duty.[152] Here she doesn't have to—it has already happened, and the woman is not responsible!

Thus, the word of a woman has drawn attention to spatial alignments, not just of herself, but of the first speaker. The ethological appeal of Jesus returns to haunt him. Just as Herakles is suspected of effeminate behaviour (including cross-dressing[153]) when he retires from the heat of battle into a house,[154] so the reading of Jesus' observable behaviour is susceptible to this negative slant. Again, without direct naming or reference, the woman's gentle words have sponsored a re-examination of the gospel hero. Significantly, in the aftermath, Mark restores the order of the universe. She enters into (εἰς) her house (v 30) and Jesus *again goes out* (πάλιν ἐξελθών v 31).

The failure in vocation

The word of the woman jolts the audience to recall that, up to this place in the narrative, Jesus has followed a vocation of large vision and large-heartedness. Gentile territory seems to have been more a barrier

147. (Ps-)Apol T *Ep* 8. Similarly, Dio Chr *Or* 6.10–11 pro Diogenes, against those who 'keep to the house'; Sen *Ep* 76.31, 82.2, Quint *Inst* 1.2.6, Luc *Sat* 1.21; *cf* Jesus' contrast of John the Baptist with those who are clothed in softness *within* kings' houses (Mt 11:7–8 par Lk 7:24–25).
148. Hirschon, 'Open Body/Closed Space', 61.
149. Plut *Mor* 72e (citing an unknown poet).
150. Hence, Sardanapalus, the infamous glutton, is described consistently in effeminate terms: Dio Chr *Or* 1.3, 3.7, 4.102 (with emphasis on the love of soft gowns), 4.113, Diod Sic 2.23. Aristotle scorns this ancient (As)syrian king for joining with women in wool carding: *Pol* 5.8.14 (1312a).
151. Hypereides fr 215.
152. Cooper, 'Insinuations', 153.
153. Quint *Inst* 3.7.6.
154. See N Loraux, 'Herakles: The Super-Male and the Feminine', in Halperin, *Before Sexuality*, 21–52.

to the disciples than to Jesus (Mk 4:35–5:1, 6:45–53) and the adulation summarily noted in 3:7–8 has received no hint of repudiation. The suggestion of restricted preferential boundaries for Jesus' ministry comes from Peter rather than Jesus (Mk 1:36–39).[155]

Jesus' words in 7:27 may be appropriate as a response to a fawning, compromised woman, but they affront the larger vision promoted by the story's main character and the narrator.[156] Indeed, this is anticipated by the woman herself (v 25b)—not that this requires the woman's knowledge of the feeding of the 5000. However, Jesus' own knowledge (and that of the audience) can be more securely asserted (so, Mk 8:19).

Regardless of how to interpret the relation of the feeding of the 5000 to the denial to the woman implicit in the command to let the children be fed, Jesus' sense of vocation, his openness to the needs of others, and most especially, his willingness to join battle with the 'strong man' all suddenly evaporate. The vocational drive (*cf* Mk 1:38) has taken Jesus into Gentile territory previously (5:1–20), has brought healing to a young girl (5:41–2) and, according to Mark's narrative comment, has affirmed that all foods are removed from defilement (7:19), a key boundary limitation for the Jew.

The Syrophoenician woman seems hermetically sealed from the benefits of Jesus' vocation. Whatever the appropriateness of Jesus' words of rejection, her proverb confronts Jesus with a failure to honour a vocation that had previously affirmed 'all', the 'whole' and 'many' (Mk 1:32,33,34). Given the daughter's possession by an unclean spirit, the particular focus of Jesus' mission in Mark—of dealing with evil—stalls. The Herculean stronger man has turned from *his* quest. If this mission is understood to be a divinely authorised battle with Satan (Mk 1:10-13), then a shadow has been cast across his fidelity to that commission in the narrative.

Manifold stories of Spartan women were repeated in the ancient world to remind men of their responsibilities to the charge that had

155. A conservative historical Jesus is raised by William Loader: 'Challenged at the Boundaries', 45–61. See, however, A Cadwallader, 'Talk of Suffering in an Age of HIV', in R Hoadley (editor), *Aids and Spirituality* (Melbourne: Spectrum, 1998), 37–62.

156. So AJ Monro, 'Alterity and the Canaanite Woman: A Postmodern Feminist Theological Reflection on Political Action', in *Colloquium* 26 (1994): 41, Schüssler Fiorenza, *In Memory*, 121, Wainwright, *Feminist Critical Reading*, 107.

been given them.[157] The same value is given a woman's voice in Jewish literature.[158] The gentle finesse of the woman has acted with surgical precision to expose the shame of a failure of vocation. The movement of the Markan narrative splutters in this pericope, right at the point of Jesus' words.[159] Its resuscitation depends on the woman's word and the response to it.

Hospitality to the stranger

We have seen already that one general application of the woman's proverb is the expectation of food dispersal to all within a household. Hierarchies built around food were retained however, by conventions related to seating arrangements, order of access to food, types and amounts of food, times and places of eating. This complexity of organization may even spill beyond the formal physical confines of the household to include clients (who may crowd about the doorway for their *sportula* handout[160]), and strangers with whom contact is made. The *Gospel of the Nazarenes*, for example, has Jesus criticising the rich man seeking (eternal) life, for having food in the house yet refusing to share it with sons of Abraham.[161] The failure of a host to distribute the remainders of a meal to others is regarded by Theophrastus as miserly.[162] Interpreted along this grid, the Markan Jesus here treads close to the very κυρίος criticised in the Lukan parable (16:19–31).

Hospitality to strangers was a key honorific value in the ancient world.[163] A welcome was seen as a measure of the nobility of the host. Ethnicity was not necessarily a barrier. But Jews were frequently accused in the ancient world of μισοξενία[164]—the hatred

157. See generally, Plutarch's *Sayings of the Spartan Women* (*Mor* 240c–242d).
158. 1 Kgs 17:18–24, 4 Macc 15:12, 16:16–24; *cf* Jud 8:9–34.
159. JC Anderson, 'Matthew: Gender and Reading', in *Semeia* 28 (1983): 14–15 (yet recognising that the Canaanite woman has no further narrative role).
160. Juv *Sat* 1.95–134.
161. From Orig *Comm Mt* 15.14 (Latin).
162. Theophr *Char* 30.16.
163. Again, underscored by reference to 'The Poet': see Dio Chr *Or* 7.83–88.
164. The substantive occurs only in Wis 19:13 in a reversal of the charge—this time laid against Egyptians. That Philo did the same (*Vit Mos* 1.36) and Josephus defended Jews against the charge (*C Ap* 2.91–102) shows how widespread and powerful such accusations were. Indeed, there is ample evidence of the allegation: Diod Sic 40.3.4, Lysim 16.1.309, Justinus 36.2, Philostr *Vit Apol* 5.33.

of strangers.

A raw nerve has been touched. The woman, through her saying, has brought the dogs inside the house, where she now is (v 25). By doing so, in the performance of a metaphorical exchange, she has used the contrast from Jesus' saying (which places the dogs 'outside') to highlight a specific cultural attitude rather than a universal order. This may have its literal application to dogs but, because of the metaphor-metonymy, is transferred to human beings.

The description of Jews as misoxenist may be the stock vilification of a despised opponent.[165] But the mere suggestion of a failure to deal honourably with a stranger faces Jesus with a choice in the very process of forcing a *distinction* between the specific woman and the general *Jewish* attitude to dogs.[166] Now, a different set of Jewish mandates are brought into play.[167] Care for the stranger is extolled (Lev 19:10, 34, 23:22, Deut 24:19–21, 26:12–13) and is fulfilled especially in the provision of food (Ex 22:21–24, Deut 10:19, Sir 29:26–27). Generosity with food was honorific (Sir 34:23–24). A person with self-control ate small portions, to enable liberality to others (so Sir 34:19–23). Disbursal of left-overs did not erase status distinctions, but could reinforce them, especially if devoid of malignant pejoratives directed at the recipients.[168]

The failure to give bread now appears culpably miserable (*cf* Sir 34:25), even though Jesus might claim that the stranger is a woman to be avoided (Sir 9:3). The critical symbolism of hospitality (as to strangers) had been refused. The parsimony of the preacher of graciousness (Mk 2:15–17) has been subtly exposed.

Of course, the final shame, as we have already noted, is one which

165. See J Gager, *Origins of Anti-Semitism: Attitudes toward Judaism in Pagan and Christian Antiquity* (New York: Oxford University Press, 1983), 82–83, 90–91.
166. There is an important issue here, which places a caveat on the repeated assertion that the woman is content to label herself a dog if it will gain her request (see, for example, Rhoads *supra*). She has not, it must be emphasised, identified herself with the dogs of Jesus' saying. Rather, she has begun the movement of separation from ethological determinism. Similarly, LA Guardiola-Sáenz argues that in Matthew the woman separates herself from collation with dogs: 'Borderless Women and Borderless Texts: A Cultural Reading of Matthew 15:21–28', in *Semeia* 78 (1997): 79.
167. This in no way suggests that the woman knew or is portrayed as knowing such precepts. The display of hospitality is a value spread through the ancient world, even if subject to local customs.
168. See, for example, Athen *Deip* 113f.

more clearly comes from a specific ethnic and cultural value. Aristotle quotes it: 'It is highly dishonourable for there to be no dog (in the house).'[169] To this we now turn.

Spatial dimensions: boundary marking and territorial protection

The Syrophoenician woman has succeeded in transferring the geopolitical intimations of the exchange from the public to the private sphere. Given that abuse is a key technique of characterisation inviting blame, the use of 'dogs' to denigrate mother and daughter is potentially tempered by this transfer to domestic space. The distinction between ὑποκάτω τῆς τραπέζης here and ἀπὸ τῆς τραπέζης in Luke 16:21 captures accurately the spatial signification.[170] Lazarus lies exposed in public at the rich man's gate (Lk 16:20). Clearly what falls from the 'Sardanapalus' banquet was to be tossed outside, just as Jesus' words suggest.

By contrast, the woman's proverb accents domestic arrangements. Certainly, the woman's presence in the house where Jesus is hiding bodily confronts the obligations and responsibilities of the household. Her words provide commentary on her current (rather than immediately prior) position and, more particularly, the (apparent) position of her daughter. They are both 'inside'. The oblique discussion of food and its provision may appear removed from the literal specifics of a girl's demonic possession, but Mark provides no indication that either the woman or Jesus were confused about the projected outcome of their words. Every context—that of the mini-narrative world of each proverb and of the players in the pericope—is measured by space. Only Jesus' dogs are 'outside'. Hence, in terms of the aptness to the spatial dimensions of the context, the woman's proverb is the more germane.

The woman has pinpointed a dissonant element in Jesus' proverb. Rightly or wrongly (depending on a specific cultural evaluation) the dogs are inside. If these are dogs of the house (that is dogs under the table), they are members of the household, albeit with low status in a household hierarchy.

The dogs under the table

Much in the argument has been predicated on a very different

169. Arist *Rhet* 2.24 (1401a).

170. The first hand of Codex Sinaiticus actually reads ἀποκάτω for Mark 7:28 (also *l*184).

appreciation of dogs. The woman has subjected the key integer of the proverbs (the dogs) to a 'level-switching.'[171] Through her proverb, she has become the architect of a different view of space, or, rather, of the placement of dogs. Such 'level-switching' was recognised to some degree in the ancient world. Aristotle, for example, understood that a word could operate differently in different cultures.[172] Boundaries in the background of the two sayings remain relatively constant in terms of house and city, but the woman's dogs are now switched to the 'inside', by reliance on an ethno-cultural convention.

The dogs in her saying are emphasised as being ὑποκάτω τῆς τραπέζης. The dogs are located by the household item that carries strong, positive symbolics. Plutarch has his symposium participant, Lucius, describe the table as a 'sacred hearth', adding that nothing sacred should ever be empty.[173] The table itself is the defining point of a household from which all (whether family, guest, slave or dog) gain their sustenance and continued life within that household, albeit in hierarchical arrangement.

The signification of the dogs by reference to the table can be traced back to Homer himself. Not only do dogs frequent the eating halls of the household, but they gain the distinction of being called τραπεζῆες κύνες.[174] In one Aesopic fable, a dog is given the title συντράπεζος.[175] This ascription carried considerable honour, intimating a sharing with, not simply taking from, those at table.[176]

Dogs under tables or with their masters are a familiar feature of Greek and Roman art, ranging across time, the geographical expanse of empire, and status associations. In this geo-culture, dogs appear on sarcophagi, as a participant in the κλίνη of death. They appear in houses in different media—from paintings, to mosaics, to pottery decoration, to statues.[177] Hence, the literary references have received

171. The term is from N Bailey, 'A Structural Approach to the Proverb and Maxim with Special Reference to the Anglo-Saxon Corpus', in *Proverbium* 20 (1972): 741. It refers to the change of application or reference of a common term.

172. His categorisation relates to 'rare' and 'ordinary': *Poet* 21.6 (1457b). A word could also be illogically deflected through homonymic puns, as in the case of the maxim about the absence of a dog already cited, which is falsely extended to valorise being a Cynic (κύων): *Rhet* 2.24 (1401a).

173. Plut *Mor* 704b.

174. Hom *Il* 22.69.

175. Babr *Aes* 74.7.

176. See Xen *Anab* 1.9.31, Eur *Andro* 658, Themist 14.7.

177. Further examples are cited in *NDIEC* 4.158.

substantial corroboration.[178] Many more instances of dogs portrayed in houses generally and in the commerce of daily existence could be paraded, just as surely as the absence of any such evidence from a Jewish context provides the contrasting backdrop.

Origen saw in the woman's reply a reference to dogs of the house.[179] However, the loss/rejection of sensitivities to the Jewish origins of Jesus or the gospel stories, has lead to repeated uncritical assumptions that there were house-dogs in Jewish homes. Again by design or default, Jesus is rescued from himself.[180]

The woman's own cultural inheritance factored dogs with many more nuances than that informing Jesus' attitude, as posited by Mark.[181] The allocation of interior space to dogs, albeit under certain careful arrangements, has enabled her to switch the metaphor's negation of her daughter's future. Significantly therefore, Jesus in this gospel has failed to accommodate the cultural conventions of the country into which he has ventured.

Mark's Jesus has therefore acted in as imperialist a fashion in his use of language as any invading power. Regardless of the shared experience between Jew and Greek—of being colonised—this has not bred a shared outlook. When this is combined with the gender dimensions of the encounter, the colonisation appears as sexual domination, in a representation of hegemonic control within the household. Jesus is male and 'master of the discourse in this encounter.'[182] Commentators have been only too happy to perpetuate that position, accenting the woman's acceptance of that discourse and the position that it enforces.[183]

But the Syrophoenician rejects pity or blame for her situation.[184] She subtly and gently substitutes her own culturally-informed construction, resisting not only the refusal to help her daughter but the spatial assumptions on which that rejection is built. The protectiveness

178. *Cf* Lucret *Nat Rer* 4.1002, 5.1070.
179. Orig *Comm Mt* 11.17.
180. Derrett, 'Law in the New Testament', 169–172, Gundry, *Matthew*, 315, Baudoz, *Les Miettes*, 264, McNamara, 'Syrophoenician Woman', 367.
181. So F Dufton, 'The Syrophoenician Woman and her Dogs', in *ET* 100 (1989): 417, followed by Kinukawa, *Women and Jesus*, 58–59, deemed a possibility by Schüssler Fiorenza, *But She Said*, 97.
182. Perkinson, 'Canaanitic Word', 74.
183. For example, Rhoads, 'Jesus and the Syrophoenician Woman', 366–367.
184. Padel, 'Women: Model for Possession', 16, Guardiola-Sáenz, 'Borderless Women', 75–77.

about space which had been so much part of Jesus' saying is now loosened by the saying of the woman. Even though the imagined territory is now the familiar domestic scene with which women are associated, it nevertheless is a space that is more inclusive of that which is 'other' than what had been allowed by Jesus.

The absence of defining masters

The vision of enclosure argued by the woman in Mark's story is therefore expressed as being more open and accommodating than that of the man. Of course, openness and accommodation is precisely the fear men voice about women in the ancient world. However, the woman's proverb has deftly contained these characteristics within the boundaries that those same males recommend for women—the house, but has done so by denying that it is merely an extension of male space.

The woman's reply makes no reference to the master(s) nor to the chance fare that might fall from his/their table.[185] As we have seen in the review of the proverb's antiquity and currency, the overwhelming impression is the hierarchical placement if not inspiration for the proverb. Matthew's reference to κύριοι in 15:27 is likely a redactional adjustment to Mark's rendition of the woman's saying, but it does make explicit the familiar contextual semantics of the proverb.[186]

The absence of masters from the Syrophoenician's rendition of the proverb defines the space by reference to the elements that are present—the table, the food, the children and the dogs.[187] This will have important implications for an assessment of the final verse where attention swings to the daughter who has anchored the entire pericope.

For the moment, a slight dissonance is imported. The distribution of food to children seems somewhat varied in the ancient world,[188] subject to permutations of age, gender, and local (ethnic) customs. Children might be served reclining on the same κλίνη as their father,[189]

185. Some manuscripts assimilate to Matthew: 157 472 485 1071 sy[s] co[sa] eth.

186. Noted by Focant, 'Mc 7,24–31 par Mt 15,21–29', 56. It is curious that Matthew's rendition of the Canaanite's saying, has a singular table with multiple masters (some Bohairic manuscripts have the plural: 'tables'). Tables for eating varied considerably. They were rarely a renaissance trestle!

187. So Schüssler Fiorenza, *But She Said*, 96–97.

188. Corley, 'Really Prostitutes?', 492–494.

189. Athen *Deip* 460a, citing Hom *Od* 19.400.

or seated at other couches or seats or even on the floor. They might be provided different portions, and subsequent to the serving of the father and his friends or guests.[190] They might eat with their mother in another room or alone after the parents.[191] All these are attested in literature and material representation in the ancient world. Much depends on the function of the meal, the status of the household,[192] the age and gender of the children themselves.

The woman's saying, however, has swung attention away from adult position to the protection of the 'inferior' members of the household. The lexicographical shift from τέκνα to παιδία asserts a different perspective,[193] in another example of 'level-switching'. Even though there is a semantic overlap between the two nouns, there is little doubt that Jesus is using τέκνα as an indication of his own people. The word has the technical connotation of free-born citizens of a country.[194] Whatever may be the semantic import, the shift alone suggests a distinction.

Even though women were frequently portrayed in the ancient world as 'soft' (a characteristic descriptor of their gender) towards their children,[195] in this context the effect is to demonstrate the woman's concern for her daughter, *contrary* to Jesus' attempts at shaming her. Indirectly, Jesus is accused of ignoring the validity of that claim because of her gender, ethnicity and status.

The multiple ambiguities over the timing and means of access to the crumbs further blur the boundaries. Do the dogs' secure provision

---

190. Athen *Deip* 143e, Theophr *Char* 5.5. One later Jewish source rules, 'When two are sitting at table, the elder begins to eat first, and the younger after him . . .' *Derek eres rabba* 7 quoted in PW Skehan and AA Di Lella, *The Wisdom of Ben Sira* (AB) (New York: Doubleday, 1987), 389.
191. Luc *Somn* 11. See generally, Osiek and Balch, *Families,* 45–47.
192. Dio Chr *Or* 7.65.
193. One which is endorsed by the narrator in v 30: M Criscione, '"There were also women": The Art and Power of Women Characters in Mark 11–16', (PhD Thesis, Berkeley: GTU, 1995), 149.
194. Theodore Beza and HA Schott translated τέκνα by *liberi* rather than *filii*. Julicher's *Itala* makes no mention of it. GP Shipp accepted this as the Latin translation: *Modern Greek Evidence for the Ancient Greek Vocabulary* (Sydney: Sydney University Press, 1979), 530, noting that Aristotle uses παιδοποιία for 'adoption' but τεκνοποιία for 'child-bearing'.
195. Eur *Phoen* 397–446, Sen *Prov* 2.5, Arist *HA* 608a–b.

contemporaneously with the children or sequential to them?[196] Do the children initiate the feeding of the dogs or do the dogs act fortuitously (as is commonly portrayed in Comedy)? These questions are not answered, and so, the issue of tight boundary maintenance is left unclear. However, the lack of clarity contributes to the opening of perspectives that necessitates a choice by Jesus. A proverb's facility for indirection has achieved the woman's purpose.[197]

Her territory is constructed differently, less protectively. Her saying registers an expansiveness that calls for greater egalitarianism in the distribution of food. Her concern for her daughter is drawn into clearer view without losing the oblique referential etiquette in which the verbal tussle is framed. And the re-shaping of a pre-existing proverb wrests it from predominantly hierarchical and male renditions into a non-humiliating or deferential scene. In Mark, Jesus' tossing of a denigrating proverb in her direction erects boundaries around his own moral standing as much as hers. The call orchestrated by the second proverb is to weigh the claims of mercy against reputation (*cf* Mk 12:14).

Boundary marking and territorial protection have been de-centred without compromise to the needs of a household. The household has been deliberately modified to recognise and embrace those who had been ignored or rejected. Informed by a different cultural background, a traditional saying has been construed to affirm the validity of the woman's claim.

Resocialisation by reference to the natural order

The inclusion of the dogs within a household points to a different cultural value, one which saw the *absence* of a dog as a mark of shame. Even a beggar was not to be denied a dog—a hedge against total abjection.[198] The woman is formed by this background and it constructs her rejoinder. That reliance does not significantly challenge the ethological understandings as such (that challenge comes elsewhere), even though the saying carefully distinguishes dogs from children. It acknowledges that culture can order nature to the extent

196. Burkill thinks the intent of the woman's reply is a simultaneous feeding, but this is not demanded by the saying: Burkhill, 'Congruence', 29; so also Lane, *Mark*, 263, JM Gundry-Volf, 'Spirit, Mercy and the "Other"', in JM Gundry-Volf and M Volf (editors), *A Spacious Heart: Essays on Identity and Belonging* (Harrisburg, PA: TPI, 1997), 25.
197. So Russo, 'Prose Genres', 54.
198. Mart *Epig* 11.32.

that the wild can be made subject. Indeed, the untamed only reaches its proper natural zenith when it is brought under control by the same order that has also constructed, explained and rationalised household borders.

Reason which has invented, shaped and recalled the saying, is the same reason that has moulded the lives of the dogs. The dogs are therefore not removed from the capacity to have their nature creatively and positively directed. Dio Chrysostom uses dogs as examples of how training can bring (moral) improvement to a creature, keeping it focussed and bounded in spite of potential distractions to left and right. Those dogs, without the benefits of the control that reason exerts, are chaotic and unproductive.[199] The natural order thus realises its high aspirations in reason alone. In fact, said Dio, it is one who is mastered that vouchsafes the designation 'noble'.[200] Wealth and descent are secondary.

The irony is that the customary notion held that the mechanism for initiating training was the provision of food. Food tames 'even the most sullen of wild beasts,' said Eustrophus.[201] Food, in the metaphor (and signification) of the provision of healing, is precisely what the woman seeks in order to tame the chaos of possession. However, unlike Jesus, she indicates this by reference to *trained* dogs (a prerequisite for the designation 'dogs of the table'); they are already subject to *logos*.

Her appeal therefore is also to the natural order, that is, to nature that *is* ordered. The subtlety of her reply itself bears witness to the power of *logos*, and adds the further irony that the creature said to be irrational proves itself as more than capable of deploying reason. The dog has spoken.

Second conclusion (the Syrophoenician's saying)

Like Balaam's ass, or Aesop's fox, the words that the bestial emits, shame the very one who is held to be the symbolic and functional (hu) man centre of *logos*. Jesus, who has shamed the woman in and through his moralising decree, finds the finality of his rejection contested at every point. The proverbial prescription has been made contingent by the woman's adroit soliciting of her own cultural and domestic experience.

199. Dio Chr *Or* 20.15–16.
200. Dio Chr *Or* 15.29–30 (*cf* Lk 3:8).
201. Plut *Mor* 703e.

In so doing, the word of the woman, voiced to prevent closure on her claim, mounts an array of causes against Jesus:

i) his saying lacks the finesse or the decorum that is fitting in exemplary speech,
ii) it is uttered in a context (a house of hiding) which places a caveat on the authority of male speech,
iii) the shock of Jesus' negative response intimates a suspension of his vocation,
iv) it violates a widespread cultural value of hospitality to the stranger,
v) it fails to recognise the cultural distinctives that operate within the geopolitical territory which he now (temporarily) inhabits,
vi) and it is exposed as restricting the range and power of reason.

The conception of male authority and superiority, masquerading under a veil of objectivity which can dispose so presumptively of the woman's claim, is exposed for its ideological and socio-cultural myopia and construction, even as it uses language to establish its position. The deft turning of the direction and form of the precept is as devastating as it is subtle and gentle.

However, at issue is whether the saying can (or ought to) be isolated from the nature/character of the one speaking. In the context of antiquity and Mark's narrative, the woman's saying of itself does not determine the result. That excruciating, decisive moment is poised in no small measure on the possibility of allowing that the Syrophoenician's saying *is* a 'word'. The complex issues involved in this adjudication are not merely the question of whether an irrational animal can deliver *logos*. They go to the heart of the critical and literary assessment of women's speech in the ancient world, and raise the contentious matter of the cost to women of any decision, negative *or* positive, that might be made within this frame of reference.

Part Three

Beyond The Word of a Woman To Somatic Restoration

6

The Eloquence of a Barking Dog
Evaluating the Word of a Woman

Introducing a different perspective on the woman's speech

The suspicion about a woman speaking

In Mark's narrative, the woman answers Jesus. Mark frames dominical words to punch out the perception that discussion has terminated, her request is denied—all within a vituperative characterisation of the woman. The moment the woman refuses to respond in an appropriately silent (and submissive) manner, she appears to confirm the stereotypical assessment that has been carefully engineered by the evangelist.

The woman who hunts out a male, who sullies public and private boundaries, who has no honourable man as guardian, who comes from a spurned environs and questionable racial background—this is the woman who fits the general characterisation of a prostitute.[1] The moment of her reply underscores how fitting were Jesus' efforts in the story to re-align the woman to a society ordered by reason.

It does not matter that the address is κύριε. Given the preparatory stereotypes, this merely confirms a duplicitous character. Martial, for example, saw in κύριε a woman's oily language of allurement,[2] a flattery designed for a purpose other than submission to the conventional hierarchies.[3] 'Oh you Flatteries,' moaned Martial, 'Wretched creatures with shameless lips . . . base, crawling and suppliant'.[4] The ethological comparison with dogs, frequently made of prostitutes,[5] is clear in

1. Liban *Decl* 25, Demosth (*C Neaer)* 59.18.
2. Mart *Epig* 10.68; *cf* Herodas *Mime* 2. Corley compares the repartee of courtesans: *Private Women* 101 and n92. Wainwright simply notes the formal, respectful address: *Women Healing*, 128.
3. See Menand *Dysk* 494–500. Flattery was a frequent *topos* precisely because it destabilised the forthrightness of language. See the plays of Eupolis and Menander, Plut *Mor* 48e–75d, Theophr.
4. Mart *Epig* 10.72. Plutarch calls flattery 'the love bites of lascivious women' *Mor* 61b-c.
5. Amphis *Gyn* 9 K-A, Anaxil *Neot* 22 K-A, Eubul fr 53 K-A, Timocl fr 10 K-A.

the allusion here. The refusal or inability to control one's tongue immediately draws the designation of 'dog'.

Suspicion therefore erodes any 'declaration of humility and trust' that early devotional and form-critical interpretation tried to find.[6] Matthew apparently was dubious and added a compliant, ναί,[7] with the deference reinforced by the displacement of παιδίων by κυρίων in the woman's reply.

The Syrophoenician's saying thwarts Jesus' closure and ignores the expectation of silent acquiescence.[8] The 'even/and' (καί v 28) subjects Jesus' sententious dismissal to re-examination and modulation,[9] and announces that the ethological mapping of person, status and space, if not rejected outright, is experienced very differently.

Now, the outcome is unpredictable. The ethologically grounded abuse might be intensified in response to any resistance. Joel Marcus points out that the opening half of Jesus' second response (διὰ τοῦτον τὸν λόγον ὕπαγε) could be, in isolation, a blunt reiteration of his oblique but abusive denial of her request: 'a final rebuff, as though Jesus were punishing the woman's impudence by dismissing her.'[10]

The issue, therefore, is not merely the question of the *content* of the woman's words but *that* she has spoken. Hanging over her words is a decision on whether they were a promiscuous undermining of speech—the linguistic extension of the resistance to boundaries assumed of a

---

6. Theissen, *Miracle Stories*, 54. Whilst denying any christological affirmation, commentators assert the woman's 'politeness': see RG Bratcher, *A Translator's Guide to the Gospel of Mark* (London: UBS, 1981), 94.
7. Mt 15:27. Many copyists assimilated Mark's text to Matthew. Some commentators agree: Stock, *Method*, 213; *cf* C Waetjen, *A Reordering of Power: A Socio-Political Reading of Mark's Gospel* (Minneapolis: Augsburg, 1989), 135, Boomershine, *Story Journey*, 108, 109.
8. See KB Jones, 'On Authority: Or, Why Women Are Not Entitled to Speak', in I Diamond and L Quinby (editors), *Feminism and Foucault: Reflections on Resistance* (Boston: Northeastern University Press, 1988), 119–133.
9. The ἀλλά of Codex D (and *it*) is teasing in its contrariness; however, the woman's reply is not an outright repudiation but a clever improvisation on the metaphors, form and content of Jesus' saying.
10. Marcus, *Mark 1–8,* 470. A few manuscripts (Δ f^{13} 565 700 it^{g1} sy^{p}) change the word order, perhaps influenced by the primacy of ὕπαγε in other stories (for example, Mk 5:19, 8:33, 10:52, 11:2, 14:13, 16:7). The transposition accents the woman's word as reason for departure.

woman's body. 'Open to all comers' is how Apollodorus put it.[11] The language forms specifically associated by men with women, such as riddles, enigmas and incantations, disturbed the precise ordering of reason.[12] Riddles, said Quintilian, are 'blemishes, in view of the fact that lucidity is a virtue.'[13] Ambiguity (ἀμφιβολία) was to be avoided.[14] The dominant assumption was that women's language was duplicitous. 'A woman is not able to coerce a man overtly,' decants the *Testament of Reuben*, 'but by a harlot's manner she accomplishes her villainy' (5:4).[15]

The assessment of the Syrophoenician woman's word therefore is to be weighed in this chapter. It will mean testing the importance and power of that word, and encountering the dangers of privileging that word exclusively. This lays the groundwork for recognising the importance, power, ambiguities and dangers of prizing the non-verbal elements gathered into the placement and deployment of her body.

The text's indication of the importance of the word of the woman
Mark highlights the importance of the reply: ἡ δὲ ἀπεκριθη καὶ λέγει αὐτῷ (v 28a).[16] Firstly, the woman's words are shifted from the aorist (ἀπεκρίθη) to the 'present tense' (λέγει). This is the only instance of the present in the pericope's *narrative*. Porter's observation is decisive: 'the imperfective verbal aspect (present tense-form) is used whenever one wishes to draw added attention to a given event.'[17]

11. Demosth (*C Neaer*) 59.20; *cf* Athen *Deip* 695e, Hor *Od* 3.6.25–32. However, even women's silence was frequently invested by men with malicious intent: Montiglio, *Silence*, 252–256. Ultimately, adjudication on the character of a woman's silence or speech was asserted as a literary male prerogative.
12. Woman was 'a Theban Sphinx who babbles not in simple language but in riddles'—Alexis *apud* Athen *Deip* 558d.
13. Quint *Inst* 8.6.52; *cf* Demetr *Eloc* 2.102, Plut *Mor* 154b.
14. Arist *Rhet* 3.5 (1407a), Demetr *Eloc* 4.196, Quint *Inst* 3.6.46.
15. *Cf* Cercid *Meliamb* 5.12f, Plut *Mor* 145c–e.
16. Acknowledged by Schüssler Fiorenza, though not developed: *But She Said*, 222n31, following Monika Fander, *Die Stellung der Frau,* 75. Fander also argued that the concentric chiastic structure of verses 26–30 placed the woman's reply at the centre.
17. Porter, *Idioms*, 31; so also EC Maloney, 'The Historical Present in the Gospel of Mark', in MP Horgan and PJ Kobelski (editors), *To Touch the Text: Biblical and Related Studies in Honor of Joseph A Fitzmyer* (New York: Crossroad, 1989), 77n27, 78.

Everything, therefore, has been preparation, not for Jesus' words, but for the woman's.

In fact, the paratactic combination of the two indicatives ἀποκρίνομαι and λέγω is unique in the gospel.[18] Elsewhere, the two words combine as participle with indicative.[19] The redundancy of expression is designed for rhetorical effect. It slows the narrative, generating a nervous anticipation by momentarily holding back the rupture of convention.[20] As Baudoz notes, this is the only occasion in the Gospel where the *direct* speech of a woman to Jesus is provided.[21]

Submission, resistance or subversion in the Syrophoenician's word

The evangelist's hand retains control of the inscribing of the woman's words as much as it has manipulated her portrait in reliance upon conventional prejudices in the previous verses. Mark has connected a (Syrophoenician-born, ethnic Greek) woman with a certain mode of speaking, and, in the unexpected twist to the story, that speech is named as '*logos*'. However, the character who *names* the speech as *logos* is male.

Feminist appraisal has moved the woman's words between submission, resistance and subversion. Monika Fander claimed the woman as the first christologian. The recognition of her word as *logos* in v 29 is taken as authenticating her standing.[22] Even the nuanced position of Elisabeth Schüssler Fiorenza followed this line. The mandatory suspicion, she argued, is that the conventional constraints implicit in the description and assessment of women's language in androcentric texts are a politicised rather than an essentialist rendition. Accordingly, the adoption of a counter-politicised platform enables the woman's speech to be affirmed independently of the androcentric

18. But see Mk 9:38 Codex D (*f*[1] 28 it).
19. Mk 3:33, 6:37, 8:29, 9:5,19, 10:3,24,51, 11:14,22,33, 12:35, 14:48, 15:2,9,12. Flammer, notes the difference: 'Die Syrophoenizerin', 475, followed by Fander, *Die Stellung der Frau*, 83. One tenuous parallel in Mark is Jesus' (non-) reply to the High Priest in 14:61 where both verbs are aorist, the middle ἀπεκρίνατο also unique in Mark. The irony from an ethological perspective, of the woman speaking here and Jesus, elsewhere, being silent ought not be lost. Silence, after all, is precisely the stance that a woman bound by convention ought to have adopted.
20. Pokorný, 'Puppy', 328; *cf* Mk 3.34.
21. Baudoz, *Les Miettes*, 282.
22. Fander, *Die Stellung der Frau*, 75–76, 83–84; *cf* Flammer, 'Die Syrophoenizerin', 474. Ross Kraemer expresses great reserve about such interpretations: *Her Share*, 132–133.

text and its androcentric transmission and interpretation.[23]

Even though the affirmation by a male character that the Syrophoenician has spoken *logos* may be read as 'androcentric' writing, the woman ends up being prized as a speaker of *logos* anyway—albeit a word crucial to the early Jesus movement. The fundamental classification remains unchallenged. Schüssler Fiorenza may impugn the aggregation of evidence from the rhetorically moulded texts of late antiquity as merely re-inscribing assessments of women,[24] but the pedestal of 'word' stands secure.[25]

There is a risk of robbing the Syrophoenician of voice if we problematise the word of a woman.[26] But, if the valorised category is itself not questioned, that voice may end up being little more than an actor's masked performance of a masculine agenda.[27] Because the 'word' is a key expression (and constructor) of the fundamental dimorphism that ethology established of old, the danger is that the woman has simply been granted honorary male status,[28] or had her word colonised by male classification. The dog remains with/as woman, just as John Chrysostom had declaimed.[29]

This is the concern named by Mary d'Angelo and Ross Shepard Kraemer. They see the affirmation of 'word' by the *male* speaker within a text written by a *male* as sufficient to register the woman's reply as conventional and submissive.[30] Kwok Pui-Lan is blunt: 'Although

23. Schüssler Fiorenza, *In Memory*, 138, *But She Said*, 13.
24. Schüssler Fiorenza, 'Challenging the Rhetorical Half-Turn', 45–47, *Discipleship of Equals*, 280–281.
25. This is in spite of Schüssler Fiorenza's recognition of the dangers of the stress on the 'word' component of a biblical story or tradition: *But She Said*, 152.
26. The immediate risk is to fall into the same problematisation of the word of a woman that was expressed by men in the ancient world, lamenting that the distaff (the sign of boundedness) had been sacrificed to wit, with all the consequences of promiscuous associations: see, for example, Sall *C* 25, Tac *Ann* 13.45 Verg *Aen* 4.340–353, Plut *Vit (MA)* 10.5.
27. Grosz, *Space, Time and Perversion*, chapter 2.
28. Schüssler Fiorenza is well aware of just this danger: *But She Said*, 182; the question is whether any variation within the privileging of reason and language can ultimately secure the woman as subject.
29. Chrysostom *Can* 52.457.43. Some doubt remains over the authenticity of the writing.
30. MR d'Angelo and E Castelli, 'Elisabeth Schüssler Fiorenza on Women in the Gospels and Feminist Christology', in *RSR* 22 (1996): 294, '(Re) Presentations of Women in the Gospels: John and Mark', in RS Kraemer and MR d'Angelo (editors), *Women and Christian Origins* (New York: Oxford University Press, 1999), 45, Kraemer, *Her Share*, 132–133.

given a voice, the woman's speech is clearly framed in a christocentric and androcentric discourse.'[31]

The retention of the key metaphor (dogs) in the woman's reply, the adoption of a foundational literary form appropriate to her gender (and the rejection of alternatives), the refusal to correct the stereotypical assessment in which she is cast, may signify a complicity if not a subjection to male linguistic cartography. However, complicity may not necessarily indicate ideological reinforcement. Her goal has been signalled as liberation for her daughter (v 25). Any 'complicity' may therefore be a strategy designed to obviate dismissal. Clues to this lie in the subtle readjustments of the configuration of the primary metaphor and in the lexical choices that are made.[32]

Such a making, however, suggests that male language, as all language, is inherently unstable. In this sense, the very ground for stability which reason and communication supposedly serve, is discovered to be continuously poetic, that is, constantly open to different permutations and meanings—tenaciously ambiguous.[33] An apocalypse hangs over every dimension of language, compromising its sententious settledness, and opening new worlds of possibility.

However, the abyss of transition from one expression to another constantly threatens any neat and efficient lineal progression of worlds. The possibility of a new world of linguistic construction was the very danger élite *literati* saw in women's speech, and manoeuvred to prevent. Within the Markan pericope, the correction of the woman's speech does not occur with a further flurry of abuse designed to reinforce the borders. However, that *logos* is 'the last word' may simply be a more subtle (re-) colonisation of the woman's speech. Eva Stehle's comment on ancient discourse relationships is sobering: 'only

31. Kwok, *Discovering the Bible*, 73.
32. This perspective is akin to Schüssler Fiorenza's rendition of contemporary women's bilingualism—the need to learn the language of a male dominated academic realm in order to subvert it and create an avenue for a language authentic to women's concerns: *But She Said*, 183–186, PP Schweickart calls this a 'positive hermeneutic that recuperates the utopian moment—the authentic kernel—from which they draw a significant portion of their emotional power': 'Towards a Feminist Theory of Reading', in EA Flynn and PP Schweickart (editors), *Gender and Reading: Essays on Readers, Texts and Contexts* (Baltimore: Johns Hopkins University Press, 1986), 43–44.
33. Monro, *Resurrecting Erotic Transgression*, 106–08.

among women could women perform as self-defining subjects.'[34]

Male adjudication of the word of a woman

A shadow obscures the discovery of a fissure of language that may attest a woman's subjectivity—the record and recognition remains under the editorial censorship of the male. Even so, any effort at censorship fuels the liberationist energy for discovery and provides an extant legacy that testifies not only to a (censored) existence but also to multiple suppressed (and often lost) companionate readings.[35]

And this is true of the Markan passage regardless of whether the evangelist's gender be clear or not. Jesus is given the last word[36] which, as it happens, acknowledges 'word' (v 29a). Thus, the reference to word operates in two ways, akin to the dialect of censorship—it draws attention to (an aspect of) the Syrophoenician's subjective initiative and constrains (or attempts to constrain) the parameters of that initiative and subjectivity within acceptable (and objectified) limits.[37]

The recognition of these two aspects has invited differing assessments of the story by both feminist and post-colonial interpreters. On the one hand the integrity of women's speech is celebrated. On the other hand, that speech is recognised and affirmed by and within the already established arena of the male voice, and the (male) reason it expresses. In other words, the woman's speech is established as valid only by male imprimatur. Diodorus Siculus records the practice of tossing a tidbit to someone (slave, courtesan or other attendant) who delighted the feasting participants with a clever reply—hardly an invitation to the banquet itself.[38]

Within the Markan pericope, the ascription of *logos* certainly overturns the stereotypical defamation of the woman invited from the audience in the narrative construction of the scene (Mk 7:24–26)

34. E Stehle, *Performance and Gender in Ancient Greece: Nondramatic Poetry in its Setting* (Princeton, NJ: Princeton University Press, 1997), 318.
35. Roland Boer, *Knockin' on Heaven's Door* (London and New York: Routledge, 1998), 1–9.
36. Schüssler Fiorenza, *But She Said*, 12–13, acknowledged this in partial correction of her earlier statement (*In Memory*, 137).
37. This is the problem flowing from Schüssler Fiorenza's concentration on the battle of words and whether the woman or Jesus snatch the last word. 'Word' itself remains unchallenged, even reified and therefore becomes the point on which both Mark and the story of the Syrophoenician become judged.
38. Diod Sic 2.8.

and confirmed by the opening words of Jesus (v 27). Accordingly, if Jesus, the great authority figure of Mark's story, has authorised the audience's assessment, he must authorise the turn-around of audiential perspective (and values?).

Two aspects therefore seek further investigation in Mark's text, namely, the (e)valuation of the woman's speech, and the ascription of value by a male authority.

The (e)valuation of the woman's speech

Mark's Jesus does not acclaim the woman's faith.[39] Rather, Mark accents that because of the word (διὰ τοῦτον τὸν λόγον), the woman's daughter is freed. The full phrase is unique in the Gospel, extending the more general διὰ τοῦτο (Mk 6:14, 11:24, 12:24). However, the pre-substantive position for the masculine demonstrative pronoun is typical of Mark's usage,[40] though the only other two instances of the accusative, τοῦτον, are post-substantive (14:58, 71).[41] This, combined with the unusual position of ὕπαγε,[42] accents its importance.

The demonstrative here has no cataphoric operation, unlike Mark 12:24 where διὰ τοῦτο does refer to what follows. The usual reference of the demonstrative in this construction is anaphoric,[43] even in classical

39. *Cf* Matthew's Jesus (15:28).
40. In Mark, the overall ratio of pre-substantive to post-substantive is 11:16 for οὗτος and 9:8 for ἐκεῖνος that is approximately 45% compared with 15% for Paul and 22% for Luke (Porter, *Idioms*, 291; *cf.* Turner, *Style*, 24. However, figures that note gender are striking: for οὗτος in the masculine the ratio is 7:2, neuter 2:1, feminine 2:11; for ἐκεῖνος the figures are 2:2, 0:0 and 7:6 respectively.
41. The stylistic balance of τὸν ναὸν τοῦτον τὸν χειροποίητον in 14:58 may have affected the choice of word-order. However, one variant to Mark 5:36 reads τοῦτον τὸν λόγον (D it). Here the expression refers back to the report of the attendants from Jairus' house (v 35). (*Cf* the variant τουτῷ τῷ λόγῳ in Mark 10:22 (D Θ f^{13}).)
42. Baudoz, *Les Miettes*, 329. The only proximate parallel for ὕπαγε governing/governed by an antecedent is in a variant to Mk 2:9 where ὕπαγε replaces περιπάτει.
43. Porter, *Idioms*, 134. Compare, on Romans 4:16 (διὰ τοῦτο), JD Dunn, *Romans* (WBC) (Dallas, TX: Word, 2 volumes, 1988), volume 1, 215, and for Pauline usage generally, L Hartman, 'The Eschatology of 2 Thessalonians as Included in a Communication', in RF Collins (editor), *The Thessalonian Correspondence* (Leuven: Leuven University Press, 1990), 475–476. The similar expression in Plutarch, Τοῦτο γὰρ λεχθὲν τὸ ῥῆμα πάντων μὲν ἥψατο ('For, thus spoken, this word arrested

usage.[44] The significance of the anaphoric usage is disturbing for those who honour Jesus as the healer of the woman's daughter: his response is *not* self-referential. Rather, his words attribute causation to the word of the woman. *Her* reply, therefore, takes on added significance in the story, just as the introduction to her words indicated.

The woman's logos in the Gospel of Mark

The significance of the woman's answer can only be appreciated by the wider use of λόγος in Mark's Gospel. Almost without exception, λόγος is directly tied to the message of Jesus. The word rarely occurs in the plural yet still comes from Jesus.[45] We have seen in previous chapters something of the semantic range of λόγος. It can have the specific reference of 'proverb', sometimes underscored by the demonstrative.[46]

In the context of Mark's gospel as a whole, λόγος has another specific reference—a synonym for εὐαγγελίον.[47] So λόγος can include parables (4:33) proverbs (2:17), teaching on transformation (9:10), ethical injunction (10:22), prayer (14:39), in fact, the sum of Jesus' teaching (8:38, 13:31) which has an authority because it effects and affects things (1:27).

There are three, possibly four exceptions to Jesus' initiative in the 21-23 instances of the word in Mark.[48] The first, in 1:45, is the preaching of the leper, or at least this appears to be the usual understanding of the phrase 'and he began . . . to spread the word'. However, it is not clear whether Jesus or the leper is the preacher. The antecedent of ὁ δὲ ἐξελθὼν ἤρξατο κηρύσσειν . . . in v 45 would appear to be Jesus.[49] *If*

---

them all' my translation), also refers to the previous words of a woman (Xenocrite): *Mor* 262c.

44. Smyth, *Greek Grammar*, §§1245–1247.
45. See GD Kilpatrick, *New Testament Textual Criticism* (edited by JK Elliott) (Leuven: Leuven University Press, 1990), 280. He explicates the meaning as 'the Christian message'.
46. Ps-Luc *As* 45; *cf* Menand *Asp* 189, Plut *Mor* 970c (both with ῥῆμα).
47. So GD Kilpatrick, in Elliott, *CH Turner's Notes on Marcan Usage*, 166, VK Robbins, *Jesus the Teacher: A Socio-Rhetorical Reading of Mark* (Philadelphia: Fortress Press, 1984), 58–59. Compare the conjunction of 'word', 'words' and 'gospel' in 8:32, 38.
48. See BM Metzger, *A Textual Commentary on the Greek New Testament* (UBS, 1971), 99–100, 114.
49. So JK Elliott, 'The Conclusion of the Pericope of the Healing of the Leper and Mark i.45', in *JTS* 22 (1971): 153–157.

it is the leper,[50] then one from the fringe of Jewish society, one of the unclean and separated, becomes a participant in the word that Jesus has 'done'.

However there are two instances where the 'word' is refused. The first is in 5:36, where Jesus ignores 'the word' that the crowd had spoken,[51] and immediately proceeds to 'speak' encouragingly to the ruler of the synagogue.[52] The 'word' that they have spoken has the quality of 'no word' in the judgement of Jesus.

It is in this light that a second striking reference in the gospel needs to be interpreted. In 11:29, the Markan Jesus says, ἐπερωτήσω ὑμας ἕνα λόγον καὶ ἀποκρίθητέ μοι. The conjunction of terminology is strongly reminiscent of the story of the Syrophoenician. Some have argued that the use of ἕνα here is equivalent to the indefinite pronoun.[53] However, the poignancy of Jesus' question is that he is seeking just *one* word[54] that may indicate that his opponents have caught something of his gospel.[55] The opponents in 11:31–33 debate amongst themselves, and refuse to answer.

The contrast with the Syrophoenician woman is manifest. Without invitation, expectation or recognised position, she enters the level of discourse that the (male) leaders in their equivocation failed to engage. Their avowal of ignorance (11:33) is tantamount to positioning themselves as fools, children and/or the effeminate.[56] They have become ἄλογα—like animals. A diametrically opposite boundary crossing is ventured by the woman from Syrophoenicia—she transgresses the threshold of the gender boundaries of reason. Her saying has been recognised as λόγος.

---

50. Marcus, *Mark 1–8*, 207, argues that ὁ δέ in Mark indicates a change of subject.
51. There is some dispute over the meaning of παρακούσας. If it simply means 'overheard' then the use of λόγος in 11:29 takes on increased significance—a refusal to speak truly.
52. The opposition of τὸν λόγον λαλούμενον to the immediately following λέγει is striking.
53. *BDF* §247 (2). CFD Moule did not include this verse in his (admittedly limited) examples: *An Idiom-Book of New Testament Greek* (Cambridge: Cambridge University Press, 1963), 125. Matthew Black's longer list also omitted it: *An Aramaic Approach to the Gospels and Acts* (Oxford: Clarendon Press, third edition, 1967), 105.
54. So Gould, *Mark*, 218; *cf* Taylor, *Mark*, 470 ('single').
55. *Cf* Mk 12:42 where 'one poor widow' is contrasted with the '*many* rich' (πολλοὶ πλούσιοι): so Myers, *Binding the Strong Man*, 321.
56. Silence may also signify abuse or defiance: Montiglio, *Silence* 86–97, 129–132.

In spite of the general perception that λόγος in Mark's gospel is a synonym for the 'gospel of Jesus', it is clear from these four instances that the realm of *logos* is not exclusively the domain of Jesus. Others can enter. It is not exclusive but potentially, and sometimes actually, permeable in its boundaries—just like a woman was regarded in socio-political convention. Indeed, the instances in 5:36 and 11:29, suggest that word is not stable but contested.

If this word of a woman in Mark's Gospel is configured lexically and semantically with the word of Jesus, then a powerful word has been located in the one who, at least initially, was equated with the ἄλογα—the beasts without reason. This raises critical implications for the ethological perspective on the woman—has the dog broken through into reason, and if so, how? This issue will be tested below.

The power of the word of the Syrophoenician woman

Something of the specific power of the word of a woman for the story is suggested by the two verbs following in v 29.[57] The imperative ὕπαγε occurs frequently in Mark's healing stories,[58] delivering not merely a word of dismissal but a confirmation that the encounter has been fruitful. The re-positioning of the imperative in this story suspends a positive assessment of the words until the exorcism itself is announced. Only then does the instruction become a demonstration that the healing has been accomplished. The daughter's release is thus confirmed *here*, not, as we will explore in the next chapter, by v 30. If the story functioned simply as a healing account, v 29 would provide a fitting conclusion.[59]

The second verb, ἐξελήλυθεν, not only redirects the meaning to be attached to the opening of Jesus' response. It also has a tense-form unusual in the gospel. 36 of the 38 occurrences of ἐξέρχομαι in Mark

57. A few manuscripts change the word order, making ὗπαγε the opening of Jesus' words to the woman (Δ f^{13} 565 700 it^{g1} sy^{p}). The transposition is probably influenced by the primacy of position it occupies in other stories (for example, Mk 5:19, 8:33, 10:52, 11:2, 14:13, 16:7), even though it has the (unfortunate?) consequence of turning the woman's word into a reason for departure rather than a cause of her daughter's release.

58. 1:44, 2:11, 5:19, 5:34, 10:52.

59. Theissen, *Miracle*, 66–67, Aune, 'Magic', 1530, B Blackburn, *Theios anêr and the Markan Miracle Traditions: a critique of the Theios aner concept as an interpretative background of the miracle traditions used by Mark* (Tübingen: JCB Mohr, 1991), 222–223.

have the aorist tense form;[60] both word and tense frequent stories of exorcism (1:25, 26, 5:8, 13, 9:25, 26, 29). *Only* this pericope uses the perfect tense. The participial form of the perfect is the last word of the pericope (ἐξεληλυθός v 30).[61] These two instances stamp the story with singularity.

A story sometimes cited as a parallel to this pericope is the royal official's son (Jn 4:46–54).[62] The lack of the perfect tense in the Johannine story highlights its significance in Mark. The command to the official to go (πορεύου v 50) is accompanied by a statement that 'your son will live (ζῇ)'. The story unfolds to confirm that Jesus' word executed the deed of healing (v 53 ἐκείνῃ τῇ ὥρᾳ). The present tense (with futuristic aspect) is used here to indicate the power of Jesus' (prophetic?) word.[63] The father's faith (*cf* v 48) becomes tied to his obedience to the instruction to depart.

Similar is Mathew's version of the story. The woman's desire is realised through Jesus' word: γενηθήτω (15:28),[64] and it is emphasised, like Jn 4:53, that the healing occurred ἀπὸ τῆς ὥρας ἐκείνης. Elsewhere in Mark, the efficacious word of Jesus adopts the present or aorist tenses. The use of ἀφίενται in Mk 2:5, for example, binds forgiveness to Jesus' word of absolution. In Mk 9:25, the aorist ἔξελθε leaves us in no doubt who achieves the exorcism of the father's possessed son.

A few Latin manuscripts of Mk 7:29 remove any ambiguity about the source of the healing of the Syrophoenician's daughter, shifting the tense from the perfect (*exiit*) to the future (*exiet*).[65] The adjustment makes the exorcism completely dependent on the word of Jesus, and relies on v 30 to satisfy the required ending of a healing story. This intensifies the necessity for scrutinising the use of the perfect in the critical text.

60. One infinitive (9:29) and subjunctive (6:10), 3 imperatives (1:25, 5:8, 9:25), 14 participles (1:29, 48, 3:6, 5:2, 13, 30, 6:12, 24, 34, 54, 7:31, 9:30, 11:12, 16:8 [16:20]), 17 indicatives (1:26, 28, 35, 38, 2:12, 13, 3:21, 4:3, 6:1, 8:11, 8:27, 9:26, 11:11, 14:16, 26, 48, 68).
61. This coheres with Porter's observation that the perfect tense is used for significant items: *Idioms*, 23.
62. For example CH Dodd, *Historical Tradition in the Fourth Gospel* (Cambridge: Cambridge University Press, 1963), 188–195.
63. There is a three-fold accent: vv 50, 51, 53.
64. It recalls Mt 8:13 but also evokes Gen 1:3, 6 LXX.
65. The Old Latin manuscripts c, g^1 contain the reading; so also a couple of vulgate manuscripts. The form *exiet* is an alternative to the more familiar *exibit* (see Mt 2:6, 5:6 vg).

Studies of verbal aspect have substantially shifted the understanding of Greek tense-forms. Stanley Porter observed that the perfect operates somewhat as a stative, 'reflecting a given . . . state of affairs'.[66] This may be attributable to 'some antecedent action' or imply 'continued duration'. Clearly, no future aspect is in view (given the repetition of the perfect in v 30).[67] Porter acknowledged that 'while the emphasis in this use falls on the state or condition existing at the time of speaking, there is also a clear implication of the anterior occurrence which produced it.'[68]

Amongst the approximate forty additional perfects in Mark, a past reference is clearly indicated for a significant number,[69] but the stative perspective encompasses most. Either way, in this instance in 7:29 the διά with the accusative stands as the rationale for a *given* state of affairs.[70] The reasonably proximate expression in Mark 4:17, διὰ τὸν λόγον, refers to the word which has been heard (from which trouble and persecution follow). There is no reason to deny a similar understanding here.

The healing does not come as a *reward* for the word of a woman.[71] Rather, the word of a woman has *performed* the healing. The mother has become the well-spring of her daughter's liberation. If the use of λόγος for the woman's words aligns her answer with the ubiquity of λόγος/λόγοι for Jesus' words, then *her* word is powerful. *Her* word effects what it says, *even at a distance*. She has engineered a freedom that has implications for herself (in terms of unshackling the fetters on potential imposed by stereotypical characterisation) and her daughter.

The larger signification of the emphasis on word

Fine words have become the succour of the soul.[72] Words were far

66. Porter, *Idioms*, 22; so also Young, *Intermediate New Testament Greek*, 126.
67. Rarely, the perfect is found bearing a future component: Porter, *Idioms*, 41. For Mark, see 6:9 (especially the variant reading: ἐνδεδύσθαι), 9:1.
68. Porter, *Verbal Aspect*, 291.
69. For example, 10:28, 11:17, 21, 14:23, 44—the 'perfect of completed action': Porter, *Verbal Aspect*, 297.
70. Porter, *Idioms*, 148–151.
71. So Wainwright, *Women Healing*, 129; *contra* Bratcher, *Translator's Guide*, 95, Cranfield, *Mark*, 249; *cf* Kwok, *Discovering the Bible*, 73, Schüssler Fiorenza, *Sharing Her Word*, 122.
72. So the ancient proverb runs: τροφὴ γὰρ ψυχῆς λόγοι καλοί (Athen *Deip* 270c).

more than representations of objects. Their combinations of sounds bore an effect far beyond dictionary meaning. Incantations exploited this capacity, a number of them in metrical form, some repeated by 'reputable' writers.[73] Words could achieve a result akin to medicine or physical manipulation.[74] A solicitous proverb could even ward off danger.[75]

Plutarch explained the power of such words by reference to the theory of emanation, namely that the sound, breath or speech, *inter alia*, of a person could travel across space and impact upon another.[76] Martial's epitaph to a seven year old acknowledged the tragic irony of a disease removing her speech which might have won her health.[77] As Dio Chrysostom held, 'not even the most skilful music can provide perfect healing'.[78] Rather, it is 'the spoken word of the wise and prudent.'[79]

However, in spite of assertions that words held some innate power, the acceptability of words was defined by socio-political convention. The force of *logos* therefore meant not only captivation by a particular turn of phrase but also that the words so spoken were *recognised as valid* within or for the ordering of society. Hence, peddling incantations was portrayed as illogical and disorderly;[80] these 'words' were subversive of conventional order. Conversely, the rationalism of a Lucian, Juvenal or Plutarch was not like our contemporary scientific scepticism but rather indicative of a social conformity.

So when the woman's word is recognised as *logos*, bearing power rather than, say, magic, it is because it has been deemed acceptable by the male in the story. The woman's proverb, with its manifold applications, has power (as an acceptable 'word') within the situation, precisely because it bears on the ordering of society.

That ordering has to do with her daughter. The interconnection of the terminology θυγάτηρ, θυγάτριον, κοράσιον and παιδίον between Mark 5:23, 35, 39, 41, and 6:22, 28 and 7:25, 26, 29, 30

73. For example Pl *HN* 27.100.
74. See Gorg *Hel* 11.
75. Athen *Deip* 701d-e.
76. Plut *Mor* 680d–682a, 734f; *cf* Democr fr A 77 (Diel), Lucret *Nat Rer* 4.712f (who relates the theory of emanations to all the senses).
77. Mart *Epig* 11.91.
78. Music frequently was used for the demonic: Menand *Theoph* 23f; *cf* 1 Sam 16:14–23, 18:10, 19:9.
79. Dio Chrys *Or* 1.8.
80. Luc *Philops* 9. The Syrophoenician's *logos* is markedly different in tone from exorcism spells.

would suggest a girl of about 12 years old, on the cusp of puberty and marriageability.[81] This was a time for the putting away of the protective amulets and talismans that signified childhood's susceptibility to predatory influences. The transition was to bring a more direct and controlling influence of reason upon the initiate to adulthood. Transitions, as we have seen, are points of greatest receptivity to the demonic, the disordering of society.[82]

The *word* of the woman thus becomes the means to effect the transition to and the ongoing reinforcement of the bounded, rational security thus achieved. The word secures release precisely because release is a restoration to society's order that is demanded if the demonic is to be dispelled.

If the word of the woman is the ground of the daughter's exorcism, as I have argued, then a series of potent consequences are released:

a) The woman's shame in relation to the daughter's condition and her failure and/or inability to prevent or solve it, has been removed through her own agency.
b) The stigma of her identity and the consequences for her speech have been obviated by the classification of her saying in honorific terms.
c) The effort to shame the woman through the finality of abusive dismissal has been effectively turned by her into a challenge that has been met and won.[83]
d) Further, in the script markers for the performance of the exchange (αὐτῇ . . . αὐτῷ), Jesus affirms that she has spoken *logos* to *him*. The word of the woman *not that of Jesus* is given the central significance and power in the story. If her words are the *logos* in/of the story, it implies that his words (in v 26) are not.
e) Finally, and most significantly of all, this one has

81. Παιδίον can mean a nursling (perhaps equivalent to νήπιος) or one up to the age of seven: Aristoph Byz fr 37–66, Phil Jud *Opif* 105 (citing Hippocrates). Yet the παιδίον of Mk 9:24 has been smitten 'since παιδόθεν'—'Usage is thoroughly inconsistent': Golden, *Children and Childhood*, 15.

82. See Crossan, *The Historical Jesus*, 315 on the connection between possession and sexuality.

83. This is no retreat into the antiquated notion of training up the woman's faith or perseverance. Rather, it accents that the woman has prevented the closure that Jesus' words (v 27) indicated.

> been distinguished from the dog. As Isocrates held, 'the power to persuade each other whatever we desire [indicates that] . . . we have escaped the life of wild beasts; . . . the power to speak well is taken as the surest index of a sound understanding . . .'[84]

As we have amply seen, the language world of the ancients presupposes that the controlling field of meaning was 'man'. The uneasiness associated with the notion of *logos* as a male construct (and male preserver) rather than as a universal essence reveals itself here. The rhetorical and poetic force of words was often felt to be ambiguous, almost dangerous, because the mysterious realm of the arrangement of sound within lexical connection resisted easy logical description and regulatory prescription. The (potential) non-compliance of *logos* had a troubling connection with the bearer of (potential) non-compliance: woman.[85] It is noteworthy that the woman's saying makes far more sophisticated use of the psychagogic potential of language. Here lies a further fissure in the edifice of *logos* waiting to be exploited.

In the standard binary edifice built on the dimorphic foundation, for the word of a woman to be pronounced *logos* brings a double bind—whether the word has the force of *logos* because of the speaker (who is a woman) or the speaker has lost her identity as woman in the speaking of *logos*. Almost all commentators, pursuing feminist concerns or not, have baulked at crediting the word of the Syrophoenician with the deliverance of her daughter. The captivity to the Word has privileged the man Jesus exclusively as the healer/exorcist and interpreted the gospel writer as complicit in that portrait.

Yet Mark has already signalled the ability of others to exorcise. The disciples are 'properly' authorised to do so in the mission (6:7, 13). The anonymous 'disciple' performs exorcisms 'improperly' (9:38),[86] and the officious followers seek to silence that powerful word (δύναμις, 9:39). The woman participates in this excess. Indeed, the anonymous exorcist narratively *follows* the Syrophoenician's

84. Isocr *Or* 3 (*Nic*) 6–7.
85. The irrational in psychagogic influence over an audience intrigued the rhetorician Quint (*Inst* 8.3.1–6), but was dangerous. He aligns this aspect/ fault of language with women (10.7.12).
86. With some irony, the incident comes after the inability of the same 'properly authorised disciples' to exorcise the dumb spirit (Mk 9:17–18).

liberation of her daughter.[87] The suggestion that the woman's word might be an exorcising word is not out of place within Mark's story. Indeed, the liberation that the woman achieved for her daughter has been confirmed and more forcefully than previously recognised.

We have consistently found that *word* in the ancient world is configured in terms which reflect a male-constructed universe. If words do not reinforce that universe, they are not recognised as *logos*—they are verbally transgressive rather than logocentrically bounded and binding.[88] It would require an inversion of the universe to press the question further by asking whether the immutable *logos* of the ancient world has been changed because the *woman* has spoken it.

In chapter four, I raised the 'Catch-22' for the Syrophoenician from the perspective being adopted in Jesus' words: speak and she is not human; silence and her daughter has no chance of healing. With the change of her speech to *logos*, that double-bind may have morphed: speak (noise) without *logos* and she is a woman (dog), speak *logos* and she is not (woman). In other words, difference in language is recognised only from the perspective of the dominance of *logos* over non-*logos* and/or multifarious (and therefore nefarious) words.[89] As Nicole Loraux distilled it: 'If silence is as necessary and natural to woman as logos is to man, a woman cannot deliver a speech without profoundly disturbing the order of things.'[90] Hence, if *logos* has been spoken, she, as woman, has become invisible right at the moment that her speech is valorised! Even in less extreme conceptualisation, a woman's praised words are praiseworthy in the male-conceptualised ancient world because they are tied in some fashion to the figure of *logos*-endowment, a man.[91]

---

87. Whilst a number of commentators have noted the significance of the Syrophoenician's story for the second feeding in Mark (for example Marcus, *Mark 1–8*, 469, 470), the relation between the disciples' exorcisms and the anonymous follower's exorcisms has not been similarly hinged on the Syrophoenician woman. The same might be said of the attitude to children which suddenly balloons after this pericope (9:36–37, 10:13–16); see however, Boomershine, *Story Journey*, 109.
88. See McClure, *Spoken Like a Woman*, 7.
89. Λόγοι ποικίλοι as used in the distinction made by Apollodorus (Lib *Decl* 25.8).
90. N Loraux, *The Invention of Athens: the Funeral Oration in the Classical City,* translated by A Sheridan (Cambridge, MT: Harvard University Press, 1986), 323.
91. The comparison of the Syrophoenician's word with courtesans' chreiai or *The Sayings of Spartan Women* (Plut *Mor* 240c–242d) is valuable for parallels to the Markan story. However, to describe these stories

Therefore, conscious of the risk to the word of a woman, we are returned to the text's characterisation of speech. The designation of the word of a woman as responsible for the child's dispossession *is delivered by Jesus*, a male character in Mark's gospel portrayed as having a natural affinity with *logos*, its recognition and its communication. There are glimpses of two fissures (at least) in the traditional conception of *logos* that await exploitation (*logos* as possessing psychagogic power and *logos* as a shared rather than a privileged site). But we have repeatedly confronted the significance of male recognition/designation of *logos* in the word of a woman.

The ascription of value by a male authority

Kathleen Jones outlines a familiar feminist critique of authority. The dichotomy between women's subjectivity and objectivity in relation to authority has frequently been established by the separation of public and private lives. Women's sphere of action is consigned to the private and affective. Consequently, they are denied the opportunity to initiate and exercise authority. This study, along with many others, confirms how long-standing and pervasive is such socialisation.

However, Jones exposes the fundamental limitation of this line of feminist critique, not because she wants to undercut the issues of justice related to women's access. Rather, she is concerned at the failure to critique the very notion of authority that has led to the dualistic structure in the first place. The arena has remained the same; the press has been to secure a greater range of players.[92] Elisabeth

---

as 'popular in antiquity' as does Mary d'Angelo, ('(Re)Presentations of Women', 140) fails to address the question of the audience of such popularity and the intention of the telling. These stories frequently, if not totally, reinforce male constructions of order. The exemplary boundedness of the women concerned and their consequent value to society, simply augment men in their public responsibilities. This is clear when Plutarch refers to the role and training of Spartan women elsewhere: *Vit* (*Lyc*) 14.3. Indeed, on at least one occasion, a saying is attributed in one place to a Spartan woman which elsewhere he credits to a man: compare *Mor* 240e (of Gorgo) and 218d (of Archidamus). As Susanna Braund writes, 'What sounded like a woman's voice turned out to be *écriture masculin*': 'A Woman's Voice? — Laronia's Role in Juvenal Satire 2', in R Hawley and B Levick (editors), *Women in Antiquity: New Assessments* (London: Routledge, 1995), 215; see also Archer, *Beyond Rubies*, 97–99, Madeleine Henry, 'The Edible Woman', in Richlin, *Pornography and Representation*, 254.

92. Jones, 'On Authority', 120.

Schüssler Fiorenza's castigation of 'malestream' patterns in education (and society) is one prominent example in this movement for justice.[93] But, as Sharon Ringe reminds us, the master's tools never dismantled the master's house.[94]

This critique plots the analysis of the story of the Syrophoenician woman, even amongst those who recognise the trap of a failure to change 'the terms of the argument'.[95] Recent feminist and post-colonial exegesis has rightly seized upon the liberating word of the woman. Thereby, the right and efficacy of the woman to enter (gospel) discourse in the public realm of text and decision traditionally occupied by men can be demonstrated.[96] The word of the woman is powerful, healing and capable of entering into dialogue with a man, even to the point of being recognised as the proper word for a situation in life. But that is precisely the point, *the word is recognised*. Little critique is made *of* the recognition, and even less about the privileging of the word. The history of interpretation has shown how easily 'the recognition of the word' can lead to the erasure of women, whether that be Tertullian's turn of the story to justify the mission to the Gentiles or nineteenth century dons purloining it to secure the humble piety of maternal faith *outside* the university.

The dangers of privileging the word of the Syrophoenician woman

I have no desire or intention to undercut the resource of this adjusted accent on word for the restoration of just relations. However, the critique offered by Kathleen Jones advises a discernment of the dangers that may flow if the accent upon word that has dominated modern scholarship (both for and against women, and in dependence on ancient progenitors) remains unquestioned. The dangers propagated by this unsuspecting embrace of word are numerous:

93. *But She Said*, 171–191.
94. *The Postcolonial Bible*, 142; *cf* 260 on the importance of challenging the governing structure not merely the dominant voices.
95. Schüssler Fiorenza, *Sharing Her Word*, 121.
96. This contemporary political dimension is openly acknowledged by Schüssler Fiorenza (for example, *But She Said*, 103–132), though mildly criticised by Kraemer (*Her Share*, 133). Indeed, current concerns have cultivated reappraisals of ancient evidence, even facilitating new discoveries. This was the very methodological foundation she wanted: *Miriam's Child*, 29.

i) The exceptional moment in the woman's story

This word of the woman may be limited to a one-off interruption which, having been delivered, is exploited thereafter by male speakers and text-controllers, remaindering the original speaker to the 'normality' from which she came.[97] Not only is her return *home* read as proof of the exceptional nature of the encounter with Jesus, but she no longer has any connection with her words.

The reassertion of conventional geopolitical arrangements requires a slight-of-hand with the text. The ὕπαγε of v 29 is hijacked to the εἰς τὸν οἶκον of v 30 as if they *necessarily* belonged together. The syntactical pattern found in Mark 2:11, 5:19 becomes the norm to which different expressions are anchored.[98] The second example (5:19) is striking. The man Legion, having been told *to go to his home*, remains in the public sphere, travelling and proclaiming throughout the Decapolis. The Syrophoenician woman, told simply to 'go' (*cf* 10:52), returns to her own home. If *logos* is the proper ordering of the cosmos, then that order appears, on such a reading, to restore the woman's proper boundedness in her home. This is one danger of accepting Jesus' ascription of *logos* as the sole determinant of meaning.

ii) The constraint of male classification

The designation of the woman's answer as λόγος by the man Jesus, at least textually constrains to masculine judgment the perception of the nature and value of what she has said. The more common διὰ τοῦτο (for example Mk 6:14, 11:24, 12:24) would at least have left open the categorisation of her response. That the last word of speech adjudicates the words *as* λόγος swings the offering of the woman to the sphere of the masculine (that is, the sphere which has conventionally characterised the masculine). It is akin to the ancient schools, where the instructor pronounced on the worth of a student's declamation.

This is where the demonstrative τοῦτον takes a sinister turn. The effect of the demonstrative may be to distinguish 'this word' not only from the woman's speech elsewhere (hence, another exceptional moment), but from 'woman' as the speaker. The issue is raised by Mary Lefkowitz in her analysis of Hortensia's speech in favour of

97. The women of the brave deeds and sayings enumerated by Plutarch (*Mor* 240c–263c) either die or are subsequently restored to their conventional place.

98. 'The woman departs to her house' apparently in response to Jesus who 'bids her depart': Taylor, *Mark*, 351; *cf* Bratcher and Nida, *Handbook of Mark*, 239 'go to your home'.

tax relief in Rome in 42 BCE. Not only is the praise for her words dependent on male approval for the sentiments uttered, but the adulation is formulated as an appreciation of the continuation of her late father's oratory.[99]

The word of the Syrophoenician woman in fact is not credited as *her* word, but as *this* word. Elsewhere in Mark, the word(s) might be further qualified as word 'of God' (7:13), 'my' words (8:38, 13:31) or 'his' words (10:24), accenting the connectedness between the word and its speaker. The demonstrative has destabilised the authorial subjectivity of the word as *hers*. Even the Samaritan woman's words are recognised as 'yours' (Jn 4:42). Only two Old Latin manuscripts make a similar connection of the Syrophoenician woman with the word that she speaks.[100]

iii) The constraint of male textualisation

From the previous potential danger of privileging the word, comes a compounding development. The one writing the text is (likely) a male and hence has one like himself (namely Jesus) identifying what he has himself written into the mouth of a woman. Men constructing women as 'acting subjects' go 'one step further in the total objectification of woman.' Susanne Kappeler sees this as the final act of victimisation.[101]

This is a *danger* of the focus on 'word' alone as the key to this story. In this, both hero and narrator, invested with the authority of adjudication, have become complicit in distancing the woman from *her* word. Moreover, the adjudicated word has itself been *supplied in the first place*: 'it is only an illusion that we encounter her and her speech directly. She is not a speaking subject but rather is an effect of someone else's speech.'[102] Those modern interpreters who describe the woman

99. Lefkowitz, *Women in Greek Myth*, 92, citing Val Max 8.3. Numerous examples occur in ancient literature where women's words are taken as exemplary of father, husband or son: see Cic *Orat* 3.45, Plut *Mor* 145b-c, *Vit* (*Pomp*) 55, Pl *Ep* 1.16.6.

100. *Hoc/hunc verbum tuum*: it[n a].

101. S Kappeler, *The Pornography of Representation* (Minneapolis: University of Minnesota Press, 1986), 90.

102. CA Newsom, 'Woman and the Discourse of Patriarchal Wisdom', in TK Beal and DM Gunn (editors) *Reading Bibles, Writing Bodies: Identity and the Book* (London and New York: Routledge, 1997), 130. I am not requiring that Mark is the author of the woman's saying but that the evangelist is the author of the (final form) of the story in which the

as seizing the opening (knowingly) supplied by Jesus' words[103] are but a hair's breadth from a total removal of the woman's subjectivity, the necessary accompaniment (cost?) to maintaining Jesus' merciful magnanimity.[104] And those who would remove any authentic kernel from the story must hear other women's voices (such as in the debates of Mark's community) to avoid the fierceness of Kappeler's removal of innocence from the text. This is where the construction of the story as a missiological text is especially threatening to the surviving presence of women either in the text or in the later community.[105]

iv) The constraint of male commentary

A further dimension of this type of danger is that my commentary in this thesis becomes part of the continued expropriation of women's speech as a means to perpetuate male identity, indulgence and/or dominance through the feminist struggle to find 'the different/ce'.[106] If λόγος, so connected by the ancients with the natural disposition of the male, is, in this light, asserted as key to the interpretation of the story, then contemporary commentary has perpetuated the standard dichotomy without question. The ethological superstructure is essentialised.

Robert Gundry's commentary on the Syrophoenician pericope set such a tone from the beginning. Jesus' 'power of attraction', 'dignity', 'divine lordship' means that he condescends to 'admiration of the woman's cleverness'. But this is all. Jesus dwarfs the woman by 'his power in accomplishing the exorcism at a distance and the supernatural knowledge displayed in his announcing the exorcism.' Gundry reduced the force of ἀπεκρίθη καὶ λέγει to the Syrophoenician's acknowledgement of Jesus as κύριε; effectively, she is rewarded for a proper address.[107] The haunting of male control remains because

saying appears. The question of literary indebtedness to traditional or historical sources is raised in the conclusion.

103. For example, Swete, *Mark*, 149, Stock, *Mark*, 213 amongst many.

104. Not all such renderings seek to exonerate Jesus: Pokorný, 'Puppy', 328.

105. G Lüdemann, *Jesus After 2000 Years: What he really said and did* translated by J Bowden (London: SCM, 2000), 50–51; *cf* d'Angelo, '(Re)presentations of Women', 139–141.

106. Similar concerns are admitted by David Halperin as a paradoxical threat accompanying the effort to expose and critique ancient constructions of women: 'Why is Diotima a Woman? Platonic *Erôs* and the Figuration of Gender', in Winkler and Zeitlin, *Before Sexuality*, 259.

107. Gundry, *Mark*, 372–375; also Pokorný, 'Puppy', 331. The hold of the Pygmalion myth on the assessment of woman (that is, of woman as

the prearranged categories continue in reified and unscrutinised presumption. The woman's *answer*, not her presence, dominates the focus, still conforming to a dominical *magisterium*.[108]

v) Logocentric valorisation masks a negation

Most potent of all, the singular concentration on the *word* of a woman, obstructs any validation of the woman *other than in those terms*. The possibility of communication other than by λόγος and the possibility of esteem for a response other than λόγος (such as the 'good deed' of Mark 14:6, 9) *in* the story are lost. The possibility that λόγος might include a wider praxis-dimension, such as we find in 4 Reigns 5:18 (ἐν τῷ λόγῳ τούτῳ), is extinguished. In other words, the focus is totally upon the *spoken* exchange between Jesus and the woman. The elements of the story's extended setting (7:24–26) are rendered inconsequential preliminaries.[109]

Jesus' words are used to remove consideration of other initiatives of the woman. The child herself, liberated from one possession, remains nothing other than a victim—hence v 30 is interpreted as a continuation (albeit diluted as a legacy) of the earlier terror of possession. The otherness of the female, which might have delivered her presence, is scripted logocentrically; otherness yet again delivers inferiority, and presence is erased in/by the headier sphere of reason. The devaluation of her body, as a *woman's* body, is secure, as readily as it is zoned by the house walls. In a bitter irony, that body is made anorexic: not only is it supposed to be sated by mere crumbs, but these scraps are not about physical well-being but cerebral elevation.

Thus, the *Gnostic Gospel of Philip* constructs the *voice* of the

---

constructed honourably by man) has governed perceptions ancient and modern: see AR Sharrock, 'Womanufacture', in *JRS* 81 (1991): 36–49.

108. Frantzen, 'When Women Aren't Enough', 450; see also JDH Amador, "Feminist Biblical Hermeneutics: The Failure of Theoretical Nerve", in *JAAR* 66 (1998): 39–57.

109. This is where Elisabeth Schüssler Fiorenza's embellishment of the Syrophoenician's story in terms of the contemporary action of breaking into the androcentric discourse of male-dominated academic institutions is especially important. Whether or not this is the intention in her rendition, she has rescued aspects of the story from dismissal and forced a reconsideration of the place of *logos* in the story (even as might challenge or modify her own interpretation): see *But She Said*, 103–4; *cf* 12–13. The irony is that the collapse of the walls of a house was precisely what women's talk in the ancient world was supposedly capable of precipitating: Herodas *Mime* 6.1–14.

bride as the scraps beneath the table for the dogs of unredeemed humanity.[110] This pale reflection of the fully rational humanity of the anointed bridegroom receives an annihilating resolution in the *Catena in Acta (Catena Andreae)*. The problem of the legacy of her gender is overcome by her transformation into a (hu)man: Συροφοινίκισσα γοῦν γυνὴ διὰ πίστιν ἐκ κύνος ἄνθρωπος γέγονεν (176.6).[111] Here, clearly, γυνή is irredeemedly set against ἄνθρωπος.[112]

vi) The romance inversion motif: or the move from 'damned whore' to 'God's police'[113]

Declamatory exercises, new comedies and romance novels in the ancient world frequently deployed the plot skeleton of the discovery of the true status origins of a woman emergent from the appearances of slave or prostitute existence.[114] *Logos* provides the point of revelation, where the true character of a person is revealed. The perception, however, is determined by the powerful figure. Thus, an explanation for the ability to speak *logos* is grounded in the honourable origins and bounded virtues of the woman not in any training in a disreputable profession. Moreover, just like other brave women, she is moved to re-orient, even police a potential disruption of the male (Jesus) commitment to proper, public order and function.[115]

This touches on a contemporary debate about the casting of the Syrophoenician woman. Amy-Jill Levine rejects the suggestion that sexuality is any part of the story,[116] yet, as we have seen, the narrative incorporates stereotypes to evoke a correlation between the woman

110. *Gospel of Philip* 82 (130/102): 21–24. (Chapter numbers differ in various editions.)
111. This overcomes the dualism with Legion (Mk 5:2) by removing any distinction from him. I am grateful to Dr Paul Tuffin of the Classics Department, University of Adelaide, for this reference.
112. Compare the famous logion 114 of the *Gospel of Thomas*.
113. The title is borrowed from a foundational Australian feminist text: A Summers, *Damned Whores and God's Police* (Ringwood, Vic: Penguin, revised edition, 1994).
114. Polyaen *Strat* 8.40, Hier *C Jov* 35, Zonar 4.9 (185b).
115. This is Martin Scott's resolution of the problem of Jesus' harsh response: the woman overcomes 'a growing sense of despair and frustration in Jesus' and 'helps the narrator to restore Jesus' sense of perspective…' See 'Matthew 15:21–28: A Test-Case for Jesus' Manners', in *JSNT* 63 (1996): 41–42. Perkinson perceives this erases the woman by making her a speaker 'for Christ': 'Canaanitic Word', 81.
116. Levine, 'Mathew's Advice', 27; contrast, *inter alia*, Dewey, 'Jesus Healings of Women', 127, Dermience, 'Tradition et redaction', 23,

and a prostitute. This forms part of the larger-scale debate about the presence of prostitutes in the early Jesus movement.[117]

The debate is a modern variation of the ancient romance form, which can only recognise *logos* in a morally and socially honourable woman. In most cases, the goal of romance and the seal on the revelation of the woman is marriage, just as occurs (in slightly varied form) in the *Pseudo-Clementine Homilies*.[118] But this is precisely what is absent from Mark's story.[119] The removal of a woman from a protective male and his house might accord with contemporary aspirations and current critique of the ancient world,[120] but the unwillingness to allow that the woman is a prostitute / courtesan before and after the exchange with Jesus, may simply be a sign of the tenacity of a logocentric arrangement of the universe, albeit in a 'white lady' form.[121]

I have outlined six dangers of an exclusive and simple assertion that the value of the Syrophoenician's story lies in the word of a woman. As Elizabeth Grosz observes, 'Even many so-called radical theories actively participate in a process of salvaging or resuscitating reason.'[122] At the same time, the necessary caution to be exercised ought not begrudge an appreciation of what the woman, as woman, says. For this also would perpetuate ancient stifling of woman's subjectivity, as Madeleine Henry has acutely accused Foucault of engineering,[123] and it would merely reinscribe an essentialism to the body as female even

---

Corley, *Private Women*, 166, Osiek and Balch, *Families*, 136; *cf.* Ringe, 'Gentile Woman's Story', 70–71.

117. Lieu, '"Attraction of Women"', 20, Corley, 'Really Prostitutes?', 520–521; *cf* Ford, 'Prostitution', 129, 133, Matthews, *First Converts*.
118. *Ps-Clem Hom* 2.20. Here, marriage forms both the backdrop for the woman (a 'widow' by separation from an unbelieving husband) and the consummation of the daughter's release.
119. See chapter 7 for the significance of the absence of men from the household.
120. H Montague, 'Sweet and Pleasant Passion: Female and Male Fantasy in Ancient Romance Novels', in Richlin, *Pornography and Representation*, 233. See also RN Brock and SB Thistlethwaite, *Casting Stones: Prostitution and Liberation in Asia and the United States* (Minneapolis: Fortress, Press, 1996), 221, 223.
121. That is, appropriating some of the commitments of feminism but in a form that ultimately either reinscribes or appropriates for itself structures of domination.
122. Grosz, *space, time and perversion*, 28.
123. Henry, 'Edible Woman', 253.

if the intent may be to revaluate it.[124]

Accordingly, an ambiguity qualifies full-blown confidence in the word of the woman. But the ambiguity is precisely what allows a positive value to be attached to λόγος as the designation of her answer. The recognition that even in the materials surviving from the ancient world women's speech is so problematised, speaks against a total scepticism about the survival of women's speech and against an unchallenged logocentric superstructure founded on an ethologically justified dimorphism.[125] Even allowing for (re-)colonisation, the hegemony of male control of language, in the face of ambiguity, cannot impose a pristine, monolithic dominion—neither in the texts themselves nor over the potential that alternate reading strategies can uncover.

Exploiting the ambiguities

A fissure in the word

In the course of the discussion, some possibilities have been raised that suggest that the standard logocentric interpretation of either the word of Jesus or the word of the woman does not have to tyrannise the reading of the text. Indeed, hints of alternative possibilities have been extracted from the text itself. These 'fissures' in the text, interpretation and convention[126] await exploitation.

Whilst there are proximities between Jesus' words of refusal and the woman's resistant reply, her saying carries substantial differences. If these differences are accentuated rather than smoothed over, then the designation of her words as λόγος must acknowledge those differences. In this sense, λόγος in Jesus' 'last word' *is* a modification

124. Neither must this be allowed to erase differences between bodies, better conceived as modes of corporeality: Grosz *space, time, and perversion*, 32.

125. Compare BK Gold, '"But Ariadne was never there in the First Place": Finding the Female in Roman Poetry', in NS Rabinowitz and A Richlin (editors), *Feminist Theory and the Classics* (New York: Routledge, 1993), 91–93.

126. I have chosen the term 'fissures' to describe those points in the boundaries of text, interpretation or convention which either lie latent or, given conducive circumstances, disclosively erupt. Elizabeth Grosz describes them as 'blindspots, points of unrecognised vulnerability . . . points of paradox or excess, sites of difference, non-identity, where the text spills over its conceptual boundaries.' (Text is here understood as anything which can be 'read'.) See E Grosz, *Sexual Subversions: Three French Theorists* (Sydney: Allen & Unwin, 1989), 28.

of his word. No longer is λόγος only to be defined by that which men speak. Indeed, if we take up the ascription of λόγος as a choice between two sayings—that of Jesus and that of the woman—then the one who is the authoritative bearer of *logos* in Mark's gospel is now not merely joined by a woman (along with the leper perhaps); his own word is rejected *by the choice for her word*. The woman's rhetorical strategy, of conjuring a clash of wisdom in order to compel a situational choice, has succeeded.

The difference(s) protects against the erasure of the woman in the affirmation of her word as (*this*) *logos*, the dangers of which we have just explored. The affirmation has exercised choice between sayings, sayings that are allocated to different genders. *Logos* must therefore encompass the speech of women, without reifying that speech,[127] or objectifying women through their speech. Indeed, the sharing of a measure of common language between men and women is what enables much communication to occur, even in Mark's story. Mischa Adams is at pains to remind us:

> A communication theory which dichotomizes female and male styles will not account for the possibility that there are times in people's daily experience when they simply communicate as a people rather than as reified symbols of the fact that they embody masculine or feminine gender.[128]

More than that, the subjectivities involved in speaking are more diverse than the binary structure of male and female, of dominant and submissive. The woman not only shares words with Jesus, she adds to his. Indeed, if Jesus be interpreted as adjusting his thinking, then, in some assessments of the ancient world, he has joined the woman, for it is the woman who is prone to the changing of mind.[129] The fundamental ethological dimorphism is struggling to maintain its alignments; the

127. Contemporary studies have seriously qualified the assertion of a language/dialect specific to women; see, generally, C Roman, S Juhasz and C Miller, (editors), *The Women and Language Debate: a sourcebook* (New Brunswick, NJ: Rutgers, 1994).

128. MB Adams, 'Communication and Gender Stereotype: An Anthropological Perspective', (PhD Thesis, Southern California: University of California, 1980), 146.

129. *Ep Arist* 250: τὸ θῆλυ . . . μεταπῖπτον εὐκόπως διὰ παραλογισμοῦ.

naturalism is breaking down.

Logos has proved to be larger in its expanse than any gendered perspective and control can allow. If this 'last word' of Jesus is reframed, it can become a confession of transformative revelation experienced by Jesus.[130] This is not to be understood as being at the expense of the woman (even though she disappears from the narrative) but rather a mutual discovery of new voice.[131]

Here is found the positive accent on *this* (τοῦτον) word in Jesus' reply. The unique Markan phrase, as *now* interpreted, emphasises the unique contribution that the woman has made. The logocentric universe controlled by the male has been potentially shifted through a fissure that has enabled the woman not merely an entry point but the opportunity to re-align the entire edifice. 'This word' can be read as more than a eulogy for its own content but as an acknowledgement of form, speaker, performance, function and even purpose of the pilgrimage. All these are involved. The word has become an event. The woman has won control of a rhetorical situation, and in so doing has not only destabilised the control of λόγος by Jesus but that of the operations of the androcentric (and/or androcentrically interpreted) text as well. It is somewhat akin to the destabilisation of the presumption of *male* disciples around Jesus by the sudden introduction of women followers from Galilee in Mark 15:41.

The fissure in the word therefore leads to a new understanding of what 'word', even the word of Jesus, might be. This word is not, or is no longer, phallically monolithic, 'whose nature it is to obscure differences and to bring them back to the same, by functioning with the familiar binary oppositions.'[132] If Mark's own textualisation of *logos* is an industry manufacturing the same immutability that Jesus' first words to the woman presupposed, then the woman's voice mounts a challenge from within the text to the text (and its author). Here, the evidence of a multiplicity of the editions of Mark's gospel, of a multiplicity of endings to the gospel, and of the very malleability of the text in transmission, offers a material witness to the success of a challenge to immutability, the very strategy of reading proposed here. At least in the first few centuries of the life of the gospel of Mark,

130. E Wainwright, *Shall We Look for Another? A Feminist Rereading of the Matthean Jesus* (Maryknoll, NY: Orbis, 1998), 88–89.

131. So Perkinson, 'Canaanitic Word', 80–81.

132. C Makward, 'To Be or Not To Be . . . A Feminist Speaker', in H Eisenstein and A Jardine (editors), *The Future of Difference* (New Brunswick, NJ: Rutgers University Press, 1980), 101.

there was a noticeable *lack* of uniformity,[133] suggesting that Mark and/or some early interpreters were susceptible to/cultivated multiple readings, multiple voices.

At the same time, the ambiguities remain. Warnings and cautions have littered this analysis, prompted by the recognition of the historical colonisation of the word of a woman. The tenacity of a logocentric approach to the interpretation of the story continually subpoenas the male to its side, whether that be Jesus himself or the arena of authorised discourse which inherently privileges the male (even when 'he' is absent). The traditions of interpretation of the Syrophoenician story amply testify to *an impoverishment of women in spite of her word.*

The fissure identified and exploited by the word of a woman must therefore seek a point of reference other than word, just as that word has pointed beyond a narrow definition of itself (especially in the potential of word being understood as an event). In standard interpretation, this potential reference point has been largely dormant. It is the most fundamental expression of the female according to ancient ethological description, namely, the body, a breathing, moving, noisy body at that. Text alone will not do. The very element seized upon in an ethological construction as demonstration of the female side of the dimorphic divide—the body—now becomes critical to the understanding, or rather communication, of the fullness of the word.

The fissure of her body

The fundamental function of a logocentric universe was to order the elements within it. Human participation in this ordering was in the recognition and communication of the order supposedly inherent in cosmic structure. Description therefore was never innocent but sought authority in its articulation of the natural arrangement of things. Given that the very act of analysis and promotion was a male activity, the woman consistently was object of study and necessarily bounded (hounded?) by the male initiation of examination.[134]

Accordingly, of far greater concern than the speech of a woman was the body of a woman. This does not deny that woman's speech was viewed as enormously dangerous (and therefore enormously

133. LM Wills, *The Quest of the Historical Gospel: Mark, John and the origins of the gospel genre* (London / NY: Routledge, 1997), 5–6.

134. See generally L Dean-Jones, 'The Cultural Construct of the Female Body in Classical Greek Science', in Pomeroy, *Women's History*, 111–137, and 'Medicine: The "Proof" of Anatomy', in Fantham *et al*, *Women in the Classical World*, 183–203.

interesting) to men.[135] But speech was an adjunct to the greater focus, given that, in the ethological dichotomy, esteemed reason was allocated to the male, the animal body to the female. The body of the woman was critical (and always on the precipice of crisis). The weight of attention given to the woman's body to genderise and sexualise as well as domesticate it functioned politically to prevent a subjectivity of speech.[136] As Plautus' character, Trachalio, quips: 'A woman's silence is worth more than her speech.'[137]

The silence(ing) of woman was 'complemented' by tabulating her body as the site for inscription. The second century (CE) psychologist, Artemidorus, offered a clear statement: 'in dreams, a writing tablet signifies a woman, since it receives the imprint of all kinds of letters.'[138] The body 'is a space for scriptural labor'.[139] The elaborate textualisation of the beloved's body in *Song of Songs* or Sarah's thighs in the *Genesis Apocryphon* demonstrates a similar Jewish attentiveness to the female body and to the requirement that it be marked out, plotted, given detailed description/inscription as a crucial part of the male responsibility to stylise a logocentric universe.[140]

The necessity inspiring such a textual practice was defensive, or at least self-positioning of the male as the stylus-holder.[141] But it has a subversive side—the body becomes essential for the communication process. As in all metaphors, what may be revelatory relies upon the subjugation and silencing of that which is to be hidden. The requisite passivity of the tablet is an integral ideological subtext of the use of such a metaphor for a woman's body.[142]

Yet, the prime capacity of a body is that it moves—otherwise it is a corpse. The stylus of course may have just this result—the slaying of the

135. Even when a woman conformed to a conventional lifestyle, male suspicion was that amongst other women or alone, convention would as readily be slipped off as the covering of clothing: see Mart. *Epig* 11.16; see generally, McClure, *Spoken Like a Woman*, 56–62, S Lewis, *News and Society in the Greek Polis* (London: Duckworth Press, 1996), 10–13.

136. So Dewey, 'From Storytelling to Written Text', 76.

137. Plaut *Rud* 1114; *cf* Sir 26:15.

138. Artemid *Somn* 2.45.

139. DuBois, *Sowing the Body*, 165.

140. Goldhill, 'Erotic Eye', 157–167.

141. The stylus received the name of Ares, the god of war and iron: *GA* 13.45, 60.

142. DuBois, *Sowing the Body*, 166.

woman's body,[143] into a literary fiction at best.[144] Even so, as Quintilian was careful to note in a section on early education, wax (like the female body) frequently caused the stylus to wander.[145] The attention to the movement of the woman in the Markan passage refuses, at least for a moment, the immobilisation of the body. The communication of *logos* by a body therefore does not reflexively require that the body be stilled by the word and its inscription. Rather the body becomes an integral, active and initiating protestor or participant in communication.

This reconceptualisation allows a move from dominance over the body by the word to the body's protest and participation in communication. It forges a joint subjectivity which does not prize word over body but body along with word. As Elizabeth Grosz perceives: 'What is mapped onto the body is not unaffected by the body onto which it is projected.'[146] Both are necessary for communication to occur. In fact, as we shall see, the medium may itself convey (and modify) the message. The introduction of this complexity into the standard dualism (pre)determining scholarly enquiry has awakened the possibility that the domestic, encapsulated in the control of the body of the woman, might become a site of female power even under the guise of submissiveness.[147] Her body provides the foundation and framework for her speech; it has become a 'narrating body'.[148]

Noticing the ambiguities

Because of the body's extensive range of rhythms, gestures and movements, it is manifestly ambiguous, open to alternate explanations. Much of the abuse in Jesus' words is directed towards the removal of *this* ambiguity; it is not merely a repudiation of words, given that Mark, unlike Matthew, withholds the woman's initial direct speech

143. Καλαμιοσφάκτης, 'one who slays by writing' Phil Jud *Flac* 132, *cf* Hom *Il* 6.167–170.
144. M Wyke, 'Written Women: Propertius' *Scripta Puella*', in *JRS* 77 (1987): 47–61.
145. Quint *Inst* 1.1.27. His solution was to cut the letters on the board itself to guide the stylus.
146. E Grosz, 'Inscriptions and body-maps: representations and the corporeal', in T Threadgold and A Cranny-Francis (editors), *Feminine, Masculine and Representation* (Sydney: Allen & Unwin, 1990), 74.
147. So MY MacDonald, *Early Christian Women and Pagan Opinion: The Power of the Hysterical Woman* (Cambridge: Cambridge University Press, 1996), 43.
148. L Marin, 'The "Aesop" Fable-Animal', in M Blonsky (editor), *On Signs* (Baltimore, MD: Johns Hopkins University Press, 1985), 334.

until *after* Jesus has spoken. Accordingly, not merely the speech, but also the body must be recognised as impacting the assessment of the woman.

Sharon McDonald observed that in societies where the appeal to nature is used to reinforce socio-political conceptions and constraints upon women, it is precisely the site of such focus that becomes the expression of resistance:

> It is perhaps not surprising that the body should itself be used as a powerful tool of defiance by groups—especially of women—seeking to challenge those in control.[149]

Hence, the body becomes a vehicle of resistance against the discourse that has sought to confine it, bearing within itself a knowledge that the dominant language system has denied.[150] It has an intelligence 'immersed in practice'.[151]

A rapid review of the story reveals the ambiguities attaching to the possibility of the Syrophoenician's embodied resistance (and communication):

- i) Her body is a woman's body—it is prized for its desirability and its procreative potential, but it is also potentially transgressive of racial purity (vv 24–25).
- ii) Her body is material—it is comprehended in direct relation to the animal (in both Jesus and her own words) but it is variously despised and desired (just like a dog) (vv 27, 28).
- iii) Her body is a procreative body—she has a daughter but there is, in the picture, no father or other male to confer an honorific value on procreation (v 25).
- iv) Her body is an accommodated body—she has a

149. McDonald, 'Socialisation of the Natural', 201.
150. The notion of 'body knowledge' is explored by MC Taylor, *Hiding* (Chicago: University of Chicago Press, 1997).
151. VY Mudimbe, *Parables and Fables: Exegesis, Textuality and Politics in Central Africa* (Madison, WN: University of Wisconsin Press, 1991), 139.

house,[152] but she moves beyond its boundaries without recognised or assumed protective entourage, thereby throwing the honour of the house(hold) into question (vv 25, 30).

v) Her body is geo-ethnically recognised—she is not without country or race but she dwells in the hinterlands and her country and race are compromised (v 26).

vi) Her body is an attentive and receptive body—she is a listener to reports but fails to respect the boundaries that have been erected around the inspiration of those reports (v 24–25).

All these ambiguities are grounded in 'her body'—the body of a woman, and a woman who, in the stereotyping conferred by the text, is a particular type of woman.

The ambiguous body of a woman

It might be argued that the ambiguities in the Syrophoenician's body are simply those that were attached, in the ancient world, to a woman's body generally, ambiguities that required resolution. This body was to be preserved from the dangers that it presented to itself and to others through its disregard of proper boundary maintenance. The Syrophoenician therefore becomes a notable example of a woman needing the control of a man. On such a reading, her prostration and address (κύριε)[153] might be reformulated as a pious request for restoration of proper boundedness—as much for herself as for her daughter.[154] Far more familiar and general than any christological affirmation, this address requests a guardian, a male with sufficient authority to expedite a woman's affairs.[155] Jesus would, functionally, be little different from the scribes that organised the affairs of widows (*cf* Mk 12:40), or the various guardians relied upon by Babatha or the

152. The ownership is accented by ἑαυτῆς in some manuscripts (א Θ 33 579).

153. Kinukawa reads the action and the word against each other: *Women and Jesus,* 54, 58, 60–61.

154. Compare *P Ent* 22 for just such a request for a κύριος. Such a dependency line is still alive and well, as in the interpretation of the Syrophoenician woman's response by Robert Gundry, *Mark*, 374.

155. Thus Joanne Dewey's imaginative re-telling of the story, refers to Jesus as a potential patron: 'From Story-telling to Written Text', 72.

majority of other women found in extant papyri.

With a κύριος, the basis is laid for allocating to the woman an acceptable deviancy—that is, a warrant for her prior action is provided because it is an action *in extremis*. It is like the young women and their mothers who risked their reputations for the sake of the temple (3 Macc 1:18) or Plutarch's examples in his *The Bravery of Women*.[156] In these, a woman's use of her body is determined by her procreative symbolism, that is, her ability to ensure the survival (territorial, racial and familial) of the male. The defence of her honour is tied to the defence of father, husband, family and state. Sarah Pomeroy commented: 'Self-sacrifice or martyrdom is the standard way for a woman to achieve renown among men . . .'[157]

From this perspective, Jesus provides a temporary embedding for the imperilled woman. His honour is enhanced because he has provided the guardianship that heals the daughter—restoring the family. It also undergirds his authority to tell her to go away, which is executed by her returning to the acceptable, familial confines of woman—the home.

The focus at this level therefore shifts to the desperation of the woman for her daughter's healing. Whatever suspicion may attach to her character is suspended or muted in the light of the exemplary concern for her daughter. The woman's procreative ambiguity is at least compensated by the depth of her maternal distress (as in 1 Kgs 3:16–27). This type of story is common in male texts. Of course, the emotional state of women that frequently drives their actions meant that they would nevertheless be characterised as irrational.[158]

For the woman's body to become an agent of honour, her words are preferably sidelined. As Plutarch sententiously stated 'It is right and proper to admire both the silence and the courage of women.'[159] The body must be dedicated to the service of the order of society; if she is to speak at all, that word must take on the construction of 'manliness'. The potential fissure of the woman's body here confronts the familiar ethological construction of the survival of the (male?) species.[160]

156. Plut *Mor* 242e–263c.
157. Pomeroy, *Goddesses, Whores*, 109.
158. Thus Plato equates women's and animals' search for health (*Thea* 171c).
159. Plut *Mor* 247a; *cf* 252a.
160. Noteworthy in the story of the two prostitutes before Solomon is the competition for an heir, and the sex of the infant—a son (1 Kgs 3: 19–22).

This brief survey of the body of the woman in the ancient world, shows the difficulties in appropriating the 'fissure' of a woman's body, certainly as a support for her speech. A woman might be held to be honourable if the use of her body fulfilled conventional values—a temporary and carefully sheltered outbreak making stronger the hold of the conventional. Almost always, this honourable positioning of the body required the abdication of a voice.

The web of stereotyped definition of the Syrophoenician woman in Mark's story, however, resists the efforts to constrain the ambiguities associated with her body, in spite of the accolade for her word. The male guardianship is temporary—a brief moment at most in the story. She returns, unaccompanied, to her daughter in her (own) home.[161]

Moreover, the ascription of λόγος by Jesus actually subverts this attention to the body of the woman. Any valorisation of the woman's body must therefore be asserted in consciousness of a resistance to the text as well, at least to this point in the narrative. It cannot readily be won by recourse to ancient texts honouring women's actions, for the woman in her body becomes subjected to the same erasure as the woman in her speech, that is, her body becomes 'manly' in the extreme moment and is then bounded in the 'deliverance'.[162]

Accordingly, one must be as careful in the focus on the woman's body as on her word. An accent on the 'distressed mother' easily devolves into an endorsement of the ethologically grounded commitments of patriarchy. Nevertheless, the difficulties of interpretation actually testify to the resistance of the body of the text and of the woman in it to conventional confinement.

The body of a courtesan

The body of the whore is a more threatening breach of the boundaries of society. As Phyllis Bird asserts, 'A fundamental and universal feature of the institution of prostitution wherever it is found is an attitude of ambivalence.'[163] Prostitutes were confined to liminal areas both in euphemistic description and in reality. Even when a courtesan or a common prostitute gained a morsel of approbation for her speech, her body remained strongly contested. She was still noted as a courtesan—her speech was both incidental to and confirmatory of

161. Some distance is conveyed in v 30 by the expression ἀπελθοῦσα εἰς τὸν οἶκον αὐτῆς.

162. Luz noted a medieval exegete, Albertus Magnus, who adduced masculine virtues from the woman's behaviour: *Matthew 8–20*, 337.

163. Bird, 'Harlot as Heroine', 121.

her designation. Thus, ancient sex manuals inscribe 'the notion that as women's nature is sexual, so are their attempts at learning.'[164] Her body, carved in the framework of desire and detestation, lay at the boundaries of society (symbolically and, frequently, architecturally).[165] Lucian's personification of oratory as a courtesan, or rather a 'woman' who plays the courtesan, describes her peeping from the roof and slyly opening windows.[166]

The threat to species survival was factored around the prostitute. Indeed, the brothel-keeper was called a 'mongrel' (κυναλώπηξ).[167] The harlot's indiscrete and indiscriminate (indeed egalitarian) mingling of male seed, her consequent ineligibility for familial and genealogical regularity, her oft-times foreign origins, all conspired to make her as dangerous as she could be desirable.[168]

The unaccompanied woman in a city street would be assumed to be a slave or prostitute or both, even for a task as simple as collecting water; she was a body on display.[169] Travel might make a man wise and honoured.[170] But a woman travelling beyond the boundaries of village or city would, in the absence of other markers, be suspected of being a fugitive, even if, from her viewpoint, escape were warranted.[171] Moreover, a travelling woman was presumed a threat to a town's security. The alien woman was dangerous precisely because she was permeable—she provided access to destructive elements.

The exemplary stories of prostitutes and slaves who remained faithful to their owner-households have a more important function than another encomium of women.[172] Rather, they are extolled because

164. HN Parker, 'Love's Body Anatomized: The Ancient Erotic Handbooks and the Rhetoric of Sexuality', in Richlin, *Pornography and Representation*, 106.

165. Rahab's house lay in walls of Jericho's city perimeter (Josh 2:15); see generally Laurence, *Roman Pompeii*, 70–78.

166. Luc *Bis* 30.

167. Lilja, *Dogs*, 77.

168. For the powerful construction of these associations in the first century, see Stowers, *A Rereading of Romans*, 53, 271–272.

169. Plaut *Rud*. Visiting a well was fraught with danger for a woman; an honourable woman would always be accompanied when gathering water (*cf* Jn 4:6–7,16–18).

170. For example, Luc *Scy* 5; *cf* Sir 34:9–11, 39:4. On the significance of travel, see S Lewis, *News and Society in the Greek Polis* (London: Duckworth Press, 1996), 27–31.

171. See the various reasons adduced for (female) slave runaways in *NDIEC* 8.36-40.

172. See, for example, Athen *Deip* 573e, 591c, 594b–c, 596e–f.

their new household/workplace has become the parameters of their world (*cf* Tit 2:9–10). Old ties have been eradicated and new loyalties established. Rahab provides the classic example of fidelity in biblical literature,[173] though, to her city, her treachery is typical of the whore. Even after her faithful confession (Josh 2:9–11), and subsequent preservation (6:17, 25), the suspicion remains: her dwelling is 'outside the camp of Israel'—status, threat and occupation are located together.[174]

The body of the courtesan therefore retains an openness of access to that which is other, even when her words carry wisdom or faith. Whereas a legitimating 'emergency' provides a glimpse and short foray into subjectivity for an honourable woman, for the woman who is described as shameless, her subjectivity may prove more extensive, precisely *because* of her transgression of male honorific frames.[175] Her self-interpretative frame may be quite different,[176] and resist the separation of body and speech.

Conclusion

The word of the Syrophoenician woman is a powerful word, perhaps more powerful than has previously been allowed. Yet, in the effort to affirm the woman by reference to 'this word', recent scholarship has, in the end, merely performed a variation on a theme of logocentricity. As Claudia Camp demurs: 'the power that might transform a world also helps to support its present form.'[177] Logocentricity has been the dominant ideology of modern critical scholarship. Whilst some

173. Josh 2, Hbs 11:31, Jam 2:25, 1 Clem 12, *cf* Athen *Deip* 572e–f.

174. Josh 6:23.

175. Without denying the sanctioned abuse and oppression often accompanying prostitution then (as now), such do not disqualify a woman's initiative or resistant construction of the world: see Brock and Thistlethwaite, *Casting Stones*, 226–227, 256–257. Kathleen Corley's study of manumission rates noticed the role of prostitution in building sufficient funds to win not only one's own manumission but that of one's mother or daughter: *Private Women*, 49–52.

176. Compare the wife of Coponius who slept with Mark Antony in order to purchase her husband's safety. Appian's remark indicates the male frame of reference adopted by one with the power of textualising: she 'thus cured one evil with another' (*Bell Civ* 4.40).

177. CV Camp, 'Wise and Strange: An Interpretation of the Female Imagery in Proverbs in Light of Trickster Mythology', in *Semeia* 42 (1988): 33.

have dared to extract the woman's 'word' from Jesus' affirmation, the ground of classification itself has not been challenged.

However, a number of fissures in the dominance of logocentricity have been identified, beginning with the very attention that logocentric industry invests in that which is 'other' to its commitments. The dualisms grounded in ethological comparison are potentially shaken by a participation of the woman in *logos*, the moreso if the choice for 'this word' implies a rejection of the saying of Jesus. *Logos* may appear as a shared activity rather than a privileged site.

The naming of the woman's saying as *logos*, for all its male derivation, has highlighted the psychagogic elements of communication. These elements presuppose a communicating agency—embodiment is needed in order to give life to the word. Textuality as an attempted totality and totalising of word ends up defeating the word, robbing it of the life of vocalisation—an inherently *bodily* function.[178] The body communicates; word is not enough. The embodiment given to the word of a woman and the movement, gesturing, and performance that have created the space for the embodied word to communicate have helped both to problematise the supremacy of the word and to suggest a possible reconfiguration.

It is a move fraught with danger because these fissures depend upon and exploit ambiguities. In the ancient world, ambiguity was especially located in woman (as a reinforcing logocentric construction). And such ambiguities inspired huge investment in overcoming them. The familiar ethological concerns—survival of the species, preservation of territory and so on—loom large even with (because of?) the efforts to decentre the word. Certainly, when v 30 is read as something of an afterthought, a silent child who is nothing more than a passive confirmation of the power of (usually) Jesus' last words to her mother, then the power of those ethological concerns has triumphed. However, the challenge to the narrative by the woman's word authorises a move to envisage something more than word. Such a move exploits the fissures identified in these chapters. But it must heed the warnings about the dangers of reinscribing attitudes that threaten the potential unlocked by the Syrophoenician woman. Those dangers are the erasure of the woman through the accent on the word on the one hand and the reifying or essentialising of the body (as female) over against word.[179]

178. So Montiglio, *Silence in the Land of Logos*, 93–97.

179. Sayers, *Biological Politics*, 3.

7

The Power of a Dog
The Syrophenician's Daughter

Setting the final scene

We have confronted a series of ambiguities involved in the assessment of the word of the Syrophoenician woman. The authorial highlighting of the saying structurally and grammatically in the pericope is matched by the valorisation of that word by the key figure of the Markan gospel, the man Jesus. This apparent complicity of author, narrator and hero has in the very act of exaltation of the word threatened to swamp with petals of triumph any visibility of the woman herself. Any removal of the woman's presence and her connection with the achievement of 'this word' generates a suspicion that there has been no real change in a logocentric universe. The dimorphic inequalities of gender, justified by reference to the animal world, survive in spite of (because of?) the recognition of ambiguities. The metonymy of dog for woman remains.

We have explored some strategies to reconfigure the word of the woman by reference to the totality of her embodied action. Instead of servility to a logocentricism that has supported the narrator's stereotypical judgement of the Syrophoenician, a possibility has been raised that *word* might be (re-)connected with body and so lose its dematerialised hegemony. The attention to such fissures has proved fruitful, but has had to combat the last words of Jesus, and the fragility of an affirmation of the worth of the woman's bodily presence and activity in initiating the exchange. The word that acclaimed word has been recognised for its menace to the integrity of the woman's act and material identity. Embroiled in that threat is the text itself, albeit not without challenge from the Syrophoenician (which is also manufactured, or at least transmitted textually).

Subsequent readers have blanketed the liberationist impulse identified within the text. On one side, longer-term, there has been the (often successful) attempt to patch the disturbing cracks that threaten the ethologically justified closure of the woman's significance. On the other, there has been the attempt to pedestal her accomplishment for the gentile mission in her own era and for contemporary feminist emergence from the zoning of women inherited from that era. As has been argued, both have privileged *logos*; consequently, regardless of intention, both threaten whatever transformation of perspective and relationship may be sought from the text.

This is where the final verse of the Syrophoenician pericope is so important. The sheer silence of speech in the last verse is crucial to the enterprise of unleashing the potential in the fissures exposed in the story of the Syrophoenician woman. The verse must be rescued from centuries of neglect.

It will mean that the dominance of the logocentric approach to the whole passage must be negotiated and repudiated. In particular, it will be forced to confront the absence of Jesus in a final scene, such that the primary relationship is not one in which Jesus, the declarer of *logos*, figures. Hence, the fragments of evidence in the ancient world dealing with the relationship of mother and daughter will need to engage the Syrophoenician woman and her daughter. And an openness to new grammatical approaches, broader semantics, and conceptualisations will be needed, at least to test whether a coherent alternate reading is possible. In what follows, the fundamental challenge to Jesus' assessment, the liberating fulfilment of the woman's aspirations, and the fracture of the ethologically justified hierarchies will be sought in the one who has dominated the entire pericope—the Syrophoenician's daughter.

The silence/ing of word

We have noted already that the power of the dialogue between Jesus and the Syrophoenician woman lies, *inter alia*, in the performance of the words. The *recognition* of a proverb is a key ingredient of its persuasiveness. And this recognition is factored according to elements of traditional referentiality. The structure, sound and rhythm of the words that make up the lineal progression of terms are the *primary* communication, more forceful than the proposition that may be contained therein. In this sense, performance is far more than the recall of words; the manner, tone and pace of delivery combined with the invitation contained in the compositional elements are not reducible to a manual of instructions that can replace the performer (or even the audience). Not just language is important, but the *embodiment* of language.

The word needs embodiment not merely as its consequence but

as its foundation and activator. In this sense, it is not merely that the word relies upon a reader for its life.[1] The word comes as an *after-word* of material and active reality. The dialogue between the woman and Jesus is fired into action in Mark's narrative only because of the woman's bodily initiative.[2]

Whether intentional or not, Mark subverts the power of the word surreptitiously from the beginning. The irony of a joust of words is that the primary function of word, the act/art of naming,[3] is undermined *by the refusal to give a name to the woman or her daughter*.[4] That irony can now be recognised in the sustained description of the woman in v.26. Whenever such attention is given to ethnic and geographic origins in the ancient world, it comes as a means of elucidating the name of a person. Here, the 'triple outsider' who is constrained by that master-frame of reference,[5] yet escapes the final pinning. The unknown woman is juxtaposed *against* the effort to categorise her. The namelessness is dangerous, precisely because it fails to heed the confinement and socialisation, the fixity that naming enforces:

> . . . language is not an element for processes of communication, but rather a determining *habitat*, a *natural oikumene* or common house of geographically reduced and naturalised realities.[6]

Language as the act/art of naming is therefore a necessary adjunct of ethological pronouncement and enforcement, bearing within itself its own naturalising function and tendency. Language in this sense is the sonorous front to a fist of coercion cocked behind it, recognised in spite of the rhetorical veil of a bestial metaphor. Silence may be the

---

1. J Svenbro, *Phrasikleia: An Anthropology of Reading in Ancient Greece* translated by J Lloyd (Ithaca and London: Cornell University Press, 1993), 84–86.
2. Compare the stories of women's performances which are then given explanation, for example Hdt *Hist* 3.34.
3. Svenbro, *Phrasikleia*, 64–65.
4. This contends with the desire to confer an identity and visibility on the woman by the effort to name her. The adoption of the Pseudo-Clementine 'Justa' as the name of the woman must be placed in the context of that writing's overall success in circumscribing the woman as 'righteous'.
5. Schüssler Fiorenza, *Sharing Her Word*, 122, 124.
6. M Althaus-Reid, *Indecent Theology: Theological Perversions in Sex, Gender and Politics* (London/New York: Routledge, 2000), 107.

acquiescent response to the deposition of moral judgement, expected of a woman. It may, by contrast, be the level of resistance/necessity that brokers bare survival. And it may also be a means to open up further possibilities.[7]

i) The silence/ing of the child

The fragility of children's lives in the ancient world is proffered as the reason for the protective adult discipline that enjoins silence. Only when maturity forms, and is revealed through the articulation of appropriate language mimetic of a child's (own) containment, does this change. This is why the learning of 'universal wisdom' in the form of proverbs, maxims and fables (all categorised as λογοί) is viewed as an agent and sign of the necessary development into proper boundedness.[8]

Until then, a child is regarded as ἄλογον, like the animals—that is, without reason, without language, the one proving the other.[9] Accordingly, the search for the speech of children in the New Testament is a far more difficult affair than the search for women's voices.[10] Only the prodigy can speak and be heard as offering a word

---

7. SL Graham, 'Silent Voices: Women in the Gospel of Mark', in *Semeia* 54 (1991): 147. She goes on, in reliance upon Susan Sontag, to claim silence as a form of speech. If this means a form of communication then performantial dynamics agree; if however silence is defined only in terms of language, then no challenge to logocentricity ultimately is made.
8. It is not without reason that Luke comments on Jesus' increase in wisdom and stature after the incident of sagacious, logocentric engagement (Lk 2:50–52).
9. Wiedemann, *Adults and Children*, 17–25.
10. In the entire New Testament, children are identified as speaking but ten times, (twelve times if the slave-girls in Acts 12:14–15, 16:17 are understood to be children): seven times in direct speech (Mt 11:17, 14:8, 21:15, Mk 6:24, 25, Lk 2:49, 7:31–32), thrice in indirect speech (Mt 7:9–10, Lk 2:46–47, 11:11; *cf* Acts 12:14–15). Even so, there are three sets of parallels in these figures (Mt 7:9–10//Lk 11:11, Mt 11:17// Lk 7:31–32, Mk 6:25//Mt14:8). In a parallel instance, a child (a girl) is the mouthpiece of an adult (Mt 14:8//Mk 6:25); in another two instances, children are the mouthpiece of some higher authority (Mt 21:16: Jesus comments on the praise of children contained in the previous verse, quoting Psalm 8:3 LXX; Acts 16:17). To give this some comparison, Jane Schaberg reported that, in Luke's Gospel, women speak fifteen times, ten in direct speech, and this to contrast with the 'din of male voices': 'Luke', in Newsom and Ringe, *Women's Bible Commentary*, 280.

that is valued—because it is unexpected.[11] Anything else that might be heard is dismissed as idle street chatter.

A cry of protest must be delivered against the silencing by the domination of the (textualised) word. However, the necessary retrieval of children's voices must be accompanied by a questioning of the justice of a decision that demands that children's worth be graded by their (retrieved) articulation.

ii) Silence as participant in word

Silence may itself be reconfigured as a political stance.[12] It can express its own rejection of the words that have been outpoured (*cf* Mk 15:5), a passive resistance to a threatened, verbally-justified intrusion[13] or a refusal to divulge.[14] Silence can be its own form of abuse, a disdain for discourse that lies beneath the station of a person to enter (so perhaps Mt 15:23a) or a weapon of contempt.

Silence may also be a compliment to the succession of words:[15] a hiatus, a poetic sense-pause, an underscoring of words, or a tacit (!) invitation to an audience to supply what has been left unsaid.[16] 'Silence, both as a "moral" behaviour in the background of one's speech and as a choice within the speech itself, emphasizes the importance of that which will be said.'[17] In Mark's Gospel there is no greater demonstration of the importance of silence than its 'premature' ending (16:8).

Such a silence is little more than an accompaniment to words and inseparable from them. Silence in this sense is itself logocentric. But this is not the silence of the untrained child.

---

11. Lk 2:47–48, Jos *Vit* 2.8–9.
12. *Cf* Plut *Mor* 249e-f.
13. Helen King suggested this as a reading of the ailing woman who pitted her silence against the invasive words and therapies of doctors: 'Self-help, self-knowledge: in search of the patient in Hippocratic gynaecology', in Hawley and Levick, *Women in Antiquity*, 136–137.
14. The courtesan Leaena died under torture of the agents of the tyrant Hippias without revealing her lover's whereabouts: Athen *Deip* 596f.
15. Cic *Orat* 3.181, 185–186.
16. There is a clear instance of this usage in Mk 9:12, 13 (*cf* 14:21), where a double reference to the citation formula 'as it is written' is followed by silence. The unfolding of Scriptural warrant, perhaps in the manner of Mk 1:2–3, 7:6, 11:17, 14:27, is the expectation/invitation thrown to the audience.
17. Montiglio, *Silence in the Land of Logos*, 127.

iii) Silence as accompaniment to body

There is a silence that redirects attention away from itself to another medium of communication and relationship, namely the body. The body not only can articulate ('embody') the word;[18] it can also assert that it is more than a mere servant for a dominant *logos*.

This silence respects that the body can be its own communicating and communicable medium.[19] The silencing of the word releases 'the material bodily principle'.[20] Hence the supposed prime realm of the animal, in which women and children were asserted to dwell *by nature*, is yet able to communicate, without recourse to the asserted centre of the universe. In so doing, it dissolves the solidity of the unified, uniform and universal *logos* as the only source of communication and relationship, and in that act fractures the dimorphism that would associate the female with body and the male with reason as an essential characterisation.

Verse 30 therefore has far greater importance than traditionally conceded. The fact that no words are spoken has diminished the importance of the verse for those who are predisposed to concur with ancient (and enlightenment) hegemonic values.[21] The accent upon action, upon the movement, gesture and positioning of bodies, may point to a level of communication that has to be fathomed beyond the hold of exclusive, logocentric thought. The absence of word makes possible a different concentration. The silence/ing of language, shared with the animal (though not demanded to be identical), opens a possibility for discovery, albeit accessed through Mark's read text.

Recovering the significance of the final verse

The final verse of the Markan pericope has received such negligible attention in commentary that it appears to function as an anti-climax rather than the apex of the pericope:

18. This is not the same as the use of the notion of 'embodiment' as the ethical expression and test of the word, important as that political examination of rhetoric is.
19. See E Tamez, 'Women's Lives as Sacred Text', in Kwok, P-l. and E Schüssler Fiorenza (editors), *Women's Sacred Scriptures* (Maryknoll, NY: Orbis, 1998), 63.
20. Patterson, *Fables of Power*, 11–12, following the thought of Mikhail Bakhtin.
21. *Cf* LC McGaughey, 'Words before Deeds; Why Start with the Sayings', in *Forum* (ns) 1.2 (1998): 387–398.

Καὶ ἀπελθοῦσα εἰς τὸν οἶκον αὐτῆς
εὗρεν τὸ παιδίον βεβλημένον ἐπὶ τὴν κλίνην
καὶ τὸ δαιμόνιον ἐξεληλυθός

Traditionally, these lines have been interpreted as confirmation that the exorcism has been successful, the necessary testimony to a miracle account. However, with such attention given to the exchange of words between Jesus and the child's mother, the verse has sometimes appeared superfluous. Their clash of wisdom seems to be resolved with Jesus' words in v 29, in completion also of the miracle form.

Petr Pokorný averred that 'on the surface of the story, the healing of the little daughter may appear as an anticlimax, a relapse . . .'[22] Barry Blackburn indeed, was happy to eradicate this verse altogether as irrelevant.[23] Jeffrey Staley does not see the daughter in the story functioning as a character at all.[24] The more subtle division of the passage to include v 31 further marginalises v 30, by making Jesus the beginning and the end of the encounter: 'and he returned from the region of Tyre . . .'[25] All this stands against the comparative evidence that 'the demon, the sick person and the miracle-worker are

22. Pokorný, 'Puppy', 335. He went on to qualify this by acknowledging that the healing reality 'becomes a metaphor of a still deeper reality', thus dissipating the child into a cipher of the gentile mission.
23. Blackburn, *Theios Anêr*, 222–223.
24. JL Staley, 'Changing Woman: Postcolonial Reflections on Acts 16: 6-40', in *JSNT* 73 (1999): 127n36. Elizabeth Malbon accords the mother the status of 'minor character' but the daughter escapes any classification: 'The Major Importance of the Minor Characters in Mark', in ES Malbon and EV McKnight (editors), *The New Literary Criticism and the New Testament* (Sheffield: JSOT Press, 1994), 60, 65. Elsewhere she sees the two healed daughters in Mark's gospel as showing that Jesus did not restrict his healing to one sex, but they 'contribute little else to the narrative': 'Fallible Followers: Women and Men in the Gospel of Mark', in *Semeia* 28 (1983): 34.
25. Burkill, *New Light*, 60, G Downing, 'The Woman from Syrophoenicia and Her Doggedness: Mark 7:24–31 (Matthew 15:21–28)', in GJ Brooke (editor), *Woman in the Biblical Tradition* (Lewiston: Edwin Mellen, 1992), 129–149, J-P Michaud and PT D'Aviau, 'Jésus Au-Delà Des Frontières de Tyr . . . Analyse de Marc 7,24–31', in A Chené *et al* (editors), *De Jésus Et Des Femmes: Lectures sémiotiques: Suivies d'un Entretien avec AJ Greimas* (Montreal and Paris: Editions Bellarmin, 1987), 37–39. The last allow that this verse functions as a 'sanction pragmatique sur le programme de la femme' (54). But this confers no identity to the child but fashions the child's function solely in terms of a proof of the mother—a re-inscription of ancient values!

"normally" principal actors'[26] If the child is no character at all, this lack of conformity at least could invite comment.

Pokorný did recognise that the final verse is really the ultimate link in a chain of control held by a hitherto invisible anchor: 'the absent and passive actant who still caused all the actions and statements.'[27] The 'child' is mentioned in a wide permutation of terms and influence throughout the pericope:

Verse	Term
25	θυγατρίον
26	θυγάτηρ
27	τεκνον
28	παιδίον
29	θυγατήρ
30	παιδίον

The semantic field is broad. Such a conglomerate is rarely found, although the longer pericope of Jairus' daughter is comparable,[28] as is Plutarch's story of *Micca and Megisto*.[29] Stylistically, the avoidance of repetition of the same word is commendable but the broad range draws in a sense of relatedness with children of different types. It expands the field of application of the story.

The final verse at last brings to centre stage the one who has controlled the direction of the engagement between Jesus and the Syrophoenician woman. Until v 30, the child has acted as the initiating and effective cause of the action and responses of the two players. The public movement of the woman, her breach of the boundaries of the house, her request and confrontation of Jesus, and Jesus' two responses are all centred upon the one who dwells off-stage.[30]

26. Theissen, *Miracle Stories*, 114.
27. Pokorný, 'Puppy', 337.
28. It contains κοράσιον but not τέκνον. Κοράσιον is common as a word used for slave-girls and dancing-girls: see the editors' comments to *P Oslo* 3.140 (*cf P Strasb* 1.79, 913, *P Lond* 2.331). This has particular relevance to Mark 6:14–29.
29. Plut *Mor* 252c-d, which has ἀπιδαρίον, παιδίον, τέκνον, νήπιον, παῖς, παρθένος, θυγατήρ.
30. It is similar to Euripides' *Children of Herakles*, where children are on stage guiding the entire performance yet without contributing one word. More pertinently, there is the myth of Demeter and Kore, where Demeter conducts most of the action and dialogue, but all is focussed on the hidden daughter: see C Kerényi, *Eleusis: Archetypal Image of Mother and Daughter* translated by R Manheim (Princeton, NJ: Princeton University Press, 1967), 26–33.

In fact, when the syntactical relations of child/daughter in the pericope are examined, *every* instance ties the woman to the child. Even Jesus' first response calls on *her* to let the *children* be fed (ἄφες Mk 7:28). Hence, throughout the passage, even though her daughter remains 'hidden', the woman acts and speaks from her relationship to the child *not* from a relationship to Jesus, actual or desired.[31]

The relationship of a woman and her daughter devoid of any (permanent) male 'head' dominates this pericope. Their alliance begins and ends the drama of the story. The encounter with the man Jesus exposes the lack of compassion inherent in rigid classifications, especially as they are deployed upon and about a woman's body. The woman's words (alone) are recognised by Jesus as the release of the daughter's body, necessary and efficacious, though still exposed to the boundaries of a male construction of *logos*. The restoration of the Syrophoenician to her daughter in v 30 does not trumpet the thrust of a colonising Jesus-phalanx into Gentile territory. Nor does it permit the continued colonisation of the woman's body inscribed by the dominant *logos*. Rather, the text offers another possible reading: the capacity of the mother-daughter relationship to control its own destiny[32] and their respective destinies within a relationship that contributes both *logos* and body.

As such, the story subverts the foundational tenet of ethology: dimorphism—that is, the unequal dyad of male and female that is said to lie at the heart of human life and society. Not only has the 'animal' spoken *logos* but this dog has paired with its own gendered kind. 'Ancient proverbial wisdom' that pronounced judgement on the 'dog' in terms of its promiscuity, greed, thieving and deception is repudiated. Initiative rather than passivity, concern for the female rather than the male, assertion of subjectivity in one's body rather than objectification by another's mind, are configured in a relationship between two women.

The finale to the pericope climaxes with a structural acknowledgement of the central role of the child in the *discovery* by the Syrophoenician woman: the indicative verb governing the entire

---

31. If the woman or daughter is a slave (which would place them at the lower end of prostitution) this relationship has no legal standing, as slave children were the property of the owner: see *PSI* 8.903.

32. *Cf* Kinukawa, *Women and Jesus*, 59, Guardiola-Sáenz, 'Borderless Women', 78–79, who, whilst not granting significance to the daughter, have seen the *relationship* of mother and daughter as critical.

sentence is focussed on the child: εὗρεν τὸ παιδίον.[33] Moreover, the finding is positioned at the centre of a group of three clauses, and acts as the syntactic hold on its dependent members. What had previously been veiled is now disclosed—the child is the centre, and in the final verse, as we shall see, she becomes an active participant in a new beginning to the story. Not only so, but she becomes the new vantage-point to (re)interpret the entire pericope. Having begun with Jesus, the pericope ends with the woman and her daughter. This is not to be robbed by drawing v 31 to close off the passage. Καὶ . . . πάλιν in Mark clearly indicates a break to a new passage rather than the formal conclusion of a previous one.[34]

Ross Kraemer observes that the condition of a woman without the respectability of a husband and as the mother only of a daughter would 'sometimes [be] so lamented in the ancient world that people who only had daughters were considered childless'.[35] The 'sometimes' ameliorates the extremity of her assertion. But her comment does draw attention to the striking relationship between the Syrophoenician and her daughter, given that it occupies the prize position as the 'last word' of the pericope, and that without Jesus. The importance of a child as the site for the ethologically justified inscription of dimorphic hierarchies[36] makes the absence of the male at the conclusion of the story highly destabilising of expectations.[37] Consequently, some assessment of the relationship between the mother and her daughter is invited.

The relationship of mother and daughter

Ties between mother and daughter in the ancient world have not received a great deal of attention even under a feminist gaze. In part,

33. The 'finding of the child' may be an ancient literary motif. Some manuscripts have the magi 'finding the child' rather than 'seeing' him in Mt 2:11 (474 892 it [b c f ff1 g1 aur] vg Basil Chrys Aug); *cf* Menand *Epit* 294, Long *Daph* 1.7, Eustath *Comm Od* 2.1123.)
34. So 2:1, 13, 3:1, 20, 4:1, 5:21, 7:14, 10:1, 11:27. Some doubt attends 8:13 and 10:32.
35. Kraemer, *Her Share*, 133; see also Ringe, 'Gentile Woman's Story', 70.
36. Laslett *et al*, *Gender and Scientific Authority*, 'Introduction', 13; see Janet Sayers' criticism of the deposition of biological universalism on particularist human relations: *Biological Politics*, 60.
37. One wonders whether this has anything to do with the loss of interest in the verse by substantially male commentary.

this is because the extant sources are so sparse, whether Jewish or Greco-Roman.[38] Moreover, daughters were usually named and known in non-literary and literary materials by reference to the significant male (father, brother or husband)[39] including, at times, the adoption of a feminine form of the father's own name.[40] Certainly the young girl in Mark 5 is known primarily as Jairus' daughter (vv 23, 35).[41] The anonymous mother is revealed only towards the end of the story (v 40) and only, it would seem, because the scene has transferred from the public encounters outside (in)to the bounded space of the household.

The Syrophoenician and her daughter are quite different. The complete anonymity of mother and daughter,[42] the absence of reference to a male, the transgression of space so that the daughter's parent asserts a place in both public and private spheres, all point to a daughter who is without the conventionally sanctioned embedding.[43] Moreover, the absence of reference to other figures—neighbours (as in Mk 5:35, 38), servants (Jn 4:51), family members (Jn 11:28–30), a great crowd (Mk 7:37, Lk 7:11, 16)—when they could readily perform a heightening or confirmatory role in the miracle story[44], brings the relationship of mother and daughter into sharp focus.[45] Indeed, as Halvor Moxnes observed, the appearance of mother and daughter as an axis of story is

38. Kraemer, 'Jewish Mothers', 89, 91.

39. A fulsome male connection for one Asklepias is found in *P Wisc* 14—she has a father, guardian and husband all named. By contrast, the generic importance of the male is clear in *P Oxy* 1.91, where a scribe, too lazy to stop for the father's name, nevertheless writes χρηματίζουσαν ἐξ οὗ.

40. Ilan, *Women*, 53–54, Allason-Jones, *Women in Roman Britain*, 28.

41. Even verse 40 has τὸν πατέρα τοῦ παιδίου καὶ τὴν μητέρα.

42. The anonymity of women in ancient literature is much debated: see Corley, 'Really Prostitutes?', 500, Tolbert, *Sowing the Gospel*, 293, DM Schaps, 'The Woman Least Mentioned: Etiquette and Women's Names', in *CQ* 27 (1977): 323–330. Here, anonymity is combined with a lack of male embedding. This was not respectful of person or preserving of status, unlike an unnamed woman known by reference to her father, husband, son or brother: see T Vestergaard, L Bjertrup, MH Hansen, TH Nielsen, L Rubinstein, 'A Typology of the Women Recorded on Gravestones from Attica', in *AJAH* 10 (1985): 179.

43. Tolbert, 'Mark', 264, Ringe, 'Gentile Woman's Story', 70. If the Syrophoenician was a slave, then the daughter would be required not to be named by reference to a father; this applied even should freed status be acquired: M d'Angelo, 'Women Partners in the New Testament', in *JFSR* 6 (1990): 68–69.

44. Theissen, *Miracle Stories*, 71–72.

45. There may be some economic implications involved here, namely, that the likelihood was that the 'nucleated' unit was at the lower end of

rare in the ancient world.[46]

Assessing the evidence of mother-daughter relationships

Non-literary evidence yields but little of mother-daughter relationships such as might give us some material, some context, for interpreting the importance and nature of the relationship between the Syrophoenician woman and her daughter. Certainly, one of the few sources of actual relationships, the Babatha papers, shows a daughter enjoying a greater bonding with her step-mother than her mother, Miriam, both older women being the wives of one Judah. The apparent friendship and support between Babatha and her step-daughter Shelamzion[47] is fraught with interpretative problems however and too much cannot be made of it.[48] By contrast, the instance of a Greek woman journeying to 'Libya' to gather her dead daughter for burial in her homeland points to strong ties, even allowing that death demands honorific displays.[49]

The paucity of material has lead a number of commentators on the mother-daughter relationship to speculate about the socio-cultural structures that predispose a woman to have closer relationships with her son(s). Ross Kraemer suggested that the significant difference in age of marriage between daughters (twelve to eighteen years) and sons (twenty-eight to thirty-five years)[50] contributed to a stronger

---

resource control (*cf* Lk 7:11–17): see Guijarro, 'Family in First-Century Galilee', 58–61.

46. Noted in his, 'What is Family?', in Moxnes, *Constructing Families*, 33. One notable exception is the story of Demeter and Kore.
47. Both Babatha and Shelamzion were only daughters, according to Y Yadin, *Bar Kokhba: Rediscovery of the Legendary Hero of the Second Jewish Revolt Against Rome* (London: Weidenfeld & Nicholson, 1971), 233.
48. However, the structural comparison between this historical example and the legendary account of Thecla is noteworthy. Thecla's rift with her own mother over the fracturing of the daughter's conventional route to marriage is compensated by Thecla's bonding with another older woman, Tryphaena: see SJ Davis, *Cult of Saint Thecla: a tradition of women's piety in late antiquity* (Oxford/New York: Oxford University Press, 2001), 17, 21.
49. The epitaph is recorded by Lefkowitz and Fant §333; *cf* also the Jewish epitaph recording three generations of women without reference to a man (*CIJ* 1007); so also a dedication to Hera (*GA* 6.265). There is a Jewish epitaph (in Greek) to Karteria, erected by her daughter Zenobia, which may indicate a return to the homeland, even as it also seeks honour for honouring the dead: *BS* 2.183.3–4.
50. These figures are for the élite class.

bond between mothers and sons.[51] She aligned this with Mieke Bal's observation that mothers are notably absent from stories of abuse of daughters in the Hebrew Scriptures. In other words, mothers in a patriarchal society, even those in a position to manipulate some advantage for themselves (as, for example, in the story of Herodias and her daughter in Mark 6:14–29), are significantly disempowered.[52] The result is an enforced if not psychological passivity in relation to their offspring, and most particularly, their daughters.[53] Even so, the bond between mothers and daughters was sufficiently strong to be identified in the fracturing potential of the early Jesus' movement (Q 12:53).

Texts, non-literary materials and inscriptions, notably epitaphs, reveal the generally agreed nature and function of the relationship between mothers and daughters. Of foremost concern was the arrangement of marriage for the daughter. This certainly is Justa's concern in the *Pseudo-Clementine* retelling of the story of the Syrophoenician woman. After the healing of Berenice, she 'gave her daughter in marriage to a certain man who was attached to the true faith, and who was poor.'[54] Marriage provided the necessary embedding of a woman, giving protection and safeguarding honour for family and individual alike.[55] Of grievous concern was not only the shame of a daughter's sexual proclivities being exercised outside of procreative

51. Kraemer, 'Mothers and Daughters', 105–110. There was also an economic aspect to the relation between mother and son. Sons were responsible for the welfare of parents in their old age (*cf* Mk 7:9–13, Jn 19:26, 27, *Ps-Clem Hom* 12.15, 1 Tim 5:4, 16 [noting, for this last reference, the manuscript variants that accent male responsibility]). Epitaphs combine with literary notices in lamenting the premature deaths of sons since this robbed parents of their hopes and expectations of final honorific care: *CIL* 6.7578, Eurip *Med* 1032; *cf BGU* 2.648.

52. David Konstan notes a mother of a non-citizen girl: the problem of low status was exacerbated to the extent that she was blurred into the figure of a procuress in any efforts to seek the betterment of her daughter: *Sexual Symmetry: Love in the Ancient Novel and Related Genres* (Princeton, NJ: Princeton University Press, 1994), 154–155.

53. M Bal, 'Dealing/With/Women: Daughters in the Book of Judges', in R Schwartz (editor), *The Book and the Text: The Bible and Literary Theory* (Cambridge, MA/Oxford: Blackwell, 1990), 16–39.

54. *Ps-Clem Hom* 2.20. 'Poor' in this text is an honorific title; *cf* 'Ebionites': see JA Fitzmyer, 'The Qumran Scrolls, The Ebionites and Their Literature', in his *Essays on the Semitic Background of the New Testament* (Missoula: SBL/Fortress Press, 1974), 439–440, 476–477.

55. Catul *Poet* 62.36–65.

marriage, but also the anguish of the death of a daughter before she had been wedded.[56] The power of marriage even spawned an image for the death of the unmarried young woman—she was abducted by Hades to be his bride.[57]

Epigraphical, literary and non-literary sources indicate other aspects of the relationship. The daughter was expected to survive the mother (and father), and not merely for economic security—examples of sepulchral grief belie such a reductionism.[58] Mothers appear as the locus of heart-felt love (φιλοστοργία)[59] in the family, which was as much transferred to children (φιλοτεκνία)[60] as to husband (φίλανδρος).[61] This trait was to be perpetuated (and reciprocated) especially in the daughter.[62] Such a transfer was also expected in other fields, notably the womanly trademark of working with wool,[63] the preparation of food and general running of a household,[64] the involvement in religious festivals[65] and laments.[66] More general education in 'letters' may or may not be involved.[67]

Much of this material reflects stereotypical constraints upon the presentation of women and their relationships (*cf* Tit 2:4), even where

---

56. *GA* 7.486, 604, 649, *CIJ* 1509.
57. Wiedemann, *Adults and Children*, 42; *cf* Eurip *Hec* 601–603, *CIJ* 1508, *Sib Or* 3.480 and Ps-Philo *Bib Ant* 40.6 demonstrate the power of the myth in Jewish imagination.
58. *CIL* 2. 3475.
59. See the discussion and examples in *NDIEC* 2.80. The editor (GHR Horsley) notes that the epigraphical usage (unlike a broader field of reference in the papyri) refers 'to the heartfelt love shown by or directed towards a mother or wife' with only one case of such love coming from an infant towards a father (p 102). See also Golden, *Children and Childhood*, 97–98.
60. *SB* 8.10162.525, 535 amongst many examples.
61. See generally Fowler, *Hellenistic Aesthetic*, 92–101.
62. Pl *Ep* 5.16; *cf* Eurip *Erech* fr 358N. Plutarch's story of Megisto's battle with the tyrant Aristotimus includes the exemplary imitation of a mother's suicide by her two daughters: *Mor* 253b-e.
63. *CPJ* 2.442, *P Oxy* 2273; *cf GA* 6.265.
64. Xen *Oecon* 7.16.
65. Menand *Sam* 37–40.
66. See M Alexiou, *The Ritual Lament in Greek Tradition* (Cambridge: Cambridge University Press, 1974), 10–23.
67. The education of daughters was variously connected with mothers and fathers: see Pl *Ep* 1.10 on the Syrian philosopher, Euphrates, and his education of two sons and a daughter; *cf* Cic *Brut* 58.211. On Jewish practice, see Archer, *Beyond Rubies*, 83-101.

the evidence presupposes a private audience.[68] As such, rhetorical expectations govern many presentations.[69] The demand for exultation and reinforcement of virtue carves the remembrance. However, non-literary sources, insofar as there is evidence, testify to a reality proximate to such public pronouncements.

This overview helps us to affirm the importance of the relationship of the Syrophoenician mother and daughter not merely in terms of Mark's story but also in relation to the small amount of evidence yielded from the ancient world. The mother's concern for the well-being of her child, especially given the vulnerability of young (and sometimes older) women to demonic (and other attack), and her distress at the potential demise of a child, even a daughter, cohere with what can be learned from her context. However, the evidence has also highlighted the distinctiveness of the mother-daughter relationship in Mark's gospel. Though propertied, there is no male embedding; nor is there any indication of a desire for male embedding.

In the ancient world, there were very few locations where this marginalisation of the influence of the male occurred. The consignment of lament to women, albeit imbued with views of female hysteria, afforded one position where self-definition was in part possible.[70] The Sapphonic circle of women becomes a typological setting on vases in late Classical and Hellenistic periods and may echo funerary clubs for women.[71]

Two further arenas of mother-daughter relationship did mute the embedding in men though neither is unequivocal.[72] The arenas may

---

68. Thus compare Pl *Ep* 5.16 with the epitaph to the young girl *CIL* 6.16631. The three ages of women: virgin, matron and wise elder are configured even for a twelve to thirteen year old (Pliny's letter overstates the age, at least according to the tomb inscription). They recur in his tribute to a friend's wife married thirty-nine years (*Ep* 6.5). For inscriptional testimony, see *ILS* 1259–1261.

69. Wiedemann, *Adults and Children*, 93.

70. In fact, the political critique that infiltrated some women's laments in Athens led to a ban on women's participation in a role that traditionally was theirs (Plat *Rep* 398e): see McClure, *Spoken Like a Woman*, 45. Other liminal moments, such as marriage, seem also to have occasioned strong linkages between mothers and daughters and other women, albeit temporary and apparently focussed on a key societal institution.

71. See, for example, the mosaic of a women's funerary symposium from the necropolis at Antioch: C Kondoleon, *Antioch: The Lost Ancient City* (Princeton, NJ: Princeton University Press, 2001), 121–122.

72. There is no attempt to speak universally here. Variations and permutations of mother-daughter relationships exist throughout the

sometimes overlap, especially in the male gaze that drew parallels between behaviours and language.[73] The arenas are those of the priestess and the prostitute.

Mother and daughter—a sacred relationship

The magico-religious field has already been mentioned as one where mothers and daughters were sometimes found without reference to men. The public conjunction of mothers and daughters in the Greco-Roman world was officially sanctioned in the Eleusian Mysteries and the Thesmophoria.[74] Here the myth of the separation of the mother (Demeter/Ceres) from her daughter (Kore/Persephone) and the restoration of that relationship in a different configuration received manifold accents. Its agricultural alliance, and perhaps origins, was symbolised in the carrying of wheat and other produce. The passage of a girl to the fecund potential of womanhood was signified in the rites, as was her role in the future of the group (whether polis or village).[75] There is widespread geographic attestation to the cult's presence in Syro-Palestine from Hellenistic times.[76] The repeated dis-ease felt by ancient writers about the cult of Demeter and Kore points to a recognition that there exists in the strength of such a relationship a 'possibility of an alternative consciousness'[77] that they could not penetrate.[78]

Lucia Nixon noted that the Demeter-Kore relationship does not find its resolution according to the pattern of the romance tales

---

extended Mediterranean arena.

73. Obscenity especially seemed a particular aspect of women's religious festivals, according to male reports: see Winkler, *Constraints of Desire*, 197.
74. For descriptions and analyses of these rites, see Kraemer, *Her Share*, 24–29, Fantham *et al*, *Women in the Classical World*, 22–33, Winkler, *Constraints of Desire*, 193–202.
75. See the detailed exploration of the contradictions involved in officially sanctioned women's rites by E Stehle and A Day, 'Women Looking at Women: Women's Ritual and Temple Sculpture', in Kampen, *Sexuality in Ancient Art*, 109.
76. GRH Wright, 'The mother-maid at Bethlehem', in *ZAW* 98 (1986): 56–72. A painted inscription at Samaria, accompanying a statue, calls Kore the 'one god, ruler of all things, great maiden, the invincible' (*NDIEC* 1.68).
77. The phrase is Jack Winkler's: *Constraints of Desire*, 188.
78. Walker, *Rhetoric and Poetics*, 223–224. A full-scale deprecation of women's rites is found in Ps-Lucian's *Amor* 42; *cf* Aristoph *Lys* 142–143, Athen *Deip* 481a.

of reversal where a young woman is honoured *after* the birth of a (male) child.[79] Rather, fecundity is *the response of the mother* as she wins the restoration of her daughter. This, Nixon demonstrated, is the 'surprising' concentration of the *Homeric Hymn to Demeter*. For all the familiar stereotypes of house, instruction in womanly tasks, prayers for progeny and the like,[80] Demeter also includes criticism of men. Moreover, she marginalises the aggressive Hades from the story;[81] the focus is her redemption of her daughter. It is 'the story of a mother using her own power on behalf of her own daughter.'[82]

But there is a further power. Nixon saw that the pomegranate seed used by Hades unwittingly provided an opportunity for the woman's reassertion of control over her own body.[83] Far from being irrelevant to cults celebrating fertility, Nixon argued that the gaining of bodily subjectivity is part of the 'secret women's business' locked into these festivals for mothers and daughters.[84]

Quite unlike romance novels where the woman generally gains wisdom from a male (father, husband, hero),[85] ignorance implicitly characterises the male in this portrayal. The anxiety of men that conception may not be under their autonomy is reflected in the custom of alluding to Persephone/Kore rather than naming her.[86] The power of her name is such as to unleash death.

Such audacious independence however was scarcely tolerated under patriarchal hegemony. Not only were significant intrusions made upon the myth and its representation so that boundaries upon fecundity

79. L Nixon, 'The Cults of Demeter and Kore', in Hawley and Levick, *Women in Antiquity*, 89; *cf* Lefkowitz, *Women in Greek Myth*, 36.
80. See *Hom Hym Dem* 118.
81. There is some debate about the presence of Hades and his rapacious action in the earliest version of the myth. However, the influence of the postulate of a primeval goddess may have directed the reconstruction. Phillips confidently speaks of 'the original pre-patriarchal evidence' but cites none (231). Though there is evidence of a unified Demeter-Kore goddess, this cannot be traced back to a primeval Great Goddess.
82. Nixon, 'Demeter and Kore', 89. See S Phillips, *Beyond the Myths*: Mother-Daughter Relationships in Psychology, History, Liter*ature and Everyday Life* (London: Penguin, 1991), 230–231. S Price, *Religions of the Ancient Greeks* (Cambridge: Cambridge University Press, 1999), 99.
83. Beans, also noted in connection with Demeter, are recommended in the Hippocratic corpus for contraception (Lefkowitz and Fant §342).
84. Nixon, 'Demeter and Kore', 88.
85. *Cf* Konstan, *Sexual Symmetry*, 111–113.
86. Eurip *Her* 608, 1104, Mart *Epig* 7.96, *GA* 7.352.

were established, but the Eleusinian celebrations and participants were themselves denigrated as much as grudgingly accepted as necessary.[87] The liturgical language was equated with brothel banter,[88] and the assertion of power over male genitalia represented in bread and clay[89] was deemed shameful.[90]

The celebration of the woman and her body is thus held within the province of women. In this relationship of mutual subjectivities, the violent boundary-marking of patriarchal shaming itself becomes hedged about and restricted. In the absence of the key integer of control of woman's sexuality, the male,[91] many of the intensities of shame are removed, and women's sexuality and fecundity is repatriated, self-interpreted, and engaged with men subject to women's autonomous decision.[92] One epitaph hints at this arrangement: a priestess of Demeter recounts her patronage of many young women seemingly as equal to her mothering of two male children.[93]

The myth of the separation and restoration of the mother and her daughter was extremely powerful in the ancient world.[94] The lines of that typology are glimpsed in the Syrophoenician's story. The

87. Pausan 7.27.4 speaks of the 'requirement of custom'.
88. Aristoph *Plut* 1014, Hesych sv γεφυρίς.
89. Athen *Deip* 109e, Scholion to Lucian cited by Winkler, *Constraints of Desire*, 194–195.
90. Winkler, *Constraints of Desire*, 196. Gooch suggests that the Demeter-Kore cult at Corinth was particularly in view when Paul repudiated eating at 'the table of demons': PD Gooch, *Dangerous Food: 1 Cor 8–10 in its Context* (Waterloo: Wilfred Laurier UP, 1993), 13.
91. Even male dogs were excluded: Pausan 7.27.4.
92. See generally M Hirsch, *The Mother/Daughter Plot: Narrative, Psychoanalysis, Feminism* (Bloomington/Indianapolis: Indiana University Press, 1989), 162–199, L Shrage, *Moral Dilemmas of Feminism: Prostitution, Adultery, and Abortion* (New York and London: Routledge, 1994), 55–77. There may be some legacy of women's autonomous and free relating to men in the frequent association of women's religious celebrations with Dionysos: see *IGL* (Syria) 714, the Xenokles cup (British Museum, reproduced in Kerényi *Eleusis* 35), Ov *Fast* 4.490, Nonn *Dion* 5.555f. There is, however, a possibility that Dionysos was an alternative to Hades in the myth.
93. *GA* 7.728.
94. Ross Kraemer commented: ' . . . the myth of Demeter and Persephone expresses important tensions in Greek society—the centrality of the emotional bond between mothers and daughters and the pain that their inevitable separation inflicts.' (*Her Share*, 29). Important for our story is the restoration of relationship and the resistance to the inevitability of separation because of male intrusion.

pervasiveness of the story of Demeter and Kore offered the possibility of an alternate consciousness of and among women, resistant to male dominance in ideas, language, and control over their own bodies. The story tells of a deliverance through the initiative of the mother and a communication of knowledge that requires neither male mediation nor embedding in male space. There is no need to imagine a direct line of influence between the Eleusinian mysteries and the construction of the story of the Syrophoenician woman. It is enough to recover the valuing of the mother-daughter relationship held in a sacred story within the socio-cultural context of the early Christian tradition and Mark's Gospel itself.

There is a second arena for the mother-daughter relationship, one which frequently overlapped with the context already outlined. Cult and courtesan are linked in epigraphic testimonial and literary description, suggesting that courtesans joined with married women in the celebration of the Thesmophoria. The festival seems often to have cultivated no distinction between these women.[95]

Mother and daughter—a secular relationship

The ability of a mother and daughter to survive in the ancient world was severely eroded when a male presence, such as father, husband or son, was removed from the scene.[96] The alternative was often to prostitute one or other.[97]

Romanticising prostitution merely perpetuates ancient male fantasies, as readily as abuse prolongs victimisation. Critical assessments of the ancient evidence as well as contemporary analysis underscores the vulnerability of women whose life survival depends on the sale of their bodies for sex.[98]

Even so, for all that the practice of prostitution may be construed as patriarchally determined, there is some oblique evidence that indicates a measure of self-determination in the lives of, at least, courtesans.

95. BC MacLachlan, 'Love, War and the Goddess in Fifth-Century Locri', in *AW* 26 (1995): 200–202. However, it appears that, at least in Corinth, the cult of Aphrodite made distinctions between freeborn women and courtesans. They were granted separate festivals: Athen *Deip* 574b.

96. Although quite late (sixth century CE), one formal papyrus barely hides the anguish of a mother unable to provide for her nine-year old daughter; she hands her over to other surrogate parents 'for all time as a lawful daughter' (ἅπαντα χρόνον εἰς θυγατέρα νομίμην): *P Oxy* 1895.

97. Mart *Epig* 9.6.

98. See Keuls, *Reign of the Phallus*, 187–202.

Some famous courtesans of the ancient world, such as Neaera, Aspasia or Metaneira, were recalled individually. The general pictorial and literary representation was of pairs or groups of courtesans.

Such groups were communities in which the trade and wider skills were acquired. They were the places of support and assistance for young and old, where the patterns of relating were not confined to the trade. Familial language infuses these relationships, most particularly that of 'mother' and 'daughter';[99] it included terms of endearment, such as μαννάδιον.[100] These terms covered fictive as well as blood ties. Certainly, courtesans bore children; and daughters followed the steps of mothers. But foundling children,[101] slaves and sometimes even free young women could be linked to experienced companions. 'Daughter' especially, is the term to describe these young women and indicate the relationship with their senior.[102] A courtesan may hope to disguise a young woman as 'freeborn' by the designation 'daughter', presumably to make the courtesan a more desirable companion.[103]

Whether or not this relationship was a blood tie,[104] the younger girl / woman was important insurance for the older courtesan's old age—a clear parallel to the responsibility of a son for his parents.[105] But there was also the capacity of a slave-prostitute to win manumission either for herself or for her mother.[106] And if the courtesan was free-born, under Roman law her children were autonomous of any male

99. Demosth (*C Neaera*) 59.19, Luc *Dial Mer* 13, Herodas *Mime* 1, Athen *Deip* 580e–581c.
100. Luc *Dial Mer* 6. The fore-grounding of the mother-daughter relationship is found in Sappho's poetry; see generally, A Lardinois, 'Lesbian Sappho and Sappho of Lesbos', in J Bremmer (editor), *From Sappho to de Sade: Moments in the History of Sexuality* (London/New York: Routledge, 1989), 21–22.
101. The raising of foundling children as slaves with many purposes in mind is a commonplace in the ancient world: *BGU* 4.1107. It even received the attention of the courts: *P Oxy 1*.37.
102. Curiously, the word 'mother' does not occur in the Syrophoenician pericope, whereas it is expressly included in the story of Jairus' daughter (Mk 5:40) and Herodias' daughter (Mk 6:24, 28).
103. Demosth (*C Neaera*) 59.19.
104. As appears to be the case for the courtesans in Plautus' *Asinaria*.
105. Pomeroy, *Goddesses*, 90–91, citing Demosth *Decl* 59.18–20 (=Apollod *C Naeara*).
106. Corley, *Private Women*, 50; see the reference to this practice in Mart *Epig* 6.71.

ownership.[107]

Lucian's *Dialogues of the Courtesans* presuppose relationships and recognised places in which those 'dialogues' could occur. It must be acknowledged that they carry a high level of satiric content, deploying formulaic stereotypes: the use of dance (inevitably lewd in satire), magic (the explanation for the hold a courtesan can wield over a man), the special tie between courtesans that borders on suggestions of lesbianism, the capacity of courtesans to become wealthy, and the ability of such women to make men lose their self-control and become governed by their passions.

Nevertheless, there are other elements which require inclusion to enable the satires to be constructed. These reveal a little of the actual lives of courtesans. Courtesans were part of an informal network that included slaves,[108] a network that enabled confidences and household boundaries to be breached. The ability to interact in public no doubt facilitated such connections.[109]

At least some courtesans were literate,[110] and occasionally to a level that rivalled philosophers.[111] They were especially adept, it seems, at pointing out the hypocrisy of those who advocated virtue. Lucian also portrays courtesans' disdain for boorish and ignorant soldiers.[112] Though the military buffoon is a stock figure, the indication is that the courtesan was far more widely read, and indeed critical of the value systems that men (of different social levels) might construct.

The religious expression of the mother and daughter relationship which we have examined, was in the main, seasonal and occasional (albeit symbolically powerful). The relationship between courtesans was continuous—the counterpoint to their casual encounters with men, even if Lucian appeals to the familiar image of a woman's interest in trapping a man for her own financial security. The women's primary relations of intimacy and support were frequently if not totally with other women, including daughters of fictive or blood kinship ties. In

107. This was rare: see B Rawson, 'Adult-Child Relationships in Roman Society', in B Rawson (editor), *Marriage, Divorce and Children in Ancient Rome* (Oxford: Clarendon Press, 1991), 26.
108. Courtesans were often drawn from such ranks or began their life there. Courtesans, as other higher-ranking slaves, were themselves authorised to own slaves.
109. It may substantiate the charge of slaves' loose lips: *Dial Mer* 2, 9.
110. *Dial Mer* 10.
111. This is confirmed in non-satirical writings—the names Aspasia, Leontion and Hipparchia are but representatives of a broader group.
112. *Dial Mer* 15.

these relationships (only?) the intensities of shame and fear might be removed, especially as attaching to status and behaviours, and the capacity for these women to define (or not define) their own bodies becomes enhanced. Even some ancient male writers recognised this as a capacity of women, albeit continuing to circumvent an actualisation.

Return to the mother and daughter in Mark's Gospel

Eva Stehle's dictum—'only among women could women perform as self-defining subjects'[113]—appears confirmed, though access to the evidence has to pass through a screen of male filters. This has important implications for the story of the Syrophoenician and her daughter. For all that society may slur their combined status—and Mark has clearly encouraged at least the recognition (if not the adoption) of such a response—their *relationship* ultimately triumphs. The wisdom of the woman is displayed in confrontation with the male. His initial discourse reinforced the damaging picture of the woman and her daughter. The female as victim (possessed) and culprit (promiscuous) are outlined more tightly by his authoritarian words. The voice of Syrophoenician authority however—persuasive, gentle and sensitive to the struggle to gain a hearing from a position of inequality—loosens the grip of such absolutes, as surely as Demeter released the grasp of Hades.

The voice of the prostitute as an authentic contemporary voice has struggled to be heard both in patriarchy and in feminism itself.[114] Even Kathleen Corley's ground-breaking work on the women of the Jesus movement, at times resiles from the suggestion of actual prostitutes in the Jesus' movement, preferring to accent the status-diminishing function of the accusation of 'harlots and tax-collectors'. Such labelling by opponents points less to the reality of the lives of the targets, as to castigate (other) unacceptable behaviours.[115]

Mark's accent in the story is on gender, not primarily her gentile

113. Stehle, *Performance and Gender*, 318.
114. Note especially, S Bell, *Reading, Writing and Rewriting the Prostitute Body* (Bloomington and Indianopolis: Indiana University Press, 1994). Shrage, *Moral Dilemmas*, 99–161.
115. See, for example, 'Really Prostitutes?', 520–521, 'Jesus' Table Practice', 458–459. A more nuanced position is developed in her book-length treatment: *Private Women*, 180–186. One of the assumptions governing the analysis is that 'harlot' had its force as a pejorative in an *urban* (Hellenistic?) setting, an assumption which has earlier been questioned (*contra* JM Ford, 'Bookshelf on Prostitution', in *BTB* 23 (1993): 129). The city merely proliferated the rhetoric of abuse.

background,[116] though this supplements the appraisal of her gender. Her 'promiscuity' is evoked as a characterisation by a series of factors, attaching to the primary accent on gender. However, that purported promiscuity is rendered inconsequential to her liberating word on behalf of her daughter. Any courtesan background could explain the refined wit that countered Jesus' attack. In other words, transforming wisdom is not divorced from the despised on the ground of promiscuity.

Here another contrast lies in the Markan narrative. The family of Herod-Herodias-Herodias' daughter shines with established structural convention (the Baptist notwithstanding) in the lead-up to the Syrophoenician story (6:14–29). We see the presence of a male guardian, a marriage and family set-up happily recognised in Roman law, and an indication of separate dining-rooms for men and women pursuant to the 'best' conservative Hellenistic practice.[117] Moreover, the male is located within a large network of clients and aristocratic connections.[118] The whole set-up breathes respectability and conventionality; then, the daughter (θυγάτηρ–κορασίον) is introduced. Suddenly, the scene is reconfigured into one of procurement with Herod and Herodias both deploying their dependant for their own ends.[119]

Traditionally, Christian commentary has seized on the female as the sirenic destroyer of John the Baptist,[120] but Mark's Gospel itself leaves

116. *Contra* Corley who accents her 'Gentile' status over against her 'promiscuity': *Private Women*, 182.

117. Note 6:24: ἐξελθοῦσα. Herod's Machaerus fortress apparently had dual dining-rooms.

118. Οἱ μεγιστᾶνες, οἱ χιλιάρχοι, οἱ πρώτοι τῆς Γαλιλαίας—this is one instance where inclusive language ought not override the gender specifics of the Greek.

119. See JC Anderson, 'Feminist Criticism: The Dancing Daughter', in JC Anderson and SD Moore (editors), *Mark & Method: New Approaches in Biblical Studies* (Minneapolis: Fortress Press, 1992), 115-133.

120. *Ibid*, 118–130. A clear example of the effort to exculpate Herod is found in Alfred Plummer, *An Exegetical Commentary on the Gospel According to S Matthew* (London: Robert Scott, third edition, 1911). He indulges in a case of special pleading, the more pointed because he recognises, at least conceptually, the evidence of abuse: 'Bad as Herod was, he cannot justly be accused of allowing his own daughter to degrade herself by dancing to please revellers at a banquet.' (202). Ross Kraemer exposes the theological bias in the revision of history that Mark achieved and which has influenced commentators ever since: see 'Implicating Herodias and Her Daughter in the Death of John the Baptizer: A (Christian) Theological Strategy', in *JBL* 125 (2006): 321–49.

no doubt. The 'leaven of *Herod*' is to be avoided (Mk 8:15).[121] The presence of the male guardian has destructive consequences, at least in the life of the daughter who bears the shame of parade before prurient men and of the exchange of half a kingdom for a head.[122] Consequently the absence of patriarchal embedding for mother and daughter in the Syrophoenician pericope—an element which had previously invited shame/ing—may be read as conducive to the *basileia's* deliverance.

Conceptualising the relationship of mother and daughter

The juxtaposition of a corrupt Herod-Herodias-daughter complexity with that of the Syrophoenician and her daughter is not to be interpreted via a nineteenth century revival to restore the moral merit of the exemplary mother's claim upon Jesus. There is another perspective. The relationship might be plotted on the 'lesbian continuum' proposed by Mary d'Angelo.[123] On this reading, intimate 'homosocial' relationships with a measure of exclusivity between women are interpreted within a wide ambit of lesbianism. Eroticism (homo- or hetero-) is not a determining element of these relationships. The term simply covers relationships between women that are 'primary and major'.

Equity is implicit in such a relationship. It is a relationship that undercuts the weight of an (expected) ethological dimorphism where male and female were required for the carving of identities, inevitably valued unequally. Moreover, the ethological extension to dogs is denied in such a relationship, not by removal of the dogs but by a refusal to align one participant in that 'primary and major' relationship with the animal. The tensions that have been asserted of mother-daughter relations[124] are here absent, replaced rather by women who find their

121. Some manuscripts read 'Herodians' (P^{45} W Θ $f^{1\ 13}$ 28 565 *pc* ik sa^{mss}). Scribes have either tried to mitigate Herod's shame (leaving Herodias confirmed?), or assimilated to Mk 3:6.

122. The scene in Mark's Gospel is a familiar type-scene: Hdt *Hist* 9.109–114, Liv *Hist* 39.42–43, Val Maxim 2.9.3, Athen *Deip* 575c. It gains its tension from the competing claims of statesmanship and household loyalties. In Mark's story, both are given mortifying twists. Abraham Smith has demonstrated how strong the typographical characterisations implicate Herod: 'Tyranny Exposed: Mark's Typological Characterisation of Herod Antipas (Mark 6:14–29)', in *Bib Int* 14 (2006): 259–93.

123. D'Angelo, 'Women Partners', 71, 'Reconstructing Real Women from Gospel Literature', in Kraemer and D'Angelo, *Women & Christian Origins*, 108. She adopted the term from Adrienne Rich, 'Compulsory Heterosexuality and Lesbian Existence', in *Signs* 5 (1980): 631–660.

124. As evidenced in the Babatha papers, *CPJ* 2.442; compare also *P Ent* 26.

affective commitment to the other.[125]

A younger and an older woman in a defining and affirming relationship is critical to an appreciation of Mark's story. But this is complemented, as we will see, by the daughter's extension of the liberation already secured by the mother. It is a generational development, an aspect familiar in the gospel. Only Mark explicitly nominates Simon of Cyrene by reference to his sons (rather than his father: Mk 15:21).[126] Mary is named in similar fashion (15:40)—not by reference to fathers but to children.[127] This is more than a generational shift of the gospel; it is a generational expansion. The expectation of a 'beyond' is woven into the gospel fabric both in characterisation and narrative.

Children therefore move beyond being mere recipients of the benefits of the gospel. The accent on the 'last word' belonging to Jesus must confront the generation beyond his speaking. The relationship between the woman and her daughter carries the potency for communication beyond Jesus' 'last word'.

The potential for a revaluation of the body, brushed into the background by the concentration on the word of a woman, now explodes in the activity of the last verse of the pericope: discovery, reclining, and departure. The centre of this action is the Syrophoenician's liberated daughter, who has, it will be argued, initiated a further action that displaces the centrality of word and affirms the body as a communication medium. Here will be found the contribution of the child, the next generation, to the relationship with her mother, and to the expansion of the possibilities won amidst all the ambiguities of the mother's activity and word. No longer a passive dependent, the child becomes an initiator within the relationship, albeit having been freed for that freedom by the Syrophoenician woman.

The daughter's somatic communication

The gesture of reclining

i) Post-exorcism distress or full deliverance

The position of the child at the moment of discovery by the

125. As is the likely representation in the Fonteia Helena—Fonteia Eleusis funerary relief in the British Museum; see d'Angelo, 'Women Partners', 65–72, B Brooten, *Love Between Women: Early Christian Responses to Female Homoeroticism* (Chicago and London: University of Chicago Press, 1996), 59–60.

126. Theissen, *Gospels in Context*, 176, Taylor, *Mark*, 588.

127. Theissen, *Gospels in Context*, 176.

Syrophoenician woman has been treated as no more problematic than a confirmatory conclusion to a miracle story.[128] The two participial phrases are taken as consecutive and mutually interpretative. That is, the child's βεβλημένον ἐπὶ τὴν κλίνην is taken as a result of τὸ δαιμόνιον ἐξεληλυθός,[129] even though the *syntactical* order is the reverse. Some commentators press this further and see the child *cast* on her bed as a result of the severity of the trauma.[130] Examples of other exorcisms in the gospel are recalled in support (Mk 1:26, 9:26),[131] explicatory comparison is drawn with Mt 8:14: βεβλημένην καὶ πυρέσσουσαν,[132] and the ending is taken as synonymous with Mt 15:28c: 'her daughter was healed instantly.'[133] Other commentators see the reference to the κλίνη as unnecessary, a mere accentuation of the departure of the demon.[134]

The transmission of the text tried to underscore the connection between the daughter 'prone' in her bed and the expulsion of the demon by accentuating the exorcism as the focus of the woman's discovery: Εὗρεν τὸ δαιμονιον ἐξεληλυθός καὶ τὸ παιδίον βεβλημένον ἐπὶ τὴν κλινην.[135] *This* word order accents the miraculous resolution of the instigating problem (v 25) and shifts attention back to the omniscience of the man Jesus. The woman has to discover what Jesus already knew and announced (v 29). Jesus' exalted position is preserved, the woman

---

128. Guelich, *Mark 1–8:26*, 388 is absolutely blunt on this. Rhoads, 352 hardly less so, apart from forcing the verse into an arbitrary parallelism with v 29—again subtly exulting Jesus, and making v 30 nothing more than an aftermath.
129. Pesch, *Das Markusevangelium*, 390.
130. Jean Héring proposes the translation 'jetée sur la couche': 'Remarques sur les bases araméennes et hébraïques des évangiles synoptiiques: prolégomenes à une nouvelle traduction', in *RHPR* 46 (1966): 26.
131. Gould, *Mark*, 137.
132. Taylor, *Mark*, 351, citing F Field, *Notes on the Translation of the New Testament* (Cambridge: Cambridge University Press, 1899), 7, amongst many supporters for the sense 'to take to one's bed'.
133. Davies and Allison, *Matthew*, 2.556.
134. Derrett, 'Law in the New Testament', 163. This suggestion probably goes back to Gustav Volkmar *Die Evangelien, oder Marcus und die Synopsis der kanonischen und ausserkanonischen Evangelien, nach dem ältesten Text, mit historisch-exegetischen Commentar* (1870), *non vide*.
135. The Majority Text plus P^{45} A W f^{13} sy^{h}.

is reduced to a witness and the child is merely the *tabula rasa* on which provider and dependant are writ.[136]

These changes in the verse indicate that ancient scribes were not happy with the better reading. They sought to work into the text a clearer presentation of the presumed intent of the final verse. A suspicion is therefore raised that another interpretation might be sustained by the critically accepted reading. The arguments for a different reading which place the child at the centre of an initiating action, follow.

a. Refuting post-exorcism distress

The violent convulsive exorcism as the explanation for the child lying on the bed is, as we have seen, deduced from other accounts of exorcism in Mark's Gospel (1:26, 9:6) and elsewhere. However, this element is never the final element in the miracle stories. The exorcism of the father's son in 9:25–26 is followed by a restoration where the child is raised up by hand. This 'two-stage' movement recalls the healing of the blind man at Bethsaida (8:22–24 and 25–26). Jairus' daughter's revival is followed by instruction for provision of food, and the daughter of Abraham has a bodily healing (5:29) followed by public testimony (5:33–34). The convulsion of the synagogue demoniac (1:26) receives no detailed attention and is not the end of the story. The testimony to Jesus follows (1:27–28). Gerd Theissen tried to overcome this difficulty by classifying v 30 as a 'recognition of the miracle'[137] and did not read the text as indicating violence.

Theissen's classification may be forced but it highlights the problem: if one adopts the notion that the final verse points to the weakened daughter exhausted on a bed, then the miracle story is incomplete.[138] There is no 'happy end'.[139] In this sense, all the Syrophoenician has won is a fragment of a miracle, a crumby remainder.

b. Narrowing the Reference of κλίνη

A further assumption made in the previous interpretation is that the phrase ἐπὶ τὴν κλίνην refers to the spatial location of a *sick* person. Occasionally comparisons are made to the κράβατος of the paralytic

136. One Georgian manuscript has the daughter 'clothed and sitting on a pallet': geo^{A} (*cf* 5:15, 2:11).

137. Theissen, *Miracle*, 65.

138. Another expression would convey this; for example, in *Joseph and Aseneth* 9.1, the Jew's inspiring words cause her to *fall* on her bed *exhausted*: πέπτωκεν ἐπὶ τῆς κλίνης ἀσθενοῦσα.

139. Pokorný, 'Puppy', 329.

(2:4), drawing the distinction between the bedding of the poor and that of the wealthy.[140] The semantic intent of κλίνη is taken as 'bed' and, in this case, the 'sick bed'.[141]

There are certainly many Scriptural examples of κλίνη referring to sick-bed.[142] Sometimes the sickness is so severe as to denote a death-bed.[143] Consequently, in a circular argument, instances of κλίνη that are uncertain as a reference to 'sick-bed', are confined to this class. But κλίνη is not only given to sickness; it also refers to sleep[144] and to sexual activity[145] (where it blurs into κοίτη[146] or εὐνή[147]). Indeed, one of the famous names for a courtesan was Cleino.[148] This association is likely to be the irony intended in Revelation 2:22 where Jezebel is thrown onto the very place where the 'adulteries' are committed.

Other commentators however, recognise that κλίνη, even in the New Testament, can have the meaning 'couch', that is, the place for dining.[149] The reference to hiding a lamp ὑπὸ τὴν κλίνην in Mark 4:21 is more likely to refer to the couch of a dining room than the sleeping quarters.[150] Swete is explicit: 'the couch of the *triclinium*'.[151] A lamp-

140. Stock, *Method and Message*, 215, Gnilka, *Markus*, 293.
141. Greg Horsley claimed that in the New Testament the word regularly means 'bed'; nowhere, he said, did it refer to a dining couch: *NDIEC* 1.1 (p.9). He did, however, point to πρωτοκλισία at Lk 14:7, 8, Mt 23:6, and noted how widespread was the practice in Palestine of reclining for meals. In the light of what follows, his judgment needs to be revised.
142. Gen 48:2, 1 Rgns 19:14–15, 3 Rgns 17:19, 4 Rgns 4:21, 32 (LXX); *cf* Plut *Mor* 159f, Sen *Ep* 17.12.
143. Gen 49:33, Jud 8:2. The familiar sepulchre of the deceased sculptured on a couch is itself called a κλίνη. *IEph* 7.1.3312, 7.1.3460 (*NDIEC* 4.101, 184).
144. Prov 26:14.
145. The feigning of sickness to encourage a liaison is found in the story of Ammon and Tamar, and may be suggested in Esth 7:8 and Jud 13:2.
146. The synonymity of the two terms is found in Job 7:13, Ps 40 (41):3; *cf* Hbs 13:4.
147. Hom *Od* 1.427, *Il* 18.433; *cf* Aristoph *Lys* 914f.
148. Athen *Deip* 425e, 576f; *cf* Luc *Dial Mer* 10.
149. *BAGD* sv; JM Robinson, 'The International Q Project: Work Sessions 12–14 July, 22 November, 1991', in *JBL* 111 (1992): 508, A-J Levine, 'Second Temple Judaism, Jesus and Women: Yeast of Eden', *BibInt* 2 (1994): 24 and K Corley, 'Salome and Jesus at Table in the Gospel of Thomas', in *Semeia* 86 (1999): 86n2, take Q17:34 as a reference to reclining on a couch at a banquet. The pairing of this saying with a reference to women preparing food supports this reading. Compare the pairing with στρωμνή in Ps 6:7, 131(132):3, Amos 6:4.
150. So Guelich, *Mark 1–8:26*, 228–229.
151. Swete, *Mark*, 82.

stand properly belongs to the more open areas of a house. The use of a 'bushel' (μόδιος) as a covering evokes a connection with food which leads naturally to the further association, as Luke takes it (8:16), of the traffic of people in the room (οἱ εἰσπορευόμενοι). In a well-known variant to Mk 7:4, the words καὶ κλινῶν[152] are added to the list of items which Jews wash—all items related to eating (7:2–3). Robert Guelich notes that the list 'does not move beyond the "tradition" regarding the relationship between eating and defilement'.[153]

Consequently, the array of meanings for ἐπὶ τὴν κλίνην is far broader than allowed.[154] And notably, it carries a strong connection with dining (*cf GT* 61). Only a pre-determination of a sick bed confines the interpretation, and this against the meaning borne of the one or two instances elsewhere in Mark's Gospel. The same problem as previously stated, is raised: if the meaning is a 'sick-bed', how does this demonstrate the *release* of the victim?

c. The semantic range of βάλλω

The syntactical unit, βεβλημένον ἐπὶ τὴν κλίνην, is where meaning must be sought. Here again, an assumption of the presumed violence of the exorcism dominates the meaning of βάλλω.[155] Some warrant for this meaning can be given, even within Mark's Gospel (9:22, 42).

However, it is difficult to see the violence in putting (βάλλει) new wine into old wine-skins—the violence is the consequence of so doing (2:22)! Similarly, just how forceful was Jesus' digital insertion into the deaf-mute's ears (7:33–ἔβαλεν)? Even moreso, it is difficult to see any turbulence in the position of the sick man brought to Jesus by his friends—after all he is paralysed. The Matthean phrase ἐπὶ κλίνης βεβλημένον (Mt 9:2) is almost identical to the phrase in Mark, and is

152. The UBS committee were quite divided, giving it a rating of {C}. Westcott and Hort consider it an intrusion from an extraneous source, written or oral. BF Westcott and FJA Hort, *The New Testament in the Original Greek* (Cambridge/London: Macmillan, 1882), 'Appendix', 25. The Authorised Version, following the *Textus Receptus*, which included the reading, translates this as 'tables'. It, rightly, perceived an example of metonymy. It is the same as in many Serapis invitations, where κλίνη means feast/banquet (see *NDIEC* 1.1, *P Oxy* 62.4339, *P Köln* 6.280).

153. *Mark 1–8:26*, 365.

154. Eva Keuls comments that the *klinai* served as places of eating, sleeping and sex, 'a domestically economical arrangement' (*Reign of the Phallus*, 162).

155. See, for example, Dermience, 'Tradition et rédaction', 26.

rightly translated, there, as 'laid on a bed' (*cf* also Mt 8:6). Significantly perhaps, Matthew's recounting of the fevered mother-in-law of Peter has her also lying down (8:14); the word again is βεβλημένον but Mark's parallel account uses κατακείμαι (1:30), a word frequently used of reclining at table.[156]

Yet again, the problem of these last few uses is that the expression seem to indicate a malignant condition rather than a healed one. We are faced with an apparent *anti*-miracle ending, *if* we follow the traditional interpretation. Even so, this short survey demonstrates that βάλλω can bear a milder sense of place or lay.[157] There is no compulsion to transfer to the *active* force of βαλεῖν in Jesus' words in v 27.

d. Reconsidering the voice of the participle

The recognition that βάλλω has a broad semantic range has also suggested that the *voice* of the verb can be a key influence on meaning. This prompts a reinvestigation of the voice of βεβλήμενον. The stock tagging of the grammatical form is that it is a perfect passive.[158] However unusual the form may be in Mark, commentators tie it to the following participle, ἐξεληλυθός, both grammatically and interpretively. The child is rendered 'passive', acted upon and devoid of initiative. There are three problems with emphasising that the neuter participle βεβλημένον is passive:

α) Firstly, the link with the main verb is rarely analysed. The use of a predicate participle following a verb of perception or cognition is classically and scripturally well-attested.[159] In this position, the verbal aspect of the participle is given special prominence.[160] This usage indicates 'indirect discourse'; that is, the participle represents the verb in direct discourse. When this indirect speech is reformulated accordingly, it reads as two distinct actions rather than one informing the other; hence: 'My child is reclined on the couch, *and* the demon is gone.'

β) Thus structured, a second problem in standard analysis

156. Mk 14:3, Lk 5:29; *cf* Pl *Sym* 185d, Hdt *Hist* 3.121.

157. Moulton and Milligan had recognised this: 'the verb does not necessarily imply *casting* or *thrusting* with some degree of violence.' (*VGT* 102, their emphasis).

158. Dermience, 'Tradition et rédaction', 26.

159. *BDF* §416.2, Smyth §2113.

160. Robertson, *Grammar*, 1108c, 1429, Porter, *Idioms*, 274.

is revealed. There are two simple sentences joined by καί. The majority of interpreters have interpreted the καί *causatively*, though the warrant for this is never given. If the phrases had been reversed, as a number of manuscripts engineered, then a case might have been made for the second to be read consequentially[161] (although the previous objection (α) would still need to be met). Even if it were to be read circumstantially,[162] the *meaning* of 'lying on the couch' is not thereby determined. Primarily, καί is a connective for 'items of equal status'.[163] It can bear an emphatic or adversative sense. Unlikely as that force may be in this case, it nevertheless clearly indicates that the two items of the woman's finding are to be distinguished.

γ) The third difficulty results in a confirmation of the lack of causal connection between the two participial phrases. βεβλημένον may be other than a passive. The morphology is identical in the middle voice of the participle. Given the possibility, and the clear use of the middle voice of βάλλω to indicate a 'doing for oneself',[164] it is surprising that interpreters have not entertained this alternative. Their *choice*, as it is now revealed, has been so decisive as to intimate absence of choice in interpretive communities. However, as Stanley Porter notes, where the morphology of middle and passive is identical, as it is for present and perfect tense-forms, 'it is a matter of deciding' or even 'whether such a distinction can be made in a given instance'.[165] The story sometimes parallelled with the Syrophoenician—Lazarus and the rich man (Lk 16:19–31)—illustrates the importance of entertaining this choice. Ancient literature on beggars shows that they *gathered themselves* around the gates and doorways of the homes or destinations of the wealthy, just as in the

161. See Black, *Aramaic Approach*, 66-67, Beyer, *Semitische Syntax*, 74.
162. See JH Moulton and WF Howard, *A Grammar of New Testament Greek, Volume II: Accidence and Word-Formation* (Edinburgh: T&T Clark, 1979), 423.
163. Porter, *Idioms*, 211.
164. LSJ sv.
165. *Idioms*, 70, 71.

> Lazarus story.[166] The pluperfect ἐβέβλητο (Lk 16:20), middle or passive in morphology, probably denotes a lengthy stay and this undermines any sense that Lazarus had attendants to transport him.[167] He placed himself at the rich man's gate.

ii) Extending the rights of access

The problems in the traditional interpretation listed above grant permission to explore a different possibility. Food has dominated the dialogue between Jesus and the Syrophoenician woman. Eating and bread figure prominently in this section of Mark's Gospel. Accordingly, one's linguistic *choice* is encouraged to be along these lines. One Old Latin variant suggests that just such a choice was exercised in the history of transmission. Instead of translating βεβλημένον as *iacentem*, indicating lying ill or weakened, some scribes opted for *recumbentem*.[168] *Recumbo* is the same verb occurring in a number of Old Latin manuscripts to Mark 6:26 of Herod's guests[169] —this time for the Greek ἀνάκειμαι;[170] and in Mark 2:15 and 14:3 for κατάκειμαι.[171] This redirects the sense to 'reclining',[172] and certainly confers greater initiative to the daughter.

The clearly recognised use of the middle voice for βάλλω is subject to the problems of distinguishable morphology in Hellenistic Greek and is exacerbated by the preference for –βάλλω compounds in literature. Future and aorist forms are recognisable however, and their occurrence indicates that a wide semantic range existed, even in the middle voice.

---

166. Athen *Deip* 71f, Luc *Dial Mer* 14, Mart *Epig* 2.19, 6.77, 10.5, 25, 11:32, 12:32.
167. *Cf* Mk 2:2–5, Jn 5:7.
168. Manuscripts a, n. These manuscripts also opt for *in* rather than *supra* as a translation of ἐπι.
169. Manuscripts b c d f ff l w² z.
170. Or συνανάκειμαι (ℵ A C² D Θ *f*¹ *f*¹³ Maj Text). See also the Old Latin for Mark 16:14. ἀνάκειμαι meaning 'recline' has a middle rather than passive sense. There is no sense in Mark 14:18 (ἀνακειμένων) that Jesus and the disciples had been 'laid up' or 'devoted' by any one (*cf* Mt 26:7). They simply adopted the common position for dining. Significantly, this verb is often translated as 'reclined at table' even though τράπεζα is omitted.
171. Some manuscripts read ἀνάκειμαι: W in 2:15 and Σ 61, 330 in 14:3, assimilated from Matthew 9:10 and 26:7 respectively. In Mark 2:15, OL is divided between *discumbo*, *accumbo* and *recumbo*.
172. Compare in particular Jn 13:23, 21:20 it, vg; *cf* Cic *C Verr* 2.3.25.61 (*in triclinio . . . recubuisset*), Pl *Ep* 4.22, Hor *Epod* 1.5.

For example, Aristobulus uses the middle aorist infinitive (βαλέσθαι) for the sowing of seed, all the more striking because the planting of trees uses a simple active infinitive (γυρῶσαι).[173] Compound verbs are even more frequent in attesting the use of the middle. The aorist middle of περιβάλλω is clear in Matthew 6:29, 31, and the perfect participle περιβεβλημένος certainly seems to be middle in its sense in Mark 14:51, 16:5.[174] This demonstrates that one ought not assume the passive for βεβλημένον in Mark 7:30; the morphology is ambiguous.

The potential unlocked by reading βεβλημένον as a *middle* participle is that the child's bodily action not only communicates *without* word but takes up the neglected potential of the Syrophoenician's example. The middle voice has frequently been difficult for translators to represent in the grammatical system of the receptor language, English. One can understand the appeal of the passive, which has at least a formal, though not literal, equivalence in translation.[175] Stanley Porter reminds us that the middle voice in Greek is far closer to an active than a passive meaning:

> *the Greek middle voice expresses more direct participation, specific involvement, or even some form of benefit of the subject doing the action.*[176]

The issue of translation may be seen in Judges 7:12. The Midianites, Amalekites and eastern peoples are *scattered* throughout a valley. The Hebrew participle, נֹפְלִים, was rendered differently in Septuagintal translations: Codex B retains the participial form: βεβλημένοι whilst Codex A adopts an active verb: παρεμβεβλήκεισαν. The Vulgate used a fulsome expression with an active, intransitive verb: *fusi iacebant*. The indications are, therefore, that Vaticanus' βεβλημένοι is to be understood as a middle rather than a passive. 'Specific involvement' is certainly indicated.

Hence, though the morphology in some tenses is indistinguishable from the passive, the meaning may be distinct. I argue this may be the case here. If this is allowed (as invited by the problems previously experienced with Mark 7:30), a new possibility of interpretation is unveiled, one more consistent with the flow of the pericope.

173. Aristobulus 13.12.6 (fr 4).
174. As in *Hist Alex Mag* B 3.28.5.
175. See O'Donnell, 'Translation and the Exegetical Process', 168 for warnings about the problems of the various voices for translation.
176. Porter, *Idioms*, 67 (his emphasis).

As we have seen, the triumph of the word of the woman left the ground of gender distinctives at least unresolved. That is, the basis on which the woman is affirmed was potentially restrained to the dominant male discourse, even if that discourse be extended to include her contribution of *logos*. Any other defining subjectivity is omitted if not precluded by such a designation. Her body remained an 'othered' inferior object, dangerously counterpoised to the snatch on valorisation gained by her word.[177]

In v 30, however, communication occurs but it establishes its exchange within the frame of the primary relationship between the woman and her daughter, namely at the level of body, more specifically at the level of the female body. The offensive presence that ostensibly disqualified a woman's equality or mutuality (with a male) in logocentric discourse because of contamination with the animal is now the critical dimension of a somatic communication. A potential loss attended the woman's word because it could be isolated and commandeered to the pre-established order of the male. The identity, action and presence of her body could easily be erased by a reaffirmation of logocentricity, even as she was affirmed as participating in word.

The daughter's silent yet somatic communication does not provide 'the last word'—for this description would merely reinforce a compromised structure. Her body, her action and gesture seal the displaced and potentially lost element of her mother's courage by bringing a somatic initiative to the fore in the climax of the story.

Of course, movements and gestures can be misinterpreted or differently interpreted. The history of commentary on this verse amply testifies to this. But it acknowledges the importance of gesture and movement to interpretation, if only by an inordinate and misdirected preoccupation with the woman's action in v 25c. Orators admitted the significance of gesture, posture and actions.[178] However, the gestures, along with the words, of a child were frequently dismissed as irrational and irrelevant.[179]

The fundamental proof of children's irrationality, however, was that 'they were no respecters of social convention'.[180] The *logos* of mind was not yet moulded sufficiently to mimic and reinforce the *logos* of society—it lacked order. More particularly, it did not control

177. See W Polinska, 'Dangerous Bodies: Women's Nakedness and Theology', in *JFSR* 16 (2000): 48.
178. Cic *Orat* 59.220, Quint *Inst* 1.11.3, 9–11, 18–19.
179. *Cf* Arist *Nic Eth* 1.9.10 (1100a).
180. Wiedemann, *Adults and Children*, 24.

or hedge about the body to its proper, inferior place.[181] Needless to say, children were only really noticed, amidst such concerns about social order, when they were breaking conventions (*cf* Mk 10:13).

The text draws attention to the discovered child in v 30: εὗρεν. Jean-François Baudoz notes that this is the only miracle story where the verb εὑρίσκω is used.[182] Every other instance in Mark's Gospel relates the word to Jesus—finding him or being found by him, finding things as he predicted, or failing to find by/against him. One might consider this finding is of a piece with these other 'findings' (for example, Mk 11:4, 14:16) even if located singularly in a miracle story. There is an epiphaneous quality to this finding for the mother and the audience.[183] Commentators have not been slow to point out the repetition of the verb in vv 30c and 29c (ἐξελήλυθεν . . . ἐξεληλυθός), along with an accent on the successful exorcism.[184]

However, unlike other predictions of Jesus that are followed by a mimetic demonstration, here an additional element is provided and given primary place in the discovery. The child *reclining on a couch* lies outside Jesus' words; this element is not included in his insight (v 29). The action is an *initiative of body* rather than a fulfilment of a word, and has its own revelatory quality. As Edward Casey wrote:

> Rather than being a passive recipient or mere vehicle of cultural enactments, the body is itself enactive of cultural practices by virtue of its considerable powers of incorporation, habituation, and expression.[185]

Accordingly, the child subverts the paradigm that sets *logos* over against body, as human over the bestial, and as male over female. The body is as culturally influential as reason claims itself uniquely to be. Lucretius, interestingly, had recognised this, claiming that gesture came before language.[186]

---

181. Arist *Rhet* 2.12 (1389a).
182. Baudoz, *Les Miettes*, 337.
183. Significantly, the fathers frequently write of the magi 'discovering the child' (for example, Basil *Holy Birth* 31.1469). They may be reliant on a variant reading of Mt 2:11 (474 892 it vg).
184. Guelich, *Mark 1–8:26*, 388; *cf* Derrett, 'Law in the New Testament', 163.
185. ES Casey, 'How to Get from Space to Place', in S Feld and KH Basso (editors), *Senses of Place* (Santa Fe, NM: SAR Press, 1996), 34.
186. *Nat Rer* 5.1019–1032.

Moreover the body itself can contain knowledge. Like the woman with the flow of blood (Mk 5:29), the daughter did not depend on the return of her mother to know that she was healed. That was the Syrophoenician's discovery; her daughter had already moved *beyond* the exorcism *to* reclining on the couch.

iii) The significance of the gesture

The standard placement of the child at a meal in the ancient world was subject to the disposition and arrangements of patriarchal concerns and favours. The child was 'full of numb imperatives' in her/his perpetuation of cultural formulations.[187] The child's performative obedience to social conventions may have been passive but it was a customary imposition from the beginning. That is, before the daughter was possessed by the 'demon', she was possessed by cultural convention. Therefore, for the child to recline indicates either that the hegemony of patriarchal convention is absent from this house or that she has broken that convention, *asserting a position for herself*. Each may be possible. What is more, she has enacted that dispossession with the very agency on which conventionality had been inscribed: her body.

Up until the last verse, the place of the woman and her child had been defined in terms of the dogs' position away from or under the table. The woman had secured an advance on Jesus' separatist words, but there was certainly no suggestion that the hierarchy symbolised in seating and eating could or would be broken by a child.

There was some variety in dining arrangements in the ancient world and ancient celebrations, but the hold of convention was strong, evident in the reconstruction of the eating hierarchies portrayed in numerous funerary *klinai* (banquet-scenes).

The appropriate position for respectable women was generally sitting rather than reclining, though the latter could occur. Inevitably, in such strong cultural codes, sitting was regarded as 'womanish',[188] even though it was noted that some cultures were distinguished by the generic use of seats.[189] The lowest position was to sit on the ground or floor, and if slaves were not involved in the meal or attending on

187. Bourdieu, *Logic of Practice*, 69.

188. Luc *Sym* 13.

189. Athen *Deip* 143e (Cretans), 443a (Illyrians). It was sometimes thought that the custom of the ancients was to sit: *ibid*, 11f, 363f citing Hom *Od* 3.471.

their masters, this would be their position.[190] If children were present, this was often their position also.[191] At best, they would sit, unlike, for example, the men (ἄνδρες) of Mark 6:39–40, 44 who recline (ἀνακλῖναι).

The liberation that the woman won was left under a shadow, at least as Mark (deliberately?) shaped the story. But the story continues, located in the body of the daughter. The gospel is expanded not merely by de-centring its focus on word to the incorporation of body and movement, but by removing the intense hierarchy configured in eating practices (whether or not the conventions were extended to acknowledge dogs).

The Syrophoenican daughter combines a movement or gesture of the body with a distinction from the dogs that had been part of her mother's reply. The dogs that secured a 'level-switching' of meaning and metaphor were dogs under the table who, themselves, were dependent on παιδία for their fare. The use of παιδίον in v 30 (rather than θυγάτηρ)[192] now is charged with significance, for *the child* is *distinguished* from the dogs. This ensures that no relapse into the equation of body with bestial occurs. The ethological confinement of body to irrationality to animal is broken. Somatic practice is the means by which the gospel, so often constrained to word(s), will be found as truly liberating. This is the breakthrough of the Syrophoenician's daughter.

Here, then, the woman-daughter relationship combines to bring benefit from one to the other. The affective primacy of their relationship has forged a hermeneutical extension of the gospel, an expansion that depends not on the relationship with Jesus but on that between the older and the younger woman. And if reclining is a demonstration of 'freedom',[193] then the daughter has exercised the freedom won for her by her mother and extended its application. Elisabeth Schüssler Fiorenza's observation that the place for these women is no longer *under* the table as dogs is accurate,[194] but this egalitarian arrangement

190. Plut *Mor* 166a; Athen *Deip* 143c. Sitting on the ground is described as the place of beggars: *Deip* 71f. The Saturnalia-style inversion in Luke 12:37 reinforces conventions related to eating.

191. Athen *Deip* 149c, 459f–460a. This can be interpreted as a place of dishonour: 153a.

192. Some manuscripts have restored θυγάτηρ in the final verse (D Θ f^1 565 700 it[a f n q]), missing the importance of the move from the mother's saying (which has παιδία) to the enactment of the daughter, so defined.

193. So GR Horsley *NDIEC* 2.26 (citing a letter from E Ferguson).

194. *Discipleship of Equals*, 296.

is secured *by the daughter*, and discovered, as already an accomplished act, by the Syrophoenician woman.

The Syrophoenician daughter as the climax of Mark's story

The argument here presented is that the Syrophoenician daughter is crucial and climactic to the entire pericope. The second generation is found to have taken up intimations in the story of the mother and developed them further. The narrative and somatic resistance to closure is just as sure as the Syrophoenician woman's refusal to accept Jesus' sententious dismissal.

Performative extension of stories is a structural pattern that can be found throughout Mark's gospel. This provides a formal corroboration for the role of the daughter in this pericope. For example, the story of Jairus' daughter tacks on an instruction for food (5:43), unnecessary to the function of a miracle story. Matthew accordingly drops it (Mt 9:25). Similarly Matthew omits the somewhat lengthy extension of the Legion exorcism that shifts the form from miracle to a commissioning story (Mk 5:19–20; *cf* Mt 8:34). These differences highlight Mark's refusal to comply with a strict replication of a miracle story. Other extensions are followed by Matthew (Mk 3:6; *cf* Mt 12:14 and Mk 10:52; *cf* Mt 20:34).

Accordingly, the daughter functions to destabilise the very story for which she has been the spine. Blackburn rightly recognised that her action in v 30 is unnecessary as an end to the miracle story, and she certainly is not required for the pronouncement story. This makes her presence even more arresting.

The fulfilment of the woman's actions and words is not dependent upon the charitable dispensation of Jesus, but in the generation that comes after. The daughter's silent yet active extension of her mother's achievements undermines a logocentric and even textual approach to the world. The daughter shifts the story from an 'ideo-story' —an invitation to improvise on the narrative (re)-presentation[195] —to a 'soma-story', the audacity to *enact* an expansion on the liberation previously experienced.

Towards a mutuality of body and word

195. Schüssler Fiorenza, *Sharing Her Word*, 122.

The discovery of this 'soma-story' by the Syrophoenician woman restores the sanctity of the interplay of relationship between these two women that stands apart from logocentric confinement. Liberation won by an action and word, and extended by further embodied action, is effected in relation to each other. The mother has won her daughter's deliverance; the daughter has moved beyond the degradation of 'beneath the table'. Their 'primary and major' interchange is with one another, at the level of their embodiment. The 'secondary and minor' interchange is with the male Jesus. The fundamental hierarchy of order, built on an ethological appeal to dimorphism, has been removed. No longer, according to the story of the Syrophoenician woman and her daughter, is the relationship between women to be defined as unnatural. The ethologically justified 'natural' relationship of male and female, inevitably inscribed with inequalities, is removed, and removed as part of a story of healing. Word is not confined to the male; nor is body inferior to the word. *Logos* and *soma* together unfold the liberation of the gospel.

Both the word of the woman and the action of two women are vindicated in the story. The words of the male Jesus (and perhaps his hiding) are set in diminished contrast to these women. They have resisted and moved beyond inscription / conscription into the ethological framework. Gender, race, age, and status do not have any bearing on access to and initiative for transformation. In the specifics of the story as interpreted here, neither one stereotyped as a courtesan nor her daughter are, by that description, to be regarded as outside the benefits of the gospel. More to the point, they are key contributors to its liberating content. Such a conclusion to the story therefore renders all the stereotypical characterisations at nought. Their 'spoiled identity', crafted so carefully in the opening verses of the pericope and inviting stigmatising perceptions from readers, has provided the basis for new conceptions of the gospel and of those who might bear it.

The Reassessment of the role of the Syrophoenician daughter

The Syrophoenician daughter has been given a much more prominent role in the Markan pericope through the reading proposed in this chapter. I have argued that this reading is sustainable within the terms of the text itself, even though the somatic action of the daughter in the story itself subverts a confinement to textuality. The gesture / movement of the daughter relativises the accent upon *logos* in the story and disrupts both conventional and feminist privileging of word. Her somatic communication functions not as a jaundiced vindication of the exorcism but as an embodied extension of the liberation won by her mother. No longer played out in terms of dogs' access to scraps, the story now authorises the place of the παιδία, the children, *at* the table, not under it. Actions, gestures, movements and behaviours become as important as communication in their own right and as the provision of an interpretative strategy for the word itself.

The integrity of this distinct mode of being, that is, of body as a valid, knowledge-bearing and communicating reality, is constructed in the narrative as a point of discovery between two women. The community of the mother-daughter relationship, as a 'primary and major' relationship of women has a number of ancient correlations. They provide alternatives to the ethological fabrication that the primary, major and unequal relationship must be between a male and female. The mother-daughter relationship dominated Mark's story from the beginning and is brought to a new level in the respective contributions of a woman and her child. In this sense, both word and body, reason and action gain their expression and exchange in a communal relationship. Neither the woman alone nor the daughter alone can achieve the extent of liberation and movement that is heard in their combined story.

Hence, through the communal and corporeal primacy given in this story to the woman-daughter relationship, the superstructure built on the asserted primacy of the dimorphic division of human beings is dismantled. Culture and nature are not and cannot be opposed in a hierarchy of value. Both communicate and both need the other for expression. This mutuality of body and word is won in the relationship of the woman and the daughter.

Conclusion

A Fondness for Bones
Reconsidering Mark's Syrophenician Women

Introduction

'Reason is more distinctive of man than is bodily effort.' So declaims Aristotle.[1] The dualistic contrast distils the hegemony of literary thought and practical outworking in the ancient Mediterranean world, regardless of whether Jew, Greek or Roman expresses it. There were modulations of course, but the basic pattern of thinking was primarily dualistic. And the fundamental building blocks on which a massive edifice of philosophical and political enterprise was erected, were the pairings of mind and body, human and animal, male and female. Indeed, as the divine was regarded as the source, activator and goal of reason, the universe was logocentrically configured. The male was therefore naturally endowed with a privileged relationship with the divine and with a natural superiority over the female. She was somatically handicapped. The *Letter of Aristeas* captures the agreed values between Hellenistic and Jewish worlds in reply to a question from 'King Ptolemy II' who had asked how one might reach agreement with a woman:

> [In knowing] that the female race is brazen, reckless for the object of its designs, effortlessly precipitous through distortions of reason, and has been established as weak by nature.[2]

The writing of such sentiments was itself testimony to the contrast of value and position between male and female. A woman's body, inscribed by 'Aristeas' in terms reminiscent of animal (especially canine) behaviour, predisposed her to seek her memorial through the generation or acquisition of bodies; bodies were the womanly realm. The proper memorial for the male was therefore literary praise,

1. Arist *Rhet* 1.1 (1355b).
2. *Ep Arist* 250 (my translation).

memorial by citation.[3] Writing, the companion to speech, and both bred from reason, became the mark of the male, the more so when it marked (out) the female.

The exaltation of mind over body is not confined to the ancient world. Social-scientific practitioners of New Testament criticism have properly warned of ethnocentric anachronism in the collapsing of cultural values between the contemporary world and the world of the past.[4] Conversely however, such scholarship is frequently inured against an awareness of the contemporary world's indebtedness to ancient formularies.[5] The subject-object dichotomy is perpetuated, the constituents of the familiar dualistic structure having merely been tinkered with.

This book has pressed that recognition to its most basic, the collation of female and bestial within a dimorphically constituted universe. The modern study of ethology is a clear successor to ancient dualistic conceptualisations as well as literary antiquity's disposition to seek interdependent reinforcement between social and scientific structures. But so also is a liturgical formulary, the Anglican *Prayer of Humble Access*, which has contributed its own 'christian' socialisation to this perspective.

A reprise of the argument

In many ways, the story of the Syrophoenician women has been a palimpsest, a text overwritten with the inherited agendas of a succession of cultures preoccupied with reason *and* the female. Up until relatively recent times, these agendas have been dominated by male inscribers. The mythological speech-maker of the ancient world, Hermes (the 'dog-throttler'), has continued his hold on scholarship in the privileging of language over body, a language which, as the delivery of godly reason, was deemed necessarily male.

Cave canem, have canis

The problem of the logocentric hold upon meaning was highlighted with a relatively simple question: how is it that a *woman*, who has been characterised as an irrational animal (a dog), can speak that which is the exemplar of rationality (*logos*)? The three key elements:

3. Plat *Sym* 208e.
4. A van Aarde, *Fatherless in Galilee: Jesus as Child of God* (Harrisburg, PA: Trinity Press International, 2001), 39–40.
5. Schüssler Fiorenza, *Politics of Interpretation*, 84–91.

the woman, the animal and *logos* in this question have directed the argument. Gender issues in Mark's story, so readily supplanted by *gentile* issues in interpretation, were argued to be mandatory for a constant, critical lens for reading, a stance required even by the text. Methodological considerations and detailed interaction with ancient materials were both necessary in order to gain a greater sense of the context within which this example of ancient literature was placed. Whilst Schüssler Fiorenza's warnings about historical positivism were heeded, critical engagement with ancient evidence has been part of a commitment to affirming materiality as a necessary interrogatory balance to rationality.

Once the key triangulation of woman, animal and reason began to be applied, a *prima facie* case was established that Mark's story could sponsor (compliantly or unwittingly) new directions about women in the ancient world. 'Dog' was found not merely to be a general term of abuse but one which was particularly applied to women as a means to confirm a dualism that held them in a position inferior to rational man.

So fundamental was the dualistic template for the scientific and philosophical assumptions that operated in the ancient world, that the use of animals for indications of character did not require justification or explanation in rhetoric. Women were understood as *by nature* belonging to the animal world. The animal world was deployed to describe, explain and justify the constraint of woman. Even though particular ancient cultures reveal differences in the appreciation of dogs, the exchange between abuse, animal epithets and the nature of women was seen to be relatively consistent.

A different line of research was therefore required, one which had to take account of the triangulation of gender, animal and reason, set it alongside an awareness of cultural specifics, and yet retain a sensitivity to the sociopolitical dimensions. Whilst a rhetorical analysis was important, it was insufficient precisely because it did not go to the heart of the interests that rhetoric served nor the presuppositions under which it operated.

A dog returns to its own vomit

Contemporary ethology aspires to provide not only comparisons between humans and animals but also biological foundations for human culture and ethics. The irony is that the ancient rhetorical term for characterisation was *ethologia*: discourse about character. The suggestive link is chillingly and expansively appropriate. Ethology reaches into descriptions of sexual differentiation and relationships, the survival of species, the marking of territory, the mutual reinforcement between science and culture and the grounding of societal arrangements in a posited natural order. Fundamental to the ethological enterprise is the dimorphism of gender. Ethology provides a scientific justification for dualistic frameworks. Dominance hierarchies are integral, argued EO Wilson, to human and animal behaviour alike.[6]

Ethology's unabashed, sociobiological determinism and its claims to ancient demonstration provide the broad lines of its methodology. It retains the realm of the divine as the explicable reflection of the natural arrangement of the cosmos. Inevitably, that realm is defined rationally and literarily. Literature, *logos*, god(s) and man belong together. Strikingly, proverbs and metaphor become especially privileged in modern ethological discourse precisely because they express literary justification for scientific claims.

The traditional proponents of ethology have received widespread feminist critique in both scientific and political analyses. The most pronounced attack has been aimed at the ethological endorsement of a massive dyadic structure that essentialises the inequalities of human gendered relationships. Here, the socio-political interests of a male-dominated scientific discipline are noted. At the same time, a different perspective of enquiry has explored a greater variety of animal practices than the socio-political agenda is prepared to tolerate, thereby challenging the ease with which correlations are derived for human beings. Both critiques have sought to undermine the naturalised, reductionist universalism given to socio-cultural values and arrangements.

However, ethology's emphasis on the animal world does compel consideration of the somatic realm; for the human species, this is particularly focussed on the development of the child. Both the critique from without ethology and that from within have the potential to resist the logocentricity even of the ethologists themselves, let alone of ecclesiastical and academic commentators. This potential has been exploited, along with key tenets of ethological description *as held accountable* by feminist critique.

Thus, when basic emphases of contemporary ethological analysis were redirected to ancient texts, it quickly became apparent how informed and, to some extent, structured were those texts by ethological commitments. Mark's gospel is not immune. The dimorphism of

6. Wilson, *Consilience*, 153, 259.

male and female with its manifold dualistic extensions surfaced in a comparison of the story of Legion and the Syrophoenician woman. A distinction of the man, Legion, *from* the animal world became a backdrop to the alignment of the Syrophoenician women *with* the bestial. Both people are gentile, and yet attract opposing connections with animals. Race cannot explain the difference. However, the fundamental ethological dimorphism *can*, not as a scientific distinction, but as a literary construction relying upon scientific justification. Accordingly, *gender* is highlighted as fundamental to the story of the Syrophoenician women, not ethnicity, and by extension, not the church's mission.

Throughout the analysis, the Markan story was read in its wider literary, rhetorical and cultural settings. Issues of the specific historicity of Jesus and an encounter with a woman were deliberately shelved so that the ethological aspects of the text-in-context could be explored.

Dog in the manger

Many of the marks of the 'traditional referentiality' of proverbs were found in a detailed analysis of Jesus' saying: its poetic balance and metrical undergirding witness to a pre-existing form. Moreover, the biting edge of the metrical cast of the proverb ensures that the use of a diminutive in the context of an address of a woman would *register* as abuse in an ancient context.

Standard grammatical assessments of diminutives that have virtually obliterated any distinction between them and the primaries from which derive, fail to recognise the status variables impacting on an assessment of a diminutive's force. In Mark's *gendered* dynamics, there is neither an equivalence between κυνάριον and κύων nor a reduction of the insult; it is *aggravated*. The proverb's incorporation into sententious and enthymemic expansion underscored the rigorous constraint of the insult operating within the gendered dynamics of the exchange between a male and a female.

The proverb itself was found to be of ancient and variegated attestation. Moreover, its antiquity of attestation was discovered to be Greek. The proverb had migrated into Jewish hands in Mark's gospel, and its transfer intensified the impact precisely because of the irredeemably denigrated status of the dog in Jewish value systems. The overall construction of Jesus' words indicates that discussion was forthwith closed.

The scent of a dog for its quarry

Jesus was not refining her faith or her quest. Her request for healing is not merely denied; the aggressive tone underscores a range of judgements. These judgements gain their force of meaning by provisions in the narrative that rely upon ancient cultural conventions. The mixture of the woman's foreignness with an absence of male embedding and an occupation of public space, arraign the power of stereotypes that the ancient world relied upon to locate a person and build a perception of character. The delayed description of v 26 is no afterthought. It is a carefully contrived addition designed to generate an assessment of the woman before Jesus' words are actually spoken. As an ethnic Greek, complicated by her foreign (Syrophoenician) birth, she is weighted with a millstone of presumptions about promiscuity, theft, deceptive talk, dabbling in magic. She is stigmatised by v 26. Her status is spoiled by a range of markers which cohere around the prostitute, a courtesan at best. And she bears the shame of the state of her daughter.

Jesus' words of ethological comparison for the woman and her daughter, execute an assessment that has been invited by the narrative. The woman's identity is impaired and her capacity to appear differently, even reduce the harshness of the gaze, is atrophied. The saying enhances Jesus' authority and maintains his honour because he has acted in continuity with the construction provided by the narrator and the perception invited of the hearers. Hero, narrator, audience and conventional values cohere in a cosy assurance that they are not like this woman: a morally bankrupt, alogical, unbounded quarry.

Jesus' response to the woman, when matched with key emphases of an ethological understanding, attempts to reimpose an order upon the woman demonstrated in nature as the proper arrangement of the universe. The fundamental basis of that order is an asymmetric dimorphism. Jesus asserts his right as a man to speak and order the woman's life. Careful reinforcements of territory are made which distinguish those ordered by reason from those who are animals. She belongs outside, the 'wall-leaner',[7] just like a dog. An ethological perspective has highlighted Jesus' words as combining scientific axioms with cultural values, reinforced in their claim on universality by long-standing proverbial tradition.

---

7. Mart *Epig* 3.82. Syrian prostitutes were often described as 'roof-dwellers', with the same intimation that they were outside the properly bounded conventional space for women: Luc *Bis* 30.

The hair of the dog that bit you

Ethological inscriptions of dimorphic relationships dictated that when the male (of the) pride spoke, the woman should be silent. But the woman refused. Risking the confirmation of the assessment mounted against her, she responds to Jesus, shaming, if not gently mocking his almost rustic reliance on conventional aphoristic tradition. The sheer creative euphony of her reply stands in sharp contrast to the plodding predictability of Jesus even as the deft craft of her answer methodically counters every point of his ethologically-charged repudiation. Taking 'the hair of the dog that bit her'—the κυνάρια of Jesus' saying—she transforms another ancient proverb and level-switches the metaphor of dogs to the positive experience known in her own Greek culture. Humility/humiliation may still linger in the air, but food is now assured in a domestic rather than public organization of space. Moreover, that space is organised without reference to masters, even though most instances of the proverb she solicits (and reforms) operate within a strongly hierarchical schema.

The suspicion of the courtesan is not removed. The brilliant aesthetics of her destabilising reply are as likely to confirm that judgement. However, she repudiates the significance of any tarnished reputation as relevant for Jesus' response to her request for her daughter's release. Judgement is restored to the merits of the case away from an inculpating and dismissive moralising about a person. Indeed, Jesus himself comes under implicit question for his readiness to abuse, his slinking into hiding in betrayal of his public responsibility and vocational calling.

The woman relies upon one of the few literary forms that male bastions of convention were prepared to grant women—the proverb. But she uses it to create an extension to dialogue. The closure that Jesus' saying had proposed by appeal to a universal arbiter, is now met by an appeal framed in the same basic form. This creates a pairing of conflicting proverbs that relativises the distancing appeal to a transcendental truth. Now choices have to be made.

The eloquence of a barking dog

The narrative itself displays how important the word of this woman is by conferring a unique form of introduction. Suspense is held about the assessment of this importance until the final phrase of Jesus' last words in the story. His conferral of value on the word of the woman indicates that a choice has been made *against* his own words, against the prejudgments that were manufactured by the text about any words that the woman might deliver and against the dominant evaluation of the words of women in the ancient world. So significant is the word of the Syrophoenician woman that it is accorded the same status as those of Jesus in the wider gospel of Mark. This *logos* is gospel; it has been spoken by one who has been characterised as a dog and its eloquence has quietened and bested the aggressive speech of the usual speaker of *logos*, the man (Jesus). The power of that word is revealed in the use of the perfect tense ἐξελήλυθεν in v 29. The word of this woman is credited with the liberation of her daughter. Jesus merely tells her what her word has achieved.

Right at the point of wonder at the power of this word, a suspicion returns to the story, generating an ambiguity in how to appraise the accolade. Elisabeth Schüssler Fiorenza's sensitivity to Jesus having the 'last word' in the story, was found to be justified,[8] albeit for different reasons. The issue runs deeper than a struggle over access to word. In such a circumstance, *logos* itself is unchallenged in its supremacy; there is merely an argument about who is credited with speaking it and who has the authority to acknowledge it. When it is a male voice that credits a woman's voice, a series of qualifications, amply reiterated in history, are raised about the woman who spoke the word, all operating to remove the woman in her own identity and subjectivity from the word. Her effort becomes an exceptional, temporary moment where 'she rose above herself'. Alternately, she is obscured by the laurel wreath delivered to her, either becoming a male at the moment of speaking or being subjected to the combined agreement of male narrator and male hero, having become merely a ventriloquist's doll for the author, still separated from *logos*. Again, even those feminists who prize her words as redirecting and expanding Jesus' vocation risk turning her into God's policewoman making sure the hero continues his quest.[9] All these concerns expose the depth and strength of the hold of logocentricity. Her somatic achievement is lost.

However, the depth of exploration into the words of Jesus and the woman in Mark's story have revealed the area where rationality begins to stall—at the psychagogic effect of language which is most powerful in performance, in its embodied expression.[10] It provided an opportunity to be exploited, fragile as it remained within the

8. *But She Said*, 12–13, *Sharing Her Word*, 123–124.
9. For example, Wainwright, *Shall We Look for Another?*, 88.
10. Precisely the realm of the *poesis* (the work of poet-makers) most distrusted by some rhetoricians and philosophers: for example Arist *Rhet* 3.4 (1407a).

ambiguities set by a logocentric dominance. If she speaks *logos* she must lose what has been the cause of her alignment with the animal by the male—her bodily presence and identity.

The power of the dog

Here the fundamental contribution of the argument is raised. The forgotten verse of the pericope has been repositioned as the climax of the entire passage. This has not involved the marginalising of the Syrophoenician woman but rather a reappraisal of the relationship between the Syrophoenician *women*. The construction that the narrator carefully provided (in v 26) to invite a demeaned representation of the Syrophoenician woman and her daughter is now returned with a different edge. Instead of the charge of courtesan closing critical appreciation, a resistant reading was pursued. The relationships of courtesans were plotted along a 'lesbian continuum' which sought to recognise those contexts in the ancient world where relationships between women were 'primary and major'. The absence of reference to a male in the lives of the Syrophoenician and her daughter was seen to offer potential for women to exercise their subjectivity without reference to patriarchal constraint. On this reading, it is the male Jesus who is marginalised.

The suggestion that the daughter has been the anchor of the entire pericope[11] was expanded beyond the assertion of the child's passivity. Her silence in the text is not taken as a subjection to the *logos* being played out in other quarters but rather as a relativisation of logocentric (self-)importance. Her somatic action, re-location and communication, discovered by her mother, appropriates not only the liberation won by the word of a woman. It extends that liberation by the adoption of the forgotten element of the Syrophoenician's mission—her bodily presence, positioning and action. This is more than the embodiment of the word. At the site of the body, logocentricism has been marginalised.[12]

The 'surplus meaning' in the final verse was exploited.[13] Problems were noted in the interpretation of the daughter's passive movement (βεβλημένον) as confirmation of the miracle and/or a debilitation resulting from the exit of the demon. The problematisation prompted

11. Pokorný, 'Puppy', 337.
12. Susan Graham calls this a 'tactile epistemology': 'Silent Voices', 147.
13. The notion of 'surplus meaning' is used by Heikki Räisänen to explain the potential for multiple meanings unlocked by the editorial activity of a writer: *'Messianic Secret'* 27.

a search for an alternate reading: an active 'reclining on a couch'. This phrase signifies a being at table where food was available. The first Syrophoenician woman had achieved the release of her daughter. That child, the second Syrophoenician woman, has asserted her right/authority to sit *at* the table rather than be collated with the crumb-mongering dogs beneath.

Rereading Mark's story of Syrophoenician women

A subtle allusion to the story of the Syrophoenician women came in a speech in Philadelphia in 1849. Lucretia Mott argued before the gathered assembly: 'Woman is claiming for herself stronger and more profitable food.'[14] The history of the characterisation of the woman and her daughter frames such a statement as resistant to the text, at least the text read as closure on women's aspirations.

The surprise, however, is that the text itself has been able to be read to accommodate Lucretia Mott's argument. Mark has provided the ground for the subversion of his own textual enterprise by pointing to the ambiguities not only in word but in how body might claim its own subjectivity and its own performance of word. The woman is accentuated in the pericope as a purveyor of word but this word is not to be read against her own movements and embodiment of that word. Jesus' response to the woman isolates her word(s). But that is not the end of the story nor the confinement of its gospel message. The action of the daughter affirms the forgotten element of her mother's courage—her somatic performance—and ensures that it will not be swamped by a disembodied word. The subjectivity and deployment of the body is now affirmed as possessing its own integrity. And word without body is judged as emaciating and demeaning, if not impossible.

So, word is not to be jettisoned as either replaced or of negligible worth. Neither is it to assert that body is itself without ambiguity or polyvalent potential. The limits of language—feared by some and exposed by others—have been seen to be fecund in potential for new meanings and significations. The same is true of body. The body *can* be possessed and controlled by the demonic. What has been disclosed, however, is that the body has been and has been sought repeatedly to be possessed and controlled by the *logos*. Without the integrity asserted of the body, writing itself becomes as possessive as the demonic. The writing of the body takes away embodiment; it becomes

14. D Greene (editor), *Lucretia Mott: Her Complete Speeches and Sermons* (New York and Toronto: Edwin Mellen Press, 1980), 144.

'buried beneath both male-developed biological scientific paradigms and a male-centred system of social inscription . . .'[15]

In the ambiguity that attends every effort to write gesture, movement, performance and embodiment, whether through text or interpretation, the body resists confinement by the word. The acknowledgment of body in written text draws attention to its presence but in the very act of recognition loses its ability to control the body as the object of its writing. The body moves. Whatever alliance has been carved between narrator and hero in Mark's gospel is subverted here precisely because the author *notices* the women in relationship together, apart from Jesus. Mark, at least in the literary dyarchy 'he' constructs, has been marginalised.

The challenge, hidden as treasure (or buried as toxic by interpretation) in this pericope, is a removal of the polarities of body and mind.[16] Body and mind are foundational, as well as, in themselves, destabilising of foundations. They cannot be made essential characteristics of a politically naturalised dimorphism, just as neither element can be discarded in any gendered subjectivity. One might be so bold as to suggest that here (again) Mark threatens the very enterprise of a written gospel. The narrative, in words, has re-membered the body as critical to communal life and as the locus of liberation from a phalanx of evil. In so doing, the *textuality* of the body thus affirmed must itself be contingent if the ultimate power of inscription is finally to be broken. Text can only ever be servant to both the oral and the community wherein the oral is exchanged and formed—indeed embodied. Otherwise, text becomes possessive, demonic.

Towards a recontextualisation

The reality of 'corporeality and subjectivity'[17] cannot be permitted to reside or fossilize in the text. This would be a sinister betrayal of all that may have been won as 'good news', a 'good news' that performs the dispossession of all that oppresses in body and mind and invites the re-establishment of access to body and mind regardless

15. E Grosz, 'Inscriptions and Body-Maps: Representations and the Corporeal', in T Threadgold and A Cranny-Francis (editors), *Feminine, Masculine and Representation* (Sydney: Allen & Unwin, 1990), 73.
16. MC Taylor, *About Religion: Economies of Faith in Virtual Culture* (Chicago, IL: University of Chicago Press, 1999), 114.
17. E Grosz, 'Notes towards a Corporeal Feminism', in *AFS* 5 (1987): 15.

of gender constructions. Gospel is not about deferring to that weapon of deterministic socio-biology—the elevation of language as a transtemporal proof of the scientific axioms which ethology has promoted.

Just as Mark's gospel resists closure by placing its resolution and hope outside of the written text, so this pericope looks to its continued life and expression beyond writing. But this entices us into historicist reconstructionism beyond the argument here.[18] Nevertheless, the lines of enquiry and analysis pursued in this book may have some contribution to make.[19]

Taking the passage in its entirety, we have seen that the accent on gender, that was adopted as prompted by the text itself and as a necessary contemporary hermeneutical awareness, has fully repaid the commitment. This is not a new discovery and my indebtedness is clear.[20] I have argued, however, that gender issues ought not be embedded automatically in the traditional interpretation of this passage as a mission aetiology. Mission merely compounds the struggle; it does not initiate it. The suggestion in the Syrophoenician women's story is that gender dynamics were not resolved in one generation, but extended into the generation of daughters.

The boundedness envisaged in the contemporary Colossian household code presupposes women embedded in men by marriage. Women outside the marriage relationship, whether as children, as slaves, or any other correlation, simply are not noticed by the letter.

18. See Burkill, Baudoz, Broadhead, Taussig for efforts to isolate the layers of historical development of the story.

19. Gerd Lüdemann, for example, claimed that 'the historical yield is nil': *Jesus after 2000 Years*, 51. By contrast, the Jesus Seminar thought there was an 'historical core' to the story, which included the recognition of Jesus as an exorcist by a Greek woman, and that there was an 'exchange of witticisms in which the woman got the better of Jesus.' Beyond this, surety collapsed: RW Funk and The Jesus Seminar, *The Acts of Jesus: What did Jesus really do?* (New York: HarperSanFrancisco, 1998), 96–97. Interestingly, their failure to take into account the gender dynamics of the story removed Jesus' reference to 'dogs' from authenticity. They retained the predominance of a general racial slur, seemingly undervaluing their primary affirmation that the authentic core of the story involved an exchange between a Jewish *man* and a Gentile *woman*.

20. Schüssler Fiorenza, *In Memory*, 138, Taussig, 'Dealing Under the Table', 268, 270, 273.

The accent is on 'every man' (πάντα ἄνθρωπον Col 1:28).[21] But non-embedded women are precisely the ones who *are* noticed in the story of the Syrophoenician women. They were likely the (type of) women connected with the same community that claimed Mark's allegiance. Hence, the gendered struggles within the early church are not to be interpreted in an undifferentiated fashion, that is, by presupposing a conventional, embedded background. Mark's literary technique in manipulating characterisation needs to be taken seriously as an indication of particular women drawing particular concerns in the early church (*cf* 1 Cor 6:15–16). The prostitutes, harlots, flute-players and perhaps even courtesans,[22] that were charged against Jesus and the early *basileia* movement cannot be reduced to a mere labelling drama of status degradation.[23] The movement towards an embrace of conventional family and household arrangements alongside the denigration of some women within the church's purview[24] suggests that it was not merely women who were at issue in the early church, but women of certain status, behaviours and occupations.

21. It is likely, as in the Legion story in Mark 5:2, 8, that ἄνθρωπος is exclusive, especially given the loss of reference to women in the modification of the 'in Christ' formula in Colossians 3:11 (*cf* Gal 3:28).
22. Mt 21:31–32, Lk 7:36–50, Jn 4:1–30; *cf* Mt 11: 16–19//Lk 7:32–34. The cultural significations within stories of the early *basileia* movement increase the yield of references to compromised women. See generally Corley, *Private Women*, *loc cit*; *cf* Schüssler Fiorenza, *Miriam's Child*, 93–94.
23. The debate appears to be forming between deviancy labelling and a *topos* of aristocratic women patronage. The former argument suggests that the charge of prostitutes in the Jesus movement was only a vilification exercise with little factual basis; the latter argues that the accrual of patronage for the Jesus movement by aristocratic women was a familiar *topos* to gain recognition for a movement that was denigrated precisely because of its association with and inclusion of compromised women: see, respectively, Lieu, 'Attraction of Women', *loc cit* and Matthews, *First Converts*, *loc cit*
24. For a general overview of the process of group conformity to prevailing social norms, see DG Horrell, 'The Development of Theological Ideology in Pauline Christianity: A Structuration Theory Perspective', in PF Esler (editor), *Modelling Early Christianity: Social-scientific Studies of the New Testament in its Context* (London: Routledge, 1995), 224–236.

A difficulty arises, however, by squaring off Mark against Colossians, if not in terms of a battle for the Pauline legacy directly,[25] at least in terms of ecclesial debates about the place and influence of (so-called 'types' of) women in the early church. Kate Cooper's observation becomes pertinent here. These debates are primarily known to us through texts, and the presumption, amply justified by engagement with literacy and the control of transmission and publication in the ancient world, is that these texts are authored by men.[26] Cooper observes that such writing about women, even when promoting diametrically opposed positions, is part of a competition between men.[27] Women are mere pawns in a larger game of chess, manipulated in text and in life by male players for whom textuality is a key instrument for the arrangement of women and demarcation of territory against one another.

Here, Mark's abdication of control of the text becomes paramount. In noticing a household whose primary and major relationship is between two women, 'he' can do no more than indicate its presence. An abdication of Mark's authority to speak within and for that household is implicit in the brevity of the final verse of the Syrophoenician women's story, startling as it is. What and how those women spoke, if at all, cannot be invented, if the voyeuristic victimisation of characters is to be avoided. Mark's own literary achievement is dependent upon what, and if, women decide to speak (16:8).[28]

But there is one further possibility of Mark's dependency—the word of the woman. At this point, her word becomes prized as a word outside an ethologically reinforced framework that services a dominant male hegemony; at least, it is outside Mark's literary capacity. It is easy enough to register the saying of Jesus at a low to medium level of literary ability. A proverb framed into iambic metre would indicate that it has already passed through powerful mnemonic interests to reach such a structure. A sententious introduction is a standard populist or

---

25. For the suggestion of a later contest about gender in the Pauline heritage, comparing the Acts of Thecla and the Pastoral Letters, see DR MacDonald, *The Legend and the Apostle: The Battle for Paul in Story and Canon* (Philadelphia: Westminster Press, 1983). Without supporting a direct contest, Joanne Dewey considered the ideology of the Pastoral Letters to be opposed to the sort of story found in Mark 7:24–30: 'From Storytelling to Written Text', 71.
26. R Thomas, *Literacy and Orality in Ancient Greece* (Cambridge: Cambridge University Press, 1992), 105.
27. Cooper, 'Insinuations of Womanly Influence', 151.
28. *Cf* Graham, 'Silent Voices', 154.

rustic characteristic. Even the rudimentary use of enthymemes has been interpreted as the basic level of argumentative strategy in the ancient world.[29] But the word of the woman is different. Whatever it owes to a common proverb has been shaped with such singular sophistication in lexical and rhythmical detail that one is compelled to face whether Mark was capable of such literary invention.

The struggle to find women's voices and women's contributions to the formation and preservation of texts has been a key concern of feminist enquiry. The territory is marked with pitfalls. However, Athalya Brenner and Fokkelien van Dijk-Hemmes generated a rigorous methodological framework that sought to enable the recognition of female/feminine voices operating within a text.[30] It resisted a perpetuation of the inequality of gender relations precisely by recognising that such voices in texts are subjugated to a dominant cultural world-view, the means of production and the generally male interests in the reproduction, representation and generic containment of those voices. But such recognition produces the actuality of those voices. One element of their methodology has particular application here, that is, the conjunction between an overall vision within a passage with the voice assigned to a female character.[31] It is not totally impregnable against male expropriation or invention.[32] But, in the light of the quality of the word of the woman in the pericope—a quality that has a narrow range of provenances—it allows the reading of the word of the woman (in the context of the total somatic communication of the story) to be called a female voice. Of course, it doesn't push the exchange back definitely to the time of Jesus but it increases the level of probability that Mark was indebted to the telling of the story by women.[33] And it is here that a sense of the breach of textual boundaries is felt. The story is not to be confined by textualisation but is fulfilled

29. Arist *Rhet* 2.22 (1395b).

30. See A Brenner and F van Dijk-Hemmes, *On Gendering Texts: Female and Male Voices in the Hebrew Bible* (Leiden: EJ Brill, 1993); for the methodological exposition, see pages 1–13.

31. Arie Troost, 'Elisabeth and Mary—Naomi and Ruth: Gender-Response Criticism in Luke 1–2', in A Brenner (editor), *A Feminist Companion to the Hebrew Bible in the New Testament* (Sheffield: Sheffield Academic Press, 1996), 179, who applies the methodology to a New Testament passage.

32. The Pseudo-Clementine adjustment of the woman is a case in point.

33. As Joanne Dewey imaginatively reconstructed: 'From Story-telling to a Written Text'.

beyond itself in a liberation such as was experienced in those who held (and extended beyond) the word of a woman.

Certainly, Mark structures the narrative and incorporates the saying with a grand flagging of its importance. Narrator and hero combine to acknowledge how critical this word is to them as indeed it is signalled as critical to the generation that follows that word. Precisely because the story climaxes with a somatic extension of the release won by that embodied and activated word, the word of the woman is enabled to assume an importance that is distinct from the standard dualistic prizing of word over body. Where and how that word began must be imagined. Perhaps Mark has offered an imagining; perhaps he has offered an other's imagining for performance. Certainly, the significance of that word cannot be separated from performance. The connection of the word *with the woman* is critical to that performance, not its connection with mission, faith, christology, avoidance of offence or any other agenda that has been used wittingly or unwittingly to remove the woman from visibility or subjectivity. And insofar as Mark has tried to notice the significance of that word of a woman in enabling release from whatever possesses the next generation of women, Mark has participated in the freedom and creativity of the *basileia* movement which Jesus also embraced.

But participate is all. Mark as a male author, like me, can only write of a presence and a speech that is absent, however much both of us may have been in dialogue with women, even the women of this story.[34] The embodiment and somatic expansion of that release does not lie in the text nor in the reading that I have proposed. Rather it moves poetically in the celebrating household of those who treasure the story of the Syrophoenician women. Oh . . . and the dogs are somewhere in their house . . . chewing on the bones of this book.

34. See the critical literary assessment by Shari Benstock of men writing (of) women, which nevertheless leaves the 'trace' that acknowledges the subjectivity of the woman's presence and initiation: *Textualizing the Feminine* (Norman and London: University of Oklahoma Press, 1991), 100–122.

Index of Biblical References

Index of Greek, Latin and Coptic Writings

Index of Papyri, Inscriptions and Ostraca

Index of Hebrew and Aramaic Writings

Index to Modern Authors

Index to Main Subjects